CQ GUIDE TO

CURRENT AMERICAN GOVERNMENT

Fall 2003

A Division of Congressional Quarterly Inc.

Washington, D.C.

Congressional Quarterly Inc.

Congressional Quarterly Inc., an editorial research service and publishing company, serves clients in the fields of news, education, business and government. It combines the specific coverage of Congress, government and politics contained in the *CQ Weekly* with the more general subject range of an affiliated service, the *CQ Researcher*.

Under the CQ Press imprint, Congressional Quarterly also publishes college political science textbooks and public affairs paperbacks on developing issues and events, information directories and reference books on the federal government, national elections and politics. Titles include the *Guide to the Presidency*, the *Guide to Congress*, the *Guide to the U.S. Supreme Court*, the *Guide to U.S. Elections* and *Politics in America*. CQ's A-Z collection is a reference series that provides essential information about American government and the electoral process. The *CQ Almanac*, a compendium of legislation for one session of Congress, is published each year. *Congress and the Nation*, a record of government for a presidential term, is published every four years.

CQ publishes *CQ Today* (formerly the *Daily Monitor*), a report on the current and future activities of congressional committees. An online information system, CQ.com on Congress, provides immediate access to CQ's databases of legislative action, votes, schedules, profiles and analyses. Visit www.cq.com for more information.

CQ Press
1255 22nd St. N.W., Suite 400
Washington, DC 20037
202-729-1900; toll free, 1-866-4-CQ-PRESS (1-866-427-7737)

www.cqpress.com

Cover photos: Scott J. Ferrell

Printed and bound in the United States of America
07 06 05 04 03 5 4 3 2 1

⊗ The paper used in this publication exceeds the requirements of the American National Standard for Information Sciences—Permanence of Paper for Printed Library Materials, ANSI Z39.48-1992.

ISBN 1-56802-806-7
ISSN 0196-612-X

Contents

Contents

Introduction

Guide to Current American Government is a collection of articles selected from the *CQ Weekly*, a trusted source for in-depth, nonpartisan reporting and analyses of congressional action, presidential activities, policy debates and other news and developments in Washington. The articles, selected to complement introductory American government texts with up-to-date examinations of current issues and controversies, are divided into four sections: Foundations of American Government, Political Participation, Government Institutions and Politics and Public Policy.

Foundations of American Government. This section examines issues and events that involve interpretation of the U.S. Constitution. This edition of the *Guide* explores the financing of the Department of Homeland Security, Congress' agenda before and during the war in Iraq, the debate over Defense Secretary Donald H. Rumsfeld's plan to transform the U.S. military and President George W. Bush's spending authority.

Political Participation. The articles in this section examine current issues in electoral and party politics, including the Republican Party's approach to race relations, the race for the 2004 Democratic presidential nomination, the House leadership in the 108th Congress and the role of Vice President Richard Cheney.

Government Institutions. This section explores the inner workings of the major institutions of American government. Congress, the presidency and the judiciary are examined in light of recent events at home and abroad. In this edition of the *Guide,* the articles focus on the domestic and foreign policy issues that President Bush and Congress grappled with in the first half of 2003, including the war in Iraq, a new Middle East peace plan, a tax cut package and judicial nominations.

Politics and Public Policy. These articles focus on major policy issues, such as technology, health care, the environment and transportation.

The *Guide to Current American Government* reprints articles largely unchanged from their original appearance in the *CQ Weekly*. The date of original publication is provided with each article to give readers a time frame for the events described. Page number references to related and background articles in the *CQ Weekly* and the *CQ Almanac* facilitate additional research. Both publications are available in many school and public libraries.

Foundations of American Government

This section covers issues that go to the heart of American democracy, including the balance of federal power and the role of Congress. The articles focus on homeland security: how to finance it and how to protect it.

The first article discusses the challenges Congress faces in financing the new Department of Homeland Security and various homeland initiatives. The creation of this Cabinet-level department—the most extensive government overhaul in five decades—received bipartisan support in Congress. But a year after passage of the homeland security bill, Congress worried whether there would be enough money to protect the homeland. Funds and resources to meet security demands were lacking. While Republicans pointed to strides in homeland security, Democrats appeared intent on making it a political issue, and discord arose over how to pay for the new department. With a war looming in Iraq, a sizable tax cut package on the agenda, and state and local officials expressing discontent over the flow of federal money for local security measures, the pressure on Congress to set priorities for homeland security increased.

The second article examines Congress' agenda and role in the weeks preceding the war in Iraq and during the war itself. In the fall of 2002, Congress authorized President George W. Bush to use force to disarm Saddam Hussein if all other options failed. Once it weighed in on Bush's war plan, however, Congress was able to do little but mark time with debates and votes on domestic issues—medical malpractice, judicial nominations and the federal budget—and wait for the war to start. As commander in chief, the president has the authority to declare war, plan military strategy and shape foreign policy. Although the major questions of war and peace, strategy and diplomacy belong to the White House, once the war began, Congress would retain a front-line role in three areas: reviewing wartime spending (only Congress can release the funds to pay for the war), watching the performance of the military and overseeing the administration's conduct of foreign policy.

The third article looks at Congress' role keeping watch over the military's performance in the war in Iraq. Defense Secretary Donald H. Rumsfeld's plan to transform the military into a lighter, more agile force—making it less dependent on ground troops and more focused on lighter weapons and technological advances—was first tested in the war with Iraq. Amid reports of success were complaints from military leaders that there were not enough ground troops. At this early point in the conflict, Congress could not judge whether the troop deployment struck the right balance, and, furthermore, no lawmaker wanted to undermine the troops' morale by being critical of the battle plan. Congress knew that the ultimate indicator of Rumsfeld's proposed "transformation" of the U.S. military would be the outcome of the war. An analysis of what worked and what didn't in Iraq would have to wait for Armed Services committees' postwar hearings.

The last article in this section addresses how Congress is reluctantly granting the "power of the purse" to President Bush. U.S. presidents have often tried to seize some of the spending authority that the Constitution grants to Congress, and in an era defined by security threats, Bush has sought, and Congress has granted him, wider latitude to decide how to allocate federal money. Some lawmakers, however, are concerned about the administration's continued requests for blank checks. Although Bush has sought spending flexibility primarily with defense funds, some congressional members fear a slippery slope as the lines between defense and domestic homeland security spending are blurred. Members worry about the pattern they may be setting.

Rhetoric Meets Reality In Security's Unpaid Bills

Congress plays middleman in fights over financing

Ridge, shown at President Bush's State of the Union speech Jan. 28, has not announced priority programs for the new Homeland Security Department. Some experts say that could make it difficult for Congress to provide adequate funding.

Securing the homeland was supposed to be one of those grand goals that transcended partisan politics and unified the nation. But nearly 17 months after Sept. 11, there is an increasing gap between the expectations created by the rhetoric of homeland security and the reality of how to pay for the policies that will make America safer.

President Bush has been successful in setting the tone and receiving much of the credit for security since the terrorist attacks. He also is working to create a public perception that the nation is indeed more secure, declaring in his State of the Union address Jan. 28 that the United States is winning the war on terrorism. *(2003 CQ Weekly, p. 267)*

Congress, meanwhile, has been caught in the middle, attempting to avoid the appearance of dawdling over the president's homeland security agenda but at the same time straining to please security constituencies that range from local police departments to border patrol agents and hospital workers.

If the tardy fiscal 2003 appropriations bills are any indication, the future of homeland security is going to be fights over every penny, whether it is radios that allow New York City police and fire departments to talk to each other or radiation detectors for ocean shipping containers in Long Beach, Calif.

CQ Weekly Feb.1, 2003

One of the largest percentage increases in Bush's fiscal 2004 budget request, set to be released on Feb. 3, will be more than 9 percent for homeland security. However, experts on the issue say that no matter how much is proposed, critics will think it is not enough, and with some reason. *(2003 CQ Weekly, p. 244)*

The fissures in what was once a fairly unified homeland security front have begun to show. Some members of Congress say they are worried there is not enough money for all the homeland initiatives, and state and local officials throughout the country complain that they do not have the resources to meet increased security demands. The administration is trying to improve intelligence sharing by proposing a consolidated terrorism threat center, but the idea has met with skepticism, given the longstanding rivalries in the intelligence community and problems that predate Sept. 11. Congress is making headway in reorganizing its committee structure to deal with homeland security, but the job is only about half done.

Democrats are not holding back in their criticism. Senate Minority Leader Tom Daschle of South Dakota has accused the administration of a "credibility gap" in homeland security and other domestic policies. Sen. Hillary Rodham Clinton, D-N.Y., has talked of "the myth of homeland security."

Spending for Homeland Security

President Bush will request $41.3 billion for homeland security in fiscal 2004, including $36.2 billion for the new Homeland Security Department. Congress has not agreed on fiscal 2003 homeland security spending, but it is expected to be close to the $37.8 billion Bush requested, which included $33.5 billion for the department.

(budget authority in millions of dollars)	Former Dept.	FY 2002 Enacted	FY 2002 Supplemental	FY 2003 Proposed*
Chemical, Biological, Radiological, and Nuclear Countermeasures				
Chemical, Biological, Radiological, and Nuclear Countermeasures R&D	DOE	$65	$45	$114
National Biological Warfare Defense Analysis Center (New)		—	—	420
Plum Island Animal Disease Center	USDA	7	23	5
Total		**72**	**68**	**539**
Information Analysis and Infrastructure Protection				
Critical Infrastructure Assurance Office	Commerce	5	1	27
Federal Computer Incident Response Center	GSA	10	—	11
National Communications System	DOD	51	89	155
National Infrastructure Protection Center (Excluding CIOS Enf.)	FBI	51	—	54
National Infrastructure Simulation and Analysis Center/Energy Assurance	DOE	6	—	29
Total		**123**	**90**	**276**
Border and Transportation Security				
Immigration and Naturalization Service — Enforcement	DOJ	4,224	537	4,855
Border-related Detention Funding	DOJ	—	—	615
Customer Service	Treasury	3,268	400	3,690
Federal Law Enforcement Training Center	Treasury	139	31	145
Animal and Plant Health Inspection Service	USDA	222	—	240
Federal Protection Services	GSA	278	102	411
Transportation Security Administration	DOT	1,250	2,435	5,346
Office of Domestic Preparedness	DOJ	251	400	—
Total		**9,632**	**3,905**	**15,302**
Emergency Preparedness and Response				
Federal Emergency Management Agency		4,294	7,478	7,946
Federal Response Assets, Including National Pharmaceutical Stockpile	HHS	113	1,161	550
Nuclear Incident Response	DOE	—	—	—
Domestic Emergency Support Team	Justice	—	—	—
National Domestic Preparedness Office	FBI	—	—	—
Total		**4,407**	**8,639**	**8,496**
Secret Service	Treasury	**1,123**	**105**	**1,214**
U.S. Coast Guard	Transportation	**5,150**	**464**	**6,183**
Immigration and Naturalization Service — Immigration Services	DOJ	**1,436**	**37**	**1,454**
Total, Department of Homeland Security		**$21,943**	**$13,308**	**$33.464**

SOURCE: Office of Management and Budget

* Congress has not passed the 2003 omnibus appropriation bill

Republicans, however, continue to hold a power position on security in terms of both policy and money. They point to obvious strides: the near doubling of spending for homeland security from $19 billion to $38 billion in the past two years; the federalization of airport security; and the enactment by Congress of a law (PL 107-296) creating the Department of Homeland Security — the most extensive government overhaul in five decades. *(2002 CQ Weekly, p. 3072)*

But those are last year's accomplishments, and Democrats now appear intent on making homeland security a political issue and using it against Republicans, just as Republicans used it as an election issue last November. *(2002 CQ Weekly, p. 2888)*

Some studies, including one from the Brookings Institution, have said the budget for all the necessary domestic security initiatives should be closer to $48 billion, instead of Bush's expected fiscal 2004 proposal of $41.3 billion. And although Bush advocates a smaller federal government in most areas, he has put more on the homeland security plate by proposing a "Terrorist Threat Integration Center" to analyze terrorism intelligence, and a $6 billion plan he calls "Project Bioshield," which would stockpile vaccines for various biological agents. It is not clear where the $6 billion would come from or whether Congress would authorize the full program once it was introduced. But such new initiatives certainly add

Appropriations Panels Remade To Oversee Homeland Spending

While the establishment of the Department of Homeland Security has led House leaders to establish a Select Committee on Homeland Security to oversee the new Cabinet department, its purse strings will be controlled by newly configured subcommittees on the two congressional Appropriations committees.

In the House, Appropriations Committee Chairman C.W. Bill Young, R-Fla., announced Jan. 29 that he will reorganize the panel to create a new Homeland Security Subcommittee that would consolidate some of the jurisdiction that had been shared by eight of the panel's 13 subcommittees. The chairman will be Harold Rogers, a trusted Young lieutenant who has spent his 22 years in Congress maintaining a low profile while tending to the needs of his poor, rural southeastern Kentucky constituents.

Before assuming the helm of the Transportation Subcommittee two years ago, Rogers chaired the Commerce, Justice, State and the Judiciary panel for six years. While considered a capable appropriator — he cut deals on several contentious domestic spending disputes during the Clinton administration — Rogers has not gone out of his way to fight members' projects or otherwise campaign for a smaller government.

He has, however, taken a keen interest in the management of several of the biggest federal agencies the Homeland Department is absorbing.

While chairing the subcommittee that financed the Transportation Security Administration (TSA) at its creation in 2001, he was vocal in his view that the new agency was submitting inflated budget requests. "We will not give them money to hire a standing army of almost 70,000 people to take off your shoes, check your briefcase three times, and perform intensive checks of white-haired grandmothers in wheelchairs," Rogers said.

At Commerce-Justice-State, he had the Immigration and Naturalization Service (INS) in his purview. Since the mid-1990s, Rogers has been an ardent proponent of splitting that agency in half, with one bureau to guard the nation's borders and another to process immigration paperwork. A version of that plan has been enacted, with both agencies as part of the new Homeland Department.

Off the committee, Rogers has not been afraid to go against the partisan grain when parochial concerns have conflicted with the wants of his leadership. This has proved especially true on trade. Kentucky's declining coal and tobacco industries have led Rogers to oppose three of the four sweeping trade laws of the past decade.

Young's move caught the Senate off guard. Appropriations Committee Chairman Ted Stevens, R-Alaska, wrote to Young and House and Senate GOP leaders urging that the first major reorganization of the Appropriations panels since the 1960s be put on hold until the mammoth wrapup fiscal 2003 appropriations package (H J Res 2), now in conference, is completed. *(2003 CQ Weekly, p. 194)*

Specter's Job

Nonetheless, Stevens said that he supports the idea of creating an Appropriations panel "to focus solely on homeland security." He has not said whether he believes the jurisdiction of such a panel should be identical to that of the new House subcommittee.

But all sides have decided against forming a 14th subcommittee, which Young initially advocated. The idea has been discarded in part because it would have made the range of the various panels' powers too disparate.

Stevens and the No. 2 GOP Senate appropriator, Thad Cochran of Mississippi, plan to stay put as chairmen of the Defense and Agriculture subcommittees, their aides said. That would put Arlen Specter of Pennsylvania, who is seeking a fifth term in 2004, in line for the job. His office declined to comment on his plans, but committee aides as well as lobbyists who closely follow the committee say he wants the powerful new post.

To take the gavel, Specter would step aside as chairman of the Labor, Health and Human Services and Education Subcommittee, freeing that

to the promise of homeland security without laying out a clear plan for how to pay for them.

"There is absolutely a disconnect" between policy proposals and funding, said Christine LaPaille, a spokeswoman for the National Governors Association, which has lobbied hard for more homeland security funding for states. "It'll take billions to make sure first responders can communicate, but the money isn't there."

Former Rep. Lee H. Hamilton, D-Ind. (1965-99), one-time chairman of the House Foreign Affairs Committee and now a member of Bush's Homeland Security Advisory Council, described security funding as a "bottomless pit."

As Congress stares into this pit, it sees billions in needs for security at every level, a growing budget deficit, states that have fiscal crises of their own, and an increasing level of discord over how to implement the Department of Homeland Security.

Congress also has made few changes in its own organization to deal with such issues. The House has created a Select Committee on Homeland Security, to be made up of other committee chairman and ranking Democrats, but the Senate has not. Both are in the process of forming appropriations subcommittees for the new department.

There also is a list of unfinished legislative business on homeland security that Congress either did not get to in 2002 or could not agree on: port security funding, air cargo security and first responder money.

With so much on the agenda, and the distractions of a looming war in Iraq and a sizable tax cut package, the central issue for the administration and Congress will be setting priorities for

chairmanship and potentially starting a game of musical chairs among the junior Senate cardinals.

The House proposal also would merge the non-homeland security remnants of the Transportation Subcommittee with the leftovers of the Treasury-Postal Service panel, which would lose significant jurisdiction under the plan. The new Transportation and Treasury Subcommittee will be chaired by Ernest Istook, R-Okla.

The Transportation panel would cede the TSA and the Coast Guard to the new Homeland Security panel, while the Treasury-Postal Subcommittee would transfer responsibility for the Customs Service, Secret Service and the Federal Law Enforcement Training Center. Treasury-Postal also is giving up stewardship of the budget for spending at the Bureau of Alcohol, Tobacco and Firearms (ATF) to the Commerce-Justice-State Subcommittee, swapping it for jurisdiction over the Maritime Administration.

Istook said he was delighted with the new post, and will use it to steer funds to Oklahoma. Appropriations has lost most of its authority over transportation funding to the Transportation and Infrastructure Committee, however, and those looking for winners and losers in the shuffle said Istook did not gain very much.

Young announced the proposal after receiving recommendations from top aide James W. Dyer. He said he won the advance blessing for his plan from Speaker J. Dennis Hastert, R-Ill., and he said Stevens "agreed to

Born: Dec. 31, 1937
Hometown: Somerset
Career: Lawyer
Last election: 78 percent
Committee: Appropriations

Born: Feb. 12, 1930
Hometown: Philadelphia
Career: Lawyer; professor
Last election: 61 percent (1998)
Committees: Appropriations, Environment & Public Works, Judiciary, Veterans Affairs

the basic concept," if not the timing of the reorganization. So did the House committee's ranking Democrat, David R. Obey of Wisconsin.

The House has led the way in prior reorganizations, and aides hoped the Senate would simply accept the plan. But Stevens seemed rankled at being informed rather than actively consulted on the plan. And if he fails to accept every aspect of the proposal, that would mean different House and Senate subcommittees would have jurisdiction over some agencies. That could make conference talks more complicated.

These are some of the other House Appropriations subcommittees that stand to see their jurisdiction taken by the new Homeland Security panel:

- VA-HUD is giving up the Federal Emergency Management Agency.
- Commerce-Justice-State gains ATF but gives up the INS and various first-responder grant programs.
- Agriculture gives up the Animal and Plant Health Inspection Service.
- Defense gives up the National Communications System and Bio-Weapons Defense Center.
- Energy and Water cedes various energy and nuclear programs.
- Labor-HHS loses the Office of Emergency Preparedness, National Stockpile, National Disaster Medical System and Metro Medical Response.

homeland security, rather than trying to be everything to everyone.

"It's going to be a major challenge for Congress and the administration to make sure they get the new department up and running without wasting money," said Michael Scardaville, a policy analyst for homeland security at The Heritage Foundation, a conservative think tank in Washington. "You can't do everything at once. If you don't set priorities and try to do it all, everything would be protected insufficiently."

The General Accounting Office (GAO) already has flagged Homeland Security as a "high risk" agency because of the size of the merger, the troubles of some of its component agencies and the consequences for the nation if it fails to curb terrorism.

Based on mergers of corporations and government agencies, the GAO said it could take five to seven years to complete the Homeland Security Department, with a risk in the meantime of lost productivity and inefficiencies.

Instead of trotting out an extensive list of homeland security needs and letting Congress sort it out, Hamilton said, the administration has to make a tough decision — publicly stating which homeland security initiatives should get the highest priority, while putting lesser threats on the back burner.

For example, he said, bioterrorism preparedness should be a top priority, while a less proven threat could wait for homeland funds.

Hamilton, who also is vice chairman of the National Commission on Terrorist Attacks, the independent panel investigating the Sept. 11 attacks, said, "The federal government is sending out all these warnings and scaring people, but they are not giving out the funds to meet the threats. I don't think the Bush administration has tackled the tough problem of priorities. They have not made clear what threats need to be made a priority and what targets need to be made a priority. . . . Government has to make judgements with regard to security, but politicians don't want to be wrong."

There is an enormous political danger in prioritizing something like security, of course. If one of the lesser priorities is somehow exploited by terrorists, it becomes a human and political disaster.

So far, homeland security accounts for a relatively small part of the federal budget. The $37.8 billion that Bush requested for fiscal 2003 would be about 5 percent of discretionary spending. The final appropriation is expected to be close to that figure.

That means a lot of arguing over a relatively small slice of federal spending. The expectation of a 9.3 percent increase in homeland security for fiscal 2004 would leave total spending at $41.3 billion. But like every budget request, that is just a starting point.

Even with strictly imposed spending caps for the next fiscal year, members of Congress do not want to scrimp on security spending for their home states or districts. Sen. Maria Cantwell, D-Wash., for instance, will probably seek more border patrol personnel for the long boundary with Canada, while Democrat Ernest F. Hollings of South Carolina will probably ask for more port security assistance. Rep. Carolyn B. Maloney, D-N.Y., is pushing for more funding to study health problems of workers at the World Trade Center site.

However, even with such a sensitive issue as homeland security, Office of Management and Budget Director Mitchell E. Daniels Jr. is going to exert his fiscal conservatism on Congress.

"We've said the largest increase [in 2004] will be in homeland security, and we did propose doubling of the homeland security budget in 2003," OMB spokeswoman Amy Call said. "Congress should pass the 2003 budget first."

If Project Bioshield is an indication of things to come, the administration may already be setting its homeland security budget priorities without expressly saying so. Carrying out such an agenda may also involve saying no to certain programs, even if doing so is politically unpopular.

"Obviously, if they don't prioritize it'll be an enormous struggle," said Robbin F. Laird, a former Defense Intelligence Agency official who now is a consultant for federal agencies such as the Coast Guard on national security matters. "The real problem is how you choose between bioterrorism defense and say, the Coast Guard. . . . [Homeland Security Secretary Tom] Ridge and the boys are going to have to make the hard choices."

> *"If they're going to mandate that the program exist, they should help us carry it out."*
>
> **— Jeff Luther, Minnesota homeland security coordinator**

How Much Is Enough?

There is always a gap between what cities, states and federal agencies say they need from the federal government and what they actually get from congressional appropriators. But with the mandate of homeland security stretching from Ground Zero to the Canadian border to nuclear facilities in New Mexico, the demand for dramatic increases in federal funding is stronger than ever. Many on the front lines worry about whether there will be enough money to fulfill their mission to protect the homeland.

New York City, for example, has received plenty of attention and billions in emergency federal aid in the wake of Sept. 11. But even its first responders — the police, firefighters and emergency medics who were the heroes of the World Trade Center — have had trouble getting federal money they believe they were promised. For example, emergency workers at Ground Zero complain that $90 million is needed to investigate ongoing health problems caused by the atmosphere around the Trade Center rubble, while only $12 million has been appropriated through federal grants.

Clinton and her fellow New York Democrat, Sen. Charles E. Schumer, say that New York has fallen short on homeland money for first responders, including police, fire and hospital workers who must handle disasters.

"We have relied on a myth of homeland security, a myth written in rhetoric, inadequate resources and a new bureaucracy," Clinton said in a recent speech. "Critically needed funds are not reaching our local communities and first responders."

The first-responder funding problem stretches to the heartland, to health care workers in Iowa who recently received a shipment of 1,000 doses of smallpox vaccine and the needles to administer the shots. But the state has not received the money to carry out the program, said Iowa's homeland security adviser, Ellen Gordon. The first phase of smallpox vaccinations nationwide is for health care workers.

Gordon said her state is still awaiting $400,000 in federal funds promised to pay for travel and administrative costs for smallpox vaccinations. Iowa has received $4 million for communications equipment but has not received funds for further homeland security training, Gordon said.

"We all understand there's a threat, but the level of frustration is very high," Gordon said. "We're at a stalled moment in time and can't go forward with some of our programs."

Further north, Minnesota is struggling to figure out how to pay for extra security at several areas considered to be "critical infrastructure," including oil pipelines, utility plants and the Mall of America, said Jeff Luther, the state's homeland security coordinator. Every time the terrorist threat level changes color in Washington, Minnesota ramps up security at the busy Mall of America as well as at water facilities and electrical plants. Even though the decisions on the threat level are being made in Washington, counties in Minnesota incur the overtime costs of ratcheting up security, Luther said.

"We don't even have money to guard [smallpox] vaccine at the local level," Luther said. "If they're going to mandate that the program exist, they should help us carry it out. We do have the responsibility for our own state, but we can't wait on the federal government."

New York, Iowa and Minnesota are not alone in their growing discontent over the flow of federal money for local security measures. The National Gov-

Federal, State or Local Responsibility For Homeland Defense?

The founding fathers employed the phrase "federalism" for a system of government that divides power and responsibility among a central authority, states and a collection of more or less self-governing local units. Now, that system is being tested by the post-Sept. 11 mobilization to prepare the country for possible doomsday scenarios.

Before Sept. 11, terrorism was primarily a federal responsibility. But the attacks on the World Trade Center and the Pentagon showed that this national issue involved states, cities, townships and counties in an unprecedented way.

The key to a strong network, say analysts and government associations, is managing the creative tension between the upper and lower levels of government to address local idiosyncrasies but enforce national standards. That means many more decisions must be made about which tasks become a federal responsibility and which duties fall on the shoulders of state and local defenders.

"It's whatever we say it is, as it is on almost everything else," said Democratic Sen. Ben Nelson of Nebraska, a former governor.

Leaders of the relevant committees in Congress say they will take a closer look at the delineation of roles this year. "I think Congress and the decisions that we make, particularly with regard to funding, will determine the division of that responsibility," said Jim Turner of Texas, ranking Democrat on the House Select Committee on Homeland Security.

Academics say they see no reason why the system that has served the country well for more than two centuries cannot adapt to the new challenge. Applied to homeland security, the federal government's strong military, its immigration and border controls, and its public health support systems cannot be duplicated by states, they say. By the same token, the federal government cannot staff every town and county with police, firefighters and paramedics.

"In general, the United States has done very well historically by giving a lot of responsibility and latitude to states and cities to develop their own ideas about how services should be provided," said Arnold Howitt, director of the Executive Session on Domestic Preparedness at Harvard University's Kennedy School of Government. The federal government cannot replace this capacity, "and we shouldn't, even if it could," he said.

Feeling the Pinch

What the federal government can do, Howitt said, is drive the state and local systems to change quickly and patch holes in the security network. It can do this by setting uniform standards for communications, emergency response and health plans, by disseminating information about terrorism risks, conducting practice exercises and convening groups to share their best practices.

The White House Office of Homeland Security started this process in July by releasing a national strategy, which began to lay out roles for each level of government. The office also assembled a 195-page report detailing the actions each state was taking. Federal officials continue to have frequent conference calls with state homeland security coordinators, and the department eventually will set up an office for state and local coordination. Howitt said the key is to keep up the coordination while the federal department looks inward at its own organization.

The grease for the system remains money, and states are feeling a severe fiscal pinch that has blocked resources from getting down to lower levels of governing. Funds promised by the federal government remain caught in the overdue fiscal 2003 appropriations bills. Turner said a Texas state senator recently called to ask him, "You all are going to make this [homeland security] stuff another unfunded mandate, are you?"

Deborah Rigsby, senior legislative counsel at The National League of Cities, said Iowa and New York have such severe problems that some of their cities have been forced to cut the police and fire budgets.

It is a problem lawmakers see clearly. "We're going to be relying on localities to do more things, and clearly that means money," said House Government Reform Committee Chairman Thomas M. Davis III, R-Va. But given the federal budget squeeze, how much money remains to be seen.

ernors Association, along with the U.S. Conference of Mayors, has increased its lobbying efforts on Capitol Hill in an attempt to increase grants for first responders. In some cases, money that was already in the budget for firefighters or police training has been reallocated and designated as homeland security money, said a lobbyist who tracks the issue.

On Jan. 24, the day his department was officially created, Ridge told a news conference that he sympathized with cities and states. "I can understand right now their huge frustration with Washington, D.C.," Ridge said. "I think we'll be able to relieve some of that frustration and concern as soon as Congress gets the omnibus bill passed, and we begin distributing these dollars, and then we move right into the 2004 budget."

To be sure, first responders may never feel like they have enough money for homeland security. And many basic security duties remain the domain of states and localities. The difference now is that security is a national mission, and if states or cities can squeeze money out of the federal budget rather than local coffers, they will. *(above)*

"Eventually, local and state governments will have to put these security costs into their own budgets,"

Hamilton said.

Port security is one of those issues that have received significant amounts of publicity, but not a lot of money.

The worst-nightmare port security scenario is frightening — a loose nuke or a radioactive "dirty bomb" is smuggled in through one of the millions of uninspected cargo containers that pass through U.S. ports every year. Only about 2 percent of the containers are now examined.

Yet coastal state members of Congress say there has not been a clear message on port security. Last year's port security legislation (PL 107-295) authorized virtually no money for programs. Schumer was able to earmark $150 million for port security in the 2003 omnibus appropriations bill (H J Res 2) but that would come from the Transportation Security Administration budget and is not new money. Port officials have applied for nearly $700 million in grants to increase security, and have said a more realistic price tag is $2 billion. *(2002 CQ Weekly, p. 3028)*

Port security is not the only unfinished business under the Department of Homeland Security's jurisdiction. With so much focus since Sept. 11 on commercial airplanes, air cargo has been somewhat overlooked. Sens. Kay Bailey Hutchison, R-Texas, and Dianne Feinstein, D-Calif., have reintroduced an air cargo security bill (S 165). *(2003 CQ Weekly, p. 208)*

Rail security also has taken a back seat, as a $1.2 billion Amtrak security amendment was taken out of the homeland security bill in 2002. Some lawmakers worried that the money would help subsidize Amtrak's operations.

"The FBI has stated that freight and passenger rail could be targets," said Sen. Thomas R. Carper, D-Del., who proposed the rail security amendment. "We've put a lot of time and energy into aviation security, but we have overlooked rail security."

Congressional Turf

Though some members of Congress have decided it is time to start criticizing Bush over homeland security funding, Congress has not completely organized its own affairs on homeland security jurisdictional matters.

The House has revived the Select Homeland Security Committee it used to draft the final version of its homeland security legislation in 2002. The panel, chaired by Christopher Cox, R-Calif., will be made up of chairmen and ranking Democrats from other committees, but the full membership has not been announced.

The Senate has not formed a similar panel, and it appears that Susan Collins, R-Maine, who chairs the Governmental Affairs Committee, will share jurisdiction on some homeland security matters with John McCain, R-Ariz., who oversees transportation and border security issues as chairman of the Commerce, Science and Transportation Committee.

On the financial front, the House Appropriations Committee on Jan. 29 announced that it was combining its Transportation and Treasury-Postal subcommittees and creating a separate Homeland Security Appropriations Subcommittee, chaired by Republican Harold Rogers of Kentucky, who previously was head of the Transportation Subcommittee. *(Appropriations, p. 6)*

The Senate probably will follow suit, though Appropriations Committee Chairman Ted Stevens, R-Alaska, has said he does not want to make any changes until after Congress clears the fiscal 2003 omnibus. He had urged C.W. "Bill" Young, R-Fla., chairman of the House Appropriations Committee, to do the same. But Young defended his panel's reorganization, saying, "It will allow us to conduct vigorous oversight of the new department and ensure that taxpayers' dollars are well spent."

Intelligence Questions

Given pre-Sept. 11 intelligence failures, nobody is criticizing the reasoning behind Bush's Terrorist Threat Integration Center, which calls for the CIA, FBI, Department of Homeland Security and Department of Defense to share information. However, there already is growing disagreement over where in the bureaucracy the center should be housed and who should run it.

Military and civilian intelligence agencies have competed for years, and their rivalry is mirrored on Capitol Hill between the Intelligence and Armed Services committees. Although the head of the CIA is the government's director of central intelligence, he does not have authority over military intelligence gathering, and periodic efforts to merge intelligence functions have been quashed by the Pentagon and its congressional allies.

Lawmakers disagreed in 2002 over whether the new Homeland Security Department should have access to raw intelligence or summaries from intelligence agencies. The legislation called for an intelligence division in the new department to integrate and analyze information from the FBI and other intelligence agencies.

Sen. Joseph I. Lieberman, D-Conn., who helped write the original homeland security legislation, believes the new analysis center should be placed in the Homeland Security Department so it is not under the CIA's control.

"The historic rivalries and lack of cooperation between the CIA, FBI and other intelligence agencies is a major problem we must overcome," Lieberman said. "Placing this fusion center in the new department would ensure analysis from an independent entity outside of the existing rivalries. The president's approach perpetuates a major part of the problem."

Cox, who has become a congressional point man for security issues as chairman of the Homeland Security Committee, also said the new department might be the best place for an intelligence analysis center.

"The biggest thing on our agenda will be implementing these programs," Cox said, discussing the terrorism intelligence center. "It's a big first step. The most essential element in preventing another World Trade Center or Oklahoma City is obtaining and sharing intelligence."

Regardless of where terrorism information is analyzed, some veteran intelligence experts are skeptical.

"They're inventing another bureaucracy to slow everything down," said Harry "Skip" Brandon, a former deputy assistant director of the FBI for counterterrorism. "I'm skeptical of creating another bureaucratic artifice. If the FBI doesn't want to share information, they're not going to share information because there's this new center."

As the war on terrorism intensifies overseas and an invasion of Iraq looms, some Democrats worry that homeland security within the United States will become a secondary priority.

Even with the increased spending Bush will call for to support the Department of Homeland Security, the funding priorities are already coming under attack. The debates over first responders, port security and intelligence are really only beginning for the 108th Congress. ◆

Congress Attends to Business, Waits for Word on the War

Financing, oversight, fence-mending roles in abeyance until Bush takes action

There has been an air of unreality to the work of Congress for about the last two weeks. The Senate spent the week of March 10 debating abortion and judges, the House voted to crack down on excessive medical malpractice awards, and House and Senate budget panels have approved blueprints that make no mention of the one future expense that is on all lawmakers' minds.

If members of Congress had any doubts about whether the United States will go to war with Iraq, they lost them after President Bush's March 6 news conference. "The price of the attacks on America, the cost of the attacks on America on September the 11th were enormous. They were significant. And I am not willing to take that chance again," he said. And then the kicker: "When it comes to our security, we really don't need anybody's permission."

Since then, lawmakers have talked about war as if it is days — perhaps hours — away. But they also know it is completely out of their hands. They had their chance to weigh in on Iraq last fall, and by lopsided margins in both the House and the Senate, they authorized Bush to use force to disarm Saddam Hussein if all other options fail (PL 107-243). Now that Bush seems convinced that all other options have failed, a view many lawmakers share, Congress has been able to do little but mark time with debates and votes on other issues — and wait for the war to start.

In the coming weeks and months, however, Congress will likely have its hands full with the duties it would have to perform when the war starts.

Only Congress can release the funds to pay for the war, and it will face pressure from the Bush administration to pass supplemental appropriations bills quickly — perhaps two, maybe more — to give the military what it needs. It also will have an oversight role, as the Armed Services committees monitor the performance of the new military hardware and decide what weapons systems will deserve funding in the future. The Foreign Affairs and International Relations committees, which will have to deal with the possibility of shattered alliances and strained diplomatic relations with other countries, will use the power of congressional hearings to shine a spotlight on the long-term problems the war could create.

None of these activities by themselves are likely to change the course of the war, or even the direction of U.S. foreign policy. Members of Congress freely admit that when the administration asks for money to support the troops risking their lives in Iraq, saying "no" is not an option. And they alone will not be able to repair whatever damage the United States might suffer in its relationships with countries that oppose the war.

The War Agenda

Still, the actions Congress will take will have lasting effects on the nation's budget, the future of its military forces, and the public debate over the administration's foreign policy.

Simply by becoming engaged in what it can do, analysts say, Congress will be able to claim a role in this likely turning point in U.S. history — the first pre-emptive military strike against a nation that has not struck first — that it has not played since the vote last fall on the resolution authorizing Bush to use force to disarm Saddam. *(2002 CQ Weekly, p. 2671)*

"Since the vote was taken in the fall, we have had no significant debate within the Congress," said Norman J. Ornstein, resident scholar at the American Enterprise Institute.

There has been plenty of unofficial debate, of course, in the form of news conferences and the occasional round of floor speeches. Officially, however, Congress has mostly stayed silent, partly because most Republicans say they accept that Bush will take the lead on foreign policy. Even Democratic leaders who have doubts about the war believe there is little point in taking up a second resolution, since there is little chance the vote would turn out much different from the one last fall.

"The president is the commander in chief. He will lead the war effort. That's how it should be," said Sen. Sam Brownback, R-Kan. "We need to get our work done here. We've got to get a budget resolution and a fiscal stimulus package."

But members of Congress also know the occasion is momentous — not only because of the stakes for the security of the United States, but also because of the precedent a pre-emptive strike could set for future military actions, the postwar relationships the United States would have with other countries, and the unpredictable impact on the nation's long-term fiscal health. "This is the first time in American history that we're going to go to war and have a tax cut," said Rep. Bob Filner, D-Calif.

If Bush decides to launch that war, Congress will have a range of duties to fulfill that will cover everything from the short-term need for military funding to the long-term questions of what would come after the war.

In the short term, Congress would have to provide the funding for the war. Politically, lawmakers have little choice but to cough up whatever money Bush asks for, but in practical terms, they can adjust how quickly or slowly the supplemental bills move and how many additional spending items are attached to them. Congress has a long tradition of loading up supplemental spending bills with pet projects — knowing the bills are too badly needed to be vetoed — so Republican leaders will have to try to keep the add-ons to a minimum.

Some lawmakers say the administration has not helped its case by refusing repeated requests to tell Congress what it thinks the war and the postwar occupation and rebuilding of Iraq would cost.

But the Pentagon is already using up its funds for the current fiscal year simply by moving the troops overseas, and Bush, as a wartime president, would be able to shame Congress into moving more quickly if the armed forces appeared in danger of running out of money. *(Supplemental appropriations, below)*

During the course of the war, Congress would keep a close eye on the performance of new weapons and equipment getting their first combat test. Those successes and failures on the battlefield would affect decisions on what weapons systems to fund in the future, and ultimately which companies and factories will receive military contracts, where military units will be stationed, and where ships and planes will be sent. *(Military operations, p. 14)*

Over the long term, the foreign affairs panels would deal with the aftermath of the war. That could involve anything from a more secure United States and a more stable Middle East free of weapons of mass destruction, according to the administration's Hill supporters, to an isolated United States that could no longer rely on the support of countries it would need to continue the war on terrorism, according to its critics.

These committees know they will play a distant second to the White House as far as the power to shape foreign policy. But they would be able to use their public hearings — and the visibility their committees give them — to raise issues about the long-term fallout in international relations, as Senate Foreign Relations Committee Chairman Richard G. Lugar, R-Ind., did March 12 when he warned that strained relations with other countries could make it harder to prevent the spread of weapons of mass destruction. *(Foreign relations, p. 16)*

Through all of this, GOP leaders are promising to forge ahead with the domestic agenda they have already planned. The war's needs and any domestic initiatives that can be even remotely linked to Iraq would take priority. If the war ends as quickly as the Gulf War did in 1991, there will be plenty of time to pick up the pace on domestic initiatives. "If the war is short and successful, the president will gain a lot of political capital, which may translate into more success for his legislative agenda," said former U.S. Rep. Robert S. Walker, R-Pa. (1977-97), now a lobbyist.

If it does not, Bush will struggle to save his agenda. In the meantime, Democrats insist they will continue to question the wisdom of his ideas for tax cuts and overhauls of Medicare and Medicaid.

They are aware, though, that any criticisms raised about domestic issues could get even less attention during a war than they did when Congress debated the Iraq resolution last fall. "We're not going to change," said Rep. Rahm Emanuel, D-Ill., a former adviser to President Bill Clinton. "Whether it gets lost in the fog of war is another question." *(Agenda, p. 65)*

What follows is a look at the burdens Congress can, in all likelihood, expect in the months ahead. ◆

THE NEAR FUTURE: Spending

When House leaders pulled a bill from the floor March 6 that would have given armed services personnel a set of tax breaks, the military's supporters on Capitol Hill oddly saw the move as a sign of hope.

The bill was pulled because it had been saddled with tax breaks for unrelated industries such as overseas off-track betting and the makers of fishing tackle boxes. And as U.S. forces stood ready for a war against Iraq, the hope that rose in the hearts of Iraq hawks such as Sens. John W. Warner, R-Va., and John McCain, R-Ariz., went like this: If House leaders were adamant that a military tax bill (HR 878) be free of extraneous provisions during a time of war, did it not follow that they would be equally disciplined about any supplemental appropriations bill headed to Congress to pay for the war?

"So far, the House showed some restraint with this military tax bill," said McCain. "You can always hope."

Whether lawmakers want it or not, war is almost certainly coming, and legislators will soon have their only say in shaping the scope of the conflict and its aftermath. While the major questions of war and peace, strategy and diplomacy belong to the White House, Congress retains a front-line role in the very near term as the institution that must determine how much to spend on the conflict. What lawmakers now must decide is whether they want to rubber-stamp the war funding request President Bush will soon submit, or fight it by placing conditions on the spending or forcing a debate on the extent to which the cost of war will burden the nation's economy.

At this moment, Congress seems to be eying the rubber-stamp option. Although many Democrats have serious questions about how much money will have to be appropriated for a war and what impact those costs will have on the economy, few are so eager for answers that they would slow down funding that is headed to U.S. troops deployed overseas.

"Once a decision has been made to start the conflict, I don't think Democrats will try to use the appropriations process to express their opposition to the war," predicted Rep. Chet Edwards, D-Texas, who sits on the House Budget and Appropriations panels.

But as Congress resolves to support the war, many legislators wonder exactly what they will be supporting. To date, estimates on the amount of any supplemental and the timing of such a request remain little more than wild guesses. Legislators are not even certain how many supplemental bills they will be asked to vote on.

House Appropriations Committee Chairman C.W. Bill Young, R-Fla., said March 12 that he has been told to expect at least two supplemental requests. The first would cover the costs incurred to date — the massive movement of troops and equipment to the Persian Gulf — even if no war occurs. Recent Congressional Budget Office estimates state that the Pentagon has spent close to $25 billion to position its forces in the Middle East and bring them home.

"Congress should not be micromanaging a war. Congress should be in a support role."

— Rep. C.W. Bill Young, R-Fla.

That request could be coming any time now, Young says. The second supplemental request would include costs incurred during the actual war. Some estimates say that bill could easily reach $60 billion.

And other legislators have been left to wonder if they will be asked to consider a third supplemental before the year is out — one that would lay down the required funds to start rebuilding Iraq after a war and to operate programs to help restore democracy and a stable economy there.

Whatever happens, Young insists it will be Congress' job to act on the requests as quickly as possible in order to make sure the Pentagon has the money it needs. Although the Pentagon is unlikely to starve for cash in the short term — managers there routinely raid money set aside for later in the year to fund near-term emergency operations — Young said it would be unseemly for Congress to take too long to get the money out to the soldiers.

What will be harder for Congress will be to act on the requests without making additions or changes to them. Supplemental spending requests are notorious targets for congressional riders, with members inserting their own spending priorities or legislative provisions. It is not unusual for a president's request to return to him with billions of additional dollars attached.

Young said that cannot be the case this year.

"We will try to keep it as lean and trim as we can," he pledged. "Congress should not be micromanaging a war. Congress should be in a support role, and that's where we'll be."

But protecting the supplemental from riders depends on knowing how much the administration wants, and so far officials refuse to say what their number is. On March 13, at a House Appropriations Foreign Operations Subcommittee hearing with Secretary of State Colin L. Powell, Young pressed the secretary, asking him when he can expect to see a request from the administration and wondering how much that request might be.

"I'm getting considerable pressure from a lot of agencies now saying, 'Hey, when are you going to get us a supplemental?' And my response to them is, 'Soon as I get a request from the administration I will move a supplemental through the committee quickly,' " Young said. "Do you have any time constraints? Are you in a hurry for a supplemental? Or does it make any difference?"

Powell parried Young's question with a joke about how he stays out of budget matters so budget people stay out of diplomacy, and the underlying issue went unanswered. However, Powell did make the point that Iraq's significant oil reserves would provide cash to fund the reconstruction.

Daniel K. Inouye of Hawaii, the ranking Democrat on the Senate Appropriations Defense Subcommittee, says he has heard all manner of estimates about what Congress will be expected to appropriate for a war. "They're high," he said. "But not high enough."

Inouye predicts that Congress will have to add money to the president's request to adequately fund all aspects of a war. "There will be differences," he said. But he adds that he is confident Congress can patch together a bill that will remain relatively focused on the war.

The Pentagon Knows Best

The question then becomes to what degree legislators might try to change the bill. Republicans are making it increasingly clear they want any request to move quickly through Congress with as little holdup as possible. House Armed Services Committee Chairman Duncan Hunter, R-Calif., noted that a war supplemental request will be carefully calibrated and should be followed to the letter, since the Pentagon, not Congress, knows what is needed for a war.

"When they tell you they need a bullet, you give them a bullet," he said.

Other legislators say the issue is not simply following orders, but meeting a political imperative to provide for soldiers in the field as promptly as possible.

"At a time of war, you're at your own risk if you want to add something and hold it up," said Sen. Larry E. Craig, R-Idaho.

Winslow Wheeler, a former aide on the Senate Budget Committee and now with the Center for Defense Information, agrees. "They've given themselves no choice but to pay for the war," he said of Congress. "They gave the president a blank check when they placed zero requirements on going to war" with last year's use-of-force resolution (PL 107-243).

But Tom Schatz, president of Citizens Against Government Waste, does not think legislators will be as cowed as Craig predicts. He notes that the supplemental passed in the wake of the Sept. 11 terrorist attacks (PL 107-38) included money for members' pet projects.

War Spending Could Create Largest-Ever Supplemental

Forecasts from the Pentagon and other government agencies place the amount of a wartime supplemental budget at sums as high as $100 billion. That figure would dwarf previous supplemental budgets shown below.

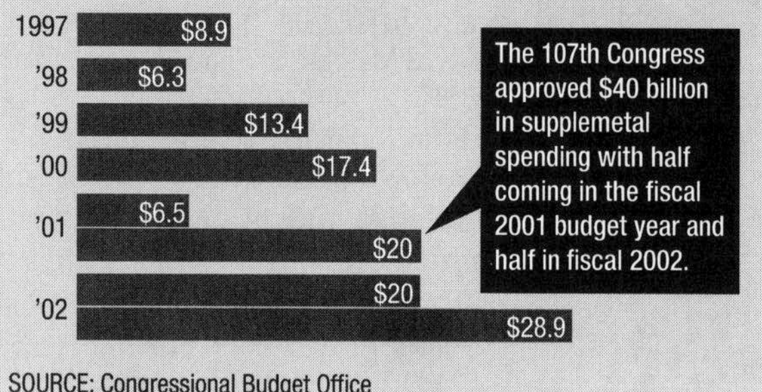

SOURCE: Congressional Budget Office

"I don't know what situation would preclude members [from adding spending for their priorities]," he said. "I cannot imagine members will restrain themselves when it comes to a supplemental for war."

Indeed, the age-old truism that "pork" is in the eye of the beholder is unlikely to be suspended by the urgency of war. At least one group, the U.S. airline industry, would like legislators to let them hitch a ride on the supplemental — or any other legislative vehicle.

Still reeling from the aftermath of the Sept. 11 attacks, the airline industry expects financial losses to deepen further if travel slows again in response to war. The Air Transport Association said the industry expects to lose $6.7 billion this year even without a war, and a conflict with Iraq would push losses to a record $10.7 billion, the association said.

Airlines are not seeking a bailout such as the $15 billion package of grants and loan guarantees Congress passed in 2001 (PL 107-42). But they have asked lawmakers for a package of concessions that would be almost as expensive: a one-year suspension of most aviation taxes in the event of war, an extension of war-risk insurance coverage and government assumption of more security costs. *(Airline law, 2001 Almanac, p. 20-3)*

The suspension of aviation taxes would cost the federal Airport and Airways Trust fund $9 billion — most of its revenue — at a time when airports are struggling with both capacity and security costs.

There is some sentiment in Congress for suspending the aviation fuel tax, but that view does not extend to the passenger ticket taxes or taxes on international arrivals and departures and cargo waybills, according to John L. Mica, R-Fla., chairman of the House Transportation and Infrastructure Subcommittee on Aviation.

The airlines say there is a $4.5 billion unobligated balance in the trust fund that could be used, along with a transfer from general revenues.

War-risk insurance provides airlines with coverage in the event of a terrorist attack and helps them avoid high private-sector rates for terrorism insurance. The airline industry estimates that the tax suspension could save companies $800 million to $1 billion a year in insurance premiums.

There is broad support in Congress for extending war-risk insurance, although the term is uncertain. Last year's homeland security law (PL 107-296) extended it until the end of this year. *(2002 CQ Weekly, p. 3072; 2003 CQ Weekly, p. 417)*

There also is support in both chambers for a government takeover of some costs imposed by the 2001 aviation security law (PL 107-71). The airlines say such costs, including security fees and unfunded mandates, such as employee background checks and screening catering supplies, amount to $4 billion a year.

But even some of the industry's biggest boosters, such as Mica, are cool to the idea of a major aid package, saying that at a time of war the airlines should do more to help themselves.

Unwilling to Choose

Meanwhile, Democrats are not eager to face the stark choice of whether to support the supplemental or not. To them, the war costs need to be considered along with a variety of issues — tax cuts, medicare spending, the federal deficit — all of which could harm the struggling economy.

That is not to say they will not support a war supplemental. They just want to see the war costs now, while Congress is considering its fiscal 2004 budget, so they can see the entire picture, including Bush's proposed tax cuts and any associated deficits.

Even Democrats who have backed the administration's aggressive posture with Iraq say they are not entirely comfortable with being asked to go ahead with the fiscal 2004 budget process and tax cut proposals when significant new costs are looming.

"I understand it's difficult to predict the true costs of a war," said Edwards. "That should be a reason to delay the consideration of massive tax cuts. We should find out how much the war costs first."

The concern is that the combined costs of a war and tax cuts, on top of a tottering economy, will bring everything crashing down, right on top of Congress.

"I think the Republicans are digging such a deep deficit hole that we'll bring down the economy," said Edwards.

To avert that ruinous scenario, Democrats are angling for ways to force a cost estimate of the war.

During the March 13 debate on the $2.2 trillion fiscal 2004 budget resolution in the Senate Budget Committee, ranking Democrat Kent Conrad of North Dakota offered an amendment that would have blocked any increase in the deficit — including tax cuts — until an estimate of the war costs was made available. The amendment was defeated on a party line vote, 11-12.

Still, House Minority Whip Steny H. Hoyer of Maryland defends the theory behind Conrad's failed maneuver. "This country is wealthy enough that we can pay attention to both our domestic needs and our foreign policy needs. [But] we cannot do so without sacrificing to meet our objectives. Therefore, many of us believe that giving the richest people in the country a tax cut so they can buy a third or fourth garage is not appropriate."

Republicans prefer to separate the issues. While the war must be fought and paid for, they argue, the troubles with the economy also must be wrestled under control. That means funding a supplemental to help fight the war and enacting tax cuts to stimulate the economy at the same time.

"There's the reality of the supplemental, and there's the reality of getting the economy moving," said Craig. "Democrats will have a deficit until their grandchildren die if they don't get the economy moving."

Hunter says he does not even see how Democrats can link the issues. He notes that the Pentagon received $6 billion for war operations in the fiscal 2003 omnibus (PL 108-7), which he says should keep operations supported in the short term. "That's essentially the front end. I think it would be a much more serious problem if you didn't have the $6 billion."

As for the rest of the potential costs, Hunter said he holds out high hopes that other nations will rally to the United States and Iraq after any invasion, chipping in for both war costs and the costs of rebuilding.

No Help From Friends

Democrats say that is an unrealistically optimistic scenario. "Even with our friends, they expect us to foot the bill," noted Rep. Nita M. Lowey of New York, ranking Democrat on the House Appropriations Foreign Operations Subcommittee.

But others insist there is yet another way to do away with any budget shortfalls: Iraq's own oil wealth. On March 13, Powell reiterated the administration's stance that Iraq will be able to fund most of the invasion on its own after a war.

"This is a country that will have a somewhat strong revenue stream," said Powell. "They can take care, to a large extent, of their revenue needs."

Still, Republicans allow that they might, at some point, have to calculate the war costs into their current efforts to craft the fiscal 2004 budget. House Budget Committee Chairman Jim Nussle of Iowa said that if the war costs look as though they might extend into fiscal 2004, it would behoove legislators to let the budget show that.

"I believe that our budget needs to reflect that . . . not follow down the road of supplemental spending," he said. "We rarely say, 'Let's absorb this emergency.' " ◆

THE MIDTERM: Military Operations

The televised images of an expected invasion of Iraq this spring may look familiar: M-1 battle tanks careening over sand dunes, shadowy B-2 stealth bombers dropping munitions within a few yards of their targets, perhaps even Iraqi soldiers waving in surrender toward the camera of an unmanned aerial drone. "You're going to see many of the machines that you saw in the first Gulf War," says retired Maj. Gen. Robert Scales, who wrote the Army's official history of the 1990-91 conflict.

But the picture would be deceiving. Up close, combat will be vastly different than a decade ago, with weapons that are more powerful and more precise, troops that move faster, and commanders that know more about their surroundings and their opponents. "Technology has made existing platforms orders of magnitude more effective," Scales says.

The U.S. commander of the operation, Army Gen. Tommy Franks, and his subordinates will try to capitalize on improvements in computers and communications to move more quickly and strike harder than would have been possible in Operation Desert Storm. These novel ways of waging war foreshadow the lighter, more agile, more lethal force that is the goal of Defense Secretary Donald H. Rumsfeld's campaign to transform the armed forces.

Separate from its impact on Middle East politics and the war on terrorism, in fact, an invasion of Iraq would be a proving ground for current and projected military weapons and tactics. Conspicuous successes or failures in the field — the winners and losers among combat weapons and equipment — could be reflected in the administration's future defense budget requests. And it is Congress that will be in position to deliver rewards and punishments based upon those on-the-field performances.

The ripple affect of these decisions would determine which companies and factories receive military contracts, where military units are stationed and where ships and planes are sent.

That is what happened after the 1991 Gulf War, when Congress requested from the Pentagon a comprehensive review of the battle that became a several-hundred-page report on lessons learned. Spectacular successes of precision-guided bombs and the M-1 tanks built by General Dynamics shored up political support for those programs. By the same token, the Army's difficulty in deploying Boeing Corp.'s Apache helicopters for the 1999 operation in Kosovo stimulated the decision by Chief of Staff Gen. Eric K. Shinseki to accelerate development of lighter, more easily transported combat units, lest political leaders conclude that the Army could not get to the scene of future fights.

The first of Shinseki's lighter "Stryker" brigades will not be ready in time for service in Iraq, and the Bell Textron/Boeing V-22 Osprey tilt-rotor aircraft is still being tested and will not accompany Marine units.

But the prospect of combat is so important for military development that the armed services may rush to the field experimental versions of some equipment and software, along with the civilian contractors needed to keep them running.

That happened in the 1991 war, when the Pentagon dispatched to Saudi Arabia the two existing prototypes of the Joint STARS ground surveillance radar planes built by Northrop Grumman. The planes gave U.S. commanders the data needed to target Iraqi forces far behind the front lines and established the Joint STARS program as a top congressional priority.

To be sure, a war may not settle every argument over tactics and weapons systems. Some debates may just be recast as each side draws its own conclusions from combat performance.

Supporters and opponents of the Patriot missile, for instance, reached opposite conclusions about the weapon's

Congressional Eyes Follow the Flight of New Patriot

The Army's new Patriot Advanced Capability (PAC-3) missile, smaller and more accurate than its Gulf War predecessor, is designed to intercept weapons such as the Scud and could be tested for the first time in combat if the United States invades Iraq. Congress will be closely watching its performance. Lockheed Martin recently received a $100 million contract to accelerate production of the PAC-3 to a total of 100 missiles by the end of fiscal year 2003. It is built in the suburbs of Dallas-Ft. Worth.

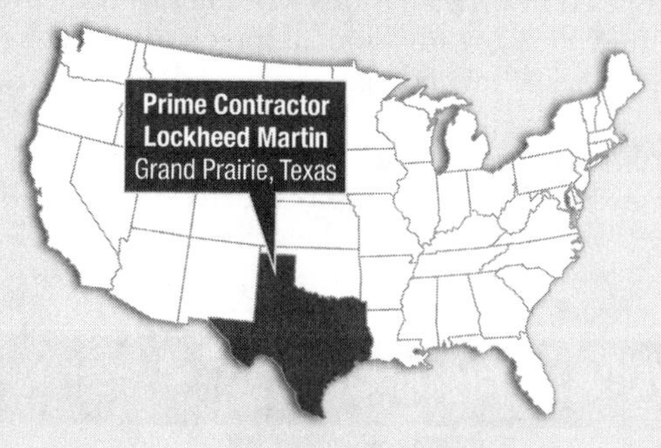

usefulness in the 1991 war. Proponents said the Patriot was vital because Iraq could arm its Scud missiles with chemical, biological or nuclear warheads. Skeptics said the weapon's woeful track record demonstrated the technical difficulty of intercepting even such primitive missiles as the Scuds.

'Shock and Awe'

U.S. forces invading Iraq would rely on the precision-guided bombs and fast-moving ground units that highlighted the 1991 campaign against Iraq. What would be different this time is the sheer volume and tempo of destruction. Rather than demolishing the Iraqi army one battalion at a time, Franks hopes to unhinge Iraqi defenses, leaving them largely intact but organizationally and psychologically incapable of resistance.

Michael G. Vickers, an analyst at the Center for Strategic and Budgetary Assessments, a nonpartisan defense think tank, notes published speculation that U.S. planes may hit 3,000 targets with precision-guided bombs in the first two days of the next war, compared with about 150 targets hit on the first day of Desert Storm. "Basically, all U.S. aircraft can carry precision-guided weapons now," he says, compared with a relative handful in 1991.

To exploit the anticipated shock of the air assault, a U.S. ground attack is expected to begin only a few days after the bombing campaign this time, compared with the six weeks that elapsed between the start of the air war and the ground assault in Desert Storm. This would increase the risk that U.S. planes might accidentally attack friendly ground troops for whom they were trying to clear the way. "In the Gulf War," Scales recalls, "we were so afraid of fratricide that there was no close air support."

In Afghanistan, new communications systems and tactics were tested that enabled even high-flying bombers to clobber enemy forces close to U.S.-backed Afghan units with dozens of satellite-guided bombs. An operation in Iraq would test whether those approaches can safely be used on a much larger scale.

One of these new communications systems is the "collaborative information environment," a network over which hundreds of commanders and staff officers in separate locations can quickly exchange information.

A prototype of the system, put together from in-house Pentagon equipment and software by Ezenia Inc. of Burlington, Mass., was demonstrated last summer in a war game called Millennium Challenge 2002. According to one senior officer, it enabled younger, computer-savvy staffers to give their commanders a very detailed picture of their situation. "They're instant-messaging 15 different guys and they're in four chat rooms at a time," he said. "It doesn't sound like much, but the ability to understand what's going on around you is tremendously powerful."

Here are some other systems that may get a trial by fire in Iraq:

- Because the tilt-rotor Osprey is years behind schedule, Special Operations units sent to capture Iraqi chemical and biological weapons dumps will be carried by modified C-130 Hercules cargo planes. The low-flying planes may have to depend on recently installed Northrop Grumman defensive lasers intended to deflect shoulder-launched heat-seeking missiles. If there are losses, it may increase pressure for the Osprey and stealthier long-range transports.
- The Army's light divisions, which have no heavy tanks, will have some new weapons at their disposal to face Iraqi armored units. The Javelin shoulder-launched missile, a joint venture of Raytheon and Lockheed Martin, is designed to allow light Army forces to kill attacking tanks as they could not have done in 1991. The war may also provide a large-scale test of the Longbow version of the Apache helicopter, equipped with radar to find targets in weather that would blind the original Apache. If the Apache is successful enough, it might weaken the Army's case for fielding the new Boeing/Sikorsky Comanche scout helicopter, still under development.
- The Army may test the basic logic of its effort to link all U.S.

units in one area by a digital network so they can view a single map of friendly and enemy forces. The 4th Mechanized Infantry Division is fully equipped with a system by TRW that networks that force down to the smallest unit. The Army has decided to network only three of its 10 existing divisions. Nevertheless, if the 4th Division gets into combat — its planned deployment through Turkey may be blocked by the Turkish parliament — a combat test of the digital system would be significant. The same network approach is at the heart of the Army's plans to develop, under the aegis of Boeing and SAIC, new technology combat units that would be lighter and more agile than the Stryker brigades.

- The Air Force would probably attack underground command centers with "bunker-buster" bombs — 5,000-pound weapons designed to punch through 100 feet of hard earth or 20 feet of reinforced concrete. If they work, it could undermine arguments by some conservatives in Congress for a new generation of nuclear weapons to destroy such targets, an effort that has significant support on the House Armed Services Committee. If they do not work, it would strengthen the argument for something more powerful.
- If Iraq's military used Scud-type weapons, U.S. forces would try out the Patriot PAC-3, the first U.S. missile system specifically designed to knock down other missiles.

The Raytheon Patriots launched at Iraqi Scuds in 1991 — with little success — were larger missiles designed to hit manned aircraft with shrapnel from an explosive warhead. The PAC-3 — a much smaller, more agile missile built by Lockheed Martin — is intended to kill approaching missiles by ramming them, the basic approach of all the anti-missile weapons the Pentagon is developing for use in the next several years.

If PAC-3 is used, unless it works flawlessly, protagonists on each side of the anti-missile debate will find support for their positions.

- Even if no chemical or biological weapons were launched at U.S. forces, some of the Pentagon's new defensive equipment would get a test of its reliability.

For instance, to replace a chemical agent warning device that frequently gave false alarms in 1991, U.S. forces in the Persian Gulf regions have thousands of new units called "advanced chemical agent detector alarms" built by Graseby Dynamics Ltd., a British firm.

Troops also will probably use up some of the hundreds of thousands of sets of chemical and biological protective clothing called JSLIST (joint service lightweight integrated suit technology) suits. Once the suits are removed from their protective wrappers, they lose their effectiveness after 45 days because of their lining material, so some are likely to be used up as a precaution. The suits are manufactured by companies in Texas, Maine and Virginia.

- Two specialized aerial bombs may get their first large-scale use. One is the so-called sensor-fuzed weapon, built by Textron Systems, designed to knock out entire columns of vehicles. The weapon is a 1,000-pound bomb that scatters 40 soup-can-sized warheads, each of which can single out and destroy a vehicle within an area of nearly 30 acres. The other is a microwave bomb that creates a jolt of electromagnetic energy that could damage or destroy any electronic system within a limited area.

Although senior Pentagon officials refuse to acknowledge the existence of such weapons, their presence is taken for granted by many defense specialists. In the 1991 Gulf War and again in Kosovo, U.S. forces shut down enemy power grids, at least for a limited period, by shorting out their transmission facilities with showers of carbon filaments scattered by Tomahawk cruise missiles. But human-rights groups objected that those widespread power outages endangered civilians by cutting power to sewage treatment plants and hospitals. In principle, the new microwave weapon could be aimed to affect only military facilities.

- Street fighting in Baghdad would be the first time U.S. troops have had to engage in urban warfare on a large scale since the 1968 battle for Hue, Vietnam, and it would test recent training and tactics. Restrictions on sightlines and radio ranges could limit the U.S. advantage in technology. Both the Army and Marine Corps are developing equipment designed to limit the risk of city battles, such as inexpensive, toy-sized aerial drones and small robots that can climb stairs and look for booby traps. A robot dubbed MATILDA (Mesa Associates Tactical Integrated Light-Force Deployment Assembly), which has been employed by domestic law-enforcement agencies for years, is being used in Afghanistan on an experimental basis to search caves and buildings for booby-traps and might be shifted to Iraq.

THE FUTURE: Foreign Relations

As geopolitical visions go, President Bush's expectations for a war against Iraq are nothing if not ambitious. No more weapons of mass destruction looming over an always-troubled area of the world. A fledgling democracy replacing a dictatorship, serving as a model of freedom that will expand in ever-growing concentric circles throughout a region unfamiliar with the concept. As Bush reiterated in his March 14 Rose Garden appearance, his ambitions also include peace between the Palestinians and Israelis. All of this would be accompanied and nurtured by expanding trade.

The vision is heartily endorsed by many on Capitol Hill, including those who are foursquare behind the president, such as Sen. John McCain, R-Ariz., who sees "an opportunity to make Iraq a showplace of democracy." *(2002 CQ Weekly, p. 3165)*

But many lawmakers doubt that attacking Iraq is the way to achieve it — especially if an attack is undertaken without support from longtime allies.

Instead, those lawmakers, figures such as Sen. Dianne Feinstein, D-Calif., a member of the Intelligence Committee, and others who are deeply involved in national security issues, foresee a grim future of repairing shredded alliances and paying tremendous costs in lives and treasure as the nation continues its war on terrorism. They also see the United States juggling future crises without the benefit of allies, lost because of a reckless haste toward an unprovoked war.

"There are a lot of people that are now afraid of the United States. That's a double-edged sword," Feinstein said. "A successful long-term war, not only against al Qaeda but against all terrorism, is going to depend on friends, allies and alliances."

Will Everyone Love a Winner?

Among the questions these lawmakers face is whether the United States will actually lose vital allies angered by the administration's war on Iraq. Or will they follow the adage "everyone loves a winner" and rapidly forgive and forget if the United States ousts Iraqi President Saddam Hussein quickly and with few casualties.

Some expect that allies — including those who oppose attacking Iraq — eventually will return to the fold and recement their alliance with the United States to help with reconstruction.

"They will all want a piece of the action," said Curt Weldon, R-Pa., a senior member of the House Armed Services Committee.

Still, many other lawmakers are anxious about the diplomatic fallout from a war. They fear that lingering bitterness over a war against Iraq could cleave ties with countries and international organizations that had "more to do with keeping peace in the world for the last 50 years than anything else," said Sen. Chuck Hagel, R-Neb., a senior member of the Foreign Relations Committee.

Senate Intelligence Committee Chairman Pat Roberts, R-Kan., says allies' hard feelings stem not merely from America's military power but from the administration's decision, after the Sept. 11 attacks, to endorse pre-emption — first strikes against enemies that have not struck America — as a new national security policy.

"Pre-emption is brand new for us," Roberts said. "It makes Americans feel somewhat uncomfortable, and obviously it makes our allies feel uncomfortable." But, he added, "people have to understand, including Europe, that this transnational threat is not going away, and I think that things will fall into place postwar, if in fact we go to war."

Hagel says the United States, as "the unchallenged superpower," must "listen to our allies and work in their concerns and not impugn their motives as to whatever their objections are."

A History of Arrogance

The Bush administration began to treat allies arrogantly long before Iraq became an issue, Feinstein says, citing its dismissal of the Kyoto Treaty on global warming; the International Criminal Court, which the administration and many Republican lawmakers did not want to join lest U.S. soldiers be yanked into its docks; and the Anti-Ballistic Missile Treaty. *(2001 CQ Weekly, p. 2986)*

Richard G. Lugar, R-Ind., chairman of the Senate Foreign Relations Committee, which does the heavy lifting on treaties, said some allies feel that "we are arrogant, that we are unilateralist, that we are dominant to a fault."

But Lugar is confident that such sentiments will not last. "They will discover their need for security again at some stage, having made their point that they can throw sand in the gears and make life miserable for us for a while," he said.

Secretary of State Colin L. Powell also has tried to allay fears of permanent rifts.

"This anxiety that exists within the international community would be gone in a heartbeat if Saddam Hussein would do what he is supposed to do, or, in the aftermath of a successful military operation, people will see that we were doing the correct thing in removing this dangerous threat from the region and from the world," Powell told a hearing of the Senate Appropriations Commerce, State and Justice Subcommittee on March 6.

At the same time, some members of Congress are less than eager to have some allies back in the fold. France and Germany are favorite targets because of their anti-war positions at the United Nations. In an emotional gesture, Bob Ney, R-Ohio, chairman of the House Administration Committee, ordered House restaurants to strike French fries from their menus and rename them "Freedom fries." In another swipe at the French, Rep. Ginny Brown-Waite, R-Fla., introduced legislation March 13 that would provide government funding to families who want to bring home from France the remains of Americans who fought and died in the two world wars.

A more sober suggestion has come from Sen. Judd Gregg, R-N.H., who has raised the possibility of barring France from reaping business benefits in a Saddam-free Iraq.

"France has had a very significant commercial relationship with Iraq, which they've continued during the period of Saddam Hussein's leadership there, and have taken advantage of that criminal regime through commercial activity," Gregg told Powell at the March 6 hearing. "What is the proper role for France and even Germany in a post-Saddam Iraq?"

Powell responded, "It is not for the United States to dictate the future of Iraq," suggesting that such decisions would be up to Iraq's new government. "But it would seem to me that the people of Iraq, now having been liberated, might glance around and see who helped in that liberation and who participated in that liberation and who did not," Powell said.

Remaking the Middle East

It is not just fissures in relationships with longtime allies such as the French that trouble members of Congress.

Some are wary of how allies among the Middle East's non-democratic nations — countries such as Saudi Arabia and the other Persian Gulf emirates, Jordan, Morocco and Egypt — will react to Bush's plan for a post-Saddam Iraqi regime that would, in the president's words, "serve as a dramatic and inspiring example of freedom for other nations in the region."

"What sort of message are we sending to the current governments, particularly at a time when we're relying on some of them for support in our war effort," asked Sen. Herb Kohl, D-Wis. "Aren't we implicitly saying, 'You're next, and if necessary, by force?' "

Powell says America's friends "know that we have no intention of forcing the overthrow of their regime or leadership, either overtly or covertly. But they also know . . . that we think that democracy is not something that is just exclusively for Western nations. Democracy should be able to thrive in Arab nations as well."

Roberts says that is not far-fetched. "If you have the resolve and commitment to provide stability to Iraq and that part of the world, you have a chance at a solution of the Palestinian-Israeli conflict," he said. Roberts added that stability in Iraq also could prompt countries such as Egypt and Saudi Arabia to emulate recent political reforms in Kuwait and Tunisia.

But Hagel cautions that democracy cannot be foisted upon people, and he acknowledges that voters might choose leaders who are anathema to Americans, such as Islamic fundamentalists.

"That's the damnedest thing about democracy, isn't it?" Hagel said. "But that's the essence of what we are trying to achieve around the world, so you respect that."

Roberts argues that democracy need not turn out that way. "It's not happening in Pakistan," he noted. "It's not happening in Afghanistan, and that's the classic example. They're making real progress. It's not pure democracy by any means, but if you compare it to a year ago, there's no comparison."

Charles Cushman of George Washington University says the United States probably will emerge from war with Iraq with "a few friends" intact — among them Britain, Saudi Arabia, Kuwait, Qatar, Bahrain, the United Arab Emirates and Oman — but that will depend on how Washington behaves as a conqueror.

"If the outcome of the war is the United States colonizes Iraq, if that's their perception, then we'll have no friends at all in the region," Cushman said.

BLOOMBERG PHOTO / CHRIS KLEPONIS

Bush, stressing his administration's commitment to an Israeli-Palestinian settlement, envisions a Middle East transformed by peace, democracy and trade following war with Iraq.

Meanwhile, other fights could follow the ousting of Saddam. "There could be several wars in northern Iraq after a U.S. invasion," Cushman said. "The Turks have made it clear they are intent on pursuing Turkish interests. Anything that looks like Kurdish autonomy causes problems at home for Turkey, and anything more independent than what [the Kurds enjoy now in neighboring northern Iraq] would not be acceptable."

The Kurds could wind up fighting three wars, he said: one against Saddam, one against Turkey, and one to prevent Iran from seizing oil fields centered in the northern Iraqi city of Kirkuk, which the Kurds also would like to control. Moreover, other experts point out, these conflicts will not spare the United States.

"Once the U.S. is on the ground in Iraq, it's a neighbor of Turkey and Iran and Israel," said Robbin Laird, a former National Security Council staffer during the Carter and Reagan administrations.

"We've never been a neighbor in the Middle East," he said. "Then you're engaged in local politics where all the local actors have their own agendas."

Israelis and Palestinians

Many lawmakers agree that the biggest local political problem is the Israeli-Palestinian battle.

Bush says ousting Saddam will ease that conflict, leading to a peace agreement featuring an independent Palestinian state that renounces terrorism and a safe Israel that stops building settlements in the West Bank and Gaza Strip.

How? Without Saddam, Bush says, terrorists would lose "a wealthy patron" who pays for terrorist training and rewards the families of suicide bombers. That would reduce terror and open the door to reform-minded Palestinians, making it easier for Israel to make concessions on the settlements.

But Israeli Prime Minister Ariel Sharon rejects that idea, and so do his many Capitol Hill supporters, including members of the Christian Right who form one of Bush's core constituencies. If these Republicans suspect that Bush's Middle East peace plan could come at Israel's expense, Bush could face political problems in 2004.

Some members, such as conservative Rep. Steve Chabot, R-Ohio, are skeptical that quick progress can be made in the peace process, saying, "Democracy and a lessening of tensions may occur over a period of years."

Still, the White House clings to its vision of a Middle East transformed by victory in Iraq. As part of that vision, the administration touts trade as a way "to promote a secure world," in the words of U.S. Trade Representative Robert B. Zoellick.

But aside from oil, the Middle East produces little in the way of exports. "Last year, the entire Muslim world received barely more foreign investment than Sweden," lamented former U.S. Trade Representative Charlene Barshefsky in a Feb. 22 op-ed piece in The New York Times.

"Today, the United States imports slightly more than $5 billion worth of manufactured goods and farm products from the 22 members of the Arab League, Afghanistan and Iran combined, or about half our value-added imports from Hong Kong alone," she noted. Meanwhile, America's trade ties to a market of more than 300 million people are limited to free-trade agreements with Jordan and Israel.

The Importance of Russia

For Lugar, it is paramount that friendly relations with Russia survive whatever ill will was stirred by Moscow's alignment with France at the United Nations against an attack on Iraq. Together with former Sen. Sam Nunn, D-Ga. (1972-97), Lugar wrote the Cooperative Threat Reduction program (PL 102-228), which funds technical assistance and other efforts to safeguard or destroy nuclear weapons in Russia and other former Soviet states. Bush requested $1.75 billion for the program and related efforts for fiscal 2004.

"There are a large number of agenda items, including destruction of weapons of mass destruction, security for fissile material and desperately needed measures in the war on terrorism, which both of us have got to be involved in," he said.

But on March 13, Russia's Deputy Foreign Minister Georgy Mamedov warned that a U.S. attack on Iraq could lead to a freeze of the Moscow Treaty, ratified unanimously by the Senate March on 6. Under that agreement (Treaty Doc 107-8), the United States and Russia must reduce their strategic nuclear stockpiles to between 1,700 and 2,200 warheads each by 2012.

It appears the diplomatic fallout from a war over Iraq already has begun to descend.

Debate Over Military's Future Will Top Postwar Agenda

War's outcome will determine fallout regarding number of ground troops

Two weeks into the war, members of Congress tried to sort out a flood of reports about the progress of the effort to disarm Iraq and overthrow Saddam Hussein. Allied forces moved to the outer edges of Baghdad, smashing Iraqi Republican Guard units along the way, and a prisoner of war was rescued. By April 4, U.S. forces had seized Baghdad's international airport.

But lawmakers also faced disturbing reports in the media of supply lines stretched too thin, troops being diverted to protect supply convoys, and unexpected guerrilla warfare tactics. And there was a growing complaint — partly from retired generals in the United States, but also from officers in the field — that the "rolling start" war strategy was flawed and there simply are not yet enough troops to do the job.

Congress has good reason to keep a close eye on these developments. It oversees the military, and serious questions are being raised about crucial elements of the war plan, from its reliance on psychological blows to the Iraqi regime — the famous "shock and awe" theory — to its balance of air power and ground power. Defense Secretary Donald H. Rumsfeld is facing the basic issue of whether the war started without enough troops to carry it out. When the war is over, that may be one of the most important points Congress will have to consider.

The political questions, however, may well be far more sweeping. Rumsfeld has become known for his ideas for a transformed military that would rely on lighter, more mobile forces and fewer ground troops, and his ideas have created friction with the Army. Those arguments spilled out into the open the week of March 31. It has been a classic example of the traditional tension between the civilian and military leaders of the armed forces. And that tension has been especially severe with Rumsfeld, who has sought to impose his ideas on the Army — and perhaps in the planning for this war — in a level of detail that goes beyond what military officers say is appropriate for a civilian.

CQ Weekly April 5, 2003

Now, the debate over Rumsfeld's ideas has taken center stage, and for all of the circumstances that are unique to this war — including a weakened Iraqi military and Turkey's decision not to grant access to ground forces — the questions regarding the number of ground troops in this war are sure to be revived in the future by critics who want to question Rumsfeld's overall vision for the future of the military.

"This war is going to prove that, despite precision bombing and technology, there comes a time when you need heavy tank divisions," said Rep. Chet Edwards, D-Texas, whose 11th District includes the Army base at Fort Hood and has the second-largest number of people in the armed forces of any congressional district.

The validity of such criticisms — and how hard critics will fight — will depend greatly on whether the strength of the ground forces is still an issue throughout the war, given that more troops are already on their way. Most Republicans in Congress have urged their colleagues, and even the officers on the front lines, to keep the difficulties in perspective and give the war effort more time.

"If you're down to one hot meal a day and you're running out of water, you're going to say, 'Hey, wait a second.' That's only natural," said Sen. Pat Roberts, R-Kan., a member of the Senate

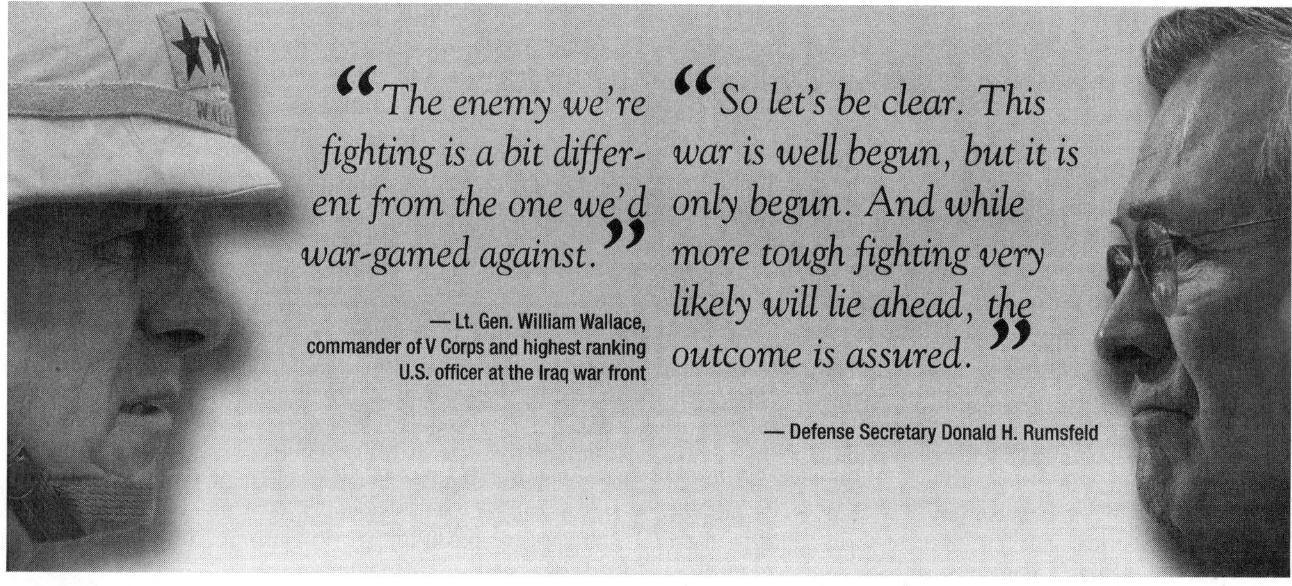

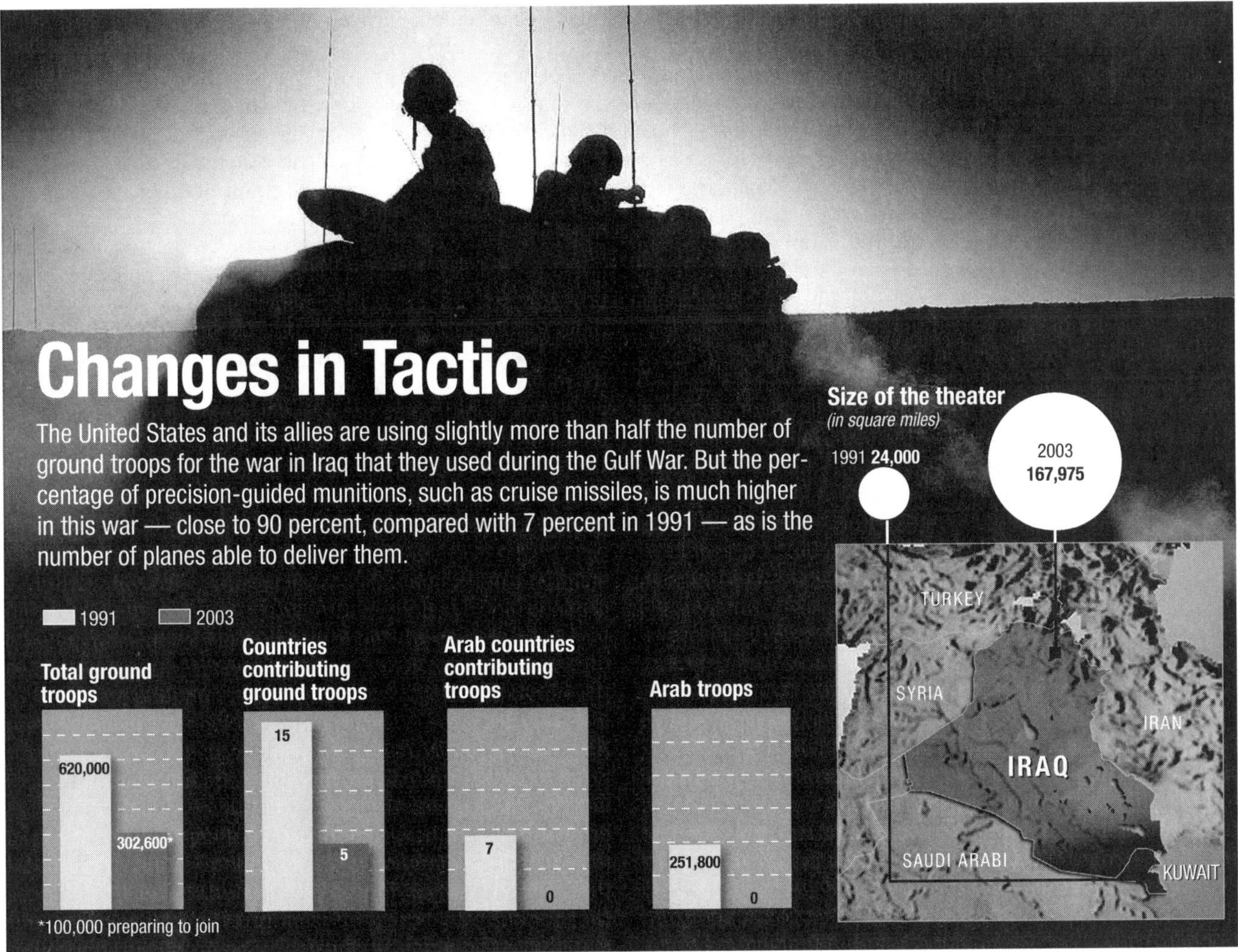

Armed Services Committee. "I just don't share their criticisms. I think it's going quite well under the circumstances."

Still, analysts say the Armed Services committees will have little choice in postwar hearings but to revisit the military transformation debate, considering how tensions between Rumsfeld and the Army bloomed in the early days of the conflict. And when the Defense appropriations subcommittees draw up future spending bills, some analysts say, they may take a more skeptical look at funding Rumsfeld's initiatives.

"When Rumsfeld asks for money to transform the military, they're going to say, 'Wait a second. You're not going to transform the military on the backs of the Army,' " said Lawrence J. Korb, director of national security studies at the Council on Foreign Relations and a former assistant secretary of defense under President Ronald Reagan.

On the other hand, he said, "If [the rest of the war] goes well, it'll be a different kind of hearing."

Strength on the Ground

This war is using fewer ground troops to secure a country the size of California than were used in the 1991 Gulf War simply to push invading Iraqi forces out of Kuwait, a country one twenty-fifth the size of Iraq. About 307,000 coalition ground troops are in the region now or on their way, including 100,000 in Iraq, compared with the 620,000 used to liberate Kuwait. There is an important caveat, however: Today's Iraqi military is far weaker than the one that was pushed out of Kuwait 12 years ago, pounded decisively and starved ever since.

It is impossible for lawmakers to judge after two weeks whether the troop deployment struck the right balance. The ultimate indicator will be the outcome of the war. But early signs of trouble, amplified by surprisingly candid comments from the ground commanders, could not help but catch the attention of members of Congress. Most said it is not appropriate to raise questions in public during the war, and some berated the military officials who already have aired their disagreements in public.

When the war is over, however, congressional committees will be asking whether Rumsfeld's military strategy truly worked as it should have.

"I'm sure there will be hearings to ask about that, as well as the overall conduct of the war," said Sen. John McCain of Arizona, the second-ranking Republican on the Senate Armed Services Committee.

"Absolutely. At whatever time we could hold hearings without being disruptive, I'm sure all of those questions will be asked," said Sen. Jack Reed, D-R.I., also on Armed Services. In the hearings after the Kosovo military campaign in 1999, Reed noted, some of the most critical assessments came from the Defense Department itself.

Politically, the timing is important, which is why members of Congress are not piling on Rumsfeld at the moment. The shooting is still going on, and no lawmaker wants to undermine the morale of the troops by being too critical of the battle plan they are carrying out. In addition, it is not clear whether the reported strains on the battlefield resources will be a lasting problem or simply a blip.

Senate Armed Services Committee Chairman John W. Warner, R-Va., and House Armed Services Committee Chairman Duncan Hunter, R-Calif., defended the war plan. House Majority Leader Tom DeLay, R-Texas, decried the "blow-dried Napoleons" who had been criticizing it on cable news networks.

And Senate Minority Leader Tom Daschle, D-S.D., who ignited a firestorm when he criticized Bush's diplomatic efforts two days before the war started, made it clear he was not about to touch any question on military strategy now. "I'm not going to get into second-guessing," he said April 2.

Troop Strength Questions

Still, as the House and Senate moved forward on the supplemental spending bill to pay for the war — practically setting new speed records for the passage of any supplemental bill — it was hard to ignore concerns that the troops might not have been given the resources they needed from the start. *(2003 CQ Weekly, p. 807)*

First, the Army's senior ground commander in Iraq, Lt. Gen. William S. Wallace, told reporters that between the Iraqi fighters' tactics and stretched supply lines, "The enemy we're fighting is a bit different from the one we war-gamed against."

Then, several officers in Iraq, all declining to be quoted by name, complained to The New York Times that Rumsfeld had not sent enough troops to fight the war as they believed it should be fought. "He wanted to fight this war on the cheap," said one colonel. "He got what he wanted."

On Capitol Hill, no one is eager to be that blunt, even those who are sympathetic to the criticisms. But some lawmakers do share those concerns, including members of the Armed Services and Appropriations panels who will have a say in the postwar analysis of what worked and what did not.

"People have concerns that we're trying to do this on the cheap" with too few ground troops, said Rep. Gene Taylor, D-Miss., a member of the House Armed Services Committee. "I would have much preferred to have had too many people there and fewer casualties than too few and lose one unnecessarily."

Edwards, the ranking Democrat on the House Appropriations Subcommittee on Military Construction, said the number of ground forces is "a major topic of conversation" in the House Democratic cloakroom. "It would be irresponsible not to" raise questions about the issue after the war is over, he said.

Underlying much of the tension is a longstanding conflict between Rumsfeld and the Army over his efforts to transform the military into a lighter, more agile force. The goal is to make it less dependent on ground troops and tanks and more focused on lighter weapons and technological advantages, such as linking high-resolution reconnaissance with the long-distance use of precision weapons.

This war will not be useful as a test of the overall strategy. Most lawmakers and military experts agree that Turkey's decision not to allow the opening of a northern front threw a wrench into the war plan and cut the size of the ground force from the beginning. The Army's 4th Mechanized Infantry Division, which would have led the northern front, began arriving in Kuwait instead the week of March 31.

"It's obvious to me, in hindsight, that we should have had a better assessment of where the politics were in Turkey and cut our losses early and moved that 4th Infantry Division early. That is a fair question," said Larry M. Wortzel, an expert on military strategy at the Heritage Foundation. But it is a different question than the overall issue of how many ground troops would be needed for the entire war.

Still, some lawmakers and former members say the war does raise fundamental questions about Rumsfeld's goals for the military, since fewer ground troops are key to the whole idea of smaller, more lethal and more agile forces.

"The view that heavy tank divisions are antiquated is about as correct as the predictions that machine guns would make foot soldiers irrelevant in World War I," Edwards said.

Some military experts say the tensions amount to little more than Army officers hoping to prove their relevance, given the success of the use of air power in the 1991 Gulf War.

"By the time we actually used ground power, there wasn't really any war to be fought. Iraqi troops were surrendering faster than we could round them up," said retired Air Force Gen. Charles Boyd. "I am absolutely certain that . . . was a driving force. The ground guys wanted to go in early."

Even so, the fact that the number of ground troops is such a contentious topic within the military as well as outside of it means Congress will have to address the issue head-on in the postwar hearings, said former Rep. Lee H. Hamilton, D-Ind. (1965-99), a former chairman of the House International Relations Committee.

"This is an enormously important question of military strategy," Hamilton said. "It's exactly the role Congress should play."

Civilians vs. the Generals

The debate also has served as a reminder of the tension that has always existed between the civilian and military leaders of the armed forces. And in Rumsfeld's case, the tension has drawn an unflattering comparison to Robert S. McNamara, the defense secretary under Presidents John F. Kennedy and Lyndon B. Johnson who often clashed with military chiefs over the strategy for fighting the Vietnam War.

"McNamara gave no ground and took no ground . . . and we paid the price for that in Vietnam," said Sen. Robert F. Bennett, R-Utah. "He destroyed the [military] establishment, and it had to be rebuilt."

No one is suggesting Rumsfeld is in as much trouble as McNamara faced, because what was fatal to McNamara was not his friction with the military chiefs, but the fact that the United States lost the war. "If we win this war as overwhelmingly as I think we will, the argument can be made that Rumsfeld is no McNamara," Bennett said.

Lawmakers say no matter what happens with this war, the tradition of civilian leadership of the U.S. military is too deeply ingrained to be revisited by Congress. "I don't think Congress is going to interfere with a historical fact," Roberts said. "We have civilian control of the military."

Still, Rumsfeld's diplomatic skills — or, more accurately, his lack of them — have proven how politically vulnerable he is when anything does go wrong on the battlefield. He has a reputation for an abrasive personal style, as well as a seeming hostility to the Army that affected his discussions with the various regional commands about how their war plans were drawn up.

"A lot of crockery had to be broken. . . . Folks were still fighting the Desert Storm model" in drawing up the war plans, one retired general said. The general added that, by contrast, William J. Perry, who served as Defense Secretary under President Bill Clinton, would "get into the details, but he did it collaboratively."

Lately, Rumsfeld has been trying to do better with his diplomatic skills in daily briefings on Capitol Hill, explaining the war plan in detail to head off concerns.

Rep. Jerry Lewis, R-Calif., chairman of the House Appropriations Subcommittee on Defense, says Rumsfeld has "been holding our hands," assuring members that the war commander, Gen. Tommy Franks, is "carrying forward a plan that's been reviewed by the Joint Chiefs and which has the necessary flexibility."

"I think the tide of opinion is turning toward Rumsfeld," Hunter said. "Listening to my colleagues, as the operation becomes more and more clear to the members, they are gaining confidence daily in the plan and in Tommy Franks and in Don Rumsfeld."

Burden of Proof

Independent experts agreed. "The war is not over, and the issue of, 'Did you send enough troops?' may come home to bite them," said Andrew Krepinevich, a retired Army officer who heads the Center for Strategic and Budgetary Assessment, a Washington think tank that promotes military transformation. "But the burden for those who say the war plan is coming apart at the seams is to explain why they believe that," he said.

"Nobody's running out of gas, like Patton's tanks," Krepinevich added. "Nobody's starving and cut off. So where's this big problem?"

Indeed, on at least one point, the war may build support for Rumsfeld's demand that the services develop lighter, more easily transported forces.

When the 4th Mechanized Infantry Division was blocked from crossing Turkey, the only Army unit that could be flown into northern Iraq was the relatively lightly armed 173rd Airborne Brigade.

But by 2010, the Army hopes to begin fielding ground combat units equipped with a tank-like combat vehicle that will be as lethal and as survivable as the Army's 70-ton M-1 tanks while weighing only 20 tons — light enough that a large force could be flown into position easily.

"If you can square that circle," Krepinevich said, "you could put a lot of those folks up in the north a lot easier than you could the Fourth."

> *"McNamara gave no ground and took no ground . . . and we paid the price for that in Vietnam."*
>
> — Sen. Robert F. Bennett, R-Utah

The plan unfolding in Iraq clearly embodies three elements of Rumsfeld's program.

In contrast to the 1991 Gulf War, the current campaign relies heavily on Special Operations forces — small groups of highly trained fighters who use guerrilla-like tactics, frequently in operations behind enemy lines.

From the outset of the current campaign, they have seized areas in western Iraq that the Iraqis would have needed to reach Israel with their Scud missiles. They also have collaborated with Kurdish forces that control northern Iraq, mounted sneak attacks on targets inside Baghdad, and seized hundreds of oil wells and pumping facilities in southern Iraq before the regime could blow them up.

"The role of Special Operations in this campaign is unsung and unappreciated, but it is powerful," said the retired Army general.

In addition, the war plan has relied on close coordination between precision air strikes and fast-moving ground forces. While U.S. forces are using far more precision-guided "smart" bombs than they did in 1991, the important difference is how they are being used, hammering Iraq's elite Republican Guard divisions after they were forced into the open to face advancing ground and helicopter units.

The most controversial of the war plan's "transformational" aspects has been the number of ground troops, and that has been determined largely by Franks' decision to launch the attack while one of his most powerful combat units — the Fourth Mechanized Infantry Division — still was scrambling to get to the scene.

After Turkey refused to allow that division to invade Iraq from the north, the cargo ships carrying the division's tanks and other heavy gear loitered in the eastern Mediterranean for several more days, while the Bush administration waited in vain for Turkey to reconsider. Thus, the ships did not begin to arrive in Kuwait until after the war began.

"We reacted very slowly," said Rep. John P. Murtha of Pennsylvania, the ranking Democrat on the House Appropriations Subcommittee on Defense. "We kept miscalculating. . . . But they adjusted the plan to fit."

Many of Rumsfeld's anonymous Army critics contend that he pushed the ground force into the fight prematurely, in hopes of proving that fewer Army troops would be needed than Army leaders argued for. Retired Maj. Gen. William Nash, who commanded an armored brigade in the 1991 war, declined to go that far but asked, "Why did you not have another division? Why not wait?"

Disproving the Critics

On the other hand, House Armed Services Total Force Subcommittee Chairman John M. McHugh, R-N.Y., insisted that the war's success thus far has undermined the argument that the attacking ground force was too small.

"Believe me, I would be one to whom those arguments would appeal, because I'm one who believes the total force is too small," he said. "In terms of future, similar conflicts, you might want to consider going heavier, but the plan has been incredibly flexible, even to the point of losing a major deployment from Turkey."

Even among Democrats, the questions over the number of ground troops have ebbed and flowed with the news coverage, and as the news from Iraq got better, those questions during the closed briefings faded away.

"It wasn't asked today," Sen. John D. Rockefeller IV, D-W.Va., said April 2, a day dominated by news that allied forces were closing in on Baghdad and defeating the Iraqi Republican Guard. "It doesn't mean the questions don't come back, but the last couple of days have kind of softened that."

But the ultimate test of the number of ground troops, lawmakers say, will be what happens when the forces storm into the heart of Baghdad. In 1982, it took about two weeks for Israeli forces heading into Lebanon to reach Beirut. But once there, they fought for three months before they conquered the city.

"I think it looks great," Rep. Norm Dicks, D-Wash., said of the war's progress. "But there's this one, last little thing called Baghdad." ◆

Has Congress Given Bush Too Free a Spending Hand?

Critics warn that exigencies of war could lead to a lasting cession of Hill authority

CQ PHOTO / SCOTT J FERRELL

Rumsfeld, left, ruffled feathers on Capitol Hill recently with aggressive words about the White House's intentions to allocate war money the way it chooses. Bush has made a habit of pressing for flexibility on spending, and some lawmakers are getting nervous.

As the war in Iraq comes to a climax, Congress appears set to give President Bush at least $9 billion to spend on the conflict however he sees fit, once again handing the president relatively unfettered use of a sizable chunk of money.

Lawmakers say they are not abdicating their constitutional prerogative over the power of the purse. They stress that they rejected Bush's request for a blank check of almost $60 billion — nearly three-fourths of the total supplemental spending bill (HR 1559). Appropriators said that by paring Bush's request substantially, they effectively blocked a president's grab for unchecked power. *(2003 CQ Weekly p. 862)*

But some members are concerned that the administration's continued requests for blank checks is establishing a pattern that cannot — and should not — be ignored. And comments such as one by Secretary of Defense Donald H. Rumsfeld on April 7 have fueled their fears. "Whatever is put forward by the Congress by way of money will be expended in a way that the president decides should be expended," Rumsfeld told reporters at a Pentagon news briefing.

Struggles between Congress and the executive branch over the spending prerogative are as old as the nation itself. Presidents always want more power over spending decisions, and typically, Congress responds by zealously resisting those efforts.

This tension is especially heightened now, however, with the nation at war abroad and in a high-alert status at home, a time when power naturally shifts to the White House. During situations like this, the administration argues, it needs maximum flexibility because Congress simply cannot react quickly enough to keep up with the nation's ever-changing defense needs and security threats.

But therein also lies the problem, as many lawmakers see it. Even if the military settles into a more predictable routine, ongoing threats to the homeland could give Bush — and perhaps future presidents — a strong argument for demanding large sums of relatively unfettered funds.

And even though Bush has sought spending flexibility primarily with defense funds, some in Congress fear a slippery slope as the lines between defense and domestic homeland security spending are increasingly blurred.

Congress may have unwittingly established a precedent for dealing with Bush on fiscal matters in September 2001, immediately after the terrorist attacks on New York and Washington. Mindful of its reputation for glacial movement, Congress wanted to demonstrate to a stunned nation that it could respond quickly to such a horrific event. It passed a $40 billion supplemental spending package (PL 107-38) that gave the president near-unilateral control over one-fourth of the total. *(2001 CQ Almanac, p. 2-59)*

The following summer, Congress handed Bush an unusual level of control over another supplemental spending package (PL 107-206) totaling $28.9 billion. Congress gave the president the authority to accept or reject a $5.1 billion package of items that lawmakers wanted, but Bush rejected the package, much to the dismay of appropriators. *(2002 CQ Weekly, p. 3183)*

In the latest case, the decision to extend billions in unfettered money to the president in the supplemental spending bill again has members thinking about the pattern they may be setting.

"It's a dreadful precedent," said Democratic Sen. Christopher J. Dodd of Connecticut. Flexibility is one thing, Dodd said, but "this is going way beyond that. . . . It's a power grab for resources . . . [that] seems rather obvious."

Some members say they are doing their best to rein in the executive branch. As the House considered its version of the bill April 3, Max Sandlin, D-Texas, congratulated appropriators "for resisting the administration's effort to wrest from the Congress its constitutional prerogative of overseeing all moneys drawn from the Treasury. Our Founding Fathers rightly understood the need for accountability among the branches of government — even in times of crisis."

But Congress is clearly striving to achieve a sense of equilibrium between the branches, a difficulty that appropriators feel most acutely. "All presidents want unlimited authority. In any time of conflict, there's a tendency to allow a little more leeway," said Ohio Republican David L. Hobson, chairman of the House Appropriations Energy and Water Development Subcommittee. "We have a responsibility to maintain a balance . . . and we're struggling with that."

From a legal perspective, the Constitution guarantees Congress the prerogative to re-assert its power over the purse anytime it chooses, and it has important reasons to do so. "It's what ultimately gives them real, real leverage," said John F. Bibby, professor emeritus of political science at the University of Wisconsin in Milwaukee.

Bibby explained that Congress is generally reluctant to give up that power because of the "constituency consequences of appropriations acts."

Winning federal money for their districts is political bread and butter for most politicians, and giving up the power of the purse means they relinquish that right.

In addition, the appropriations process is a powerful tool for Congress to exert control over federal departments and agencies.

To hear appropriators tell the story, relations between the executive and legislative branches started downhill when George Washington took office in 1789. "There's never been a president who didn't think that Article I of the Constitution was a serious mistake," said the House Appropriations Committee's top Democrat, David R. Obey of Wisconsin.

Long History

Hyperbole aside, presidential efforts to secure discretion over military budgeting — and congressional resistance to these attempts — are hardly new. Benjamin Ginsberg, professor of political science at Johns Hopkins University, argues that Congress' power to restrain the president from going to war has diminished over the past century, and the assault on Congress' power of the purse has accompanied that trend.

Ginsberg noted than in 19th century conflicts, Congress would say, " 'You can have $500 for cannonballs.' . . . What we've seen since is a steady erosion of Congress' ability to determine exactly what the money is going for."

During Operation Desert Shield in 1990 and Operation Desert Storm in 1991, Bush's father sought authority to allocate as he saw fit $53.5 billion in expected contributions from foreign allies — plus the authority to shift around $15 billion in appropriated funds. Instead, Congress granted, as part of a $42.6 billion supplemental package, a flexible $7.8 billion "Combat Costs" fund to cover "operations and maintenance" and procurement costs. It rejected his request concerning contributions from allies. *(1991 CQ Almanac, p. 680)*

In 1995, President Bill Clinton asked Congress to create a "Readiness Preservation Authority" that would allow the Pentagon to shift tens of billions of dollars, without congressional approval, to meet military-readiness requirements. Congressional committees declined to take up the proposal.

The current administration has been more persistent. Last year, the administration asked Congress to give the secretary of the fledgling Homeland Security Department (PL 107-296) permanent authority to shift up to 5 percent of its funding without congressional approval. Appropriators balked, and Congress granted a much more limited provision — the authority to transfer up to $640 million for two years to ease the transfer of agencies and functions into the new department. *(2002 CQ Weekly, p. 3191)*

In his fiscal 2003 budget request last year, Bush requested a $10 billion defense contingency fund. Congress never seriously considered the proposal, and instead allocated the $10 billion to specific accounts in the fiscal 2003 omnibus appropriations bill (PL 108-7). *(2002 CQ Weekly, p. 3178)*

THE SPLIT OVER WHITE HOUSE SPENDING PREROGATIVE

"In any time of conflict, there's a tendency to allow a little more leeway."

— Rep. David L. Hobson, R-Ohio

"...this is going way beyond [flexibility]. ... It's a power grab for resources."

— Sen. Christopher J. Dodd, D-Conn.

The fight over control of the purse strings has even gotten personal at times. The report accompanying the Senate Appropriations Committee's version of this year's supplemental bill scolded the White House Office of Management and Budget (OMB) for requesting only $125 million for legislative branch security needs, when the actual funds requested by the individual legislative branch agencies had totaled $130.8 million. The White House and Congress try to avoid fighting over each others' budget request, and they generally grant each other the funds they say they need. "The committee is concerned that OMB has violated normal protocols dictated by the separation of powers between the two branches of government by not including in the supplemental request precisely that which was requested by the legislative branch," the report read.

Demanding Information

In cases where Congress has acquiesced to requests for funding flexibility, it sometimes has tried to compensate by insisting on extensive reports from the administration. In this year's supplemental request for the Iraq war, the Senate version of the bill called essentially for an $11 billion blank check. The House version would have imposed more requirements on the money, but left $25.4 billion somewhat flexible.

In conference, Republicans initially wanted to allow Bush to spend the funds without notifying Congress beforehand. However, conferees adopted an amendment on April 11 that established a five-day requirement.

Appropriators cited the supplemental spending bill enacted in response to the first war with Iraq as a precedent for this year's supplemental. But the 1991 supplemental request was backed by a 109-page Defense Department report with detailed war cost estimates. This year, the administration submitted a 33-page justification to Congress on March 25 which included far broader cost estimates and only one combat scenario — "a short, extremely intense period of combat operations."

Members acknowledge they are bequeathing the president a large amount of budgetary trust, and although the supplemental has broad bipartisan support, some senior Democrats are nervous. "It's the job of Congress to make sure we keep control" of spending authority, Obey said. "You don't do that by giving Cabinet-level agencies slush funds."

Robert C. Byrd of West Virginia, the Senate Appropriations Committees' top Democrat and the Senate's foremost protector of institutional prerogative, had harsh words for the administration and his colleagues. "This administration wants to extend its power wherever it can," Byrd said. "And Congress is recreant in going along with that in many instances . . . The power of the purse is here, and we ought to defend that."

Many Republicans have also been uncomfortable granting the president sweeping authority to spend billions of dollars. Arizona GOP Rep. Jim Kolbe said the administration's desire for flexibility on the supplemental spending bill was ambitious and "a bit unusual."

As chairman of the House Appropriations Foreign Operations Subcommittee, Kolbe knows money can shape policy. He said the State Department should control $2.5 billion in Iraq reconstruction funds included in the supplemental. Late in the week of April 7, it appeared he would be overruled by

A Familiar Budget Battle

Appropriators who assembled spending measures to pay for the first war with Iraq 12 years ago have something in common with the 108th Congress: They wrangled with a White House trying to extract budget authority from the legislative branch.

After Iraq invaded Kuwait, President George Bush sought two broad grants of spending flexibility. The first came in September 1990, as U.S. and coalition troops massed in the Persian Gulf. Bush asked for $2.1 billion to pay for the costs of Operation Desert Shield, and asked Congress to set up a "National Defense Gift Fund," where foreign allies would deposit their contributions.

Under the proposal, then-Defense Secretary Dick Cheney would have been able to transfer those "gifts" directly to defense coffers without congressional approval, an idea that left appropriators laughing.

"That would have been very amusing, but it didn't happen," said Benjamin Ginsberg, a political science professor at Johns Hopkins University. "Congress was much more specific about what the president could do."

Congress gave Bush the $2.1 billion (PL 101-403), but kept control over the new account for foreign contributions. *(1990 Almanac, p. 896)*

On Feb. 22, 1991, the president made another supplemental funding request. This time, he asked for a $15 billion "Desert Shield Working Capital Account" from which Cheney could draw and transfer funds as needed, while the administration waited for the $53.5 billion in foreign pledges to stream in. Once those funds arrived, Bush wanted authority to transfer them as he saw fit.

Again, Congress balked, rejecting such a broad cession of congressional prerogative. As hostilities ceased Feb. 27, the House Appropriations Defense Subcommittee prepared to mark up the request and allot it to specific accounts. The panel ended up paring requests whose cost estimates were particularly uncertain.

"What they called notional costs we funded with notional money," then-Defense Subcommittee Chairman John P. Murtha, D-Pa., said at the time. *(1991 Weekly, p. 546)*

However, Congress did allow for some White House flexibility as part of a $42.6 billion supplemental package (PL 102-28), which included $7.8 billion in a flexible account for procurement and operations.

But appropriators kept a relatively tight rein on the bill as a whole. In outlining how members expected the money to be used, Congress cited extensive documents provided by the Pentagon outlining the need for the money.

Democratic leaders also managed to keep foreign assistance grants and other extraneous provisions out of the bill, and loaded all those provisions onto another measure (PL 102-27). *(1991 Almanac, pp. 668, 680)*

Senate Appropriations Committee Chairman Ted Stevens, R-Alaska, and House Appropriations Committee Chairman C.W. Bill Young, R-Fla. They leaned toward supporting the president, who wants to give that money to the Defense Department.

Indeed, many members of both parties have been loath to deny the commander in chief the resources and tools he says he needs to respond to the most devastating foreign assault on U.S. soil in history. Young said the elusive nature of terrorist networks must be matched by flexibility in the nation's defenses. "After 9/11, we're dealing with an unknown," he said. "In times of crisis, the president is responsible for the country's [security]. He needs flexibility."

Van Doorn Ooms, a senior fellow at the Committee for Economic Development, said who controls federal funds can have a big impact on the actions of the government, as demonstrated by the State-Defense struggle. "Clearly there are policy issues that lie behind this. . . . Those policy differences get rolled into this," said Ooms, who has served as chief economist for the House and Senate Budget committees and the OMB.

Robert L. Bixby, executive director of the nonpartisan budget watchdog Concord Coalition, argues that this grant of discretion is "Congress' way of saying, 'We support you in a time of war.' " However, it is also a way to ensure that Congress does not get blamed if the right funds do not end up in the right account quickly enough, which could cost lives on the battlefield, Bixby said.

That shifts the burden onto the president if troops run short of fuel, or do not have the right type of equipment for combat. "Frankly, people will hold him responsible," said Ralph Regula, R-Ohio, the chairman of the House Appropriations Labor-HHS-Education Subcommittee. Regula said he doubted that Congress will ever grant the president much leeway on domestic spending.

As conferees deliberated the supplemental, House Majority Leader Tom DeLay, R-Texas, attempted to quell speculation that the GOP leaders were getting rolled by the president. "In my opinion, we gave them more than enough flexibility in spending money," DeLay said. "We are bending over backwards to give them flexibility while maintaining our own responsibility to oversee spending."

Still, many members say Bush appears more eager than other recent presidents to push for expanded budget authority.

"This [president] seems to be more aggressive about it," said Rep. Martin Olav Sabo of Minnesota, ranking Democrat on the Homeland Security Appropriations Subcommittee.

Rumsfeld's comments shrugging off Congress' role in allocating funds only serve to sharpen that perception. "That kind of thing doesn't help," Kolbe noted.

But so far, the aggressive approach is paying off for Bush. "He's asking for much more discretion than past presidents have asked for . . . and the president's ending up with much more than previous presidents," said Brian Riedl, lead budget analyst at the Heritage Foundation.

"Even after Congress pares it down, they're ending up in between," he said. "In that way, the White House can claim victory."

James W. Dyer, the longtime Republican staff director of the House Appropriations Committee, said the administration "absolutely" has been more aggressive in trying to wrestle spending authority from Congress. Dyer said his biggest frustration has been the "giant pots" of funding requested by the Defense Department. Dyer and his boss, committee Chairman Young, have clashed with OMB Director Mitchell E. Daniels Jr. on spending issues over the last two years.

Dyer said that Congress is "trying to be . . . a partner in the process," noting that "the power of the purse is really the last power we have." Dyer said Republican congressional leaders have done a good job of signaling to the White House that Congress can only be pushed so far.

Containing the Battle

The biggest battles over budget control have for the moment been confined primarily to defense measures during wartime, and members insist they will not allow this tendency toward administration flexibility to creep into other areas. Congress and the administration will be tested when military action subsides, and when the new focus on "homeland security" funding becomes more routine.

For now, Congress is keeping an eye on how carefully the administration abides by the reporting requirements and other restrictions placed on these more flexible spending approaches. "If this experiment fails, it may not be replicated in the future," said Christopher Hellman, a senior research analyst at the Center for Defense Information and former Appropriations Committee staffer. "Congress' historical objections will reappear."

Mary L. Landrieu, D-La., a member of the Senate Appropriations Committee, said the flexibility granted to the president so far is "temporary, because this is something new." She predicted that as the war scales down, and the Homeland Security Department establishes itself, normalcy will return. "As we settle in . . . it'll revert back in some ways to the way it normally is," Landrieu said.

Some signs of this are already evident. The White House criticized Republicans for putting too many restrictions on homeland security money in the fiscal 2003 appropriations omnibus (PL 108-7). And new Homeland Security Subcommittee Chairman Harold Rogers, R-Ky., has been sparring with the administration over its failure to provide timely justifications for its fiscal 2004 budget requests. "It's frustrating . . . we've had spotty success. We need justifications of how they intend to spend the money . . ." he said. "There's no reason why it can't be furnished."

But at the moment, many members of Congress still seem content delegating authority to the president on homeland security matters. For example, the Senate voted, 51-46, on April 3 to table, or kill, an amendment to the supplemental from Byrd that would have allocated about $1 billion in homeland security funding requested by the White House into specific accounts.

The Concord Coalition's Bixby predicted that as long as terrorism is a significant source of concern for the public, members of Congress may show the president some deference on homeland security. "You can't really tell at the moment where that will end up. . . If it looks more like a commander in chief function, Congress will allow more flexibility," Bixby said. "How long do you define this as war spending?"

Bixby noted that the war on terrorism "is not likely to have an end that can be defined in time."

Many Democratic appropriators hope that their GOP counterparts take such concerns to heart before getting into the habit of turning over the checkbook to the president.

"This is a matter of short-term temporary convenience," Obey said. "We damn well better keep congressional oversight." ◆

Political Participation

Sen. Trent Lott's (R-Miss.) tribute to retiring Sen. Strom Thurmond, who fought a segregationist campaign for president in 1948, led to a change in the Senate majority leadership. As the first article in this section notes, it also raised broader questions about the ability of the Republican Party to put race relations at the top of its agenda as President Bush had promised during his campaign. After Lott's blunder, his party was eager to replace him, and elected Sen. Bill Frist (R-Tenn.) Senate majority leader. The Republican Party has not been known for focusing its agenda on improved race relations, and the Lott episode offered the party an opportunity to rethink its agenda. However, what happens over the next two years will determine whether the leadership change will be perceived as a turning point—pushing race relations and Bush's "compassionate conservative" social policies to the top of the Republican agenda—or whether Bush and congressional Republicans will treat Lott's withdrawal as just another example of damage control.

The second article examines the race for the 2004 Democratic presidential nomination and how it is affecting the Democratic Party and the work of the 108th Congress. Because so many sitting members of Congress are on the campaign trail, the race amplifies the party's differences and makes it even harder for congressional Democrats to present a unified agenda against President Bush and the GOP majority. Additionally, the race will affect the daily work of Congress. Candidates will deliver an unusually large number of floor speeches and press releases, introduce several high-profile bills, miss votes while they are on the campaign trail and put their committee work on the back burner.

As the GOP approaches the decade mark as the majority party in the House, its power has become concentrated in three unusually close-knit leaders: Speaker J. Dennis Hastert of Illinois, Majority Leader Tom DeLay of Texas and Whip Roy Blunt of Missouri. The third article discusses how this triumvirate works together without rivalry and engenders loyalty within the Republican Party. The degree to which House GOP leaders are effective in exercising their power has tremendous implications for the future of their party, including whether President Bush is successful in getting his initiatives through Congress and whether he is reelected in 2004.

After nearly three decades in various political positions in Washington, Vice President Richard Cheney, the subject of the final article in this section, has cultivated relationships and trust that transcend institutional divisions between the House and the Senate, and between Congress and the White House. Cheney has used his constitutional prerogative as president of the Senate to cast tie-breaking Senate votes six times during his 28-month tenure. And, as President Bush's right hand, he plays a key role in pushing priority legislation forward and making deals that advance the president's agenda.

GOP Faces Turning Point In Handling Race Relations

Lott episode forces party to examine its philosophical direction

Flash back to July 10, 2000. Texas Gov. George W. Bush is in Baltimore, making that most awkward of appearances for a Republican presidential candidate: a speech before the National Association for the Advancement of Colored People. He knows full well that the African-American vote has been going overwhelmingly to Democrats since the 1960s, that the modern Republican Party is not known for putting better race relations at the top of its agenda, and that a GOP candidate has a lot to prove.

But Bush has been campaigning as a "different kind of Republican," and he uses this event to raise the stakes even higher. The candidate suggests that if he becomes president, he will transform the Republican Party. "There's no escaping the reality that the party of Lincoln has not always carried the mantle of Lincoln," Bush tells the legendary civil rights group. "That's my job: to say, 'Here's where we have fallen short and here's where we will improve.' "

Now, flash forward to Jan. 7, 2002. The 108th Congress is about to convene with Republican majorities in the House and Senate, and GOP leaders will be eager to talk up their plans for the next two years. There is just one problem: The Senate Republican leader is a newcomer who has been on the job barely two weeks. The presence of Bill Frist, R-Tenn., as Senate majority leader rather than Trent Lott, R-Miss., will be a constant reminder to the nation — and to President Bush — that the Republican who was expected to run the Senate for the next two years will not do so because he failed to carry the mantle of Lincoln.

That episode may seem to be in the past now that Lott has left center stage, but the implications are not. What happens over the next two years will determine whether the leadership change will be perceived as a turning point, pushing race relations and Bush's "compassionate conservative" social policies to the top of the Republican agenda. It is possible, however, that Bush and congressional Republicans will treat Lott's withdrawal as just another example of successful damage control.

"The only way the Republican Party can be the majority party in the future is to broaden our support, and we haven't done a very good job," said Sen. Olympia J. Snowe, R-Maine. "Traditionally, Republicans have just been resolute in not understanding the issues that minorities face in America . . . and the tremendous racial inequality that still exists."

The drama that led to the change in power started with Lott's tribute to retiring Sen. Strom Thurmond's segregationist campaign for president in 1948. It was, perhaps, one of the most disastrous birthday speeches ever. In reality, however, the issue ceased to be just about Lott within days after he gave the speech. Instead, argument started to focus on whether the Republican Party had met the challenge Bush laid out in that campaign speech two and a half years ago.

After one thundering condemnation of Lott's blunder, Bush tried to keep out of the fray as much as possible. But his longtime supporters barely were able to restrain themselves. They feared that if Senate Republicans did not take a strong enough stand against Lott's comment and show a greater appreciation for the sensitivities of racial politics, much of the point of Bush's candidacy would be lost.

"That's what 'different kind of Republican' means. It means a more tolerant Republican, one who welcomes people of all different backgrounds," said Mark McKinnon, a former Democrat who served as Bush's media adviser during the 2000 campaign.

"A lot of the messages that were coming out of the Republican Party in the 1990s were very negative, and that's what the president campaigned against. That's why a lot of Republicans and former Democrats like myself were attracted to him," McKinnon said. "He talked about issues that Democrats typically owned, and in a very inclusive way."

Those are many of the same qualities that made Frist the instant front-runner to succeed Lott. After his election as the new Senate Republican leader Dec. 23, Frist said he hoped to turn the situation into "a catalyst for positive change" and that, "We must dedicate ourselves to healing those wounds of division that have been reopened so prominently during the past few weeks." And some Republicans say it is a sign of progress that Lott's comments generated such an uproar that his own party would no longer have him as a leader, a reaction that would have been unthinkable in the past.

Still, the qualities that elevated Frist to the leadership had less to do with race relations and more with his strengths as a spokesman for "compassionate conservatism," Bush's term for a broader category of social policies that present uniquely Republican ways of helping needy people. They include proposals on education, health care, social services, homeownership and aid for people with disabilities, all issues more traditionally identified with Democrats.

Frist, a heart surgeon, is known more for his expertise on health care issues — such as overhauling Medicare and creating a prescription drug benefit — than for civil rights and race relations, issues on which he has had little to say. Meanwhile, other Senate Republican leaders have emphasized their plans to revive proposals such as school choice and Bush's "faith-based initiative," another social policy benchmark.

If they make good on those statements, the Lott episode could give the Republican Party a new commitment to those compassionate conservative policies, all existing proposals that they simply can bump up a few notches on the priority list. But that will happen only if a war with Iraq does not overshadow the party's renewed attention to social issues, the way homeland security and the war on terrorism did for most of 2002.

The challenge on race relations, however, is much greater — and may be so fundamental that Republicans will not know what to do with it.

Remaking a Party

There is a difference between reshaping a party and simply repackaging it. If Bush truly is trying to reshape the GOP to get rid of its greatest vulnerability — the perception that it is insensitive to minorities and perhaps even benefits from racism — the past few weeks have taught him how hard it is for a president to bring along an entire congressional wing.

Just as President Bill Clinton faced friction from congressional Democrats as he tried to reshape that party by shedding some of its vulnerabilities, including its image as a free-spending group that refused to address crime or welfare dependency, Bush has faced resistance from Republican senators as he appeared to be taking away their right to choose their own leader.

Compared with Bush, however, Clinton had it easy. He took heat for proposing a balanced budget and signing the 1996 welfare overhaul legislation (PL 104-193), but those changes in direction have lasted. Though critics said Clinton adopted those policies more to help his re-election campaign than to help his party, the end result was the same: Democrats now can talk about fiscal responsibility, and welfare is no longer a major liability for them.

REUTERS PHOTO / JEFF MITCHELL

"That's what 'different kind of Republican' means. It means a more tolerant Republican, one who welcomes people of all different backgrounds."

— Mark McKinnon, Bush's campaign media adviser

For Republicans, however, the issue of race relations has proven to be a more fundamental liability than Democrats faced even in their worst days of infighting over budget and welfare policies.

The scope of the problem has been obvious since the 2000 election, when Bush received only 9 percent of the African-American vote. And in a Washington Post/ABC News poll of 1,209 adults conducted Dec. 12-15, only about three of 10 African-American respondents said Republicans are committed to equal opportunity for minorities, compared with the two-thirds who held that view of Democrats.

Despite the presence of prominent African-American officials in the Bush administration such as Secretary of State Colin L. Powell and National Security Adviser Condoleezza Rice, "There are a lot of African-Americans who still see the Republican Party as exclusive and supportive of the kinds of views that Sen. Lott expressed," said Martin Luther King III, president of the Southern Christian Leadership Conference, the civil rights organization founded by his father.

Many African-American leaders say that in order to transform the Republican Party into one with broader appeal to minorities, Bush will have to confront challenges that go well beyond the Lott crisis. They are pushing Republicans to take positions that conservatives say would contradict their basic philosophy, such as supporting affirmative action, backing fewer conservative judges, and raising the minimum wage.

The GOP "must come up with a concrete agenda to improve the lot of minorities — not just African-Americans, but Hispanics and Native Americans," said Rep. John Lewis, D-Ga., the former civil rights leader who was injured in the 1965 "Bloody Sunday" march in Selma, Ala. "Taking a picture with a group of young black kids or visiting a soup kitchen may be symbolic, but people need more than that."

That pressure to turn leftward, however, is being rejected by conservatives who say Republicans cannot reverse their position on affirmative action and other issues without violating their core philosophy of not targeting their policies to different racial groups.

"I don't believe that Republicans are going to start endorsing quotas and preferences, and that's really the area that tends to divide us," incoming Senate Majority Whip Mitch McConnell, R-Ky., said on Fox News Sunday the day before Frist was elected as the new majority leader.

That view is being seconded by prominent African-American conservatives. "Any Republican agenda that is intended for all Americans should remain a conservative agenda," said Peter N. Kirsanow, a black Republican who sits on the U.S. Commission on Civil Rights.

"Republicans and conservatives have come a long way on social policy in the last 10 to 15 years. They should have confidence in themselves," said Shelby Steele, author of "The Content of Our Character," which argues that African-Americans should embrace individual responsibility rather than group remedies.

The Lifespan of a Crisis

So far, the odds are not good for a sustained dialogue about how the party addresses race relations. In an age of media saturation, the nation already tends to lurch from crisis to crisis; with the exception of a catastrophic event such as Sept. 11, each tends to be all-consuming for a few weeks or months and then fade away.

Some Republicans already are suggesting that they expect the Lott controversy to fade quickly. "In the long sweep of American history, this is going to be a blip," McConnell said. "The image of our party is the president of the United States. He has a very good image on race and on reaching out to others."

Democrats, meanwhile, plan to get as much political mileage as possible. That could lead to new momentum for stalled initiatives such as hate crime legislation, but it also could backfire by allowing Republicans to dismiss the entire debate as politically motivated.

"There are many Democrats that want to keep this race issue alive, who want to actually prevent us from moving forward," McConnell said. "They do it around election time every year. It's quite irritating."

To Senate Republicans who say they want to use the episode as an opportunity to rethink the party's agenda, however, Lott's comments cannot be brushed aside as merely an embarrassing incident.

"There has to be a better way than sending the messages that we have sent in the past," Snowe said. "We've just been consistently against everything, rather than having a positive agenda for the future."

It is likely Republicans will put more of their focus on the compassionate conservative agenda by pushing proposals on issues such as education, health care and social services.

The education overhaul of 2001 (PL 107-110) is considered the model for the agenda. At Bush's urging, Congress passed a bill that leverages federal aid to require annual testing and better performance from the public schools, particularly those in low-income and minority neighborhoods. *(2001 Almanac, p. 8-3)*

Senate Republican Conference Chairman Rick Santorum, R-Pa., and other Republicans are vowing to put more emphasis on such themes. Santorum already was planning to make another push for Bush's faith-based initiative, which would steer more federal funds to religious social services. Conference Vice Chairman Kay Bailey Hutchison, R-Texas, said Republicans will steer more money toward historically black colleges and universities and Hispanic-serving institutions.

And Frist said Senate Republicans will put a new emphasis on overhauling Medicare, creating a prescription drug benefit for seniors and individuals with disabilities, and helping the uninsured.

In the Spotlight

Meanwhile, the Bush administration is trying to ramp up its own efforts. On the same day Frist was elected the new Senate Republican leader, Bush created a White House Task Force for Disadvantaged Youth to determine why so many federal programs intended to help young people have failed. And Bush said his State of the Union address will include a new pitch for the compassionate conservative agenda.

"People of faith led the struggle against slavery. People of faith fought against child labor. People of faith worked for women's equality and civil rights," Bush said in a Dec. 12 speech in Philadelphia on the faith-based initiative, the setting for his public scolding of Lott. "By promoting the compassion of our people, by promoting the great strength of America, we will bring new hope to neighborhoods all across this land."

The test, of course, is whether such an agenda would continue to receive a high priority if the war on terrorism flares up or the United States goes to war with Iraq. But if it does, conservative scholars such as Steele said Bush and the Republicans can build a new credibility on social policy.

REUTERS PHOTO / DAVID GRAY

"There are a lot of African-Americans who still see the Republican Party as exclusive and supportive of the kinds of views that Sen. Lott expressed."

— Martin Luther King III, president of the Southern Christian Leadership Conference

"In many ways, compassionate conservatism has given the Republican Party a relevance in racial issues that they haven't had before," Steele said. "It says that social reform has to, in some way, engage individual responsibility. That idea has a lot of legs to it . . . and people seem to buy it."

But critics say Republicans have undermined their credibility in other ways, such as their failure to provide more funding to support the 2001 education overhaul or reach an agreement with Democrats to extend unemployment benefits before the 107th Congress adjourned. Senate Republicans say that will receive immediate attention at the beginning of the 108th, but that is more of a mop-up action than a new agenda item. *(2003 CQ Weekly, p. 33)*

In addition, the Bush administration has taken heat for floating ideas for shifting more of the tax burden to lower-income workers to correct what some administration officials believe is an oversized burden on the rich.

And Bush is being watched closely to see if he will submit judicial nominees in the same vein as U.S. District Judge Charles W. Pickering Sr., who was criticized by civil rights and liberal interest groups as insensitive to civil rights and women's rights when Bush nominated him to the 5th Circuit Court of Appeals. Bush has not said whether he will renominate Pickering, though conservatives said he was the victim of a smear campaign and prominent Republicans such as incoming Senate Judiciary Committee Chairman Orrin G. Hatch, R-Utah, have said he should be renominated. *(2003 CQ Weekly, p. 36)*

"There's the atmospherics, and there's 'Are you better off today?' " said Hugh B. Price, president of the National Urban League. "Is there a housing initiative of any consequence? Does the president support affirmative action? What kinds of judges is he appointing?"

Civil rights historians say a more basic challenge is that Republicans cannot reexamine their policies on race relations too closely without confronting the fact that they have gained more from racial tensions than they would like to admit.

How They Rose to Power

Before the controversy over Lott's birthday tribute to Thurmond, a smiling Bush had his picture taken with the 100-year-old senator at a separate birthday party at the White House, with Lott standing in the background. That picture has a special symbolic power now, historians say, because of the chain of events Thurmond set in motion that helped the Republican Party become the power it is today. *(2003 CQ Weekly, p. 24)*

In 1964, Senate Republicans cast more of their votes for the Civil Rights Act (PL 88-352) than Senate Democrats, who had to contend with a bloc of Southern lawmakers in their party who opposed all civil rights legislation. When the landmark bill passed on a 73-27 vote on June 19, 1964, there were 27 Republicans who voted in favor of the bill and six who opposed it. Democrats were more split, with 46 voting in favor and 21 voting against. *(1964 Almanac, p. 696)*

One of the Republicans who voted against it was Barry Goldwater of Arizona (1953-65, 1969-87), who went on to become the party's standard-bearer in the presidential election. And one of the Democrats who voted against it was Thurmond — who switched to the Republican Party just three months later and campaigned for Goldwater, warning that if the Democrats stayed in power, "Freedom as we have known it in this country is doomed." *(2002 CQ Weekly, p. 3117)*

That switch, historians say, was the moment that foreshadowed the Republican Party's rise to national dominance, including mass conversions of Southern Democratic officeholders to the Republican Party and the attraction of Southern white votes that made it possible for Republicans to win control of Congress in the 1990s.

"That was what showed [Thurmond's] prescience. It was a giant leap into the unknown because no one else was doing it," said Taylor Branch, author of "Parting the Waters" and "Pillar of Fire," the first two books in a planned trilogy about the civil rights movement.

Since then, political scientists such as Merle and Earl Black, the authors of "The Rise of Southern Republicans," have noted other GOP strategies that have played off racial divisions. For example, they cited the GOP strategy in the redistricting of the early 1990s, in which black votes were concentrated into certain districts to make it easier for African-American Democrats to win election — but also easier for Republicans to win in other districts.

More recently, the party has been urged to take a more aggressive stand against racially charged tactics such as appeals to the Confederate flag and the attempts in some states to suppress black voter turnout in last year's elections.

Democrats have criticized Georgia's governor-elect Sonny Perdue, a Republican who unseated Democrat Roy Barnes, for endorsing a referendum to reconsider last year's change in the state flag to minimize its use of the Confederate battle emblem. "The Republicans have repeatedly exploited the issue of race," said incoming House Minority Leader Nancy Pelosi, D-Calif. "What happened in Georgia was a shameful manifestation of the same sentiment that was expressed by Sen. Lott."

Democrats also have attempted to link Frist, who chaired the National Republican Senatorial Committee in the 107th Congress, to tactics aimed at suppressing black voter turnout in last year's elections. The tactics included pamphlets distributed in New Orleans housing complexes in December that falsely told residents they could wait until the Tuesday after Election Day to vote in the runoff for Democratic Sen. Mary Landrieu's seat.

Frist has not responded to that criticism, and Democrats have offered no specific evidence to back the accusation.

Both Sides Vulnerable

The race relations issue carries some risks for Democrats as well. As much as the party has won the confidence of African-Americans and other minorities since 1964, it still has vulnerabilities.

For example, Sen. Robert C. Byrd, D-W.Va., who filibustered the Civil Rights Act of 1964 and belonged to the Ku Klux Klan in his youth, was in the Senate Democratic leadership throughout much of the 1980s and remains a powerful member of the caucus today. Byrd has said he has deep regrets about both of those chapters in his life.

And as much as Thurmond's past has been revived as an issue now, it basically had been set aside by both Republicans and Democrats in the days before Lott's speech. On Sept. 24, as Thurmond approached his 100th birthday, the Senate chamber rang with tributes to him from such diverse speakers as Sen. Edward M. Kennedy, D-Mass.; Sen. Hillary Rodham Clinton, D-N.Y.; and Frist.

The difference was that unlike Lott, everyone else focused on the more positive aspects of Thurmond's career, such as his service in World War II and his lengthy public service, and carefully talked around the most notorious part of his background. Although Thurmond changed his voting practices on civil rights after the 1960s, he told the Charlotte Observer four years ago that, "I don't have anything to apologize for" on the 50th anniversary of his segregationist campaign for president.

"You can have these kinds of skeletons in your closet, but the nature of congressional leadership is that no one's interested in asking these kinds of questions," said David J. Garrow, author of "Bearing the Cross," a biography of Martin Luther King Jr.

Meanwhile, Senate Democratic Leader Tom Daschle of South Dakota still is trying to recover from criticism of his initial reaction to Lott's comments, when he wrote them off as just another case in which "he and I go to the microphone . . . [and] say things we meant to say differently."

One reason the episode has been so difficult for Congress is that "people don't know how to respond to race issues," said Angela E. Oh, who served on the advisory board of Clinton's Initiative on Race in the 1990s. "Once you get into the dialogue, it becomes very contentious because then you have to talk about economic realities and privilege. Then you get to people who don't care about race very much. They don't want to talk about it. You bring up race and they say, 'Please don't waste my time. This is my private set of opinions.' "

Some Republicans say this has been a learning experience. "We all have learned, we're more understanding, I think, than some might have been otherwise," said George Allen, R-Va., the incoming chairman of the National Republican Senatorial Committee. "But most importantly we're looking forward. And we're looking forward to creating opportunities for all Americans, passing legislation and laws and programs that'll have a positive impact on people's lives."

To do that, Branch said, Republicans will have to start by disavowing "a fairly consistent strategy since 1964 of using code words on race." The code that stands out the most, he said, is "states' rights" — a phrase that dates back to the civil rights struggle, when it was the rallying cry for opponents of the federal laws that now are credited with ending segregation.

Republicans say their current ideas for shifting power from the federal government to the states have nothing to do with race, and instead are about making programs more efficient and responsive to the needs of different states. If so, Branch said, Republicans need to state that distinction clearly.

They also will be urged to consider solutions that are not on anyone's agenda now. For King, of the Southern Christian Leadership Conference, a significant step forward would be diversity training — for both Republicans and Democrats. "Nobody should be so arrogant as to think they don't need it," he said.

For Lewis, who put his life on the line many times for civil rights, everyone deserves a chance to prove their commitment to racial justice. "Maybe, just maybe, the Lott episode will be a wake up call — not just to the Republican Party, but to the whole country," he said.

If so, there would be a genuine competition between the parties in the new Congress for one of the greatest challenges of all: carrying the mantle of Lincoln. ◆

Party Unity Elusive as 2004 Hopefuls Shout, 'Look at Me'

Democratic candidates balance Capitol Hill business with campaign priorities

GETTY IMAGES PHOTO / MIKE THEILER (LEFT); KRT PHOTO/ CHUCK KENNEDY

Edwards, left, and Gephardt were among seven White House aspirants who wooed party activists at the Democratic National Committee's winter meeting Feb. 21-22.

It is a new day for Democrats, the cheering crowd of activists at the Democratic National Committee winter meeting was told. No longer would congressional Democrats simply blow spitballs at President Bush's economic proposals without telling the country what they stand for.

"We are united behind a fair, fast-acting, fiscally responsible plan to create at least 1 million new jobs this year," House Minority Leader Nancy Pelosi of California announced in her Feb. 21 speech.

Really?

Pelosi was talking about the official House Democratic economic plan, which the leadership unveiled in January. But the two-day parade of presidential candidates did not exactly line up behind that economic plan. Sen. Joseph I. Lieberman of Connecticut had one of his own. So did Sen. John Edwards of North Carolina. If Sen. John Kerry of Massachusetts had not been recovering from prostate cancer surgery, the crowd could have heard about his plan too.

For that matter, Rep. Richard A. Gephardt of Missouri, Pelosi's predecessor as House minority leader, framed his entire platform — including an international minimum wage, portable pensions and tax credits to pay for employer-based health coverage for everyone — as an economic plan.

It is not unusual to have a crowded field of presidential candidates from one party or another, and they will naturally stake out positions that may or may not agree with their congressional counterparts. But the race for the 2004 Democratic presidential nomination is unusually well-stocked with sitting members of Congress. When that many lawmakers hit the presidential campaign trail, the race is bound to collide with the work of Congress — and make it even harder for congressional Democrats to present a unified agenda they can use to counter President Bush and the GOP majority.

So far, four Democratic senators are in the race, and two more are thinking about entering. In addition to Kerry, Edwards, and Lieberman, Sen. Bob Graham of Florida, who recently had heart surgery, established a campaign committee Feb. 27 and will run if he gets final approval from his doctor next month. Sens. Joseph R. Biden Jr. of Delaware and Christopher J. Dodd of Connecticut are pondering the race, though they are considered less likely to run. *(2003 CQ Weekly, p. 86)*

Two House members, Gephardt and Rep. Dennis J. Kucinich of Ohio, are in the race as well. They round out a field that includes former Vermont Gov. Howard Dean, civil rights activist Al Sharpton and former Sen. Carol Moseley-Braun (1993-1999).

The contest appears likely to include more members of Congress than even some of the recent Congress-heavy presidential primaries, such as the 1988 Democratic race that included Gephardt, Biden, and Sens. Al Gore of Tennessee (1985-93) and Paul Simon of Illinois (1985-97). Even the classic 1960 race, which included Sens. John F. Kennedy of Massachusetts (1953-60), Lyndon B. Johnson of Texas (1949-61), Hubert H. Humphrey of Minnesota (1949-64; 1971-78) and Stuart Symington of Missouri (1953-76), comes up short by comparison.

"We'll have enough [presidential candidates] to field a football team pretty soon," noted Senate Democratic

History Fails to Dissuade Senators From Long-Shot Run at Presidency

In 1958, Massachusetts Democratic Sen. John F. Kennedy told the Washington Gridiron Club a joke about a purported poll of senators' preferences for president. The result: each senator received one vote.

The 2004 campaign to pick the Democratic challenger to President Bush will feature at least four senators who see the president staring back at them when they look in the mirror: John Edwards of North Carolina, Bob Graham of Florida, John Kerry of Massachusetts and Joseph I. Lieberman of Connecticut. They will be joined by at least two House incumbents, Richard A. Gephardt of Missouri and Dennis J. Kucinich of Ohio.

Yet Congress has been a notoriously poor platform for would-be presidents. The last elected directly from the Senate was Kennedy, in 1960; the only other one was Republican Warren G. Harding, in 1920.

And the record is even worse for House members: Republican James A. Garfield, in 1880, was the only president elected directly from the House.

Fifteen presidents once served in the Senate, but most held another office or temporarily left politics before assuming the presidency. Even those examples go back a while: The most recent were Republican Richard M. Nixon, a former vice president, who came back from retirement to win in 1968, and Democrat Lyndon B. Johnson, who was elected vice president in 1960 and became president when Kennedy was assassinated in 1963.

The nation has turned more often to governors, who run for president touting executive experience. Four of the five most recent presidents served as governor but never in Congress.

Yet the pull remains strong. Virtually all members of Congress have visited the White House and understand the awesome power the president holds. Many members have national fundraising networks, appear on the Sunday news shows and delve

"It doesn't help your candidacy."

— Former Sen. Paul Simon on the conflicts between running for president and keeping up with Senate business

into the foreign policy and military issues that are central to a president's duties as commander in chief.

But members who have run for president while serving in Congress compare it to holding two full-time jobs. "It's not an ideal situation," said former Sen. Paul Simon, D-Ill. (1985-97), who sought the 1988 Democratic nomination. Senators running in 2004, he said, "will have to recognize they're just going to have to miss a lot of roll call votes."

Being a Broker

In 1996, Majority Leader Bob Dole, R-Kan., resigned after 27 years in the Senate to focus on his ultimately unsuccessful challenge to President Bill Clinton.

Political analysts say Dole and other presidential candidates from the Senate struggle to demonstrate leadership and decisiveness — qualities that are associated with the presidency but are not prized in a legislative chamber.

"Being a broker is not helpful to a presidential candidate," said Harvard University political scientist Barry C. Burden. "You need to be an independent leader, someone who appears decisive, strong-willed, and someone with vision. It's just hard to convey that if you have that Senate experience of working with both sides."

Simon said President Ronald Reagan, a former California governor who never served in Congress, was "terrible on knowing about the details of issues, but he knew where he was going and was willing to step on some toes to get there." He added, "I think the public tends to want that."

The 2004 Democratic candidates seem to recognize this, focusing more heavily on their broad vision and life experience outside Congress than on their legislative experience.

Kerry's status as a decorated Vietnam War veteran is integral to his campaign and heightens his credibility on foreign and military affairs.

Edwards, a trial lawyer, is a self-styled "champion of the regular people." In a speech to the Democratic National Committee on Feb. 22, Edwards said the Bush administration practiced "government of the insiders, by the insiders, for the insiders."

But there are limits. Gephardt, a 26-year House veteran who was Democratic leader from 1995 to 2003, said in his candidacy announcement that he will not try to pretend that he is a Washington outsider. He portrays himself as a leader of the Democratic opposition to Bush and his policies, and contends that his long years of experience — and his cross-country travels promoting Democratic policies and candidates — leave him much better positioned to pursue the presidency than when he ran a failed campaign in 1988.

Gephardt said Feb. 20 during a campaign visit to New Hampshire — the site of the traditional first presidential primary — "I've met a lot more people than I knew before, and I think people have more interest in this race."

Policy Committee Chairman Byron L. Dorgan of North Dakota.

"I think it's sort of uncharted territory," said Democratic political consultant David Axelrod. "Until this year, we didn't have all that many prominent governors. Our bench has atrophied a little bit. The Senate is a wellspring of potential candidates for us."

This early in the race, the impact on Congress is visible mainly as an unusually large number of floor speeches, press releases and high-profile bill introductions. And jokes, of course. At the weekly Senate Democratic policy luncheon Feb. 25, Edward M. Kennedy of Massachusetts, who had his own presidential ambitions for years, told his colleagues he was the only one who could introduce their guests — a group of Democratic governors — because he was the only one who was not running for president.

"I haven't seen [the race] impede on good will," said Sen. Mary L. Landrieu, D-La. "Right now it's just good-natured jostling."

Down the road, however, the impact could become more serious. It may not be strong enough to alter the course of legislation, but it will be noticeable all the same.

The Shrinking Minority

Many senators and aides expect that Senate Minority Leader Tom Daschle of South Dakota, who passed up the race to focus on his Senate work, will see his voting bloc shrink as the four Senate Democrats begin to miss votes while they are on the campaign trail.

Daschle said he does not expect major problems, saying he has an understanding with the candidates that "on those critical issues where their votes would make a numerical difference, that they'll be there to make the difference." Other Democrats, however, expect that Republican leaders will not bend over backwards to schedule those votes at the most convenient times for the presidential candidates.

And those who have experienced the presidential campaign trail say its demands are simply too great to keep up with Senate votes. "I had a 55 percent voting record," said Sen. Ernest F. Hollings of South Carolina, who sought the Democratic nomination in 1984.

In addition, some say the Senate Democrats' committee work will suffer. That could deprive Daschle of crucial expertise on high-profile panels such as the Finance Committee, where Graham and Kerry are both members, and Governmental Affairs, where Lieberman took charge of homeland security issues last year as the committee's top Democrat. "You've got to let your committee work go" during the campaign season, Hollings said.

Some analysts say Daschle may have to turn to other senators to take the lead on critical issues once dominated by the presidential candidates, such as prescription drug coverage. Graham sponsored the main Senate Democratic proposal last year.

Daschle himself left the door open to such a switch, though he played down its significance. "The nice thing is that we have the depth in our caucus to be able to turn these issues over to others," he said. Graham spokesman Paul Anderson, however, said prescription drug coverage "has been and will remain one of his top priorities," and "I can't imagine he will let other activities interfere with that."

Senate GOP leaders, meanwhile, predict the Democratic candidates will use their Senate seats as a platform for their campaigns. "There's always the possibility that some of the candidates will try to run their campaigns out of the Senate well, and put their own agendas ahead of the interests of the Senate," said Senate Majority Leader Bill Frist, R-Tenn. "I've not seen that yet, but there is that potential."

There already are signs of jockeying for ownership of key issues, however. Edwards, for example, has introduced seven bills related to homeland security this year, asserting himself on a subject closely associated with Lieberman. Edwards also has vowed to lead the opposition to Bush's "Clear Skies" initiative, implicitly challenging Kerry on the environmental issues the Massachusetts senator is emphasizing in his campaign.

How Much Crossover?

The Democratic candidates have different views of how much campaign crossover is appropriate in their congressional duties. Edwards, for example, makes no apologies for introducing campaign proposals as Senate legislation. "It means we can actually do something about our campaign proposals," he said. Kerry and Lieberman also are likely to introduce bills related to their proposals.

Others, however, do not see the point. Aides to Gephardt, who outlined at least half a dozen specific proposals in his speech to the DNC gathering — notably his proposal to require employers to provide health coverage and give them a tax credit to pay most of their costs — say he does not plan to introduce them as legislation because he knows they would never pass.

Kucinich, who co-chairs the 54-member Progressive Caucus, which often offers substitute bills on the House floor, says the caucus will not become a vehicle for his candidacy.

"I'm going to continue to be the active member of Congress I've always been . . . I'm not going to let a presidential campaign stand in the way of that," said Kucinich. "But the Progressive Caucus is not a platform for anyone's candidacy."

Even in the Senate, none of the side effects of the presidential campaign are expected to have a major impact on the outcome of legislation. No matter how many bills Edwards, Lieberman, Kerry or Graham introduce that might be related to their campaigns, they are still in the minority, and they would have trouble getting their bills through even if they were not candidates.

Likewise, even if Daschle cannot round up all of his votes during the height of campaign season, there is not as much pressure on him as there would have been last year, when Democrats were in the majority. As minority leader, Daschle is not expected to win votes.

What the race does, however, is amplify Democrats' differences even more than usual, as was the case with the economic plans. Likewise, the party's split over war with Iraq will become even louder. Kucinich is framing his campaign as an anti-war candidacy, while Gephardt, Kerry, Edwards and Lieberman all supported last year's resolution (PL 107-243) authorizing Bush to use military force in Iraq. Graham voted against it. *(2002 CQ Weekly, p.2679)*

"It's hard to get political coherence out of a group with such different political needs," said Axelrod. "There will be ownership of particular parts of the agenda."

The Democratic jockeying also puts the White House in the awkward position of pretending not to care about the potential challengers while dealing with a Congress that could be a substantial base for the campaign to unseat Bush.

That is no small concern. In a CNN/USA Today/Gallup poll of 1,004 adults conducted Feb. 24-26, the percentage of registered voters who said they would support Bush for reelection fell below 50 percent for the first time. The poll, which had a sampling error of plus or minus 3 percentage points, found that Bush's drop in support appeared to be caused by voters' economic anxieties.

Officially, the White House line is that the administration is not paying attention. "The president is focused on the challenges this country faces, both at home and abroad," said White House spokesman Scott McClellan. "2004 is the farthest thing from his mind right now."

Unofficially, there are signs that people within the White House are paying attention. In January, when Bush gave a speech advocating limits on medical malpractice awards, an unnamed White House official was quoted by the Associated Press as calling the event "whack John Edwards" day, a reference to the North Carolina senator's previous career as a trial lawyer. Edwards' defense of his career — "bring it on" — brought the biggest applause of his DNC speech. *(Malpractice, p. 101)*

There is no doubt that Republican operatives are watching the Democratic candidates closely. Opposition researchers at the Republican National Committee have churned out papers listing the numerous weaknesses they see in Edwards, Dean, Lieberman, Gephardt and Kerry.

"I think the White House is being clever in letting the RNC put this stuff out," said Republican strategist Scott Reed, who served as campaign manager for former Senate Majority Leader Bob Dole, R-Kan., (1969-1996) in his 1996 presidential race. "They know the only issue right now is Iraq, and everything else is semantics until Iraq is settled."

Campaigning From Congress

So far, Edwards appears to be the lawmaker who is seeking the most crossover between his presidential campaign and his activities in Congress. His centerpiece homeland security proposal, a bill (S 410) to create a Homeland Intelligence Agency to take over intelligence duties from the FBI, is promoted on his campaign Web site.

In addition, Edwards has introduced bills to improve the cybersecurity of the federal government (S 187), give first responders more access to classified intelligence information (S 266), create a national emergency warning system (S 118), improve building and fire codes to make buildings safer (S 216), and increase support for neighborhood watch programs so they can look out for terrorists as well as criminals (S 329).

The most recent bill (S 479), introduced Feb. 27, would offer up to $10,000 a year in college scholarships to students who commit to serving in professions related to homeland security for five years after they graduate.

The homeland security bills will be followed by other legislation that overlaps with his campaign. Edwards said he plans to introduce a bill to provide $50 billion in aid to the states to help them with homeland security, health care and other costs. Another possibility, according to aides, is a legislative version of his campaign proposal to provide a free year of college tuition at public universities and community colleges for students who pass their courses and perform part-time work or community service.

A Little Help

Getting the Republican majority to act on his bills, however, would be a tall order even for a Democrat who was not trying to unseat a Republican president. In addition, Edwards likely would need help from the ranking Democrats on the committees with jurisdiction over his bills, and some of them are unlikely to be enthusiastic about helping him. His cybersecurity bill, for example, was referred to the Governmental Affairs Committee, where the ranking Democrat is Lieberman.

Edwards is not the only senator whose legislative activities are taking on presidential overtones.

Lieberman, who delivered a speech to the Council on Foreign Relations Feb. 26 on the importance of rebuilding Iraq, says he is preparing legislation with Sen. Chuck Hagel, R-Neb., to create a "Marshall Plan for the Muslim world" — a program to improve the economies, health care and educational systems of Muslim countries. He also has introduced a resolution (S J Res 6) urging the Bush administration to spell out its plans for a postwar Iraq.

Lieberman said the presidential campaign has not affected his ability to work with Republicans on legislation. But as for getting it passed, "let's be honest — nothing's moving in the Senate right now anyway," he said.

Kerry, who already has been crowned the Democratic front-runner by some political reporters, may introduce legislative pieces of his economic and environmental proposals, according to spokesman David Wade. While the components have not been determined, Kerry has proposed a payroll tax holiday as part of his economic package, and he has said the nation should set a goal of getting 20 percent of its electricity from alternative and renewable sources by 2020.

More Bills

Still, Kerry insists he is not trying to make a point of turning his platform into legislation. "John Kerry has a long and accomplished legislative record, so he has nothing to prove by introducing a flurry of bills related to the campaign," said Wade.

Kucinich, meanwhile, said he will continue to introduce legislation on issues that might overlap with his campaign, but insisted they will not be any different from the bills he has sponsored for years before becoming a presidential candidate. They include bills to establish a national, single-payer health care system, protect Social Security from being privatized and establish a Department of Peace, he said.

Even with the presidential race taking off rapidly, it is not unheard of for the candidates to team up with each other when the issue is right.

Kerry and Edwards were among the 11 Senate Democrats who joined Daschle in filing an amicus brief with the Supreme Court supporting the University of Michigan's affirmative action program, taking a stand against Bush's support of the lawsuit against the school.

And Lieberman and Edwards, along with Daschle and eight other Democrats, are cosponsors of a Kerry bill (S 318) to give emergency aid to small businesses hurt by the drought.

On the bright side, some Democrats say a presidential race based largely in Congress will give the party's ideas maximum exposure.

"So far, I don't see it having a negative impact on the Democratic agenda," said Ed Kilgore, policy director of the centrist Democratic Leadership Council. "It may even help, because it earns more attention than it would otherwise."

And if that means earning attention for several agendas rather than one cohesive one, most congressional Democrats simply shrug off the notion that a unified Democratic agenda will become difficult to find.

"No more difficult than it usually is," said Sen. Thomas R. Carper, D-Del. ◆

The Record: Democratic Contenders Since '99

Six of the nine Democratic presidential hopefuls are sitting members of Congress, each with a voting record that spans at least four years. Hundreds of votes in the House and Senate offer voters and interest groups ample opportunity to size up the candidates, comparing and contrasting where they stand on issues that will be key to the 2004 presidential race.

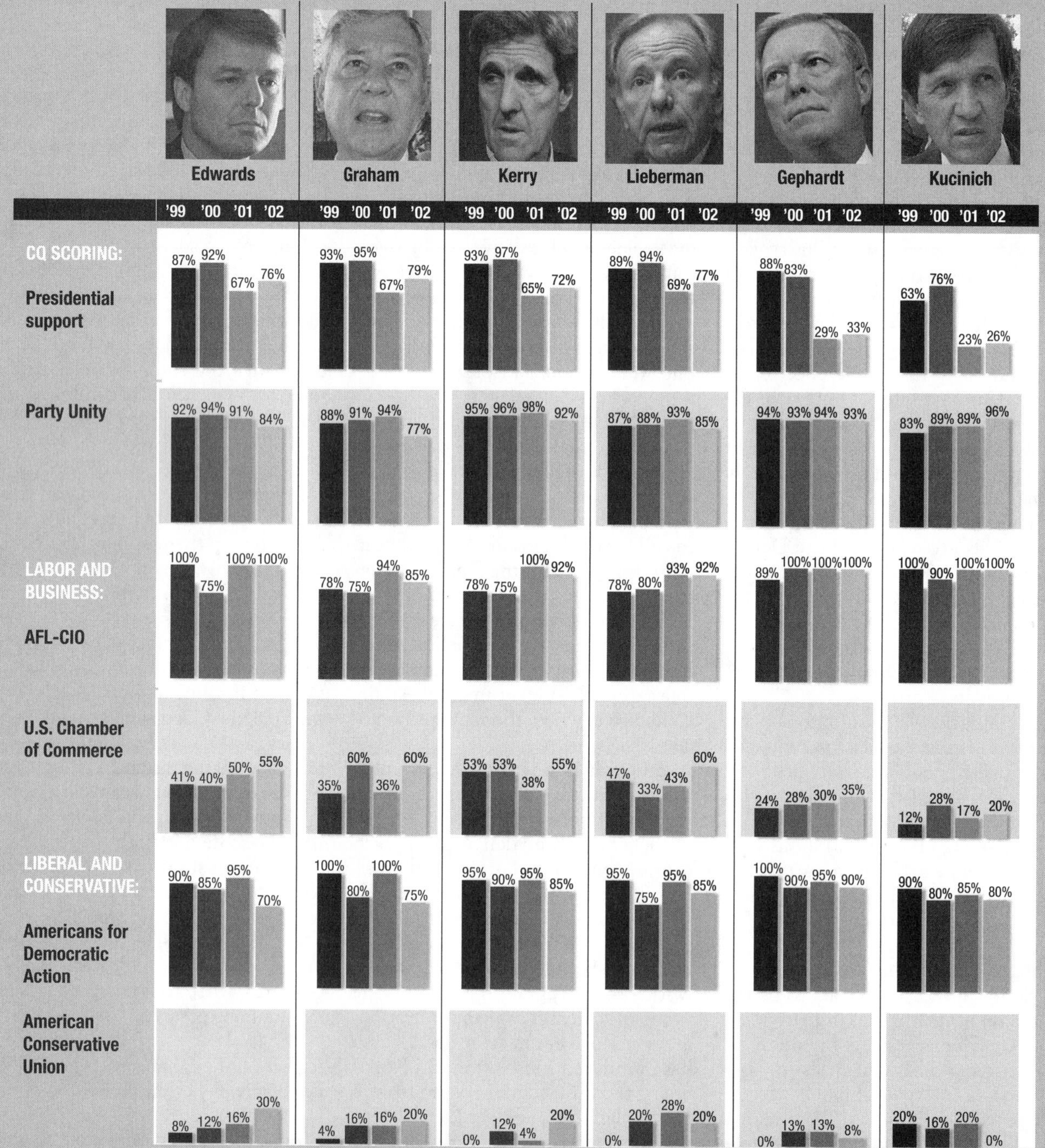

EXPLANATION OF STATISTICS

CQ's presidential support scores show the percentage of time members voted in agreement with the president. Votes are from the last two years of Clinton's presidency and the first two years of Bush's term. The Senate scores during 2000-01 are higher than those in the House because of "yes" votes on Bush Cabinet and judicial nominees.

CQ's party unity scores are derived from roll call votes on which a majority of Democrats opposed a majority of Republicans.

Ratings by the four interest groups are compiled by CQ based on information provided by each organization.

Effective House Leadership Makes the Most of Majority

GOP has consolidated political power to a degree not seen in decades

Republican leaders looked surprisingly calm in the early morning hours of March 21 even though time for voting on the all-important House budget resolution had expired and "nay" votes outnumbered "yea" votes by one.

Moments later, two Texans — Republican Larry Combest and Democrat Ralph M. Hall — switched their votes, giving GOP leaders a milestone victory on the blueprint for President Bush's domestic agenda, which calls for $726 billion in tax cuts and a $400 billion Medicare overhaul.

As it turns out, GOP leaders had presented this threshold vote to members without knowing for certain the outcome. "We didn't have the votes when we went to the floor," a source close to the Republican whip organization acknowledged.

The roll call vote, which wrapped up just short of 3 a.m., provided high drama for the limited few in the galleries. More important, it was a pointed show of strength from the increasingly emboldened House Republican leadership.

Combest's vote was secured by a promise from the Budget Committee chairman, Jim Nussle of Iowa, that farm subsidies would not take a hit to make room for the tax cuts. His was the last of many votes won with eleventh-hour promises — made while the path between the House chamber and the office of Speaker J. Dennis Hastert was being worn by House leaders, recalcitrant Republicans and White House lobbyists.

As the GOP now approaches a decade in the majority, the centralization of power in the current triumvirate at the top — Hastert of Illinois, Majority Leader Tom DeLay of Texas and Majority Whip Roy Blunt of Missouri — is greater than ever. And the loyalty these three leaders engender — made easier by the increasingly homogeneous nature of the GOP conference and a whip organization intently focused on member service — is more devoted than any in the eight years of GOP rule.

CQ PHOTO / SCOTT J. FERRELL

Speaker Hastert, center, presides over a weekly strategy session March 11 with other members of the House Republican leadership team.

The degree to which House GOP leaders are effective in exercising their power has tremendous implications for the future of their party, including whether Bush is successful in getting his initiatives through Congress and even whether he is re-elected in 2004.

The vote on the budget resolution (H Con Res 95), for example, was a satisfying culmination for the Republican leaders, whose preparation proved just meticulous enough to deliver a domestic victory for Bush as he sought military victory in Iraq — an objective repeatedly made clear in the leadership's efforts to win votes.

Two weeks earlier, DeLay had pulled a bill (HR 878) granting tax relief to military personnel and their families off the floor at the last minute, sparing the rank and file from having to cast a tough vote on legislation that had been loaded up with tax breaks for special interests. *(2003 CQ Weekly, p. 560)*

At the time, a senior Republican aide insisted leaders would have won a floor fight, but they chose to reserve their political capital for tougher battles. Their judgment paid off — they did need all the firepower they could muster for the budget — and their adroit command of the Republican troops has seldom been more evident.

Longworth-Like Power

Powerful leadership has been a cornerstone of Republican rule since the party took control of the House in 1995. But the way this current team has consolidated power is extraordinary even by more historical standards.

Ronald M. Peters Jr., a political scientist at the University of Oklahoma who has written several books on the Speaker's office, says the current team may be the strongest House leadership in 75 years.

Comparisons are difficult, but Peters

said today's leadership reminds him of the power structure that developed under Ohio Republican Nicholas Longworth (1903-13; 1915-31). Longworth was not a tyrannical individual powerhouse in the mold of Joseph G. Cannon, R-Ill. (1873-91; 1893-1913; 1915-23; Speaker 1903-1911). Rather, as Speaker from 1925 to 1931, Longworth established a group of trusted associates to help him run the House. *(History, p.39)*

Today's Republican leadership is a cohesive group, nearly all of whom rose through the ranks of the whip operation established by former Whip DeLay. Both Hastert and Blunt served as chief deputy whip under DeLay before ascending to their current positions.

So, for the first time since the GOP took control of the House, there is virtually no rivalry within the leadership team. The men in charge — tacticians to the core — all honed their consensus-building and vote-counting skills in the same shop.

The GOP leadership was fragmented under Newt Gingrich of Georgia (House 1979-99; Speaker 1995-99), and rivalries ultimately led to an aborted coup attempt in 1997. Even after Gingrich left Congress, fissures remained, as DeLay on occasion butted heads with Majority Leader Dick Armey of Texas (1985-2003) and Conference Chairman J.C. Watts Jr. of Oklahoma (1995-2003).

But even then the foundation of the current leaders' power was being built. The Republican revolutionaries sworn into office in January 1995 immediately began consolidating power in Gingrich's hands. John A. Boehner of Ohio, a member of the "Gang of Seven" Republican freshmen who agitated for change in the early 1990s, says concentrated authority has served the Republicans well. Boehner himself later served four years in the leadership, as conference chairman, before losing his post after the disappointing 1998 election.

"The problems and the issues tend to get dealt with at a much earlier point in the process . . . they used to get resolved right out here on the House floor," Boehner said, motioning from the adjacent Speaker's Lobby as he recalled watching the Democratic majority "disintegrating" right before his eyes.

During their final years in power, Democratic leaders at times had trouble with even the most basic functions. In large measure, they became victims of more than three-quarters of a century of efforts to decentralize authority in the wake of a revolt in 1910 against Cannon, the iron-fisted model of House authoritarianism.

While Democrats, unhappy with the immense power wielded by committee chairmen, had sent some authority back toward party leaders in the 1970s, they also continued a general decentralization by enhancing the role of subcommittee chairmen.

When Republicans took over in 1995, they set about ensuring that their leader would have broad authority to pass their agenda quickly. They instituted a rule forcing committee chairmen to give up their gavels after three terms, eliminated three committees, denied a chairmanship to Rep. Carlos J. Moorhead, R-Calif. (1973-97), who was in line to head either Energy and Commerce or Judiciary, and brought subcommittee chairmen back under the domain of committee heads.

But some of the more powerful panel chiefs became displeased with the degree to which Gingrich dominated the process. In perhaps the biggest affront to chairmen, Gingrich established ad hoc task forces to draft legislation on major issues such as health care.

Despite his charismatic and vision-driven leadership, Gingrich could not quell his underlings' constant jockeying for position. And his colleagues' ultimate loss of faith in his ability to hold the majority did Gingrich in. "Gingrich was not able to sustain that level of centralized leadership, and it was one reason . . . that he ran into trouble," said Peters.

The controversial Georgian stepped down after Republicans nearly lost their majority in the 1998 election, and DeLay, then the majority whip, backed Hastert, his top lieutenant, when Speaker-designate Robert L. Livingston of Louisiana (1977-99) resigned amid revelations of extramarital affairs. *(1998 Almanac, p. 7-4)*

Regular Order

In contrast to Gingrich, the tenet of the Hastert era has been a return to "regular order," meaning bills should be considered first by the committee of jurisdiction. Still, the leadership team does not hesitate to let committee chairmen know when they are displeased with their positions on issues or with the direction of legislation.

For example, DeLay is mounting a battle against raising the federal gas tax, putting himself in direct opposition to Alaska's Don Young, chairman of the Transportation and Infrastructure Committee, who is readying a reauthorization bill for federal highway programs with the stated intention of raising the gas tax to pay for highway construction.

And at a conference meeting a day before the budget resolution vote, leaders admonished Veterans' Affairs Chairman Christopher H. Smith of New Jersey for rounding up votes that threatened to defeat the measure. Smith was concerned about possible cuts to veterans programs and withheld his support for the budget until he got a letter promising that House leaders would seek at least the Senate committee-approved levels for veterans spending.

"They called Chris Smith out on the carpet," said one Republican lawmaker, making it clear that committee chairmen were expected to toe the leadership line.

The episode was typical of how DeLay tends to lead, members say. "What I see is a guy who's very strong in his conviction . . . [who] is not particularly tolerant of people who are trying to lead in the opposite direction," said moderate Sherwood Boehlert of New York.

Indeed, the leaders' influence helps them observe regular order without allowing panel chairmen to drift too far afield.

Traditionally, committee chairmen pose the greatest threat to the authority of the leadership. Charged with shaping and moving legislation, chairmen can exercise great control over the details of policy, including the special items favored by colleagues.

But a hallmark of Republican control of the House has been a shift of power from committee chairmen to the leadership. The shift helps leadership pass legislation in the form favored by a majority of the mainly conservative Republican Conference.

"The House can act as a body, whereas when committee chairs were little czars it didn't act as a body," said Grover Norquist, president of Americans For Tax Reform and a close ally of DeLay.

One significant reason for the shift in power was the adoption in 1995 of three-term limits on committee chairs. Now the roster of committee chairmen changes at the start of each Congress. Just three members who had won gavels in 1995 — Young, Bill Thomas of California and Henry J. Hyde of Illinois — are currently committee chairmen. None chairs the same panel he did then.

As chairmen cycle out, the Republican Steering Committee decides who replaces them. It is dominated by members of the leadership. And while seniority was once the sole factor in determining chairmanships, today loyalty and fundraising ability can trump longevity. Even after they have been given a gavel, chairmen are forced to defend their tenure every two years to the Steering Committee, which has the power to remove them.

At the start of the 107th Congress in 2001, GOP leaders ignored the seniority of New Jersey's Marge Roukema (1981-2003), the longest-serving Republican woman in the House at the time and in line to run the Financial Services Committee. Instead, they chose Michael G. Oxley of Ohio, a top fundraiser and a loyalist, to run the panel.

This year, Republican leaders reached far down the ladder to select Californian Richard W. Pombo to head the Resources Committee over five more-senior members of the panel. And Christopher Shays of Connecticut, the senior Republican on Government Reform, was bypassed for Virginian Thomas M. Davis III, who led the House GOP campaign committee last Congress. *(2003 CQ Weekly, p. 89)*

Wisconsin Democrat David R. Obey and other critics say the erosion of the seniority system — the awarding of gavels to junior members — hurts the outcome of legislation.

"The strength of a legislative body, the strength of the Congress [is that] people get on committees and develop expertise," Obey said. "[That] turns a political body into a legislative body."

But Shays, who angered his leaders last year by repeatedly beating back their opposition to his signature campaign finance legislation (PL 107-155), understands the need for centralized power even though it was used against him in the past. "All of us want a strong leadership because we want to get things done," he said.

For Republicans, moving big-ticket items — the budget, fast-track authority, the 2001 tax cut package and Bush's education overhaul, to name a few — has been the primary reward of centralized power. They have moved those top agenda items while wielding a historically small margin of control in a remarkably polarized House.

Hastert's authority "really allows for him to build the kind of team that's really necessary for getting anything done around here," said Ray LaHood, R-Ill., a parliamentary expert who frequently presides over the House and served as chief of staff to former Republican Leader Robert H. Michel of Illinois (House 1957-95; minority leader 1981-95) before being elected to Congress with the Class of 1994.

The Hastert Touch

Seen by some as a caretaker when he succeeded Gingrich, Hastert quickly became known as a "healer" and has now served longer than his predecessor. Hastert also is widely acknowledged as the conference's "coach," a moniker that carries over from his days as a successful high school wrestling coach.

Says Blunt: "The Speaker . . . is always willing to step back after the game and let the star of the game that day get the applause, knowing that at the end of the season people look back at the whole season and they begin to realize really what we have here is a great coach as well as some good individual players."

A package of rules changes adopted in January was both a testament to Hastert's popularity within his conference and a demonstration that GOP leaders are secure enough to backtrack on reforms first adopted in the heady days of the Gingrich revolution, when a primary goal was to make the House a more open, accountable place where minority rights were strengthened.

On a party-line vote, the House adopted a rules package (H Res 5) that eliminated a four-term limit on the Speaker, gave chairmen the power to postpone committee votes, loosened a strict ban on gifts to lawmakers and made it harder for the minority to assert its positions through "motions to instruct conferees." *(2003 CQ Weekly, p. 90)*

Two months earlier, Republican leaders had made an internal conference change that proved their determination to take hold of the House:

Six Speakers' Legacies

The Speaker of the House is regarded widely as the most powerful position in Congress, but his authority and ability to rule the House has fluctuated greatly over the years. The following six men are among the most effective Speakers in history, each using the office in his own way to advance his own or his party's agenda.

Clay
U.S. HOUSE OF REPRESENTATIVES PORTRAIT

■ **Henry Clay, Democratic-Republican of Kentucky** (Speaker, 1811-14, 1815-20 and 1823-25) was the first Speaker of national prominence and the first to use the position to achieve his own ends. He packed key committees with war hawks, pressuring President James Madison to declare war against England in 1812. And he established new standards of order for conducting business on the floor.

■ **Thomas Brackett Reed, R-Maine** (1889-91 and 1895-99), expanded the powers of the office more than any Speaker except Clay, using rulings from the chair that were later incorporated into the rules of the House. He, in essence, established the absolute right of the majority to control the legislative process.

■ **Joseph G. Cannon, R-Ill.** (1903-11), used the centralized power of the speakership established by his predecessors to tyrannize the House. He disregarded seniority in making committee assignments, used consideration of "unanimous consent" bills to reward friends and punish enemies, and used the Rules Committee to block bills he opposed. Ultimately, his powers were stripped in a bipartisan revolt in 1910, a year before his term as Speaker ended.

■ **Nicholas Longworth, R-Ohio** (1925-31), sought to centralize power in the Speaker's office once again after more than a decade of decentralization in the wake of Cannon. He never had all the

They decided to make the 13 appropriations subcommittee chairmen subject to approval by the Steering Committee.

For decades, it had been the Appropriations Committee chairmen and their subcommittee chiefs, forming the so-called college of cardinals, who drove the deals with Democrats to send large amounts of federal largess to members' districts to pay for bridges, roads, farm payments and other pet projects. The process went on almost without questioning from higher-ups.

But in the last Congress, as lawmakers grappled with a rising budget deficit and expensive demands to improve homeland security, Republican appropriators increasingly clashed with their party leaders. The two chairmen of the big-dollar subcommittees overseeing education, health, housing and other domestic programs — Ralph Regula of Ohio and James T. Walsh of New York — demanded full funding for their programs and, as a result of their demands, made governing even more difficult for their party chiefs.

The rule change, approved by the conference in mid-November, essentially forced the cardinals to re-interview for their chairmanships before the start of the 108th — and before 11 holdover fiscal 2003 spending bills had been completed. *(2002 CQ Weekly, p. 3015)*

"We were not told in advance that was going to be offered at the conference meeting," recalled Appropriations Chairman C.W. Bill Young of Florida, who was caught off guard by the rule change. In hindsight, he added, it was a good exercise because it helped the leaders understand the pressures facing appropriators.

But Young and other appropriators got the message. "We understand the chain of command. We understand who the leaders are," Young said. The point was underscored by Regula: "Every ship has got to have a captain."

Two Captains?

Hastert and DeLay have developed a finely tuned working relationship in which they generally present a united front and rally their members around a cause. They have had few public disagreements; a notable one was on gun-control legislation that Hastert backed and DeLay fought in the wake of shootings at Columbine High School in Littleton, Colo., in 1999. But usually their battles are private.

"If they're spilling blood in the back room, that's where it should be spilled," said John M. McHugh, R-N.Y.

The consummate deal-maker and facilitator, DeLay has used every implement available to him to build loyalty within the party ranks. His effective use of the whip operation as a vehicle to provide services to members cemented his constituency.

No task was too small for DeLay, whose operation handled travel arrangements for members and provided food when House votes dragged into the late hours of the night.

Those smaller goodies were icing on the cake once Delay's ability to help members win money for pet projects or his hard-driving efforts to raise cash for their campaigns were taken into account. At election time, DeLay has dispatched aides to walk precincts for GOP candidates across the country.

The result: He is roundly praised on the Republican side — even by those with whom he does not always see eye-to-eye — for his integrity and his drive to advance Republican goals.

DeLay also earned respect from colleagues for owning up to his role in the coup attempt against Gingrich and for pushing impeachment proceedings against President Bill Clinton when it looked like they might be dropped.

DeLay earned his nickname, "The Hammer," during the early years of GOP House control. Though some have forgotten, it was the former exterminator's aggressive approach with K Street lobbyists — suggesting that access to leadership is related to money and fealty for GOP causes and candidates — that earned him the nickname, not his dealings with colleagues.

The reputation lends DeLay an advantageous mystique within the Republican ranks, particularly with newer members. As Speaker Thomas P. "Tip" O'Neill, D-Mass. (1953-87; Speaker 1977-87), once said, "Power is when people assume you have power." But the true source of DeLay's influence is an ability to meet the needs of colleagues while using a pinch of vinegar and a heavy dose of honey to get what he wants.

LIBRARY OF CONGRESS PHOTO

Longworth

authority of Cannon but was an effective leader, nonetheless, using a collegial style and the power of persuasion to achieve his goals. A small circle of advisers helped him govern the House, and he often would reach across the aisle to work with Democrats on both policy and scheduling issues.

■ **Sam Rayburn, D-Texas** (1940-47, 1949-53 and 1955-61), was an effective and respected Speaker despite the fact that in his era the seniority system dominated the House. Committee chairmen were the power brokers after decades of relatively weak Speakers. Rayburn won the loyalty of his colleagues by dealing with them as individuals rather than members of his party. He built friendships and did favors for members, knowing that would help secure their votes when necessary. He downplayed partisanship and counseled young lawmakers "to get along, go along."

■ **Thomas P. "Tip" O'Neill Jr., D-Mass.** (1977-87), modernized the speakership and served as his party's spokesman when President Ronald Reagan was in the White House and Republicans ruled the Senate. Faced with demands from the rank and file for more participation in decisions, he enlarged the whip operation and set up task forces to help plot strategy. He broadened the use of restrictive rules for floor debate and kept favored legislation alive by referring bills to more than one committee and setting time limits for action.

REUTERS FILE PHOTO

O'Neill

"Nobody listens more than he does, and nobody takes care of their members more than he does," said GOP Rep. Adam H. Putnam of Florida.

That is lofty praise from a man who offers a case study in DeLay's tactics and effectiveness. In December 2001, Putnam voted against the fast-track trade bill (PL 107-210) despite heavy lobbying from Bush, Cabinet officials and GOP leaders — plus a rare public dressing down by DeLay on the floor as the cliff-hanger vote was under way.

As he left the floor that day, a shaken Putnam allowed: "I feel like I'm going to throw up." *(2001 CQ Weekly, p. 2918)*

When the conference report on the fast-track bill came before the House eight months later, Putnam voted with his leadership. He said he had won a provision that would help protect Florida's citrus and sugar industries.

"There was no retribution," Putnam says today. In fact, the second-termer was awarded a subcommittee chairmanship in the 108th. Still, Putnam acknowledges that his less-than-robust support of trade does have repercussions.

"My hope of ever serving on the Ways and Means Committee is probably closed off," he said, because he opposes the proposed Free Trade Area of the Americas. "It would be unfair for me to expect them to put someone who has trepidation on some aspects of trade on the committee with jurisdiction."

Ultimately, Robin Hayes of North Carolina cast one of the last votes to put Republicans over the top on fast track in December 2001. With a tough re-election bid looming, Hayes, whose family made its money in textiles, found the vote an especially difficult one. He gave party leaders a list of 10 concessions they would have to make to secure his vote. Not only did Hayes receive assurances that his policy demands would be met, but GOP leaders rallied to his electoral cause.

Hayes ended up winning re-election with 54 percent, after outspending his opponent more than 3 to 1. "Expectations have been exceeded at every step of the way," Hayes recently said of promises to meet his demands for tempering the impact of the trade bill.

Even some Democrats praise DeLay's ability to deliver on his promises. John P. Murtha of Pennsylvania says there are two ways to gain power on Capitol Hill: Develop expertise on an issue that makes you vital to colleagues, and keep your word. Murtha, an influential voice on defense issues who quietly operates in the back corner of the Democratic side of the House, says he has dealt with DeLay and found him to be an honest broker. When DeLay wants something, Murtha says, "He comes over to the corner and we work it out."

Monolithic Ranks

Another important reason for Republican leaders' success in keeping their herd in line is the increasingly monolithic nature of their conference.

Veteran GOP moderates, including Roukema, Constance A. Morella of Maryland and Benjamin A. Gilman of New York left the House at the end of the 107th. And for every moderate Republican newly elected, such as Jeb Bradley of New Hampshire, there are several rock-ribbed conservatives, such as Tennessee's Marsha Blackburn, Colorado's Marilyn Musgrave, New Jersey's Scott Garrett and Iowa's Steve King.

While Republican moderates often estimate their ranks to be three dozen or more in the House, voting records and other evidence pin the number closer to two dozen. And while that is more than enough to change the outcome of any given vote if moderates vote as a bloc, in practice, they rarely do.

Norquist of Americans for Tax Reform says the solidarity results from a two-decades-long rightward shift within the party. And such ideological unity facilitates governance.

"From time to time, you have to work very hard to get the last two votes," said Norquist, who sat in DeLay's office as the majority leader rounded up budget votes. But "90 percent of your caucus is with you before you call them on the phone."

Meanwhile, conservative groups, most prominently the Club for Growth, have targeted moderates for defeat in GOP primaries, funneling thousands of dollars to challengers. While the club has yet to knock off an incumbent, many of the candidates it has backed have won open-seat primaries.

Maryland's Wayne T. Gilchrest, the target of a club-funded challenge this year, defiantly says he will not change the way he votes. "I don't have a second thought about Club for Growth when it comes down to my votes here on the House floor," he said.

But the specter of a primary challenge can lead members to think twice before defying their leadership. And the Club for Growth, which received $50,000 in checks from a political organization run by DeLay last year, fans those flames.

"We have said anybody in the House or Senate that votes against the Bush tax cut is someone we'll give strong consideration to fielding a primary challenger against," club President Stephen Moore said.

The Democrats' Take

Veteran Democrats, including Obey, say the current leadership has gone too far in its dominance of the floor — particularly when it comes to using "closed rules" that preclude the minority from offering amendments and substitutes to bills under consideration.

"Things don't get debated, issues aren't open," said Massachusetts Democrat Barney Frank, a student of parliamentary procedure.

Democrats say the closed rules usually approved by the Rules Committee — an arm of leadership — undercut both parties' responsibilities: the duty of the minority to question the majority and that of the majority to defend its positions. "That way, [bills] were insulated from all evaluation," Obey said.

Rules Chairman David Dreier of California says Democrats have a short memory. "They put into place very unfair rules," he said, noting that his party routinely allows the opposition a chance to send legislation back to committee through a "motion to recommit," the penultimate floor vote before final passage. "I point to that motion to recommit, which was often denied to us," Dreier said.

But Frost says that Dreier and the once-revolutionary Republicans have changed their tune on the rules for debate.

A Frost news release March 13 quoted Dreier saying the following when Republicans were in the minority: "I oppose closed rules, Mr. Speaker. I believe they are anathema to the concept of deliberative democracy."

Bickering aside, longtime observers note that each side uses the rules to its advantage; controlling the rules is the ultimate spoil of a majoritarian body. Indeed, Republicans say that focusing on the narrowness of their majority — and how easy it would be to lose any given vote — has helped Republican leaders keep their troops in line. ◆

GOP Turns to Cheney To Get the Job Done

Vice president's reputation gives him key role at both ends of Pennsylvania Avenue

President Bush wanted an economic stimulus bill on his desk by Memorial Day, and it was Vice President Dick Cheney, more than any other single player, who gave it to him.

It was Cheney's tie-breaking vote that got the second substantial tax cut of the Bush presidency through the Senate on May 23, clearing it for Bush to sign (HR 2 — PL 108-27) five days later.

But more important, it was Cheney's intervention in the final hours that yielded an agreement from what had promised to be a lengthy and divisive conference committee, one preordained weeks before when House and Senate Republican leaders had a serious and very public falling out over how large the tax cut would be in the end.

KRT PHOTO / DAVID BOHRER

Cheney celebrates with Treasury Secretary John W. Snow, left, and Commerce Secretary Donald L. Evans in Cheney's Capitol office after the tax cut cleared.

As Senate Majority Whip Mitch McConnell, R-Ky., put it, Cheney was "the indispensible element" in bridging the substantive differences and deep-seated mistrust between Republican leaders on Capitol Hill, closing a deal that gave all players room to claim at least some measure of success. Meeting over two days with lawmakers behind closed doors in the Capitol, the vice president served as sounding board, conciliator, deal-cutter and a determined president's firm right hand, pressing all parties toward a compromise that would allow Bush to declare victory on his top domestic priority.

"Without Dick Cheney's intervention, there would not have been a bill today," Finance Committee Chairman Charles E. Grassley, R-Iowa, said May 23, shortly after the Senate cleared the $350 billion budget reconciliation measure. *(Congress, p. 77)*

It was not the first time Cheney played such a key role in pushing priority legislation over the final hump, and it probably will not be the last. In the five months since Republicans once again secured one-party government — with control over both chambers of Congress as well as the White House — the 46th vice president of the United States has become the steady hand that can get things done when personality conflicts, institutional jealousies and internal philosophical differences threaten to derail the Republican agenda. Along with mediating the final agreement on the tax plan, he struck key compromises that helped end an intractable dispute over fiscal 2003 appropriations.

Since winning back the Senate last November and slightly expanding their majority in the House, Republicans have seen their internal differences occasionally spill into the open, not only between conservatives and moderates but between the Senate and the House and between Congress and the Bush administration. They have fought over the size of the latest tax cut, the composition of it and whether to include fiscal aid to the states. They have also tangled over whether to allow oil and gas exploration in Alaska's Arctic National Wildlife Refuge (ANWR).

And as they return the week of June 2 from their Memorial Day recess, they are likely to face differences this summer over Medicare, gas taxes and domestic spending priorities. *(2003 CQ Weekly, p. 1331)*

Mediating the Squabbles

At the same time, Senate Republicans have had to regain their footing under a new and relatively inexperienced majority leader — Bill Frist of Tennessee — one who made a rookie mistake in April when he blessed a deal with two Republican senators to hold the tax cut to $350 billion but failed to tell his House counterparts. *(2003 CQ Weekly, p. 931)*

Despite their visibility, the party's differences are relatively minor compared with past intraparty squabbles in Congress. Democrats were far more deeply split over health care, budget, trade and crime policies in the 103rd Congress of

1993 and 1994 — the last time they controlled both the White House and Congress — and President Ronald Reagan faced bigger revolts from House Republicans over tax policy in the early 1980s. (*2003 CQ Weekly, p. 1309*)

But as the past several weeks have shown, any internal differences and missteps become magnified when one party controls both the legislative and executive branches, which makes Cheney's role all the more crucial.

Cheney listens more than he talks, and he is widely viewed as having no personal ambition higher than his current office. When he does speak, he is taken on Capitol Hill as the undiluted and trusted voice of the president.

That perception is a source of great power in his dealings with congressional leaders and committee chairmen. No one in the GOP considers the president of the Senate — Cheney's other title under the Constitution — to be anything other than a clear line to their president, with the authority to make deals on behalf of the White House that will stick.

After nearly three decades in Washington that have included time in the House leadership and stints as secretary of Defense and White House chief of staff, Cheney has cultivated relationships and trust that transcend institutional divisions between the House and Senate — and between Congress and the White House. That, too, is a source of power.

"He has the confidence of people at both ends of Pennsylvania Avenue," said James W. Dyer, Republican staff director for the House Appropriations Committee. "Those are the people who get things done in Washington: the people who inspire confidence at both ends of the avenue."

Pragmatic Operator

At times, Cheney is deployed by the White House, usually as a deal-closer — those times "when the chips are down," said Nancy Dorn, the top General Electric Co. lobbyist, who worked as Cheney's legislative liaison in 2001. At other times, congressional leaders and committee chairmen call him for help sorting out their differences with each other or the administration — again, in the endgame.

"The vice president brings the weight of the administration to the table to make the final sale," Dorn said.

Such was the case the week of May 19, as Republicans worked to finish the tax bill.

House Ways and Means Committee Chairman Bill Thomas, R-Calif., wanted a tax cut that would be deep enough to satisfy the party's conservative base. Grassley envisioned a package with added sweeteners, such as fiscal aid to struggling state and local governments, to get the bill through the closely divided Senate. Grassley also could not get around the earlier GOP pact that he, Frist and Budget Committee Chairman Don Nickles of Oklahoma had made with George V. Voinovich of Ohio and Olympia J. Snowe of Maine to keep the size of the tax cut to $350 billion. The differences seemed certain to produce an arduous conference.

Bush moved to cut the process short May 19, telling congressional leaders he wanted a deal by the end of the week. Thomas and Grassley outlined a plan that would cost $380 billion, but it quickly became clear that Voinovich and Snowe would not support it. On May 21, a tense meeting between Thomas and Grassley ended with Thomas storming out of his own office. Cheney was called in that day and the next to mediate and sort out the differences.

Meeting first with Thomas alone, then with Thomas and Voinovich together, the vice president helped broker a deal to fit both the tax cuts and additional spending under the $350 billion ceiling by moving the expiration date of the capital gains and dividend tax cuts to 2008 from 2009, saving $29 billion. Cheney then went to the north side of the Capitol to seal the deal with Frist and Grassley.

Cheney stepped in May 22 to clear away one last hurdle. It was put up by House Energy and Commerce Committee Chairman Billy Tauzin of Louisiana, who threatened to lead a revolt by Republicans on his panel over the conference report's $10 billion in Medicaid money for states.

Tauzin was concerned that the money would become a permanent part of the budget, changing how the cost of the low-income health insurance program is divided between the federal government and the states. But Cheney helped Frist and House Speaker J. Dennis Hastert, R-Ill., persuade Tauzin to back down by promising the additional Medicaid funds would not make a permanent change.

Cheney's low-key approach and well-modulated temper appear to keep him on good terms even with the most irascible and independent-minded GOP chairmen, who jealously guard their authority and often bristle at outside interference.

"He's not the kind that would agitate people, even

Cheney Casts Deciding Vote on Six Key Issues

Vice President Dick Cheney has cast tie-breaking Senate votes six times during his 28-month tenure. How his tie-breakers compare with those of previous vice presidents:

MOST*

Vice president	Tie-breaking votes
John Adams (Washington)	29
John C. Calhoun (Adams and Jackson)	28
George M. Dallas (Polk)	19
Richard M. Johnson (Van Buren)	17
Schuyler Colfax (Grant)	17

*Eleven vice presidents have broken no ties. Most recently, Dan Quayle.

CHENEY'S TIE-BREAKING VOTES

107th Congress

Vote 65: Amendment to the fiscal 2002 budget resolution (H Con Res 83) to reserve $300 billion over 10 years to overhaul Medicare and create a drug benefit.

Vote 79: Amendment to the 2002 budget resolution to increase the tax cut by $69 billion to ensure that it was large enough to fix the so-called marriage penalty.

Vote 119: Motion to table an amendment to the fast-track trade legislation (HR 3009) to make low-interest loans for mortgage payments available to displaced workers.

108th Congress

Vote 134: Adoption of the fiscal 2004 budget resolution conference report (H Con Res 95).

Vote 171: Amendment to a $350 billion package of tax cuts (HR 2) to exempt 50 percent of dividends from taxes in 2003 and to eliminate such taxes in 2004 through 2006.

Vote 196: Adoption of the conference report on a bill (HR 2) providing $350 billion in tax breaks over 11 years.

CQ GRAPHIC

when he's sort of laying down the law. His approach is not aggressive," said Sen. Trent Lott of Mississippi, who served in the House leadership with Cheney.

"It's not the kind of thing that makes a profound impression. It just kind of happens," Lott said. "It's not that there's a great moment of exhilaration because of an inspiring speech or a great moment of anger because you've just been hammered."

Brokering the Omnibus

Early this year, when House and Senate appropriators clashed with Mitchell E. Daniels Jr., outgoing director of the White House Office of Management and Budget, over long-delayed spending bills for fiscal 2004, it was Cheney's counsel and aid they sought. And it was Cheney who brokered the final compromise on an omnibus spending bill (PL 108-7) after appropriators mostly shut out Daniels. *(2003 CQ Weekly, p. 385)*

While Cheney pushed hard to keep lawmakers close to Bush's $750.5 billion discretionary spending limit, he also offered key concessions that kept the talks rolling. For example, the bill contained $1.5 billion for grants to states for new voting equipment, and that money was supposed to count toward the cap. After appropriators appealed to Cheney, the administration relented.

"Everyone understood the Senate and House committees both had problems with Mitch," said House Appropriations Committee Chairman C.W. Bill Young, R-Fla.

"We called on the vice president numerous times to try to intercede for us to the administration. And most of the time, he was able to help us through problems," Young said. "A lot of the work we got done — even though it was late last year, early this year — a lot of it we'd probably still be haggling over if it wasn't for Dick Cheney."

Still, the vice president has had his failures: The administration's high-pressure lobbying in 2001 for the first package of tax cuts, in which Cheney played a central role, alienated Senate GOP moderates. When one of them, James M. Jeffords of Vermont, threatened to bolt the Republican Party, Cheney failed to persuade Jeffords, his friend and colleague from the House, to stay put. *(2001 Almanac, p. 1-3)*

Cheney's efforts to secure the Senate votes to open ANWR also have so far come to nothing. *(2003 CQ Weekly, p. 822)*

As an outspoken advocate of a strong executive branch, the vice president has come into conflict with Capitol Hill. For a year, he successfully battled in federal court a demand from the General Accounting Office that he turn over records from his energy task force — a lawsuit that Congress' investigative arm finally dropped in February. *(2003 CQ Weekly, p. 343)*

In the midst of the tax negotiations, GOP senators complained that they had been whipsawed by the White House when parts of the plan they had supported were eventually abandoned by the administration. And House Republicans, who had loyally passed a package closer to the size Bush wanted, grumbled that the final deal was less than half the size of the original Bush plan.

Still, Republicans in both chambers routinely portray Cheney as an honest broker and a sympathetic ear. "He really is a conciliator, and a damn good one," said Senate Appropriations Committee Chairman Ted Stevens, R-Alaska.

"I've always assumed that he was the majordomo in this administration when it comes to legislative relations," Dyer said.

But Cheney does not spend most of his time lobbying Congress. That function is reserved for David W. Hobbs, the administration's congressional liaison, and his staff. *(2003 CQ Weekly, p. 182)*

"He has a constituency of one, and that's the president. If the president wants him to resolve issues on the jobs-and-growth package, he'll do that," a White House aide said of Cheney. "If the president wants him to be the point person on the first comprehensive energy legislation in a generation, he'll do that."

On both the tax package and this winter's spending package, the vice president displayed a willingness to take a narrow and even qualified victory if necessary to get priority legislation to the president's desk.

Rather than reaching for a broad bipartisan consensus, he has focused his efforts to bridge congressional divides on a handful of centrist Republicans and Democrats, the votes that clearly are in play. He appears comfortable using his constitutional prerogative to break a Senate tie and has done so six times. *(Tie votes, p. 43)*

When the margins are tight, lawmakers know that every vote gained costs precious ground. Still, some feel pressured to reach for a wider victory, said Michael Franc, vice president of government relations for the conservative Heritage Foundation think tank in Washington.

"I think Cheney is immune to that temptation," Franc said.

On the tax bill, Cheney's task was eased considerably by the fact that, as a reconciliation measure, it could not be filibustered in the Senate. Therefore, Republicans needed just 50 votes to pass it, plus Cheney's tie-breaking "aye."

Man of the House

Like Cheney —Wyoming's only congressman from 1979 to 1989 — the previous two vice presidents, Republican Dan Quayle of Indiana and Democrat Al Gore of Tennessee, served in the House. But they moved to the vice presidency from the Senate and were most closely identified with that chamber.

Cheney, by contrast, is considered by House Republicans as one of their own. He succeeded Lott as minority whip in 1989, and served 10 weeks before becoming Defense secretary in the first Bush administration.

The only book he has written — with his wife, Lynne — was "Kings of the Hill," a 1995 study of nine lawmakers who made effective use of the power of the House, including GOP Speakers Joseph G. Cannon of Illinois (1873-91; 1893-1913; 1915-23), and Newt Gingrich of Georgia (1979-99).

Tellingly, GOP House leaders have given Cheney an office on their side of the Rotunda to complement the quarters assigned to him as president of the Senate just outside that chamber. It is the first time anyone can recall a vice president having offices at both ends of the Capitol.

Frist said Cheney plays a particularly important role as Republicans learn how to govern effectively, to work in a "coordinated or complimentary way," from both halves of Congress and the White House. Not since the Eisenhower administration has the GOP controlled both Congress and the White House for a sustained period. So Republicans are under tremendous pressure to produce before the 2004 election.

Cheney "gets involved when asked by me personally, and of course when the president wants him to," Frist said. "I'm very careful not to abuse that. . . . When I ask him to get involved, it's usually after we've exhausted all the normal interactions among colleagues, between the houses." ◆

Government Institutions

The articles in this section provide insight into the inner workings of the major institutions of American government, focusing in turn on the presidency, Congress and the judiciary. As many of the articles illustrate, President Bush and Congress grappled with both domestic and foreign policy issues in the first half of 2003. Among them were the war in Iraq, a Middle East peace plan, a tax cut package and judicial nominations.

The section on the presidency examines how Bush's handling of national security issues and the economy became the subject of debate and dissension, even within his own party. In January 2003, his policies on North Korea and Iraq came under scrutiny, as some GOP members favored strong assertions of U.S. power and others favored diplomacy. In his State of the Union address, Bush presented an ambitious domestic agenda and spoke forcefully about the need to oust Iraq's leader, Saddam Hussein. His first significant foray into foreign policy brought a swift victory. However, once the war ended, debate began again as Congress and the White House turned their attention to the struggling economy and the Middle East. Bush's tax cut proposal and his multilateral "road map" for Middle East peace both failed to garner unanimous approval from the GOP. Aware that the outcome of the tax cut battle and his Middle East diplomacy tactics would play a significant role in his campaign for the 2004 election, Bush tried to rally support within the fractured GOP.

The section on Congress illustrates how the war with Iraq affected the role and functions of the national legislature. As the first article discusses, Congress not only disagreed about whether the United States should go to war but was divided over Bush's domestic agenda to such an extent that even a war could not put differences aside. Once the war in Iraq began, the second article notes, many in Congress felt that the White House showed little inclination to consult with Capitol Hill on issues of war and diplomacy. With U.S. soldiers fighting abroad, congressional members were reluctant to debate the war and foreign relations, but some still struggled with the outcome of the Iraq war resolution, arguing that it was not necessarily meant to authorize war but to strengthen Bush's diplomatic power with the United Nations.

The third article discusses interest groups' "scoring" of congressional members' votes on a particular issue. These legislative scorecards are used not only to assess a lawmaker's record and mobilize grass-roots supporters at election time but are an effective tool of the lobbying trade.

The final article in the Congress section returns to the tax cut debate and examines how the Republican Party reached a compromise that was acceptable to both House conservatives and Senate moderates. The $350 billion economic stimulus package was half the amount of Bush's proposed plan, but it still allowed the White House and each of the principal factions within the GOP to claim some measure of success.

The first article in the judiciary section analyzes the Supreme Court's copyright ruling, *Eldred v. Ashcroft*, which affirmed Congress' power to legislate on intellectual property. The ruling could have significant implications for the 108th Congress, which is set to weigh the rights of creators to profit from their copyrighted works and the rights of the public to reasonably free access to the material.

The final two articles examine the Senate's unprecedented use of the filibuster to block judicial confirmations. This normalization of the once-rare filibuster increases the chances that Democrats will employ the filibuster on a nominee to the Supreme Court. Since at least one Supreme Court justice was expected to step down in 2003, Republicans were looking for ways to loosen the Democrats' grip on the judicial confirmation process.

Eroding Support Leaves Bush In Foreign Policy Minefield

Challenges from his own party on Iraq, North Korea embolden Democratic critics

Warner, center, wants more information from Rumsfeld, right, and Joint Chiefs Chairman Gen. Richard Myers, left, about the administration's war plans — one of several complaints Republicans have about Bush's foreign policy.

REUTERS PHOTO / WILLIAM PHILPOTT

Until recently, Republican lawmakers were more than happy to line up squarely behind their wartime president.

And no wonder. President Bush's leadership on national security issues had not only toppled the Taliban in Afghanistan and scattered the al Qaeda terrorists, but he also had delivered rich political dividends for GOP candidates in the 2002 midterm elections. Indeed, it was the public's approval of Bush's performance on these issues that helped Republicans win control of the Senate and expand their majority in the House.

But as Bush now struggles with international crises in Iraq and North Korea, that phalanx of GOP support is fracturing. Hard-liners complain that Bush is bungling the escalating nuclear standoff with Pyongyang. Moderate Republicans fret about his impatience with United Nations weapons inspections in Iraq. And all sides grouse about what they regard as the administration's obsessive secrecy and apparent indifference to their views on these issues.

"I would hope the White House would uphold the principle that we can't give in to blackmail," conservative Sen. Jeff Sessions, R-Ala., said of Bush's efforts to strike a deal over North Korea's nuclear weapons program. Maine's moderate Republican Sen. Olympia J. Snowe urged the administration to provide a "stronger demonstration of the [unconventional military] capabilities of Saddam Hussein" before launching a war against Iraq.

This lack of support from his own political base has emboldened Democrats to challenge Bush on what had been his strongest turf. It also parallels a sharp drop of public support for his foreign policies, according to recent polls.

The result threatens to turn into a vicious spiral for the administration. Only months ago, Bush's strong domestic political standing helped him secure United Nations support for confronting Baghdad. Today Bush needs to keep his fellow Republicans in line with his Iraqi and North Korean policies to prevent further resistance from already reluctant allies. And the lack of international support is fueling further domestic criticism.

Now, as a Republican president prepares to deliver a State of the Union address to a fully Republican Congress for the first time in half a century, Bush is facing crunch time for his presidency. He now has to find a way to tamp down his fellow Republicans, outsmart the Democrats and soothe nervous allies, or risk damage to his international standing and his domestic political agenda.

A Crucial Test

"He's got a lot of balls in the air, and now we have to see if he'll catch them," said Stephen Hess, a presidential scholar at the Brookings Institution. "This is a very key moment for his administration."

Within Republican ranks, Bush's most crucial test will come over his handling of North Korea. Early on in the crisis, Bush faced criticism from GOP moderates, such as incoming Senate Foreign Relations Committee Chairman Richard G. Lugar, R-Ind., for not talking to North Korea about its efforts and threats to develop nuclear weapons. *(2003 CQ Weekly, p. 40)*

Now, Bush is drawing criticism from GOP conservatives for offering to talk with North Korea and for offering economic carrots to the Asian nation after it announced it would withdraw from the nuclear Non-Proliferation Treaty and threatened to end a moratorium on missile testing.

On Jan. 14, after South Korea, Russia and other U.S. allies urged the United States to seek a diplomatic solution to the standoff, Bush said if North Korea abandoned its nuclear weapons program, he would consider putting forward a "bold initiative" to bring food aid and energy assistance to the isolated communist nation, along with unprecedented diplomatic and security agreements.

"We expect this issue to be resolved peacefully, and we expect them to disarm," Bush said. "We expect them not to develop nuclear weapons. And if they choose to do so — their choice — then I will reconsider whether or not we will start the bold initiative that I talked to Secretary [of State Colin L.] Powell about."

Leading the charge against this approach is John McCain, R-Ariz., Bush's rival in the 2000 Republican presidential primaries and a senior member of the Senate Armed Services Committee. McCain launched the attack with a broadside in the conservative Weekly Standard, saying, "The rapid deterioration of our resolve is as reckless as it is disingenuous."

McCain and two conservative colleagues — Sessions and fellow Arizona Republican Jon Kyl — then joined Democrat Evan Bayh of Indiana in introducing legislation (S 145) that seeks to punish and isolate the North Korean regime, rather than engage its reclusive dictator, Kim Jong Il.

"We need some sticks out there as well," Kyl, the chairman of the GOP policy committee, said on the Senate floor Jan. 15. "We need to put an 'or else' to any negotiations."

Messages From the Hill

While administration officials give the legislation little chance of passage, they recognize its political significance — an attempt by conservatives to hold Bush's feet to the fire on North Korea.

The bill calls for tough measures against Pyongyang, including economic sanctions and stepped-up broadcasts of U.S.-government radio programs into North Korea. It would void a 1994 agreement under which North Korea agreed to freeze its plutonium-based nuclear program in return for the construction of two light-water nuclear power plants and an annual supply of heavy fuel oil while the plants were being built. In essence, it would reverse the Clinton administration's efforts to use economic levers to entice North Korean cooperation on nuclear matters.

But that is just the beginning. The measure also would withhold all aid to North Korea until Pyongyang dismantled its nuclear program, including the planned transfer of reactor technology. And it would call on the president to seek United Nations sanctions against North Korea equivalent to those against Iraq and to reinstate some sanctions on Pyongyang that President Bill Clinton lifted in 1999. *(1999 Almanac, p. 23-24)*

Moreover, in a bid to threaten the very survival of the

Opposing the President

As President Bush attempts to tackle international crises involving North Korea and Iraq, he finds his ability to conduct U.S. foreign policy limited by disputes with moderate and hard-line Republicans on Capitol Hill.

HARD-LINERS

Favor strong assertions of U.S. power and see negotiations with rogue regimes as largely pointless.

Kyl

Sessions

McCain

ON IRAQ: Do not want the U.S. military timetable for attacking Iraq slowed by allied demands. Place little faith in further U.N. weapons inspections and insist that Iraqi President Saddam Hussein must be overthrown.

ON KOREA: Deride Bush's recent moves toward a diplomatic solution to the nuclear standoff. Want to use economic and political pressure to squeeze Pyongyang.

MODERATES

Favor close coordination with U.S. allies in Europe and Asia, and diplomatic solutions when possible.

Lugar

Hagel

Warner

ON IRAQ: Have pushed for Bush to work with other countries at the United Nations and to allow the U.N. weapons inspections process to play out as long as possible to shore up international support.

ON KOREA: Want direct negotiations between the United States and North Korea. Have encouraged Bush to dangle economic and diplomatic carrots as an inducement for North Korea to begin talks and eventually end its nuclear program.

White House Feelers to Iran Employ Lawmakers' Touch

In confronting the three countries that make up the "axis of evil," President Bush favors military action against Iraq and diplomacy to tame North Korea. But with Iran, the White House is trying an unconventional approach that relies in part on a helping hand from Congress.

National security adviser Condoleezza Rice and Secretary of State Colin L. Powell quietly have encouraged Joseph R. Biden Jr., D-Del., the ranking member of the Senate Foreign Relations Committee, and Chuck Hagel of Nebraska, the panel's second-ranking Republican, to pursue a channel to Iran.

Biden and Hagel are preparing to meet Mohammad Javad Zarif, Iran's permanent representative to the United Nations, who invited the two to New York for talks. They were scheduled to meet with Zarif on Jan. 13, but their discussions were postponed because of the death of Hagel's mother.

This is the second time in recent months that Biden and Hagel have acted as freelance foreign policy troubleshooters. In December, they traveled to northern Iraq to meet with Kurdish leaders.

Their talks in New York with Zarif are intended to pave the way for further discussions with Iranian parliamentarians, Biden said, bringing to fruition an idea that he first proposed in a speech to the American-Iranian Council last March.

"I am prepared to receive members of the Iranian Majlis [parliament] whenever its members would like to visit," Biden said then. "If Iranian parliamentarians believe that's too sensitive, I'm prepared to meet them elsewhere." The United States and Iran have not had formal diplomatic relations since the 1979 takeover of the U.S. Embassy in Tehran by Iranian students.

While Iranian officials did not respond to Biden's initiative last year, they now appear ready to take him up on his offer. John Calabrese, an Iran expert at the Middle East Institute, says Tehran and the United States once again have a common enemy in Iraq. Iran and Iraq fought a bloody eight-year war in the 1980s.

In particular, Calabrese said, Tehran is looking for reassurances that the United States will not follow a military victory against Iraq with a similar effort against Iran. Iranian officials also are concerned they could end up encircled by U.S. forces based in neighboring Afghanistan, Pakistan, Turkey and Iraq.

Mutual Interests

"If I'm them, I'm concerned as to what U.S. intentions are — in terms of what comes after Iraq," Calabrese said. "Iran is next in the firing line."

He added that Iranian officials might prefer a meeting between legislators, rather than the direct government-to-government talks, because they may feel Biden and Hagel are more accessible than the hard-line Bush administration.

A meeting among lawmakers also would carry significantly less political risk in Iran's ongoing domestic political struggle between the moderate pro-Western supporters of moderate President Mohammad Khatami and the conservative anti-American forces backing spiritual leader Ayotallah Khamenei, which dominate Iran's national security apparatus.

Biden said he hoped the talks would focus on common concerns, such as Tehran's continued neutrality during a military campaign against Iraq and the development of Iran's oil and natural gas resources.

"We have a lot of mutual interests," Biden said.

So far, Iran has expressed its willingness to stay on the sidelines of any conflict between the United States and Iraq.

"Iran's stand is crystal clear," Foreign Minister Kamal Kharrazi said Jan. 15. "We are neither supporting the United States nor Iraq. We are concerned with our own national interests."

But Biden said he and Hagel also would express U.S. concerns about Iran's atomic energy program, its alleged attempts to build nuclear weapons, and U.S. allegations that Iran sponsors terrorism.

In some ways, the administration's nod to the Biden-Hagel gesture toward Iran appears at odds with its stated policy. Last year, the White House said it would abandon its policy of cultivating the moderates surrounding Khatami, saying they had little influence. The administration said it was opting instead for direct appeals to the Iranian people through U.S.-funded radio broadcasts and other programs.

"Our policy is not about Khatami or Khamenei, reform or hard-line," said Zalmay Khalilzad, a Middle East adviser on the National Security Council. "It is about supporting those who want freedom."

Some Republican lawmakers strongly support the Biden-Hagel initiative. "If you're looking for progress with a member of the 'axis of evil,' the best chance is probably here," said Pat Roberts, R-Kan., the incoming chairman of the Senate Intelligence Committee.

But others see the effort as futile. "People go in there and meet the moderate foreign minister and the moderates around him, and they fool themselves into thinking the regime will change," said John McCain, R-Ariz., a senior member of the Senate Armed Services Committee. "The religious mullahs will never let them."

Indeed, the likelihood of Biden and Hagel securing a breakthrough with Tehran are remote. But with U.S. troops busy confronting Iraq and U.S. diplomats scurrying to calm tensions with North Korea, it appears to be a chance that both Iran and the White House see as worth seizing.

North Korean regime, the measure would make it easier for North Korean refugees to flee the famine-stricken country and authorize the president to impose new sanctions — such as interdicting missiles and other weapons-related shipments to and from North Korea. Sales of the weapons to other nations are a major source of Pyongyang's foreign currency.

"They want to show the administration that this is the sense of Congress and that if Bush goes against it, it's going to cost him," said a senior State Department official who asked that his name not be used.

Meanwhile, as Bush faces pressure from the right to maintain a hard-line stance toward Pyongyang, more moderate Republicans such as Lugar have encouraged the administration's new diplomatic initiatives. *(2003 CQ Weekly, p. 104)*

Like Bush's Democratic critics, Lugar says the administration has little choice but to step back from a confrontation, given that South Korea fears the current situation could lead to a devastating conventional war, or even a nuclear conflict.

"Before we even think of what North Korea might do with their nuclear forces, we have the public concern in South Korea about what they might do with their conventional forces," said John M. Spratt Jr., D-S.C., a senior member of the House Armed Services Committee. "That's why this has to be treated delicately," he said.

Such criticism of the president's foreign policy skills is playing into the hands of Bush's Democratic rivals for the 2004 elections. Indeed, a staple among Democratic contenders these days is to blame Bush's earlier tougher tack toward Pyongyang for creating the crisis in the first place.

Sen. Joseph I. Lieberman, D-Conn., in his Jan. 13 speech announcing he would run for president, panned the way Bush has handled North Korea, saying he has "made a difficult problem into a dangerous crisis.

"I wouldn't have feared to negotiate," Lieberman said.

Nation Favors Non-Military Action In Hot Spots

Polls show that Americans view both the Iraq and North Korea situations as serious. But in both cases, they prefer diplomatic solutions to war.

Do you approve of the way President Bush is handling foreign policy?

SOURCE: The Gallup Organization telephone polls of more than 1,000 adults nationwide. Margin of sampling error: plus or minus 3 percentage points.

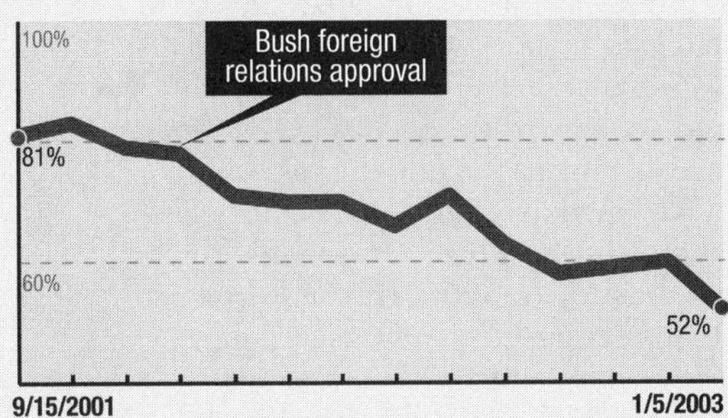

North Korea has nuclear, chemical and biological weapons and recently revived its nuclear weapons program. Do you think the U.S. should treat North Korea like Iraq and prepare to take immediate military action to disarm the country OR that the North Korea situation should be resolved diplomatically without the use of military force?

Right now, which ONE of the following do you think is more important for the United States? To move forward QUICKLY with military action as the only way to effectively deal with the threat posed by Iraq OR to take more time to try to achieve our goals in Iraq WITHOUT going to war?

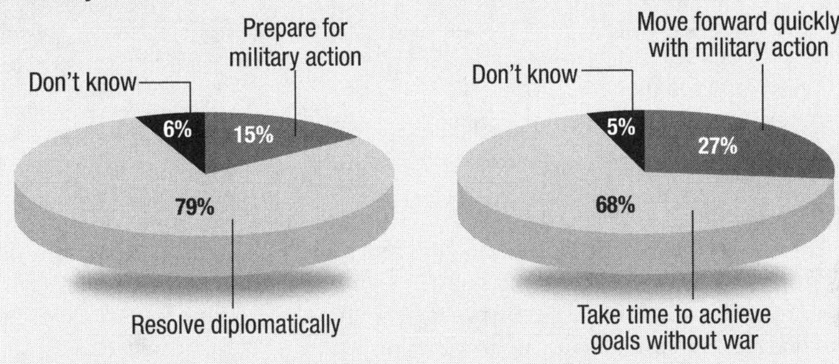

Source: Knight Ridder telephone poll of 1,204 adults nationwide conducted Jan. 3-6, 2003, by Princeton Survey Research Associates. Margin of sampling error: plus or minus 3 percentage points.

Caution Urged on Iraq

Republican moderates also are joining with Democrats and international players in saying the president may be moving too quickly toward a war with Iraq.

On Jan. 14, Bush indicated that his patience with Iraqi President Saddam Hussein was wearing thin. Once again, he accused Saddam of failing to cooperate with a November U.N. resolution that threatens "serious consequences" if Iraq fails to relinquish its unconventional weapons. *(2002 CQ Weekly, p. 2897)*

"I'm sick and tired of games and deception," Bush said. "Time is running out on Saddam Hussein. He must disarm."

A number of milestones lie ahead as the president decides whether to go to war. On Jan. 27, U.N. weapons inspectors are to report their progress to the Security Council. The next day, Bush is scheduled to deliver his State of the Union address to a joint session of Congress. And on Jan. 31, the president will host his closest ally, British Prime Minister Tony Blair, at Camp David.

All these events take place against the backdrop of a huge buildup of U.S. forces in the Persian Gulf. Defense Secretary Donald H. Rumsfeld in recent weeks has ordered 62,000 additional troops to join an equivalent number already in the region. And military experts warn that these troops will have only a limited window for regime-changing action before the desert heat makes their chemical warfare suits unbearably hot.

Yet while these events are placing pressure on Bush to act, other members of the U.N. Security Council, including Britain, are counseling patience, urging that U.N. inspectors be given more time to carry out their work. They also insist the Security Council first be given the option to decide whether the use of military force against Iraq is warranted.

Likewise, Russia, a veto-wielding member of the U.N. Security Council, and chief U.N. weapons inspector Hans Blix are sparring with the White House over whether a 1999 resolution calling on inspectors to report in late March is still relevant. The date is significant because it comes near the end of the time frame by which Iraq's winter climate would facilitate a military campaign.

GOP moderates and Democrats are making similar protestations, saying Bush has to show the international community and the American public more compelling evidence of Iraq's weapons development before he can initiate hostilities unilaterally.

Such comments reflect increasing public concern about the potential war. Major protest demonstrations are scheduled to take place in Washington and other cities Jan. 18.

Powell says that by the end of January, the United States will present a "persuasive case" that Iraq is not cooperating with U.N. weapons inspectors. "If you are looking for proof of weapons of mass destruction, I can show you pictures," Powell was quoted Jan. 17 as telling Germany's Sueddeutsche Zeitung.

Hanging Tough

But just as with North Korea, Bush faces pressures from conservative lawmakers to resist allowing U.N. inspectors to dictate the timing of any U.S.-led attack on Iraq. These lawmakers — including Sessions, Kyl and McCain — always have doubted the utility of inspections, especially after a four-year hiatus following their ejection from Iraq in 1998, and do not want to lose the military and diplomatic momentum that Bush set in motion last fall.

They argue that the burden should be on Saddam to prove he has come clean, rather than on the United Nations or the United States to prove that he has cheated on his agreements.

"It appears to me that Mr. Blix has not been as aggressive and determined as I would like, and I've never been convinced that inspections would work anyway," Sessions said. "If they've been developing weapons of mass destruction, they've got to help us find them. If it's simply 'catch me if you can,' that's not enough for me."

Yet Bush's ability to sway lawmakers has been harmed by the perception that his administration is too secretive and indifferent to their concerns.

At a GOP senatorial retreat at the Library of Congress on Jan. 8, White House Chief of Staff Andrew H. Card Jr. heard complaints from nearly a dozen lawmakers, including Senate Armed Services Committee Chairman John W. Warner of Virginia and Senate Appropriations Committee Chairman Ted Stevens of Alaska about what they said was the White House's and Pentagon's disrespect and secrecy on military matters toward members of Congress.

> *"He's got a lot of balls in the air, and now we have to see if he'll catch them . . . This is a very key moment for his administration."*
>
> — Stephen Hess, presidential scholar at the Brookings Institution

In a subsequent interview, Warner said he was speaking for less experienced senators who believed they had not been kept well-informed on developments in North Korea and Iraq.

"It's not a problem for me," Warner said. "I spent five hours over at the Pentagon the other day. But Iraq alone is the most complicated issue I've ever seen, and I would have kept a more active consultation going, especially with the more junior members."

Senate Minority Leader Tom Daschle, D-S.D., seized upon the dispute to indict the White House — and to implicitly warn that Bush was jeopardizing continued Democratic backing for his handling of these foreign policy crises.

"I don't see how Congress can function as a co-equal partner if we are locked out of the information that should be provided to us on a regular basis," Daschle said Jan. 15.

Seeking to tamp down the criticism, Rumsfeld briefed members of the Senate Armed Services Committee on Iraq, North Korea and the war on terrorism in a closed session Jan. 15. And the White House followed up the next day by sending Deputy Secretary of State Richard L. Armitage to provide a closed briefing to the full Senate on North Korea.

The erosion of confidence in Bush's stewardship of foreign policy is already having a legislative impact. Appropriators, eager to maintain control of Pentagon funds, have refused since last fall to provide $10 billion requested by the White House for the war on terrorism.

To Rumsfeld's frustration, that will force the Pentagon to dip into its operating funds and then request a supplemental funding bill from Congress late in fiscal 2003 to pay the rest.

"Every month that goes by, you're robbing Peter to pay Paul in a way that's not good management," Rumsfeld said.

Legislative Sniping

The ongoing crisis also is encouraging other legislative potshots at the administration. For example, Ike Skelton of Missouri, the ranking Democrat on House Armed Services, has expressed the frustration of many lawmakers about the extended deployment of reserve forces to the Persian Gulf and other regions. Employers in some districts are complaining that their employees are overseas for months at a time.

In response, Skelton has called for the active military force to be enlarged, a suggestion Rumsfeld has asked the military services to study. And Rep. Charles B. Rangel, D-N.Y., has called for the military draft to be reinstated so all Americans can share the burden of war. *(2003 CQ Weekly, p. 9)*

Still, the most telling indication of Bush's slipping hold on the foreign policy and broader political debate comes in recent public opinion polls.

A January 10-12 CNN/USA-Today/Gallup survey showed only 58 percent of voters approve of Bush's performance, the lowest percentage since the Sept. 11 attacks. And in one week alone, the public's approval of his conduct of foreign affairs had dropped from 60 percent to 53 percent.

Of course, Bush still has plenty of opportunity to halt the slippage. If his moderate course on North Korea and his hard-line policy on Iraq succeed in ending the threats from those countries, the murmurs of dissatisfaction on Capitol Hill are likely to die down, and Bush is likely to rise again in public esteem. But until then, Bush's handling of national security issues will remain a double-edged sword. ◆

Bush Uses State of the Union To Solidify Grip on Agenda

President pitches an array of proposals designed to attract voters of many stripes

With his ideas for the economy, health care, the environment, homeland security and an array of other topics, the State of the Union address that President Bush delivered at the midpoint of his term asked more of his Republican allies in Congress than they can ever deliver — and everyone in the House chamber the night of Jan. 28 knew it.

Still, Bush's one-hour speech, his fourth before a joint session of Congress, was no rote exercise. By laying out an ambitious domestic agenda — even as his administration prepares for war with Iraq — Bush seized control of the conversation with Congress and the nation on issues critical to both parties as they begin positioning for the election 21 months from now.

For now at least, the defining debates for the 108th Congress are playing out on ground of the president's choosing, with lawmakers on both sides reacting to what he has proposed. This, historians and lawmakers in both parties agree, is one of the main advantages a president has when the Capitol is under the control of his own party. *(2003 CQ Weekly, p. 180)*

"A constant characteristic of this president and the Bush team is to want above all to control the agenda — if possible, to dominate the agenda," said Charles O. Jones, an expert on Congress and the presidency and a fellow at the Brookings Institution. "These guys are planners. In planning, you want as much as possible to be in charge, to be proactive rather than reactive."

At the same time, by stressing the need to make health care affordable and renewing his commitment to a "compassionate conservative" agenda, Bush continued to position himself as a "different kind of Republican," to reach out to swing voters and challenge Democrats on turf where they historically have had an advantage.

CQ PHOTO/ SCOTT J. FERRELL

President Bush spoke passionately about the need to oust Iraq's Saddam Hussein, and presented a long wish list on domestic policy in his State of the Union speech on Jan. 28.

Bush, who has taken a beating from Democrats for his record on the environment, stayed on that line when he spoke of cleaner air and hydrogen-powered cars.

It reminded presidential historian Richard Norton Smith of President Richard M. Nixon's use of the same podium to call for expanding clean water programs in an effort to moderate his conservative image and drive Democrats to the left. "Nixon used the State of the Union to steal the opposition's clothing," said Smith, director of the Robert J. Dole Institute of Politics at the University of Kansas.

Choosing His Shots

Bush spoke to the GOP's traditional conservative base with demands that Congress cut taxes, control federal spending and ban human cloning. But significantly, in addressing the divisive issue of abortion, he highlighted a measure with broader bipartisan support than most legislation to curtail abortion rights: a ban on the procedure doctors call "dilation and extraction," but abortion foes call "partial birth" abortion. *(2003 CQ Weekly, p. 101)*

"You didn't hear him say, 'I want a reversal of *Roe v. Wade*,'" noted Republican strategist Daniel J. Mattoon.

Bush struck a balance of another kind on foreign policy, mixing threats against Iraq with a ringing and unexpected call to throw America's wealth and energy behind efforts to fight AIDS in Africa. "It very much blunts the notion that he is a hard-hearted conservative," Jones said. *(2003 CQ Weekly, p. 266)*

With that proposal, Bush also spoke to African-Americans, a group that Bush and other Republicans have pledged to reach out to in the aftermath of the leadership downfall of Sen. Trent Lott, R-Miss. *(CQ Weekly, p. 28)*

Black leaders, though still critical of Bush's stand on health care, affirmative action and other issues, applauded him for his AIDS proposal, as well as his call to expand mentoring programs to disadvantaged children and to pass, with some caveats, his "faith-based initia-

President Sets His 2003 Agenda

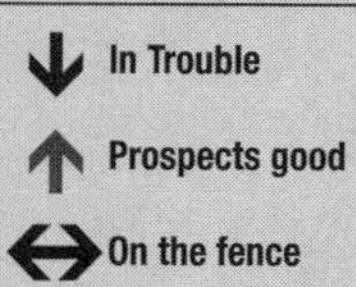

In his second State of the Union address, President Bush talked tough on Iraq and challenged Congress to enact an ambitious domestic agenda. Below are summaries of his main proposals and their prospects.

TOPIC	PROPOSALS	OUTLOOK
TAXES ↓	Bush's economic plan includes eliminating taxes on stock dividends paid to individual investors and immediately implementing several tax changes scheduled for future years, including income tax rate cuts and an increase in the child credit.	Democrats and some moderate Republicans worry that the plan would deepen the deficit. Critics also say it would help the wealthy disproportionately. Tax writers in both parties are drafting alternatives.
MEDICARE ↓	Seniors could get expanded coverage — including prescription drug benefits — only if they joined a private-sector plan.	The proposal has met resistance, with lawmakers from both parties objecting even before the administration has fleshed out the details fully.
AIDS ↑	Bush has proposed spending $15 billion over five years for AIDS treatment and prevention in African and Caribbean nations.	The plan is broadly popular, but some liberals criticize aspects of it — saying, for example, that the funding would phase in too slowly. Social conservatives might object to the administration's acquiescence to contraceptive distribution.
ENERGY ↔	Bush wants to boost U.S. production with tax incentives and by opening more federal land to exploration, including Alaska's Arctic National Wildlife Refuge (ANWR). His plan includes incentives for conservation, energy efficiency and alternative fuels. He also wants to boost funding for research into cleaner-burning hydrogen fuel cells for cars.	Democrats can be expected to oppose drilling in ANWR and other provisions, which is why the Bush plan stalled last year. Republicans may have to cut the plan into pieces to get anything moving. Some Democrats called the hydrogen-fuel cell initiative "timid," but it is popular.
ENVIRONMENT ↓	Bush's "Clear Skies" plan would phase in mandatory cuts for sulfur dioxide and other emissions. Power plants that produced too much could buy credits from those that cut emissions below standards. The plan would not regulate carbon dioxide, which many scientists say causes global warming.	Democrats and environmentalists say Bush's plan would result in less regulation of power plants than under the current Clean Air Act. Some Republicans also have concerns with the plan. It seems destined to be rewritten.
SOCIAL PROGRAMS ↔	Bush is again promoting his "faith-based initiative," which would allow religious charities to compete for federal grants for social programs. He also proposed an expansion of drug treatment programs and an initiative to recruit mentors for disadvantaged youth and those with a parent in prison.	Democrats have blocked the faith-based initiative, saying it would allow religious charities to discriminate in hiring while using federal funds. Congress might pass a stripped-down compromise. The drug treatment and mentoring plans will be popular, but there could be a fight over money.
HOMELAND SECURITY ↑	Bush is seeking a "Terrorist Threat Integration Center" to analyze intelligence gathered by the FBI, CIA, and departments of Homeland Security and Defense. He also proposed "Project Bioshield," under which the Food and Drug Administration could approve treatments and vaccines against biological and chemical threats and then stockpile the drugs in case of a terrorist attack.	The Integration Center is likely to survive in some form, but questions remain about who will be in charge of the program. Widespread support for Project Bioshield is expected, but lawmakers might question the $6 billion price tag and the broad authority given to the FDA.
ABORTION AND CLONING ↔	Bush wants to ban what opponents call "partial birth" abortion and has called for a comprehensive ban on human cloning.	A partial-birth ban has a chance of becoming law, although many Democrats and some Republicans oppose it. Efforts to pass a cloning ban stalled last year in a Senate dispute over whether to allow cloning to create tissue for research.
MEDICAL LIABILITY ↓	Bush wants to cap damage awards in medical malpractice cases.	Republicans will try to move a bill early. But Democrats, who say caps would deny injured patients justice, will stand in the way.

tive" to direct more federal social services spending to religious groups.

With guaranteed coverage by all the television broadcast networks as well as a handful of cable TV news networks, the State of the Union affords the president his largest and most demographically diverse audience of the year, making it perhaps his best opportunity to frame the agenda and define the tone of his presidency as much for voters as for lawmakers. This year's audience of 62 million was the largest for a presidential speech since President Bill Clinton's inaugural address, according to ratings compiled by Nielsen Media Research.

A wave of polling before the speech suggests that Bush addressed a nation with growing doubt about his handling of the economy and foreign affairs — and a need to burnish anew his image as a leader 16 months after the Sept. 11 terrorist attacks. His most passionate words came in the second half of the address, which he devoted to making his most detailed case yet for ending the regime of Saddam Hussein in Iraq. *(2003 CQ Weekly, p. 261)*

But Bush used the first half of his address to make clear that he expects Congress to deliver solutions to problems that are of most concern to average Americans, such as job insecurity and rising health care costs.

"We will not deny, we will not ignore, we will not pass along our problems to other Congresses, other presidents and other generations," the president said. "We will confront them with focus and clarity and courage." *(2003 CQ Weekly, p. 267)*

At stake are both Bush's legacy and his party's fortunes in November 2004, when the president plans to stand for reelection and the GOP hopes to expand its House and Senate majorities. With Republicans expecting to control for the first time in 50 years both ends of Pennsylvania Avenue throughout a two-year Congress, the pressure is on to deliver a strong record of legislative victories.

Furthermore, by putting concerns at home first in his speech, Bush again signaled that this White House understands it cannot afford to appear out of touch with everyday concerns, no matter the magnitude of foreign policy challenges.

A Tall Order

Political reality came crashing down less than 24 hours after the president's address. Democrats, who with 49 votes can easily tie up the Senate on almost any issue, continued a drumbeat of criticism. And even some Republicans expressed strong reservations about key provisions of Bush's economic stimulus package, his plan to overhaul Medicare and the effect of his agenda on the deepening deficit. *(2003 CQ Weekly, p. 248; p. 255; p. 244)*

Democrats pounded Bush before and after the speech, arguing that despite the rhetoric his agenda would shortchange homeland security, undermine environmental protection and conservation, weaken patient protections, and threaten the separation of church and state. *(Homeland, p. 2; 2003 CQ Weekly, p. 99; p. 156; p. 128; 2002 CQ Weekly, p. 3207)*

Democratic Gov. Gary Locke of Washington, in the official Democratic response, called Bush's economic plan "upside-down economics" that will "create huge, permanent deficits that will raise interest rates, stifle growth, hinder home ownership and cut off the avenues of opportunity that have let so many work themselves up from poverty." *(2003 CQ Weekly, p. 273)*

Starting Out Bold

Republicans say Bush knows the practical difficulties that lie ahead and accepts that compromise will be necessary. "He recognizes the process here," said Sen. Larry E. Craig, R-Idaho. "It's his job to challenge us. It's his job to set the agenda. I said before the speech that I hoped he would be aggressive and bold, and he was that."

In his first two years in office, Bush showed himself to be a realist in dealing with Congress. On his priority issues, he focuses on a few essentials, cedes ground when necessary to reach his ultimate objective and relies on Republican leaders to keep the troops in line. *(2002 CQ Weekly, p. 3235)*

Taking aggressive stands early on his economic plan, health care and other issues helps move the final compromise as close as possible to his position, strategists said. "He lays out where he wants to go, but he understands to move the ball forward that he's going to have to incorporate other ideas," said GOP strategist David Winston. "He's shown that he's willing to do that."

Despite softening poll numbers, Bush's approval ratings are still high by historical standards. He has strong allies in the GOP leadership, and deep good will for helping his party win the Senate in November. So Republican leaders rallied predictably behind his proposals. On his plan to cut taxes by $674 billion in the next decade, they took particular pains to defend a provision that has raised doubts even among some in the rank and file: ending the taxation of most corporate dividends paid to individuals.

Senate Majority Leader Bill Frist of Tennessee, a surgeon and one of the GOP's leading voices on health care, went to the floor to endorse the president's approach on Medicare a day after the speech. But when asked afterward how much of his plan the president could expect to see passed, Frist said, "Realistically, I can't predict how much we can do."

Prospects for Bush's $15 billion global AIDS initiative appear brighter. The proposal, which would direct funding for treatment and prevention to the most affected African and Caribbean nations, has been put on a fast track by Frist, who has treated AIDS patients in Africa, and by Foreign Relations Committee Chairman Richard G. Lugar, R-Ind.

Senate Environment and Public Works Committee Chairman James M. Inhofe, R-Okla., said he will introduce sometime in the next few weeks Bush's air pollution plan — the "Clear Skies" initiative, which the administration says would cut emissions from power plants by 70 percent over the next 15 years. But "the bill passed is not going to be like the bill that is out there right now," Inhofe warned.

Bush made only brief mention of a comprehensive energy bill in his address, but his words prompted quick action from Hill Republicans. Pete V. Domenici of New Mexico, chairman of the Senate Energy and Natural Resources Committee, said he would work to move the legislation by summer. Joe L. Barton of Texas, chairman of the House Energy and Air Quality Subcommittee, said he would work to move it by spring.

Domenici's comments were a reversal from his indications at the end of 2002. In December, he said he planned to take "a long time" to offer new legislation. A two-year effort to pass a comprehensive measure stalled in the last days of the 107th Congress. It foundered particularly over a provision that would open the Arctic National Wildlife Refuge to oil drilling. ◆

For Bush, Tax Cut Package Is Next Must-Win Battle

President hustles to overcome intraparty division over deficits

When George V. Voinovich was governor of Ohio, he urged President George Bush, whom he considered a "very, very close" friend, to talk more about the economy on the campaign trail in 1992. Otherwise, Voinovich warned the president, "People will think you don't think it's a problem — or you don't care."

But Bush was not buying the advice. Voinovich recalled the president protesting, "The economy is doing better." A few months later, voters told Bush they disagreed.

His son watched and learned. This year George W. Bush wasted no time proposing a bold prescription for the still-struggling economy — more tax cuts on top of those enacted just two years ago (PL 107-16). (2001 Almanac, p. 18-3)

Voinovich, left, and Bush are at odds over the size of this year's tax package. Bush is pressuring moderate Senators who want a smaller tax cut because they are nervous about the deficit.

The tax plan is more than just the second act of President Bush's fiscal program. It is a nod to the political imperative for the White House to act when the economy struggles.

The problem for Bush is that a small but pivotal group in his own party, including Voinovich, is standing in the way of his 11-year, $726 billion growth package.

Now Bush is scrambling to salvage as much of his tax initiative as possible, and he must deal with a longstanding fracture within his own party: those who favor tax cuts regardless of the deficit impact, vs. balanced-budget hawks like Voinovich who are loath to support tax cuts that are not paid for, particularly when the budget is in the red.

And on April 24, Bush barnstormed straight into Ohio with Voinovich square in his sights. Voinovich — a longtime advocate of balanced budgets who supports a tax cut but also frets about the impact on the deficit — helped force a secret Senate budget deal among Republicans on April 10 that would limit Bush's tax cut to no more than $350 billion. *(2003 CQ Weekly, p. 866)*

The move blindsided and angered the White House. Bush and top administration officials are working furiously to undo the damage as Capitol Hill tax writers prepare to move their bills.

"Some in Congress say the plan is too big," Bush said at an appearance in Canton. "Well, it seems like to me they might have some explaining to do. If they agree that tax relief creates jobs, then why are they for a little bitty tax relief package?"

Even though he opposes the size of Bush's tax cut plan, Voinovich praised the president for trying to boost a fragile economic recovery. "The people know he knows there's a problem and he cares about it. He wants to see people have jobs," Voinovich said.

Tax Plans Trimmed

In 2001, Senate moderates forced Bush to trim his $1.6 trillion, 10-year tax cut proposal to $1.35 trillion. This year, with the Senate still closely divided and the Democrats more unified in their opposition, moderates appear intent on forcing Bush into a much deeper retreat: a tax cut of less than half the White House's original $726 billion proposal.

Even in the House, where GOP leaders generally have a stronger grip on their troops than in the Senate, the Bush proposal was trimmed to $550 billion to appeal to moderates in the party. Now Bush has accepted that House defeat as his goal.

Bush needs to win the coming battle over tax cuts to guard his economic flank heading into next year's election campaign. If his latest tax cut proposal is to improve the economy — a topic hotly disputed by economists — it must be enacted soon in order for it to make a difference before next year's elections.

Limiting the package to $350 billion would force tax writers to gut Bush's key proposals, particularly his plan to eliminate taxes on stock dividends. The White House believes eliminating taxes on most dividends would lift the stock market, increase investment and spur job growth.

If the economy improves, Bush and the GOP are likely to benefit regardless of what happens with his tax proposal. But if Bush manages to get less than half of the growth plan he has proposed and the economy continues to stumble, voters could come to view Republicans as unable to lead.

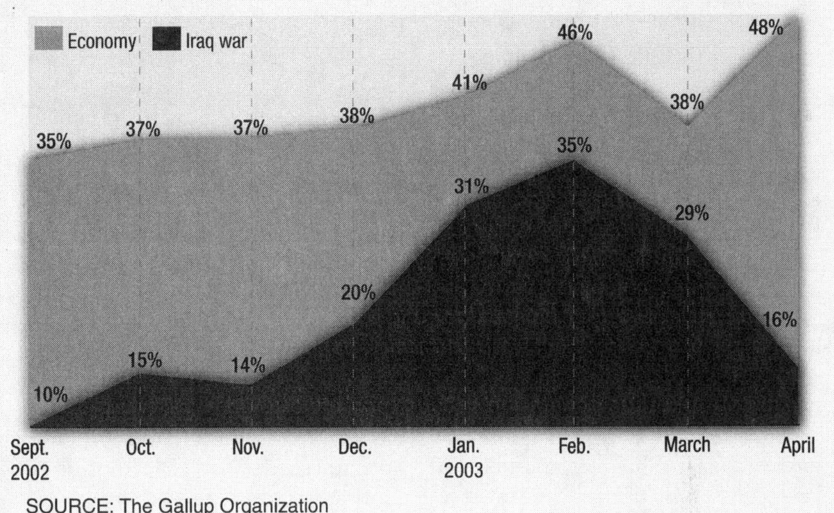

'Things Have Changed'

With budget projections showing deficits totaling about $2 trillion over the next 10 years, deficit hawks have a lot more to worry about than they did during the tax cut debate two years ago, when a 10-year surplus of $5.6 trillion was forecast.

Voinovich originally opposed Bush's 2001 tax cut, arguing that budget surpluses should first be used to pay down the debt. But a week after Bush visited Ohio that year, Voinovich supported the proposal.

However, he insists he will not buckle this time.

"Things have changed since 2001," Voinovich said, citing the return of deficits.

The tax-cutting faction within the GOP rose from the "stagflation" of the 1970s. Then, Keynesian economic prescriptions to boost faltering demand through government spending failed to help. A group of conservative economists developed a theory that the best way for Congress to improve the economy was to create incentives for work and investment by lowering marginal tax rates.

Rep. Jack Kemp, R-N.Y.(1971-89), and Sen. William V. Roth Jr., R-Del. (1971-2001), were convinced by the supply-siders' growth prescription and offered the Kemp-Roth tax cut in 1978. Their bill would have cut marginal income tax rates across the board by 33 percent.

The bill failed, but it became the centerpiece of Ronald Reagan's economic agenda during the 1980 presidential campaign. After Reagan defeated President Jimmy Carter, he won passage in 1981 of a large package of tax reductions including a 15 percent income tax rate cut, business tax cuts and a capital gains rate reduction. *(1981 Almanac, p. 91)*

Although some of those tax cuts were scaled back in 1982, an economic boom followed even as deficits soared. For many, that was sufficient validation of supply-side theory, and the number of deficit hawks in the GOP has been declining ever since. *(1982 Almanac, p. 29)*

"Kemp and his gang turned out to be 'righter' than traditional conservatives, myself included, on the committee," said former Rep. Bill Frenzel, R-Minn (1971-91), then a Ways and Means Committee member, now a scholar at the Brookings Institution.

Even as taxes crept back up through the 1980s, Frenzel credited the supply-siders for denying the government access to tax revenue that could have been used for "mischievous" spending.

Many Republicans support reducing taxes not only to expand the economy, but as a way to restrain government programs, another source of irritation for GOP moderates who are more inclined to support an activist federal government.

The number of "Rockefeller Republicans" obsessed with deficit reduction are so few that some in the party bristle at the notion that a major schism still exists within the GOP.

"Don't say 'some' Republican senators. There are three," said Sen. Jim Bunning, R-Ky., a member of the Finance Committee, which will draft the Senate's version of a tax cut. "That makes a difference when you're 51 and 48 and 1. They voted against the majority of the Republican caucus. That's their privilege. Then they have to be responsible if the economy falls on its face."

Still, with only a one-vote majority in the Senate, the White House and Republicans leaders have few options for turning the tide against the deficit hawks in the party. Zell Miller of Georgia is the only Senate Democrat to endorse the president's economic plan, but Republicans John McCain of Arizona and Lincoln Chafee of Rhode Island are steadfastly against any tax cut during wartime. The administration has not bothered to target McCain or Chafee.

At times, the tax cut fight within the GOP seems less like a schism than a mixed bag of philosophic approaches. Despite their deficit fears, even Voinovich and the like-minded Olympia J. Snowe, R-Maine, support a tax cut of $350 billion — a figure that would have seemed substantial if Bush had not started the debate with proposal more than twice that size.

High-Pressure Sales Pitch

The White House stepped up its tax cut lobbying blitz on April 15, just six days after U.S. marines toppled a statue of Saddam Hussein in Baghdad. Bush talked up his plan in the Rose Garden to a friendly audience including representatives of the National Association of Manufacturers, the Na-

Bush Determined Not to Repeat Father's Politically Fatal Errors

Early in 1991, fresh from triumph in a war with Iraq, President George Bush enjoyed record approval ratings. He seemed almost invincible.

But the American people quickly turned their attention from the war to the economy, and they did not like what they saw. The following year, the voters sent Bush back to Texas.

Despite the striking historic parallels, the current President Bush is planning for a different end to his first term.

Bush senior's stature as the international statesman who assembled a large, diverse coalition to reverse Saddam Hussein's land grab in Kuwait did nothing to improve his image on domestic policy. He had already angered his Republican base in 1990 by reneging on his "read my lips: no new taxes" campaign vow. Meanwhile, Democrats hammered him as out of touch and unfocused amid an economic recession. Bush scoffed at the pessimism of his critics, and he avoided even uttering the "R word." *(1990 Almanac, p. 111)*

To underscore the duality of Bush senior's persona, Time magazine gave him the title "Men of the Year" in January 1991. The cover featured a Janus-type figure of Bush the world statesman and Bush the domestic no-show. In a famous incident in February of 1992, he gushed in amazement over a checkout line price scanner, which by then was part of daily life for most Americans.

He refused to acknowledge that there were any serious problems with the economy until just weeks before the 1992 elections, but by then it was too late. Arkansas Governor Bill Clinton recognized early on that "it's the economy, stupid," and made that the central message of his campaign. Hints of a similar strategy by some of the Democratic presidential hopefuls are already in evidence this year. *(1992 Almanac, p. 3-A)*

Presidential scholars say the current president has never forgotten how his father let a second term slip through his fingers. In three key ways George W. Bush is charting a different course: He has stayed on good terms with the base of the Republican party; he has aggressively sought to use his political capital to achieve policy aims; and he is taking nothing for granted on the domestic front.

Keeping the Base Happy

In sharp contrast with his father, Bush has carefully tended to his conservative base on both economic and social policy, said Grover Norquist, president of Americans for Tax Reform and a long-time conservative political activist. Bush senior, Norquist said, "screwed, double crossed and sold out" his base on a number of fronts.

Cutting taxes, Norquist said, is "the central unifying theme of the modern Republican party." As a direct result of raising taxes, "Bush got 38 percent of the vote — something like Goldwater in 1964," Norquist said.

Lee Edwards, a senior fellow at the Heritage Foundation, said he recalls raising concerns with the first Bush's top aides and being told with "arrogance" that conservatives had nowhere else to go.

Another advantage Bush has over his father is that he has an enormous amount of political capital — not so much because of the war against Iraq, but because of Sept. 11. The terrorist attacks on the United States shattered the American sense of security and gave the president wide latitude in taking steps to restore it.

"The two things that get people to the polling booth are the economy and their security," said Stephen Hess, a senior fellow at the Brookings Institution. Hess said the economy generally trumps physical security, but the terrorist attacks changed that. "It has really crept up as an issue — almost equal to the economy — and Bush has a lock on it," Hess said.

And the current president has not shied away from freely spending that political capital. With the economy still shaky and a war on the horizon, he made the congressional election of 2002 about his presidency, and Republicans picked up seats in both the House and Senate, a rare event in off-year elections.

And despite growing deficits and the looming war, Bush in December called for a $726 billion "growth" tax cut. "When he proposed a $726 billion tax cut — everyone gulped," observed Hess. "That was really big."

The move was particularly bold considering the $1.3 trillion tax cut (PL 107-16) enacted just two years ago. *(2001 Almanac, p. 18-3)*

Larry Sabato, a political scientist at the University of Virginia, said the elder

tional Association of Wholesaler Distributors and the U.S. Chamber of Commerce.

The following week, Bush hosted a roundtable of personal finance columnists to mobilize investors. To underscore his focus on the economy, Bush endorsed Alan Greenspan for another term as the head of the Federal Reserve Board.

Ratcheting up the pressure on Congress during the two-week April recess, the White House dispatched more than 25 administration officials and staged 60 events in more than 40 cities in 26 states as part of an effort to sell Bush's plan.

Six Cabinet secretaries were recruited for the barnstorming effort, including Agriculture Secretary Ann M. Veneman and Energy Secretary Spencer Abraham. Treasury Secretary John W. Snow even took the marketing tour to Brazil, where on April 21 he insisted that Bush would win at least $550 billion in tax cuts.

At each domestic stop, the salesmen were armed with talking points on just how many taxpayers would benefit. The administration calculated that 4 million Pennsylvania taxpayers, more than 2.9 million New Jersey taxpayers and nearly 5.9 million New York taxpayers would have lower income tax bills in 2003 if the president's plan were enacted.

Public Perception and the Bush Presidencies

Presidential approval ratings during the two Bush administrations were very high after major events involving national security. But the senior Bush suffered from a perceived weakness on economic issues.

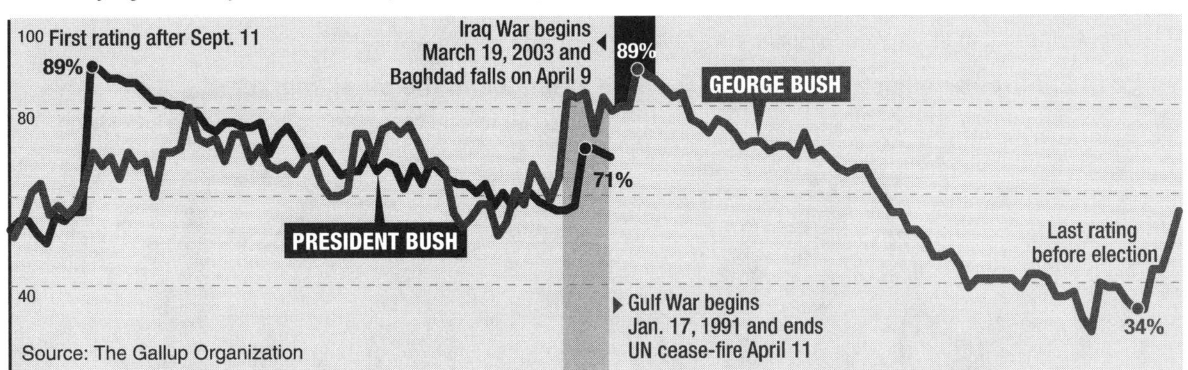

Source: The Gallup Organization

Bush was as inclined to store political capital as the son is eager to use it.

Strong Domestic Focus

The determination to stay focused on the economy — or at least to be perceived as doing so — arises from lessons learned the hard way. Sabato said his father's loss in 1992 has stayed with Bush "like an open wound."

Bush demonstrated his focus on the economy late last year by unceremoniously dumping his first Treasury Secretary, Paul H. O'Neill, who was widely viewed on Capitol Hill as a poor salesman for the president's economic program. O'Neill's replacement, John W. Snow, was promptly dispatched to begin selling Bush's tax cut plan — before the war in Iraq has even been declared over.

Hess said the first President Bush delayed getting his re-election campaign in full gear, but his son, aided by the deft political talent of Karl Rove, is apparently taking nothing for granted. "These folks are off and running, maybe under the radar screen," Hess said.

The elder Bush lacked a trusted intimate whose sole job was to look after the president's political fate, noted Sabato. James Baker had run the campaign in 1988 and then quickly settled into being secretary of State. "The dirty work was behind him, and he was being a statesman," said Sabato.

Had Lee Atwater lived, he might have played that role and gotten Bush re-elected in 1992, said Edwards.

Rove, an Atwater protégé, began thinking about the 2004 campaign as soon as the U.S. Supreme Court settled the disputed 2000 presidential election, Sabato said.

And the president must know that, with the war over, the media will quickly focus more on the economy, Sabato said.

"Nearly every unemployed person in the country will be giving his or her personal interview in the coming year," said Sabato. "That will be hard to deal with. But the president has practiced empathy."

With the House and Senate in Republican hands, Bush will not be able to run against Congress if the economy remains a trouble spot next year. He will have to pitch a more refined argument, said Sabato. If he gets his economic program through, he can ask voters to help him continue his fiscal plan with even more Republicans. If he is thwarted, he can argue that he needs a stronger Republican majority to respond to the economy.

Despite his current strong approval ratings, Bush will not have an easy walk to re-election next year, unless the Democrats nominate some one "goofy" who is well outside the mainstream, Norquist said.

Bush probably knows that to win he cannot simply ignore the demands of anxious voters and the assaults of an aggressive Democratic challenger. "They won't defer to some staffer too busy being a policy wonk to think about political considerations," Norquist said.

The White House carefully selected the locations of its sales stops. Snow paid a visit to Louisiana, the home state of one of the Senate's most conservative Democrats, John B. Breaux, who brokered the deal to pass Bush's $1.3 trillion tax cut of 2001. Housing and Urban Development Secretary Mel Martinez followed down to New Orleans a week later. But Breaux, who rallied moderates around the $350 billion figure this year, probably will be tough to sway.

Then, Bush swooped into Voinovich's backyard. Voinovich greeted the Bush on the tarmac in Dayton, but did not join the president at public events in Canton and Lima. White House spokesman Ari Fleischer told reporters Voinovich was invited to both events, but was unable to attend because of scheduling conflicts.

Bush's public message links an appeal to Americans' pocketbooks with his expectation of creating 1.4 million jobs by the end of 2004. Bush told the staff of a Boeing F-18 fighter production facility in St. Louis on April 16, "Congress must pass this jobs package as soon as they come back from their recess . . . that will give you more of your money in your pockets so you get to decide how to save or invest and spend."

How Economic Measures Compare Between the Two Gulf Wars

The perception of economic woes following Operation Desert Storm sent President George Bush to defeat in the election of 1992. Now, as the end of the Iraq war sinks in, his son faces similar concerns for the election of 2004. How economic barometers compare for the two periods.

Change in the gross domestic product
(growth or loss from previous quarter)

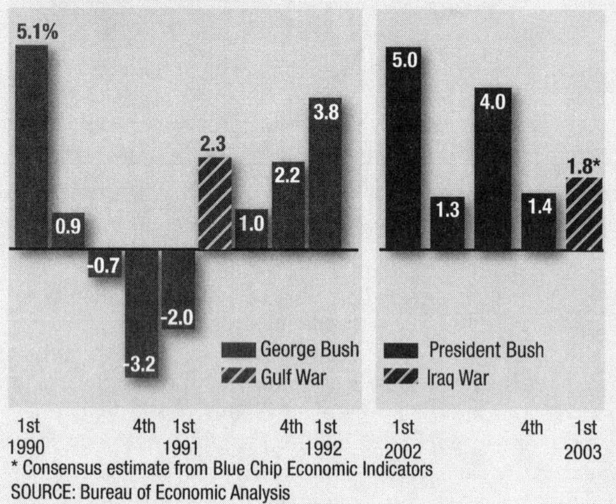

* Consensus estimate from Blue Chip Economic Indicators
SOURCE: Bureau of Economic Analysis

Changes in the stock market
(monthly increases or decreases in the Dow Jones Industrial Average)

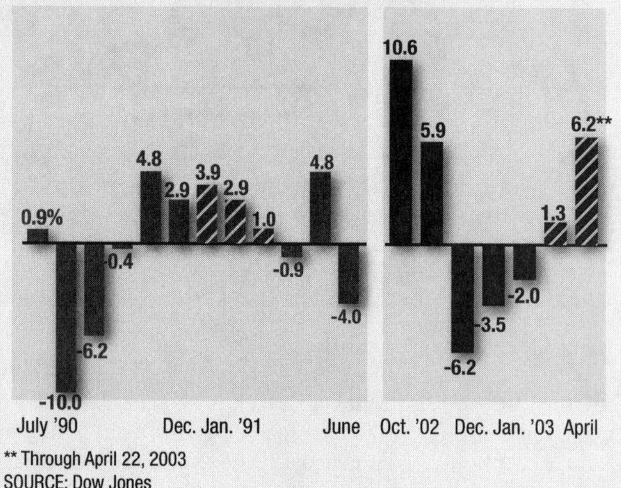

** Through April 22, 2003
SOURCE: Dow Jones

Mixed Messages

Indeed, Bush has emphasized the rate cuts in recent weeks — while saying relatively little about the dividend proposal.

The White House has sent conflicting signals on what parts of the package it feels most passionate about preserving. The Wall Street Journal on April 21 quoted Snow saying he would settle for half the dividend tax break this year and delaying the reduction of the top marginal income rate from 38.5 percent to to 35 percent.

But Fleischer rushed to deny the story, calling it "a misread of what the secretary was saying." And the Treasury Department issued a written statement, reinforcing that Snow would press for a tax cut of "at least $550 billion . . . including 100 percent exclusion of the double tax on dividends."

Prior to the flap, Snow had been lobbying members of the House Ways and Means Committee to insist on a full elimination of the dividend tax even if it meant sacrificing all the rest of the president's tax cut proposals. Snow's aim was to kill a proposal by Chairman Bill Thomas, R-Calif., to draft a modified and much less costly dividend tax break that would effectively cut dividend taxes to 18 percent — halving the rate for upper-income filers. *(2003 CQ Weekly, p. 991)*

However, if the choice comes down to the dividend cut vs. other elements of Bush's plan, and the administration chooses the former, it could hurt Bush's assertion that he is seeking a quick boost for the economy.

"If [he] says 'I want a dividend tax cut and nothing else,' that says their biggest commitment is a certain vision of the tax code, which is defensible, as opposed to whether the economy gets a lift or not," said Ed McKelvey, senior economist at Goldman Sachs.

In practical terms, Wall Street is not expecting much of an economic boost from the president's growth package, even if he gets almost everything he wants. McKelvey's forecast, for example, estimates that the plan could add just one-half to three-quarters of a percentage point to the nation's economic output. Of far greater concern are the war in Iraq, whether nervous consumers will spend or save, how much state and city budget problems will drag down the economy, and the potential for deterioration of foreign trade.

Looking for Two Democrats

Still, Wall Street firms themselves have much to gain from Bush's proposals to eliminate most taxes on dividends, and the best way to ensure that it survives is for the tax cut package to total $550 billion. Supporters of the dividend tax cut are not overlooking any options for turning the tide in the Senate.

"It could be two Democrats," said Richard Hunt, a lobbyist for the Securities Industry Association, which represents large Wall Street firms. "Everyone who supported the 2001 tax cut is on the hit list." He cited his targets: Voinovich; Snowe; Breaux; Blanche Lincoln, D-Ark.; Ben Nelson, D-Neb.; and Finance Committee Chairman Charles E. Grassley of Iowa.

Wartime popularity can assist Bush in using the bully pulpit to pressure legislators on the fence. But he will have to persuade Senate moderates to undo a hard-won budget deal forged under intense pressure on the Senate floor, and sealed with an unusual floor

Index of Consumer Sentiment

The index began with a baseline of 100 in 1985. It moves based on how people feel about the economy. Highs and lows were 112 in January 2000 and 63.9 in October 1990.

Month	Index	Month	Index
July '90	88.2%	Oct. '02	80.6%
Aug.	76.4%	Nov.	84.2%
Sept.	72.8%	Dec.	86.7%
Oct.	63.9%	Jan. '03	82.4%
Nov.	66%	Feb.	79.9%
Dec.	65.5%	March	77.6%
Jan. '91	66.8%	April	83.2%
Feb.	70.4%		
March	87.7%		
April	81.8%		
May	78.3%		
June	82.1%		

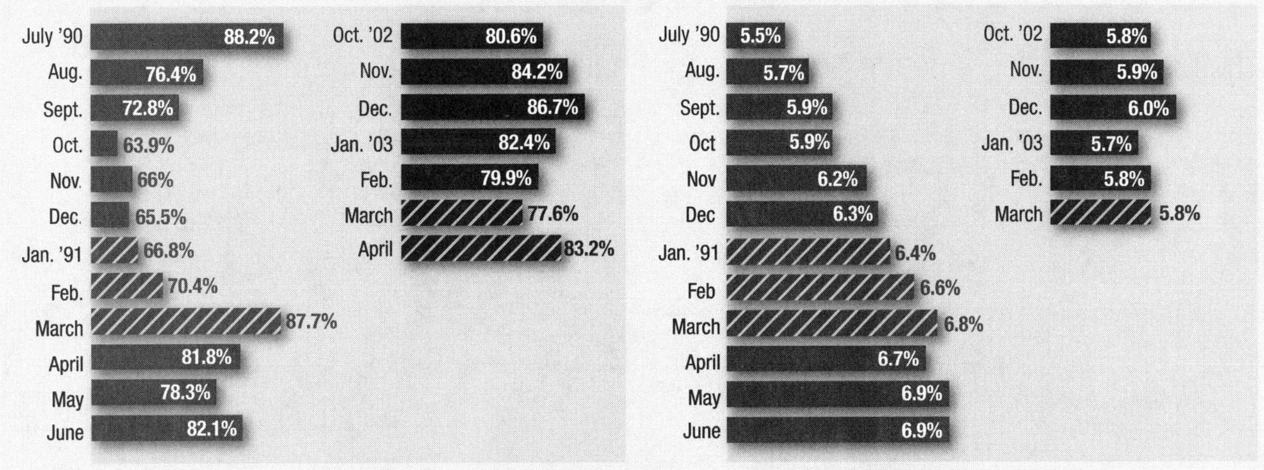

SOURCE: University of Michigan

Unemployment rate

Month	Rate	Month	Rate
July '90	5.5%	Oct. '02	5.8%
Aug.	5.7%	Nov.	5.9%
Sept.	5.9%	Dec.	6.0%
Oct	5.9%	Jan. '03	5.7%
Nov	6.2%	Feb.	5.8%
Dec	6.3%	March	5.8%
Jan. '91	6.4%		
Feb	6.6%		
March	6.8%		
April	6.7%		
May	6.9%		
June	6.9%		

SOURCE: Bureau of Labor Statistics

statement by Grassley.

Although the budget resolution adopted by Congress (H Con Res 95) on April 11 would provide key procedural protections in the Senate for a tax cut of up to $550 billion, Grassley promised Voinovich and Snowe that he will "not return from the conference on the growth package with a number greater than $350 billion."

If the moderates do not budge, the focus of conference debate will not be about size, but whether to include any dividend tax cut in a $350 billion package. "At this point, the hard-nosed calculation says that the dividend tax cut is dead," said Goldman Sachs' McKelvey.

Attack Ads

Other interest groups are joining an aggressive effort to flip senators. The Club for Growth, a conservative, tax-cut advocacy group, began airing television advertisements in Ohio and Maine aimed at Voinovich and Snowe. The ads equate the actions of these "so-called Republicans" to the obstacles raised by France to the U.S. war effort in Iraq. Voinovich is pictured next to a waving French flag.

"These Franco-Republicans are as dependable as France was in taking down Iraqi dictator Saddam Hussein," Club for Growth President Stephen Moore said in a statement.

The White House has offered no public objections to the advertising campaign.

"These ads really backfired in Maine," said Snowe's spokesman, Dave Lackey. "Twenty percent of the population is of French-Canadian background. Being Franco-American is a matter of pride, not a criticism."

And many senators, including Snowe, are listening to state legislators who complain about the revenue that states would lose under the dividend tax cut. Many state income taxes are calculated in part using filers' federal taxable income.

Breaux also has complained bitterly about what he sees as strong-arm tactics by the White House. Two Washington-area groups, the Seniors Coalition and the 60 Plus Association, recently took out a full-page ad in the New Orleans Times-Picayune urging Breaux to support the dividend tax cut.

Still, the new GOP message appears to be a conscious one to equate tax cuts with patriotism.

Like Voinovich, Bunning is up for re-election in 2004. But while Voinovich believes voters want him to exercise fiscal restraint and keep his eye on the deficit, Bunning fears that limiting the tax cut because of deficit fears would hurt job creation.

A $350 billion tax cut "would be the most unfortunate thing I can think of," Bunning said. "When our troops come home, I hope they have jobs. The Reserves and Guardsmen coming back, their jobs are on the line."

Bunning said he believes a $350 billion tax cut would be too small to have a meaningful impact on a $10 trillion economy.

"I'm sorry if Chuck Grassley made a promise," Bunning said. "He didn't ask me before he made it. In the [Kentucky] State Senate, we used to roll chairmen a lot. It's much more difficult when you have a one-vote majority in the Finance Committee."

To defend themselves against attacks for which they would be held responsible if the economy tanked, Snowe and Voinovich are emphasizing their impatience to pass a $350 billion tax cut package that could kick in quickly. Snowe would focus on business tax breaks for investment, increasing the child tax credit and the married couples tax break.

"Many Democrats think $110 billion is enough. Snowe thinks a larger one is important because we don't want to revisit the jobless recovery we saw after the 2001 recession," said Snowe spokesman Lackey. ". . . Economists have acknowledged that a near-term stimulus of a dividend cut is small. It's a long-term growth plan. And you pay for long-term growth plans. She'll work on that."

Voinovich also is shrugging off the heavy arm-twisting from the White House. "I don't consider it to be pressure," said Voinovich. "I support a stimulus package." ◆

Middle East 'Road Map' May Have Wrinkles for GOP

Timetable for Mideast peace process could become a big problem for Bush

REUTERS PHOTO / KEVIN LAMARQUE

Bush's next big foreign policy challenge will be diplomatic, not military. He has embraced a road map for Middle East peace, but many in Congress want no part of a plan that could endanger Israel.

For neoconservatives, President Bush's war speech aboard the aircraft carrier *Abraham Lincoln* on May 1 struck the double chords of triumphalism and the threat of American might.

By declaring an end to major combat operations just six weeks after the war began, Bush confirmed what the neoconservatives had predicted for months — that the war would be swift and that coalition forces would prevail. And by threatening further action against terrorists and those who seek weapons of mass destruction, Bush appeared to side with those hawks both in his administration and Congress who have suggested that Syria and North Korea now could be candidates for some Bush-style regime change.

And then, of course, there was the telegenic setting — Bush framed against a 22,904-ton symbol of American power and global reach, an image neoconservatives hope will help Bush win re-election in 2004.

Despite this triumph of neoconservative thinking in the administration's national security policy on Iraq — a victory so forceful that the neoconservative military posture has looked as if it might become a permanent feature of the Bush White House across the board — the president's next major foreign policy challenge probably will not be military but diplomatic. Just a day before his Iraq speech, Bush released a long-awaited multilateral "road map" to end the Israel-Palestinian conflict, launching the first major Middle East peace initiative after nearly three years of grinding communal warfare.

The timing of the events was not coincidental: Like his father after the 1991 Persian Gulf War, Bush wants to use his success in Iraq to move forward on Middle East peace to preserve stability in the oil-rich region. And to underscore that point, Bush has joined the European Union, the United Nations and Russia — the other members of the so-called quartet of mediators — in endorsing the main tenet of the road map: parallel concessions by both Israel and the Palestinians as they move toward a final settlement by 2005.

The road map's timetable threatens to become not only a major diplomatic issue but also a political problem for Bush as well. Conservatives, one of Bush's core constituencies, are strongly pro-Israel, uncomfortable with diplomacy that pressures Israel into concessions that could compromise its security, and deeply distrustful of the European Union and the United Nations, whom they regard as pro-Palestinian. With Israel already demanding major changes in the road map, a confrontation between Bush and the conservatives over the Middle East seems only a matter of time.

And one of the first places that clash will be felt is on Capitol Hill, where neoconservative support for Israel has been strengthened by the religious right and pro-Israel Democrats who together now form a broad bipartisan coalition of lawmakers who do not like the road map as it is currently written.

'I don't think Congress will sit on the sidelines and let the European view . . . dominate the road map," said Sen. Lindsey Graham, R-S.C., a leader among Christian conservatives and a strong supporter of Israel. "There needs to be a check and balance, and Congress can play a check and balance role here."

AP PHOTO / THE FACTS, ERIC LYLE KAYNE

DeLay has been one of the most outspoken lawmakers in criticizing the Middle East road map.

Timing Is Everything

Sen. Charles E. Schumer, D-N.Y., said, "With the road map, the key issue is timing." Schumer is referring to Israel's demand that there should be no negotiations on sensitive issues, such as the Israeli settlements in the occupied territories, before all violence ends. If Bush insists on such negotiations prematurely, Schumer warns, Congress will respond.

"It could be resolutions, could be speeches, could be appropriations measures," he said.

Schumer's conditions echo the changes that Israeli Prime Minister Ariel Sharon is demanding. Among other things, the road map calls on the Palestinians to restructure their security services and crack down on terrorist groups. At the same time, it calls on Israel to immediately dismantle settlements in the West Bank that have been established since March 2001, freeze all settlement activity, and "progressively" withdraw its troops from Palestinian areas occupied since the current uprising began in September 2000. But Sharon insists the road map be implemented sequentially, not in parallel, as it now stipulates. In other words, the Palestinians must make their concessions first, and Israel will follow only if satisfied with their performance.

For now, the White House says the timetable of the road map is not negotiable, although it has invited both the Israelis and Palestinians to "comment." And while Israeli diplomats say Sharon is dealing directly with Bush in private, much of Israel's comment on the road map is coming out through the statements of congressional supporters such as Graham, Schumer and others.

"Dotting the i's and crossing the t's of Israel's security is very important to me," Graham said. "And I think Congress will be a key player in whether or not this road map gets implemented."

Larger Foreign Policy Concerns

Lawmakers' fixation on the Middle East road map appears to be part of a larger concern among conservatives about the direction U.S. foreign policy has taken under Secretary of State Colin L. Powell.

In what has now become a touchstone event for many in the right wing of the Republican Party, former House Speaker Newt Gingrich, R-Ga. (1979-99), castigated the State Department in an April 22 speech at the conservative American Enterprise Institute.

While he did not mention Powell by name, Gingrich called the State Department's pre-Iraq war strategy of seeking a diplomatic solution to the crisis both "ineffective and incoherent." He blamed the State Department for blurring "President Bush's clear choice between two worlds," and "descend[ing] into a murky game in which the players were deceptive and the rules were stacked against the United States." And he also attacked Powell for his "ludicrous" decision to meet with Syrian President Bashar al-Assad during an upcoming trip to the Middle East, saying the secretary was jeopardizing momentum gained by the Pentagon.

"The United States military has created an opportunity to apply genuine economic, diplomatic and political pressure on Syria," Gingrich said.

While the White House let Gingrich know it was not pleased with his attack, some conservatives on Capitol Hill have come to the former Speaker's defense. GOP Sen. Jon Kyl of Arizona insists that Gingrich's remarks were misinterpreted.

"We have healthy debates about Congress," Kyl said. "Why can't we have healthy debates about the State Department?"

But Gingrich is not the only one challenging the State Department's stewardship of the country's most sensitive foreign policy issues. In a leak that appeared calculated to undermine delicate negotiations among the United States, North Korea and China over Pyongyang's nuclear weapons program, an internal memo from Defense Secretary Donald H. Rumsfeld appeared in The New York Times on April 21, suggesting that "regime change" was the way to resolve the standoff.

That is a position that also has its supporters among conservatives on Capitol Hill. John McCain, R-Ariz., has repeatedly warned that the United States cannot rule out military action against North Korea. South Carolina's Graham agrees, saying a nuclear-armed North Korea would be "the most serious threat to our nation outside of another al Qaeda attack."

Powell has responded forcefully to his critics. In an April 30 appearance before the Senate Appropriations Foreign Operations Subcommittee, he said those who hurl blanket criticisms at his department are "in for a fight."

"Ever since Thomas Jefferson was sworn in as the first secretary of State, an uninterrupted line of secretaries of State have all been criticized for being quiet diplomats, for trying to find peaceful solutions," he said. "That's what we do, and I'm not going to apologize to anybody."

A day earlier, appearing before the Senate Foreign Relations Committee, Powell politely warned against a congressional move to press ahead with the "Syria Accountability Act" (HR 1828), a wide-ranging sanctions bill, in advance of his May 3 meeting with Assad.

"We are dealing with a very serious problem, but we're

Road Map to Middle East Peace

The so-called road map lays out a series of steps that Israel and the Palestinians must take together to reach a permanent two-state solution to their bloody, historic conflict. Here are the highlights:

PHASE I: Ending Terror and Violence, Normalizing Palestinian Life and Building Palestinian Institutions — Present to the end of May 2003

• The Palestinians reiterate Israel's right to exist in peace and security and declare unconditional cease-fire. Israel reaffirms its commitment to a viable, independent Palestinian state living in peace alongside Israel and declares an immediate end to violence against Palestinians. Both sides end all official incitement against the other.

• With the help of the United States, Egypt and Jordan, the Palestinians rebuild their security forces and begin sustained operations aimed at confronting all those engaged in terror. This includes confiscation of weapons. Israel takes no actions to undermine trust, including deportations, attacks on civilians, confiscations or demolitions of Palestinian property.

• Joint Israeli-Palestinian security patrols resume. As security improves, the Israeli army gradually withdraws to positions held before Sept. 28, 2000. Palestinian security forces redeploy to areas vacated by Israeli troops.

Palestinian Institution-Building

• Palestinians appoint interim prime minister and Cabinet with executive authority.

• Palestinians begin the process of drafting a constitution for Palestinian statehood, based on a strong parliamentary democracy and Cabinet with an empowered prime minister. The draft constitution is submitted for approval by appropriate Palestinian institutions after elections.

• Palestinians establish independent election commission. Palestinian Legislative Council reviews and revises election law. As early as possible, Palestinians hold free, open elections. Israel fully facilitates travel of Palestinian officials and non-governmental organizations involved in institutional reforms and elections. Israel reopens Palestinian Chamber of Commerce and other closed institutions in East Jerusalem.

Humanitarian Response

• Israel lifts curfews in Palestinian areas, eases restrictions on the movement of people and goods, and allows unfettered access of international and humanitarian officials.

• Israel transfers taxes, arrears and other funds to Palestinian authority.

Settlements

• Israel immediately dismantles settlement outposts erected since March 2001 and freezes all settlement activity, including natural growth.

PHASE II: Transition — **June 2003 -December 2003**

• After Palestinian elections and approval of draft constitution, an international conference is held to establish an independent Palestinian state with provisional borders. The United States, Russia, the European Union and the United Nations promote international recognition of the new Palestinian state, including possible U.N. membership.

PHASE III: Permanent Status Agreement and End of the Palestinian Conflict — **January 2004 - 2005**

• A second international conference is held to begin Israeli-Palestinian negotiations over final borders, the status of Jerusalem, settlements and refugees.

• Israelis and Palestinians reach final and comprehensive agreement on these issues in 2005, thus ending their conflict.

• The Arab states accept full normal relations with Israel in the context of a comprehensive Arab-Israeli peace.

dealing with it in a changing environment," he said, referring to the aftermath of the Iraq war and the renewed Middle East peace process. "It would not be helpful for me right now to also have something that would be pending in the way of legislation. I hope that this is one that Congress will allow the diplomacy to remain in the hands of the president."

Congress has deferred to the administration on the Syria legislation for the time being, but its deep skepticism toward the Middle East road map is not likely to go away.

Driving the issue is the powerful pro-Israel lobby, which insists that Bush reaffirm his June 24, 2002, comments about the road map. In those remarks, Israel's supporters say, Bush appeared to embrace Israel's demand for a sequential implementation of the plan, with the Palestinians making their concessions first. *(2003 CQ Weekly, p. 831)*

With the biggest lobbying group, the American-Israel Public Affairs Committee, or AIPAC, watching closely, some 313 House members and 88 senators have signed two separate letters to Bush that urge him to stay faithful to his June 24 remarks. The House letter also urges Bush to require a complete cessation of all Palestinian violence before any "concrete actions" could be expected from Israel. Both were delivered to the White House the day the road map was formally unveiled.

The White House has said repeatedly there is no contradiction between Bush's remarks of June 24 and his later statements about the road map, maintaining that the plan is a "vehicle for implementing the vision of the June 24 speech."

But many lawmakers and activists appear to be less than convinced. House Majority Leader Tom DeLay, R-Texas, for example, restricts his support for the "president's view that he laid out a year ago." Meanwhile, he has attacked the administration and its international partners as the "quartet of appeasement."

Indeed, DeLay, a leader of the Christian right, has been one of the most outspoken lawmakers to criticize the Middle East road map and the administration's diplomats. The Christian right's support for Israel is rooted in its religious belief in the second coming of Christ. *(2002 CQ Weekly, p. 1136)*

"The moral ambiguities of our diplomatic elites notwithstanding, Israel is not the problem; Israel is the solution," DeLay said at an April 2 gathering of Stand for Israel, an interfaith alliance co-chaired by Ralph Reed, former chairman of the Christian Coalition.

On the central question of timing, DeLay stuck to a hard line, rejecting the road map's parallel progressivism: "The violence must stop, period. When it does, and not before, the Palestinian people will have a viable opportunity for peace."

Though legislatively innocuous, these letters might presage future legislative action. In an internal document, AIPAC said one of its legislative priorities this year is Congress' "codification" of the major changes that Israel is seeking in the road map: Palestinian governmental reforms, an overhaul of the security apparatus, and the cessation of violence before Israel takes any action.

Such legislation could take the form of a non-binding resolution or an appropriations bill that could restrict the president's ability to fund any peace-related projects.

Enough Troops to Fight

Some lawmakers, such as House Minority Leader Nancy Pelosi, D-Calif., refuse to speculate on future congressional action until Abu Mazen, the new Palestinian prime minister, is given time to perform. But Tom Lantos of California, the ranking Democrat on the House International Relations Committee, who co-authored the House letter with committee Chairman Henry J. Hyde, R-Ill., is confident of Congress' ability to successfully challenge the road map.

Asked if he foresees a legislative role, Lantos simply notes the number of signatures on the letter. "That's my answer," he said.

Should such legislation be introduced, some lawmakers say, more than pro-Israel sentiments would be at play. Mark Steven Kirk, R-Ill., a former State Department official and member of the House Appropriations Foreign Operations Subcommittee, says that in the wake of the Iraq war, a stronger consensus emerged in Congress that supports a "more robust and more militarized policy" backed by Rumsfeld and Vice President Dick Cheney, and adopted by Bush.

"In that sense the road map looks a little anachronistic," Kirk said.

"This is a new era in the Middle East, and we are pressing for democracy throughout that region," adds Sen. Sam Brownback, R-Kan. "I think the administration has made a brilliant, wonderful move in Iraq, and it should expand on that. This is the real road map to peace — through democracies, not dictatorships."

Danger on the Right

While Bush faces no real political consequences by offending Democrats such as Lantos and Schumer who oppose most of his policies anyway, he cannot afford to underestimate the challenge coming from his Christian conservative base or neoconservative policy activists speaking as proxies for many in his own administration. With the 2004 election looming, Bush faces a delicate political challenge in pursuing his current agenda without offending his conservative base.

"The president has made a mistake," said Frank Gaffney, president of the conservative Center for Security Policy in Washington. "It's likely to have domestic political repercussions before it's over."

Conservative Christian activist Gary Bauer, who challenged Bush in the 2000 Republican presidential primaries, also has raised the foreign policy divide as an issue with Bush's political base.

"There is a deep, deep division . . . on issues ranging from the creation of a Palestinian state to how we deal with North Korea and Syria," he told townhall.com, a conservative Internet publication, on April 24.

"The State Department bureaucracy has had its own foreign policy for years, and it has tended to be a very U.N.-oriented, 'peace at any cost,' anti-Israel, anti-defense spending, 'diplomacy can solve everything' sort of approach," Bauer said. "And, as of now, Secretary Powell shows no inclination to take on that liberal bureaucracy."

But Bush and Powell still have some powerful allies among Republican moderates, such as Richard G. Lugar of Indiana, chairman of the Foreign Relations Committee, and committee member Chuck Hagel of Nebraska, neither of whom signed on to the "Dear Colleague" letter.

Lugar says he withstood intensive pro-Israel lobbying on the road map issue. "I have listened to good friends who have come in from various American groups . . . who are suggesting, to me at least, amendments and even wholesale changes [to the road map]," Lugar said.

But he describes himself as "intensely supportive of the president and Secretary Powell" and the road map's parallel approach to resolving the Israeli-Palestinian conflict.

April 30, the day of the road map's release, was also Holocaust Remembrance Day — which saw an assemblage of lawmakers and Holocaust survivors packed in the Capitol Rotunda. With the strains of the World War II Jewish resistance anthem, the *Partisan Hymn*, filling the Capitol Dome, Israeli Ambassador Daniel Ayalon praised Congress for being a "moral beacon" of support, adding that his government would continue to press for changes in the road map.

"We have always been counting on the great support of Congress," he said.

Ayalon would not comment on a specific future role for Congress. But he suggested that if the road map continued to remain unacceptable, his government might simply scrap it.

"With all due respect to the road map or any other paper, what counts is the vision of President Bush," he said, alluding to the president's June 24 speech. "No matter what is written here and there, we will have our own road map. Israelis and Palestinians, mark my words, will have their own road map for direct bilateral negotiations."

In what could be a political escape hatch for Bush, the White House says such an outcome would be acceptable. "If Sharon and Abu Mazen meet and come up with steps on their own that don't track the road map exactly, I don't think anybody here is going to object to that," said a White House official.

But as long as the administration remains involved in the negotiations, Bush will have to deal with a Congress that has far more faith in his military skills than his diplomatic acumen. ◆

War Won't Unify Congress

Party divide over domestic agenda too wide to bridge this time

During the days after the terrorist attacks of Sept. 11, Republicans and Democrats in Congress made a point of minimizing their differences and presenting a united front as they responded to the tragedy. For a while, Tom Daschle of South Dakota, who was then the Senate's Democratic majority leader, and Trent Lott of Mississippi, then the GOP minority leader, even held news conferences together.

But when he was asked whether Congress could put aside its partisan differences once again if the United States goes to war with Iraq, Senate Judiciary Committee Chairman Orrin G. Hatch just laughed.

He was not trying to be flippant. The Utah Republican was simply acknowledging the political reality that lawmakers from both parties are seeing. The conventional wisdom is that the nation always has united at the beginning of a war, and that Congress will do the same after a military conflict with Iraq begins, just as it did after Sept. 11. But this time, Democrats and Republicans say, don't expect that to happen.

It is not just the disagreement over whether the United States should go to war, although that is part of the problem. The bigger difference between now and 2001 is that the House and the Senate are so bitterly divided over the agendas they have been working on — tax cuts, budget priorities, a possible overhaul of Medicare, abortion restrictions and judicial nominations — that lawmakers from both parties say it may be too difficult to put their differences aside or minimize them, even during a war.

Republican leaders are preparing to reshuffle that agenda to give war-related initiatives top priority over domestic legislation. A supplemental fiscal 2003 appropriations bill to pay for the war — and possibly a second such measure — would bump any other legislation off the House and Senate floors once it was ready, GOP leaders say. And the 108th Congress would probably adopt a resolution in support of the troops in the first days of a conflict. *(Spending, p. 10)*

But such a resolution, which Congress routinely rallies behind at the start of any armed conflict, might be the only item that wins broad bipartisan support.

President Bush is continuing to push for a $726 billion tax cut at the same time the nation could launch a war, a decision questioned by Democrats and some moderate Republicans.

GOP leaders expect the first supplemental spending package to quickly become law, but other lawmakers say it will not go that smoothly if it gets caught up in the debate over whether the tax cuts should wait until after the war. Democrats are already hammering at Republicans' spending priorities in budget resolutions (S Con Res 23, unnumbered House draft) that will be on the House and Senate floors the week of March 17 — and they say they have no intention of quieting down even if the nation goes to war. *(2003 CQ Weekly, p. 608)*

A Reshuffled Agenda

If war with Iraq breaks out, Congress will shift gears to war-related appropriations and other legislation, delaying some domestic priorities.

Likely to be on a faster track

- A resolution in support of U.S. troops
- 2003 supplemental appropriations bill
- Comprehensive energy bill (S 597)
- Bioterrorism defenses legislation (S 15)

Those that may be pushed to the back burner

- Faith-based initiative (S 272)
- Medical malpractice limits (HR 5)
- Welfare reauthorization (HR 4)
- Individuals with Disabilities Education Act reauthorization
- Medicare overhaul

"There will be no opportunity to have light between us and the men and women of the armed forces," said House Democratic Caucus Chairman Robert Menendez of New Jersey. However, he said, "We will feel absolutely no prohibition to disagree when there is not common ground on all other domestic issues."

Democrats tried to make a similar distinction after Sept. 11, uniting behind Bush on the war on terrorism while continuing to disagree on domestic issues. But the shock of the terrorist attacks did lead the two parties to play down their usual domestic differences for awhile, particularly on spending priorities. Republicans agreed to more generous domestic funding levels in the fiscal 2002 appropriations bills to appease Democrats, while Democrats signed off on the defense buildup Bush wanted. *(2001 Almanac, p. 2-3)*

Cuts and Competition

This time, however, it could be impossible for Congress to separate the war — which could cost close to $100 billion — from the expensive initiatives already on tap, such as tax cuts to stimulate the economy and a Medicare prescription drug benefit. They will all be competing for resources at a time when the Congressional Budget Office has projected a $200 billion budget deficit for fiscal 2004 — increasing to $338 billion if Bush's budget and tax proposals are enacted.

At a time when House and Senate budget writers are already facing a backlash over their proposals for painful domestic spending cuts even before the costs of a war are factored in, such competition is sure to make this year's debate over education, health care and other spending decisions all the more bitter.

But Republican leaders insist they will not put off work on the budget resolution or the tax cuts simply to avoid a public argument over those issues during wartime.

"No. Why?" asked Senate Republican Policy Committee Chairman Jon Kyl of Arizona. "We've got to do our jobs, and one of the things we have to do is pass a budget resolution. Democrats didn't get a budget resolution done last year. Maybe even with a war on, we can."

Asked whether the House would keep its budget resolution on the floor if war broke out, Majority Leader Tom DeLay of Texas said, "Absolutely, because that's how you pay for the war. You've got to pay for the war."

So, the war vs. tax cuts debate appears unavoidable. "Instead of asking people to sacrifice, he is going to say to the richest 1 percent, 'Here's another tax cut'," Rep. Bob Filner, D-Calif, said of the president. "This is not a time to ask that."

"They want to raise taxes," countered House Speaker J. Dennis Hastert, R-Ill. "We want to make sure we have economic growth."

No Turning Back

It also may be impossible for Democrats to defuse their anger over what they perceive as Bush's arrogance — in refusing to disclose estimates of the likely costs of the war or addressing their concerns over his judicial nominees — just as it may be impossible for Republicans to put aside their anger over Senate Democrats' opposition to the nomination of Miguel A. Estrada to serve on the U.S. Court of Appeals for the D.C. Circuit. *(2003 CQ Weekly, p. 615)*

"Nothing's going to be any easier," said Hatch, who has been at the forefront of the troubled effort to confirm Estrada. "The game plan is, gum everything up and obstruct, obstruct. That's what it boils down to. They've just been using judges as an example."

Democrats say Bush and the Republicans have brought it upon themselves because they have chosen to pick too many fights on the eve of a possible war.

At the time of the Sept. 11 attacks, "we weren't talking about the most divisive issues in society, whether it's [abortion] or affirmative action or the makeup of the Supreme Court," said Sen. Jon Corzine of New Jersey, chairman of the Democratic Senatorial Campaign Committee. "They're creating an agenda that's intended to be divisive. It's a strategy."

The partisan distrust is so high that some Democrats suspect Republicans would be happy to see issues such as Medicare and education knocked out of the spotlight. "I think there will be less national attention on it, and maybe that's the intention," said Sen. Charles E. Schumer, D-N.Y.

Republican leaders say they are hardly trying to avoid domestic issues and have stressed that they will make a point of carrying on with their domestic agenda if war breaks out. DeLay and House Majority Whip Roy Blunt, R-Mo., have discussed adding days to the House schedule if necessary in order to accommodate debate on war-related measures without shortchanging their priorities at home.

If war comes, "I will, as majority leader, put my primary focus on the war and on the war on terrorism," said Senate Majority Leader Bill Frist, R-Tenn. "At the same time, I will move forward with a domestic agenda that is consistent with what we have outlined. It'll be a balancing act as we go."

Lawmakers did not make the same kind of attempt at the beginning of the Persian Gulf War in January 1991. "There was an effort to have a lighter schedule so members could spend more time in their districts to be closer to their constituents," said former Rep. Robert S. Walker, R-Pa. (1977-97), now chairman of his own lobbying firm. "By the time we got back, the war was over."

Today, Republican leaders remember the fate of the first President Bush after critics charged that he had no domestic agenda. Blunt said his view is that "members will want to work more."

In 1991, Blunt said, "you had a Republican president and a Democratic Congress that opposed everything he was trying to do. That was another reason not to do anything. We don't have that excuse. We have an agenda to move forward." *(1991 Almanac, pp. 437, 3)*

Shifting Priorities

Still, a certain amount of reshuffling is a given as foreign policy rises to the top of the agenda. New items such as financial assistance to the airline industry could be added, Republican aides say, while some domestic bills already on the agenda could be given higher priority if they are related to the war.

For example, energy legislation — an as-yet-unnumbered bill already is on course for a House vote before the spring recess begins April 11. The Senate legislation (S 597) could accelerate as well, since Republicans say the measures are needed to reduce the nation's dependence on foreign oil. Likewise, a bill (S 15) to improve the nation's defenses against a bioterrorism attack could be put on a faster track.

Other domestic initiatives not related to the war could remain on the agenda but get delayed. In the Senate, issues such as the faith-based initiative (S 272), limits on medical malpractice awards, and reauthorizations of the 1996 welfare overhaul (PL 104-193) and the 1975 Individuals with Disabilities Education Act (PL 94-142) could take longer to reach the floor. *(2003 CQ Weekly, p. 629)*

The House passed its welfare bill (HR 4) and its medical malpractice legislation (HR 5). But it could take longer to overhaul pension rules and reauthorize the special-education law. *(2003 CQ Weekly, p. 398; p. 626)*

The biggest substantive impact may be on the proposed Medicare overhaul. Although Bush administration officials insist a war would not delay the effort, lawmakers are not anxious to talk about where they will find $400 billion over 10 years for a prescription drug benefit — the amount Bush has proposed — after the war extracts its huge costs.

"I don't think people have faced up to that very much yet," said Marilyn Moon, a senior fellow at the Urban Institute.

A war also would make it hard for congressional Republicans to get Bush's attention for crucial feedback as they work their way through the Medicare legislation.

But that may be less of a problem than it might appear, Moon said, since Republicans are still trying to decide what they want to do and Bush has backed away from proposing as detailed a plan as he originally had in mind. *(p. 105)*

"It may be that a war gives them some time to put their heads together and actually think about this," she said. ◆

Congress Seeks to Find Its Voice as Iraq War Rages

Relegated to the sidelines, lawmakers struggle with irrelevance

CQ PHOTO / SCOTT J. FERRELL AND U.S. NAVY VIA BLOOMBERG NEWS

As war against Iraq begins, Republicans say they feel no diminution of Congress' role in matters of war and foreign relations. But fights over resolutions to support U.S. troops underscore Congress' desire to assert its voice alongside that of the president.

When President Bush announced March 19 that the war against Iraq had begun, it was as if someone had suddenly switched the sheet music that lawmakers had been singing in ragged harmony for the preceding weeks. Overnight, most Democrats and the few Republicans who had been openly skeptical of Bush's Iraq policy dutifully muted their criticism and fell in line behind the president. On March 20, the Senate unanimously passed a resolution (S Res 95) expressing support for U.S. forces and their commander in chief. Early on March 21, the House passed its own version (H Con Res 104) on a vote of 392-11, with 22 members voting "present." *(2003 CQ Weekly, p. 725; p. 722)*

As Rep. Robert Menendez, D-N.J., put it before the vote, "Today, there are no Democrats and no Republicans. There are only patriots."

But just as when Congress voted overwhelmingly last October to approve the Iraq war resolution (PL 107-243), the roll calls did not tell the whole story. Even as American forces poured into battle, Democrats and Republicans in both chambers fought over the proper way to recognize President Bush. Democrats, many of whom tried to keep the United States from going to war with Iraq, found it difficult to vote for a resolution commending Bush's leadership. The Senate compromised by dropping Bush's name, honoring only "the president." House Democrats were mollified only when the qualifier "as commander in chief" was added, thus limiting their praise to his war leadership without endorsing Bush's diplomatic skills. The Senate resolution used the same modifier.

Though seemingly petty, such concerns underscore not only lingering reservations over Bush's stewardship of the Iraq crisis. On a deeper institutional level, they also highlight Congress' struggle to assert its voice alongside a popular president and an administration that has shown little inclination to consult with Capitol Hill. Among many lawmakers, there is the uncomfortable feeling that on the issues of Iraq, war and diplomacy, the administration has consistently outmaneuvered Congress, leaving lawmakers as mere spectators. *(2003 CQ Weekly, p. 682)*

"Congress leaves the field," Sen. Richard J. Durbin, D-Ill., said on the eve of the war. "We're not even on the sidelines. We're in the stands watching from this point forward."

Yet Congress bears some responsibility for its predicament. Despite a handful of 11th-hour misgivings over the

Bush and Cheney, far left, receive an update on Iraq from CIA Director George Tenet. Chief of Staff Andrew H. Card Jr. is at the president's left. Many lawmakers feel the administration has ignored Congress' demands for similar briefings.

BLOOMBERG PHOTO / ERIC DRAPER

"Congress leaves the field. . . . We're not even on the sidelines. We're in the stands watching from this point forward."

Sen. Richard J. Durbin, D-Ill., in a floor speech on the eve of the war.

war and Bush's diplomatic efforts to avoid it, there has been little congressional debate over the Iraq issue to speak of. If anything, Congress appears to have relegated itself to the sidelines, its views on Iraq policy rendered largely irrelevant by its own vote last October that gave Bush broad authority to wage war against Saddam Hussein as he saw fit. Since then, administration officials moved ahead with their war plans, while lawmakers found themselves in the frustrating position of pleading for administration briefings on Iraq and information about the war's cost — all to little or no avail. *(CQ Weekly, p. 9)*

In retrospect, the administration appears to have maneuvered Congress deftly last year, using both the clamor in the then-Democrat-controlled Senate for a debate on Iraq, as well as Democratic divisions over the war, to push a vote on the resolution before last November's midterm elections. By winning passage of that resolution, the administration gained a free hand for the six months that followed.

"It was a no-brainer from the viewpoint of the White House that it was a win-win situation," said James M. Lindsay, a political scholar at the Brookings Institution. "I don't want to suggest that [Bush political adviser] Karl Rove had scoped this out in January. Maybe he did. But by the time you got to August, it didn't take a rocket scientist to realize they could put Democrats in a very difficult spot."

Lindsay adds: "Congress voluntarily removed itself from the debate over Iraq and went up into the cheap seats with the reporters and the pundits."

As lawmakers now watch the war unfold on television, students of Congress say its current bout of irrelevance should come as no surprise. Historically, the legislative branch always has handed control over foreign relations to the president. And congressional deference is especially pronounced during wartime — with some notable exceptions, such as the last years of the Vietnam War, when Congress used appropriations measures to limit the war in Southeast Asia.

But one question now is whether Congress, with its Iraq war resolution, made the same mistake it committed at the beginning of the Vietnam War, when it passed the 1964 Gulf of Tonkin Resolution and gave President Lyndon B. Johnson broad discretion to deepen America's involvement in that conflict. It took Congress nearly a decade to re-establish its voice and pass a series of measures that denied U.S. forces the money they needed to remain engaged in Vietnam. *(1970 Almanac, p. 120)*

The answer of how and when this new Congress can find its own voice lies not only on the Iraqi battlefield, but also with the modern media that are bringing the war, and later its aftermath, to Americans' television and computer screens in real time. Given the speed of today's information flow and the compression of the news cycle, the answer is likely to require months, not years.

"The timing and tempo of the news cycle, with the Internet and cable TV, is so different now than in the 1960s," said Alton Frye, an expert on Congress and foreign policy at the Council on Foreign Relations. "You'll see an acceleration of the war's consequences in public opinion."

A Free Hand

While Congress has steadily allowed its war-making authority to erode since the end of World War II — the last time Congress formally declared war — legal experts note that the war powers it gave Bush in the Iraq resolution are unprecedented.

The war resolution grants Bush virtually a free hand, with no provisions for congressional review once hostilities begin, no expiration date, and no constraints on the military action. More important, for the first time in U.S. history, it sanctions the use of force for a pre-emptive attack. *(2003 CQ Weekly, p. 678)*

While some scholars and lawmakers believe the Bush administration adroitly manipulated Congress to win the Iraq war vote, others say Congress was fully aware of the resolution's scope and how much authority it would be granting the president.

Some Democrats now insist they expected a more successful diplomatic effort to disarm Saddam Hussein, but the fact remains they granted the president the green light when the key moment came for the vote. If Congress' power was diminished as a result, the experts say, the lawmakers were the authors of their own woe. *(Democrats, p. 69)*

"Congress had a role to play, and it played it," said former Rep. Mickey Edwards, R-Okla. (1977-93), now a professor at Harvard's Kennedy School of Government. "They chose to make a decision early, and they were willing to approve it. That's not having your hands tied."

Strengthening Diplomacy

Charles H. Stewart III, professor of political science at M.I.T., also dismisses the idea that Congress went into the vote unaware. "Only a fool would have believed that there was any other course than going to war," he said.

But many in Congress did expect that the resolution would strengthen the U.S. diplomatic effort, even though they knew that war could be a consequence, says Frye.

"Congress went along with the resolution because it voted with its hopes, not fears," he says. "Many wanted to give Bush leverage to disarm Iraq without war."

As the war gets under way, many members now defend their votes, arguing today as they did six months ago — that the Iraq war resolution was meant to strengthen Bush's diplomatic hand at the United Nations, where he was seeking a Security Council resolution commanding Saddam to disarm or face "serious consequences."

"I think we pursued the course of action that gave peace the best chance," said Sen. Evan Bayh, D-Ind., who supported the war resolution. "In the end, it didn't work. But that's because of Saddam Hussein."

But several lawmakers, including some Republicans, used the debate on the resolutions to support the troops to express their disappointment over the failed diplomacy that led the United States to war against Iraq.

Arlen Specter, R-Pa., called it "regrettable" that the United Nations was not in the end united against Iraq, "because had that been done, I think it might have been possible to back Saddam Hussein down."

Another key factor shaping the outcome of last fall's resolution — especially the lack of a drawn-out debate over Iraq — was the political composition of Congress, says Stewart.

Gephardt's Ghost

At the time the vote was held, Republicans controlled the House, and Democrats held the Senate by a tenuous one-seat majority. But backers of the war resolution also had the added advantage that Democrats were deeply divided over the Iraq issue. That allowed Bush to peel away the support of then-House Minority Leader Richard A. Gephardt, D-Mo., leaving behind other Democrats who sought a resolution that placed more constraints on Bush. *(2002 CQ Weekly, p. 2671)*

As a result, the makeup of Congress, with no strong Democratic majority in either house able to challenge the president on the resolution, was critical in strengthening Bush's hand. Scholars also point out that this constellation is historically rare. Since World War II, Americans have generally opted for divided government, with Congress in opposition to the president.

In that respect then, what happened last fall was not so much a diminution of Congress' role but a narrow Republican majority projecting its power, granting the president the backing for a war that it also supported.

Two other factors also bolstered Bush: the traditional Republican advantage in projecting competence in national security issues and the tendency of Americans to rally around the president during wartime — in this case the lingering aftermath of the Sept. 11 terror attacks.

"In times of peace, power flows to Capitol Hill. In times of war, power flows to the White House," said Lindsey.

By and large, congressional concerns over that branch's loss of power correspond with members' views on the war. Democrats, especially those who did not sign on to the resolution, are most worried that the resolution's legacy will be enhanced power for the executive branch. But most Republicans, who support Bush's policies, express no such fears.

In contrast with Democrats, who have complained bitterly about the administration's lack of consultation with members of Congress, Sen. John W. Warner, R-Va., chairman of the Senate Armed Services Committee, said those consultations have been "very adequate." Warner adds that he expects Congress to play a significant role in shaping the policy in the aftermath.

Sen. Jon Kyl, R-Ariz., says policymaking for postwar Iraq will be "a joint operation with Congress and the White House. We're going to work with him, and they'll work with us."

Even the independent-minded chairman of the Senate Foreign Relations Committee, Richard G. Lugar, R-Ind., does not see congressional power weakened as a result of the resolution's broad authority.

"Congress is never constrained," he chuckled. "Three-quarters of us in the Senate felt that the administration was on the right course when it came time to vote. And since then the administration has been very forthcoming with us as far as information is concerned."

Democrats in the Dumps

By contrast, it is mostly Democrats who say Congress has been sidelined. But they, too, say it will not take the legislature long to restore its role in overseeing the administration's foreign and war policies.

The first test could come as early as the week of March 24, when the administration is expected to request a fiscal 2003 supplemental spending measure of as much as $100 billion to pay for the Iraq war and homeland security. Congress also will become relevant once again if the administration, as expected, returns to Capitol Hill with further requests to pay for Iraq's postwar reconstruction.

"After the war, everything about maintaining forces, spending money, that's all still on our plate," said Sen. Joseph R. Biden Jr. of Delaware, ranking Democrat on the Foreign Relations Committee. "That's how we stay in the game."

The war resolution "wasn't an eternal authority," agreed Sen. Russell D. Feingold, D-Wis. "After the war, Congress should assert its oversight authority, and I hope that the administration doesn't try to rely on this authorization to prevent us from asking what we need to ask."

But the fact that Congress holds the power of the purse does not mean that it will exercise it as its own foreign policy lever anytime soon. At least for now, most lawmakers say it would be highly

Democrats Divided Over Voicing Anti-War Sentiments

The Democrat vs. Democrat confrontation in a small room in the basement of the U.S. Capitol displayed the intraparty struggle to find a right time and method to criticize President Bush for waging war against Iraq.

A band of anti-war Democrats gathered for a press conference March 20, the morning after hostilities began, to lay out their plans within the Democratic caucus, and eventually before the House, for arguing that Congress had never exercised its authority to declare war, and that diplomatic efforts should continue at the United Nations. But mostly, they simply asserted that they would not be silenced.

"The debate must continue. This is not over because the president unilaterally decides to start a war," said Rep. John Conyers Jr., D-Mich. "Will it intimidate some people who don't want to be considered unpatriotic? Probably."

This group would not be intimidated. But it was taken aback moments later when freshman Rep. Jim Marshall, D-Ga., arrived, and upon being invited to the microphone, calmly announced that their plans to restart the war debate at a party caucus later in the day were in technical violation of party rules.

Rep. John Conyers Jr., D-Mich.

"The time for debate is past," said Marshall, a Vietnam War veteran who recalled how servicemen were demoralized back then by the anti-war demonstrations back home. His objection forced the Democratic caucus meeting to be canceled and prompted angry complaints from the anti-war lawmakers that Marshall had breached informal protocol by crashing the press conference to disagree with their position.

As a party, the Democrats found themselves the week of March 17 walking a fine line between exercising their right to protest the war and wanting to wave a patriotic flag to boost troop morale.

For some, such as Marshall, the only resolutions worthy of discussion once war had begun were the bipartisan House and Senate resolutions (H Con Res 104 and S Res 95) in support of U.S. troops, their families and the president.

Others, such as Conyers, argued that the best way to support the troops was to bring them home. He was among those who did not back the troops resolution because it included support for the president.

In between were lawmakers such as Senate Democratic Leader Tom Daschle of South Dakota, who began the week being strongly critical of Bush's policies. By March 20, he stood shoulder-to-shoulder on the Senate floor with Majority Leader Bill Frist, R-Tenn., as they offered the resolution backing the military. *(Iraq, p. 66)*

unusual for Congress to refuse the administration's supplemental request while American forces are in the field.

Even those who voted against the war resolution now say that Congress should not exploit its power of the purse to challenge the president and leave the troops hanging.

"The decision to go to war was arrived at democratically," said Sen. Carl Levin, D-Mich., who opposed the resolution. "Now it's our duty to give the troops everything they need."

That sort of unity did not prevent some Democrats from demanding that the administration provide an early estimate of its war costs. But that demand reflected broader concerns about the budget resolution and the affordability of Bush's proposed tax cuts. *(2003 CQ Weekly, p. 687)*

Even if Congress does start to reassert itself by controlling funds for the war, some experts say the past record does not suggest that lawmakers will necessarily opt for fiscal prudence.

"Throughout history, nations have been willing to accept economic ruin as they pursue military goals," says Stewart, the M.I.T. political scientist.

Levin, ranking Democrat on the Armed Services Committee, says the outcome of the war will decide the question of congressional assertiveness in foreign and war policy.

"If the war is quick and casualties are few, then the president will probably use that to increase his authority," Levin said. "But if the war is messy and the aftermath is chaotic, especially without U.N. authorization, then Congress will have learned to be more cautious before giving broad authority to the president."

Democratic Rep. Ellen O. Tauscher of California, who backed the war resolution but now expresses dismay over the collapse of diplomatic efforts to avert a conflict, underscores Levin's prediction, cautioning that moderate Democrats will be more skittish about cooperating with Republicans on national security policy in the future.

"I don't believe the U.S. had a credible commitment to peaceful disarmament [of Iraq], and I never would have believed last fall that the president would ask me to authorize force for something that was in fact pre-ordained," she said.

"We may have had differences of opinion about what brought us to this point, but the president of the United States is the commander in chief, and today, we unite behind him as well," Daschle said in a floor speech before the Senate voted 99-0 for the resolution, with Zell Miller, D-Ga., absent. *(2003 CQ Weekly, p. 725)*

As the Senate vote proved, Democrats strived to show that despite policy differences with the administration, Congress could be united in a time of war.

But in the House, unity was more elusive as members haggled over the wording of the latest resolution. For months, opposition to the war has run deep among House Democrats, with 126 of the 208 Democrats in the 107th Congress voting against the resolution (PL 107-243) authorizing use of force against Iraq. Eventually, the House voted 392-11 on the troops resolution, with 22 members voting "present." Democrats cast all but one of the dissenting and present votes. Republican Ron Paul of Texas voted present. *(2003 CQ Weekly, p. 722)*

During a speech to a labor group just three days earlier, Daschle had touched off a firestorm of criticism when he observed the U.S. was being "forced to war" because "this president failed so miserably at diplomacy."

Replied House Majority Leader Tom DeLay, R-Texas, "Is Tom Daschle the official Democrat hatchet man or just a taxpayer-funded pundit?"

CQ PHOTO / SCOTT J. FERRELL

Rep. Jim Marshall, D-Ga.

Democrats rallied to Daschle's defense, arguing he was stating the reality of diplomatic failure.

House Democratic Whip Steny H. Hoyer of Maryland noted that in 1999, it was DeLay who had labeled the U.S. campaign against Slobodan Milosevic in Kosovo "Clinton's War," and had lobbied against the House-passed resolution supporting the campaign. *(1999 Almanac, pp. 14-21)*

"If that was not raw partisanship designed solely to embarrass President Clinton, then I don't know what is," Hoyer said.

"If we don't raise questions, then we are in trouble," said Democratic Sen. Dianne Feinstein of California. "This is the first real instance of the carrying out of the doctrine of preemptive attack as an offensive posture by the U.S."

Rep. Charles B. Rangel, D-N.Y., who voted against the latest resolution, called Daschle a "patriot" because he had the courage to voice an unpopular opinion. "Being a patriot is more than having a flag on your SUV."

As war approached, House Democrats vowed to pursue anti-war resolutions, including one by Rep. Dennis J. Kucinich, D-Ohio, that would second-guess evidence cited by the administration in its arguments for a strike against Iraq. "Their war is based on lies," Kucinich said.

But even the most ardent critics of the march toward war, such as House Democratic Leader Nancy Pelosi of California, abruptly halted Kucinich's plans once military strikes began on March 19.

Pelosi quickly dismissed the anti-war resolutions, signaling that she would not question the president's decision during the first hours and days of war.

"We have moved on from that place," she said.

"I'm a moderate who believes in bipartisanship, but I've learned my lesson," she said. "We were played."

Yet such attempts by Democrats to distance themselves from what some on Capitol Hill already are calling "Bush's war" might go only so far. By voting to approve the resolution last fall, lawmakers put themselves on the record as well. If the war goes badly, voters could hold them accountable for not only the consequences of the war but also its aftershocks.

No Crying in Politics

Because of that risk, say Congress watchers, the recent comments from some Democrats that have criticized the administration's pre-war diplomacy and its reluctance to provide more concrete cost estimates could be seen as attempts at self-inoculation.

"The fact that some Democrats are expressing concern over war costs just means that they're hedging their bets in case the war turns out badly," says Stewart. "It's the nature of Congress to grant authority for war to the president, but then be in the position to criticize the administration when things go wrong."

A small number of liberal Democrats, including Sheila Jackson-Lee of Texas and Barbara Lee of California, want the party caucus to get behind legislation that would limit Bush's power to wage war in Iraq.

Party leaders have kept their anti-war members at bay, aware of the political embarrassment that would come from trying to retract congressional authorization for a war that already has started.

But in an attempt to take themselves out of the bleachers and reclaim Congress' voice in foreign relations, other lawmakers may consider one more resolution over the coming days, this one saluting countries assisting the U.S. war effort.

A senior Democratic aide notes that lawmakers also are working to ensure that such a resolution will not further antagonize relations with nations that are not supporting the war effort — although there are temptations to single out some.

"There are certainly not too many friends of the French on either side of the aisle," he said. ◆

Interest Groups Make Sure Lawmakers Know the 'Score'

Scorecards prove a powerful tool to affect legislative outcomes

Compromise legislation to tighten bankruptcy law was always going to be a tough sell in the House. Though Republican leaders had signed off on a hard-fought deal with the Senate months earlier, the package was spurned last fall by many conservatives, who objected to a provision aimed at keeping anti-abortion protesters from escaping court-imposed fines by filing for bankruptcy.

But the deal really began unraveling when influential conservative advocacy groups, including the Eagle Forum and Concerned Women for America, sent a simple message to lawmakers.

They would be "scoring" House members on how they voted on the resolution setting the ground rules for debate on the bankruptcy bill conference agreement. In other words, how each member voted on that rule — balloting that is normally a straightforward test of party discipline — would become part of the legislative scorecards that the groups post on the Internet or distribute by the thousands to their members and affiliates across the country.

CQ PHOTO / SCOTT J. FERRELL

Eagle Forum Executive Director Lori Waters says the group's scorecard lets members know 'we are watching.'

In essence, the groups' message to the House membership was this: "Vote 'no' on the rule if you want our support on Election Day."

The groups' decision to make the vote one of their "key votes" of the year pleased one of the leading abortion rights opponents in the House, Republican Joe Pitts of Pennsylvania. But it did not surprise him. He had asked them to do it and was counting on their help to win enough votes to compel GOP leaders to strip out the abortion provision before advancing the bankruptcy bill. And the strategy worked: The bankruptcy deal, the culmination of six years of debate at the Capitol, died for the 107th Congress the night of Nov. 14 when the House rejected the rules resolution. *(2002 CQ Weekly, p. 3021)*

In March, the House passed bankruptcy legislation (HR 975) without the provision that abortion opponents objected to. *(2003 CQ Weekly, p. 704)*

As the tale of the bankruptcy bill makes clear, interest groups — and members of Congress themselves — use legislative scorecards for much more than reflecting an assessment of each lawmaker's record or mobilizing supporters at the grass-roots level at election time.

Scorecards, interest groups and lawmakers agree, have become an effective tool of the lobbying trade.

News that an influential advocacy group is scoring a vote can help solidify support for a bill or undo it, something lawmakers use to their advantage when they can. Especially in the House, both Republican and Democratic leaders also have sought to coordinate with these groups — asking them to either score or refrain from scoring a particular vote — in hopes of attaining shared legislative goals.

And, as in the case of the bankruptcy bill, maverick factions in the House have combined with powerful advocacy groups to use the scorecarding process to triumph over the vaunted House GOP whip organization.

"It definitely weighs on members' decision-making process if you tell them a vote is going to be scored by a particular group," said a former top aide to the House GOP leadership who is now a Washington lobbyist. "Is it the be-all-end-all? No. Will it help push people over the line? Yes."

The groups maintain that it is their own agendas, and not the tactical needs of either party, that drive their decision-making about their scorecards. But they welcome the notion that their decision to include a vote in their scorecards can help determine a close outcome.

"It's very helpful in lobbying when members know we are watching them," said Lori Waters, executive director of the Eagle Forum. "And watching them like a hawk."

Influencing Votes

The most influential ratings are those created by large and engaged grass-roots networks — as well as those that influence campaign contributions, donated either by associated political action committees (PACs) or by the groups' members and allies.

The National Federation of Independent Business (NFIB), the U.S. Chamber of Commerce, the League of Conservation Voters, the AFL-CIO, the International

Rankings: From Zero to 100 — Literally

Below are four lawmakers and how their voting records were scored last year by several of the outside groups considered most influential on Capitol Hill. The four are the members of the 108th Congress who voted either most often or least often in favor of the president's position in each chamber during the 107th Congress, according to an analysis by CQ.

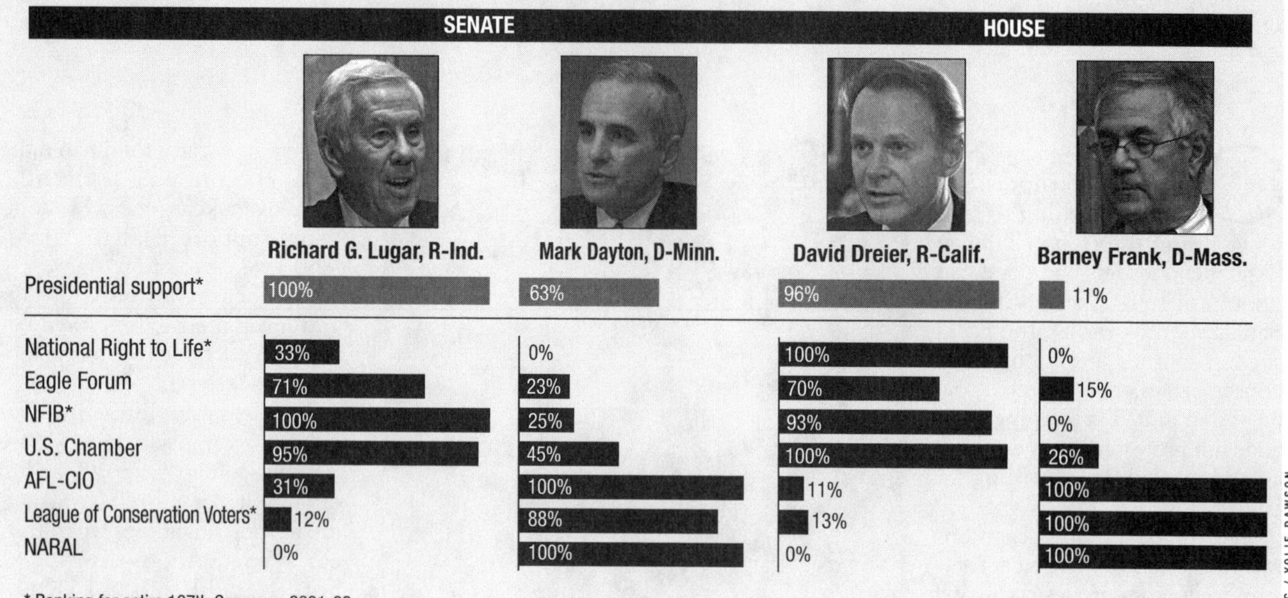

* Ranking for entire 107th Congress, 2001-02

Brotherhood of Teamsters, National Right to Life, NARAL Pro-Choice America and the National Rifle Association (NRA) are among the groups whose scorecards carry the most weight on Capitol Hill, lawmakers and informed observers say. *(Influential groups, p. 73)*

Some groups report annually to their membership, some at the end of each Congress. Many, such as National Right to Life and the Eagle Forum, update their scorecards on their Web sites as votes important to the groups are taken.

Others, such as the Teamsters, simply report each lawmaker's vote and note how it squares with the group's position. Still others, such as the NFIB and NARAL, calculate the percentage of the time each lawmaker stands with them on issues they care about most. The NRA gives each lawmaker a grade, A+ through F, based in part on votes on key issues.

Nearly all the most influential groups notify lawmakers in advance of any vote that will, or may, appear on scorecards. (The AFL-CIO is an exception to that rule.) The Chamber sends letters to House and Senate offices on special "key vote" stationery. NFIB "blast faxes" letters to every congressional office, and the group's five lobbyists distribute "key vote" cards door to door on Capitol Hill. The 8fi-by-6 inch cards, emblazoned with the group's logo, describe the upcoming vote and the group's position.

NFIB lobbyists handed out such cards last month urging House members to vote in favor of legislation (HR 5) that would limit attorney fees and cap awards in malpractice cases. The bill passed with a 33-vote margin. *(2003 CQ Weekly, p. 622)*

Early this month, NARAL announced that it would be scoring the Senate vote on confirming one of President Bush's judicial picks, Priscilla Owen, whom the group views as hostile to abortion rights. NARAL activists are calling for a filibuster of Owen, whom Bush has nominated for the U.S. Court of Appeals for the Fifth Circuit. And the group promises to score two votes, if necessary: a vote to invoke cloture, or shut down debate, as well as a straight up-or-down vote, if Owen gets one. *(2003 CQ Weekly, p. 944)*

Groups say there are two main reasons for giving such advance warning: They do not want to blindside, and potentially anger, members by signaling after the fact that a vote was of particular importance to them. But more important, the heads-up, although described as a courtesy, adds weight to a group's lobbying efforts by signaling to lawmakers that a vote is of particular importance to its membership.

"To the people who find political value, fundraising value and credibility value in the endorsements, it means a lot," Bruce Josten, the Chamber's executive vice president for government affairs, said of the key vote letter. "It's telling you that that's one you don't want to vote against."

Calling for Help

Political scientist Larry J. Sabato of the University of Virginia said the use of scorecards up front, to influence votes before they are cast, is a change from past practice.

"In the post-Watergate era, this was considered unethical," said Sabato, who has studied the use of scorecards. "Interest groups were not supposed to reveal which votes they were rating. They wanted an objective measure, and they also thought it would be better for members to not know, to be off balance."

Nonetheless, the practice of notifying members of key votes has become fairly routine, as has using that information for whipping purposes.

Influence-Packed Groups Score Big on the Hill

Scorecards matter because they go to highly motivated voters: individuals committed to an agenda or a cause who look to the ratings for help sorting friend from foe in Congress. The most influential groups are those with an organized grass-roots membership that hits the pavement in the weeks before an election. Below are some of those most watched on Capitol Hill.

NATIONAL FEDERATION OF BUSINESS

The group: The NFIB bills itself as the "voice of small business," the largest advocacy group representing small and independent businesses.
The membership: 600,000
The scorecard: Reports go out twice each Congress, once at the end of the first session and again before Election Day. The scorecards, posted online and distributed to members, listed 14 House votes in the 107th Congress and eight Senate votes.

U.S. CHAMBER OF COMMERCE

The group: The Chamber calls itself the "largest business federation in the world," representing businesses of all sizes and in all sectors.

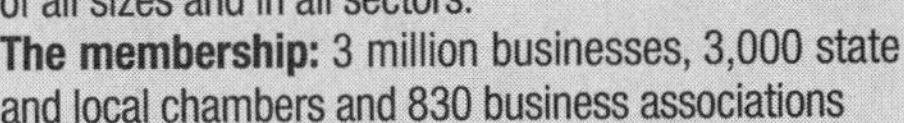

The membership: 3 million businesses, 3,000 state and local chambers and 830 business associations

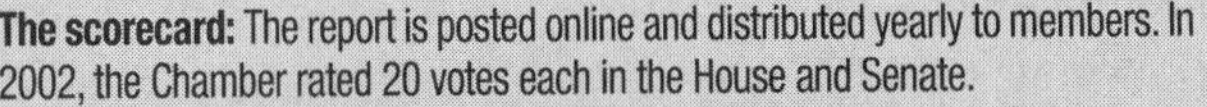

The scorecard: The report is posted online and distributed yearly to members. In 2002, the Chamber rated 20 votes each in the House and Senate.

NATIONAL RIGHT TO LIFE COMMITTEE

The group: Founded in 1973 in response to the Supreme Court decision legalizing abortion, NRLC says its goal is "to restore legal protection to innocent human life." The group lobbies for restrictions on abortion, euthanasia and human cloning.
The membership: NRLC has 50 state affiliates, but does not keep track of membership. Its newspaper, the National Right to Life News, has a circulation of about 400,000.
The scorecard: NRLC regularly updates a "rolling scorecard" online and publishes a less expansive version before Election Day in its newspaper. The printed scorecard for the 107th Congress listed three key votes in the Senate and 16 in the House.

NARAL PRO-CHOICE AMERICA

The group: NARAL calls itself "the political arm of the pro-choice movement" and lobbies to protect access to safe and legal abortions, as well as effective contraception and reproductive health care.

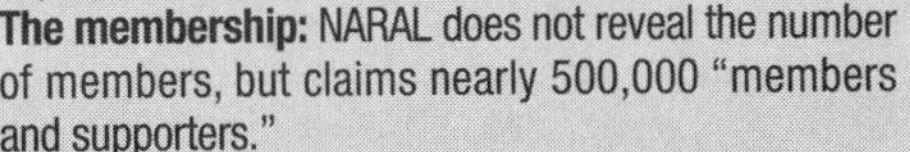

The membership: NARAL does not reveal the number of members, but claims nearly 500,000 "members and supporters."

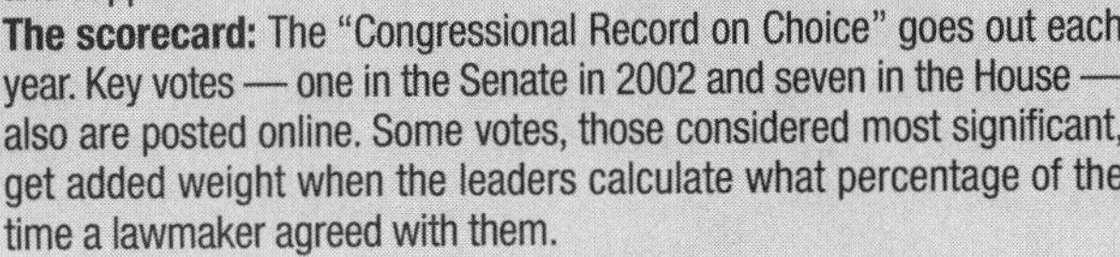

The scorecard: The "Congressional Record on Choice" goes out each year. Key votes — one in the Senate in 2002 and seven in the House — also are posted online. Some votes, those considered most significant, get added weight when the leaders calculate what percentage of the time a lawmaker agreed with them.

LEAGUE OF CONSERVATION VOTERS

The group: The League calls itself "the political voice of the national environmental movement" and the "only organization devoted full-time to shaping a pro-environment Congress."

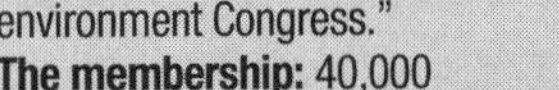

The membership: 40,000
The scorecard: The League's "National Environmental Scorecard," issued at the end of each session of Congress, is the most watched environmental scorecard. Representatives of more than 20 national environmental organizations determine the key votes — 16 in the Senate for 2002 and eight in the House.

THE NATIONAL RIFLE ASSOCIATION

The group: The NRA lobbies for gun rights.
The membership: 4 million
The scorecard: The group releases no general scorecard of key votes, but it does keep an internal record of all votes on gun-related issues, used when compiling ratings and endorsements of lawmakers in "political preference charts" distributed to its membership. Lawmakers get letter grades, A+ though F, on the political preference charts, based primarily on their voting records.

INTERNATIONAL BROTHERHOOD OF TEAMSTERS

The group: Many Teamsters work in the freight industry, but the union now also represents police officers, hospital employees and others.
The membership: More than 1.3 million in the United States
The scorecard: The scorecard is posted online and distributed to members. The 2002 scorecard identified 10 key votes in the House and 11 in the Senate. The Teamsters union reports each lawmaker's position, but does not rate them.

The AFL-CIO

The group: The AFL-CIO is a federation of 65 national and international labor unions representing workers in nearly every sector of the economy.
The membership: More than 13 million
The scorecard: The report is posted online and distributed to members. The AFL-CIO says it does not identify key votes in advance. The group's 2002 scorecard identified nine key votes in the House and 13 in the Senate.

"I've heard it mentioned as there's a debate, but it's always in the tone of, 'For those of you for whom this matters, you should know that this is a vote that fill-in-the-blank is scoring,' " said Robert F. Bennett of Utah, the chief deputy Republican whip in the Senate. "It's particularly mentioned if the leadership wants you to vote that way. I can't give you any examples where anybody's vote was changed, but there's no question that some senators who pay attention to those kinds of ratings will be informed. . . ."

On the House floor, letters circulate telling members when groups are scoring a vote. Sponsors of the bill under consideration sometimes hand them out at the door.

Former Rep. David E. Bonior of Michigan (1977-2003), who was the House Democratic whip for a decade, said he would spread news of scored votes to put pressure on his colleagues. He sometimes would take note of scored votes in his regular "Whip Wind-up," distributed to House offices.

"It's significant, particularly if there's going to be a close vote," Bonior said. "That's part of the lobbying effort, part of putting pressure on members."

Bonior and the current House Republican whip, Roy Blunt of Missouri, both said leaders of each party have approached groups to ask them to score certain votes as a means of motivating members of the rank and file. Conversely, both party leaderships have asked advocacy groups to refrain from scoring a vote that is politically problematic, such as when the caucus is torn between two constituencies.

But only occasionally will an advocacy group agree either to score or not to score a vote at the leadership's request, Bonior and Blunt say.

"Sometimes, if the relationship is strong enough, you could get them to change their minds," Bonior said. "But that was rare."

Blunt said there is never a guarantee that a group will respond when leaders call. "There's no group I'm aware of that we can call and have them automatically score a vote," he said.

On occasion, Blunt said, he does not know a vote is being scored until he walks onto the floor of the House "and the sponsor of a bill is handling out a sheet saying this bill is endorsed by a particular group."

A Subtle Coordination

A former aide to the GOP House leadership said scorecards are one tool among many in the majority's effort to advance its legislation with the assistance of lobbyists and advocates. "There is definite coordination," the aide said. "And those ratings do mean something."

Another former House GOP leadership aide described the coordination as informal: When lawmakers call interest groups to seek help in rallying support on a bill, groups understand that sometimes one of the most helpful things they can do is announce that they will score the vote, the aide said.

Senators said no such coordination of whipping and scoring occurs in their half of the Capitol. And while interest groups acknowledge that they regularly get requests from House members to score certain votes, they emphasize that their decisions are made independently and in the best interests of their memberships.

Mike Schwartz, vice president of government relations for Concerned Women for America — which seeks to "bring Biblical principles into all levels of public policy" — said the group decided to score the procedural vote on the bankruptcy bill in part to assist Pitts' campaign to derail the legislation. Waters of the Eagle Forum, a "pro-family" group founded by conservative activist Phyllis Schlafly, said her group had decided to score the vote before Pitts asked.

Dan Blankenburg, NFIB's top House lobbyist, takes issue with any suggestion that his group decides which votes to score based on what congressional leaders want. "We're not a wing of the Republican Party or a wing of the Democratic Party," he said. "Are we asked to key vote things sometimes? Yes. Do we ever turn them down? Yes."

Asked if his group ever scores votes at the request of lawmakers, legislative director Douglas Johnson of National Right to Life said, "I'm going to take the Fifth on that one. But I will tell you that we would never put a vote on our scorecard unless it met our criteria, and that is that it's a clear, fair vote that measures a member's position on issues of importance to our members."

Fair or 'Cooked'?

Coordinated with congressional leaders or not, some lawmakers and staff aides say the scorecards reflect a cynicism in the process. They complain that advocacy groups sometimes go through contortions to find votes that make their allies look good — choosing meaningless procedural votes or issues far from the group's core agenda.

"In many cases it's a political exercise: Trying to reward those people you are closest to, the people you want to be close to," said one senior GOP House member. The member — who requested anonymity — said he knows of at least one instance when GOP leaders worked to persuade a pro-business group to alter the roster of votes on its scorecard so more House Republicans would get on a list of "pro-business" lawmakers.

"We got them to more accurately reflect their organization's view in terms of what was rated," the lawmaker said. "You have some pro-business members who weren't quite pro-business enough, but you didn't want them being portrayed as anti-business, which was tending to happen."

A senior Democratic legislative aide wondered why the American Farm Bureau chose to score a 2002 Senate vote on permitting oil and gas drilling in Alaska's Arctic National Wildlife Refuge (ANWR); he suggested that the vote was added to inflate the scores of Senate Republicans. The Farm Bureau denied that. Brad Eckart, its director of public policy, said a vote to allow the drilling was scored positively by the Farm Bureau because the group believes oil from ANWR would lower retail gasoline prices, a major concern for farmers.

Republican Christopher H. Smith of New Jersey, one of the lawmakers who helped engineer the bankruptcy bill's defeat last year, is also one of the Republicans in the House who is friendliest toward labor unions, and he recently complained to AFL-CIO President John Sweeney that the group's 2002 scorecard appeared designed to make primarily Democrats look good. Smith lamented that his 22 percent support score inadequately reflected his support for labor's "core" causes.

The scorecard took points off, for example, for Smith's vote in favor of the GOP plan to add prescription drug coverage to Medicare. Smith argues that the matter was not a central issue for labor groups, but a spokeswoman for the AFL-CIO, Kathy Roeder, said that "having access to affordable health care is a core labor issue." *(2002 CQ Weekly, p. 3196)*

Mike Rogers of Michigan, a deputy House GOP whip who is in charge of coordinating the whip organization's dealings with advocacy groups, said he knew of no evidence to support the view that scorecards are cooked to favor anyone — or either party. "I have never seen that; I've never heard of that," he said. "I've never seen anyone try to alter a scorecard."

Schwartz, of Concerned Women for America, said maintaining the independence of the scorecard process is key to his organization's credibility. "Any group that wants to be around for the long haul and is not a partisan organization is going to avoid reporting on votes in a way to make their friends look good and their enemies look bad," he said.

In most cases, the broader issues that will top a group's agenda are chosen by the wider membership or a governing board, and then the group's Washington staff chooses the votes that they conclude best reflect member sentiment on those agenda items.

Vulnerable Lawmakers

It was in that spirit that Pitts appealed to the two conservative groups last fall to add the bankruptcy vote to their scorecards. He was not trying to manipulate or bully anyone, he said, but he did want his colleagues to know the importance of the issue to the anti-abortion lobby. "For those members who want a 100 percent pro-life score, it's a character issue," Pitts said. Such lawmakers "feel very strongly about that, and they have voters who look at that, he said, and those voters "don't want you to wobble."

At times, the lines in a legislative fight are so clearly drawn — so hardened and well known — that a letter from an outside group promising to score a vote is moot.

For example, in the Senate last month, the League of Conservation Voters circulated a letter telling lawmakers that the League would include in its 2003 scorecard the upcoming vote on an amendment to the fiscal 2004 budget resolution (H Con Res 95) that would have made it easier to enact legislation opening ANWR to energy exploration. But senators knew environmental groups would be watching the vote, which went their way, 52-48. (*CQ Weekly, p. 108*)

"You didn't need a letter," said Barbara Boxer, D-Calif., the sponsor of the amendment. "I mean, that's been one of the biggest issues of the large environmental groups for years here."

Boxer played down the importance of scorecards as influencers of congressional behavior. "I think people know what they want to do," she said. "I'm not saying they don't think about it, but I don't think it decides their votes."

That may be so in the Senate, but the dynamics of the House are quite different. A committed bloc of voters, energized by an interest group publicizing a scorecard, can more easily decide the outcome of a close House race than in a statewide Senate campaign, said Burdette Loomis, a political scientist at the University of Kansas.

And because House members are generally less well known than senators, scorecards can be more important in determining the public's perception of them, Loomis said.

Members of interest groups — whether organized to advocate for an industry or an issue — are among the most committed and energized voters, and they look to their groups' scorecards to help guide their votes in congressional elections. The "key vote" cards that NFIB lobbyists distribute include a pointed reminder of the muscle backing them up: They urge lawmakers to support the NFIB position, taken "on behalf of the 600,000 members of the National Federation of Independent Business."

The cards tell lawmakers, "This isn't just a random vote for small business," Blankenburg said. "We're going to put out to our members how you voted on it, and we're going to use it to judge whether you are supportive of small business."

"People power" is the greatest weight behind the most influential scorecards, more so than money, lawmakers and staff say.

"Scorecards go out and you know there is shoe leather hitting the streets out there," said Terry Holt, a lobbyist who was previously communications director for House Majority Leader Dick Armey, R-Texas (1985-2003).

The 2002 NARAL scorecard, for example, is seen as having motivated abortion-rights supporters to lend crucial support to Republican Nancy L. Johnson, who defeated another House incumbent, Democrat Jim Maloney (1997-2003), by 23,000 votes after redistricting forced the two to compete for one seat in Connecticut.

Johnson had a 100 percent rating from the abortion rights group; Maloney's score was a 65. Under the group's weighted scoring system, he was penalized substantially for his vote in favor of legislation to outlaw the procedure labeled "partial birth" abortion by its critics — even though it was the only one of the seven key NARAL votes on which he broke from the group's position. (*2002 CQ Weekly, p. 3186*)

Scorecards also help determine the flow of campaign contributions. For example, Save America's Free Enterprise Trust, the PAC affiliated with the NFIB, looks at the group's scorecards when deciding which candidates to back and rarely donates to any incumbent who has not been named a "Guardian of Small Business," which means he has voted with the group's position on at least 70 percent of its key votes.

CQ PHOTO / SCOTT J. FERRELL

NFIB's Blankenburg says the group's 'key vote' cards tell lawmakers 'this isn't just a random vote for small business.'

Eyeing the Next Election

Lawmakers say colleagues in vulnerable districts or at risk of a primary challenge do pay close attention to scorecards — and take care that they receive the "right" score.

"It has an effect on members, particularly members with a primary," said Thomas M. Davis III of Virginia, who chaired the National Republican Campaign Committee for the 2000 and 2002 elections. "They want to protect their flanks."

A Republican with less than a 100 percent rating from National Right to Life, for example, could be vulnerable to a primary challenge from the right.

Scorecard ratings can be powerful political ammunition. Punchy and easy to communicate in 30-second television advertisements, they are "manna from heaven" for campaigns, said Sabato of the University of Virginia. "It takes complex ideas and boils them down to a simple number . . . that can be used in TV ads, direct mail and phone calls."

Ratings can be a great annoyance to an incumbent seeking re-election, because they can be unfair and oversimplified and gloss over the nuances of an issue, said former Rep. David E. Skaggs, D-Colo. (1987-99), executive director of the Center for Democracy and Citizenship at the Council for Excellence in Government.

"Life is a good bit more complex than these scorecards would suggest," said Skaggs. But "in a democracy, these interest groups are entitled to have a voice in the process."

Announcements that certain groups consider a vote "key" have the most effect on members who are taking a position on a question for the first time, are not sure how to vote and are looking for guidance, Skaggs said.

Armey said he did not pay much attention to scorecards during his 18-year career. Once, when he was berated at a gathering of conservatives for scoring an imperfect 97 percent on a scorecard assembled by conservative activist Paul M. Weyrich, he dismissed the complainers by saying that "Paul Weyrich was 3 percent wrong." Armey acknowledges that was a "fairly cavalier attitude for a member," one he says he could afford to take because he was on "thick ice electorally" at home in Texas.

Armey said House members with marginal holds on their seats pay close attention to scorecards because they believe poor ratings could cost them votes they cannot afford to lose.

Although he declined to give specifics, Armey said that as a House leader he would hear members explain their votes by describing them as essential to maintaining high scores from interest groups representing their political base of support.

A former senior House Democratic leadership aide cited the NRA as having particular power to alter the dynamic of a debate by promising to score the vote. "When that word got out, I watched votes flip among members of our caucus who care about what the NRA thinks," he recalled.

The same goes for the NFIB, particularly among moderate Democrats such as the "Blue Dog" coalition, Bonior said.

Aides and lobbyists recall the NRA's announcement that it was scoring votes in its internal key vote index — used for its ratings and endorsements — as important to the scuttling of gun control legislation in the 106th Congress. The Senate passed new restrictions in 1999 a month after 15 people died in a shooting rampage at Colorado's Columbine High School. But the House, with the NRA monitoring every vote, defeated a more modest approach — which gun rights advocates said went too far and gun control advocates said did not go far enough. *(1999 Almanac, p. 18-3)*

NRLC PHOTO / PATRICIA COLL

Johnson's group, National Right to Life, has a scorecard that can move votes.

And lawmakers and aides say National Right to Life helped delay House consideration of what became the 2002 campaign finance overhaul law (PL 107-155) by promising to put any vote on its scorecards. *(2001 Almanac, p. 6-3)*

Aides of both parties say lawmakers are keenly aware when votes are, and are not, being scored by interested groups. "If I don't send up a letter, I will sometimes get calls from members wanting to know our position," said Mary Minette, legislative director of the League of Conservation Voters.

Looking the Other Way

To be sure, some lawmakers insist they pay little attention when groups announce they will score a vote.

"My positions are pretty clear and stable," said Rep. Ted Strickland, D-Ohio. However, Strickland says he believes a scorecard by the Christian Coalition contributed to his narrow defeat in 1994, when he was seeking a second term. The group pilloried him for his stands on abortion and other issues, he said, and in his socially conservative district, the guides moved enough votes to elect Republican Frank A. Cremeans. Strickland won the seat back two years later.

Strickland said he has known only one House member — whom he declined to name and says is gone now — who visibly fretted about which votes might appear on scorecards of various groups. Strickland said he and his colleagues poked fun at that member's hand-wringing. "I just think he was cowardly," Strickland said.

Rogers, who is serving his second term, played down the influence of scorecards. "I don't know any members who say, 'I've got to vote this way because this is being rated,' " he said. "Maybe some do, but I've never heard anyone say that."

Still, knowing the position of a group whose outlook matches your own can provide a guidepost for lawmakers trying to make sense of the swirl of competing interests and arguments, Rogers said. In that sense, advance word from the Chamber of Commerce, for example, that an upcoming vote is important enough to score can help clarify an issue for an undecided member, he said.

"This can be a confusing place," Rogers said. "Getting information here is like drinking water through a fire hose."

Knowing that an outside group intends to score a vote also assists the leadership in making its arguments to members, Rogers said. "It can cut a conversation a lot shorter sometimes if you can say this is important to a group whose philosophy matches yours," he said. "You don't have to have a six-hour discussion with charts and diagrams."

That was the case with last month's medical malpractice measure. Several lawmakers, including James C. Greenwood, R-Pa., the bill's sponsor, said the Chamber's announcement that it would be rating the vote helped define the bill as an important one for pro-business lawmakers, particularly freshman members who were wading into the complex debate for the first time.

"I think certainly for some members who might have been on the fence, knowing that this was an issue that matters to a wide audience, including the groups that buy health insurance, like the Chamber and NFIB, probably helped tip the scales," Greenwood said. ◆

Tax Cut Package Clears Amid Bicameral Rancor

House and Senate Republicans finally close ranks, but rift remains

The third deepest tax cut in American history, and the second substantial tax reduction of George W. Bush's presidency, is about to become law.

Spurred by the president to put aside their deepening differences and send him a bill by Memorial Day, House and Senate Republicans grudgingly closed ranks the week of May 19 behind a $350 billion economic stimulus package that allows Bush and each of the principal factions within the GOP to claim some measure of success.

Doing so was something of a political imperative for the Republicans. Since the start of the year, they have controlled both the White House and the Capitol, and yet until now the 108th Congress has completed no marquee legislation that would be noticeable to the typical outside-the-Beltway voter.

Bush pronounced himself happy with the fiscal 2004 budget reconciliation measure (HR 2), which the Senate cleared the morning of May 23 only because Vice President Dick Cheney was in position to break a 50-50 tie. The conference report had been adopted by the House, 231-200, before dawn. *(2003 CQ Weekly, p. 1292)*

The administration betrayed no annoyance that the legislation's bottom lines — $320 billion in tax cuts between now and fiscal 2013, and another $30 billion in spending on state aid and refunds this summer to parents of youngsters — added up to just 48 percent of what Bush had requested when the year began. Nor did the president signal frustration that the final deal contained only a shred of his proposal for ending the federal taxation of corporate dividend checks sent to investors.

When it became clear that Congress was not going to come close to endorsing a tax cut as deep as the $726 billion figure Bush wanted, the president derided the $350 billion consensus forming in Congress as a "little bitty" amount inadequate for providing a stimulus to a sluggish economy. But when he visited Capitol Hill on May 22, the president was ready to thank lawmakers for their work.

And, in fact, the package ranks third on the all-time list. Measured in inflation-adjusted dollars, it is almost five times the size of the recession-fighting package (PL 88-272) promoted by President John F. Kennedy and enacted in 1964 soon after his death. The $1.35 trillion cut Bush pushed through two years ago (PL 107-16) is No. 2, and the Ronald Reagan tax cut enacted two decades before that (PL 97-34) is the biggest of all: worth $1.51 trillion as adjusted for inflation. *(1964 Almanac, p. 518; 1981 Almanac, p. 91; 2001 Almanac p. 18-3)*

Moreover, the legislation Bush will sign — a ceremony is expected by the week of June 2 — reflects longstanding GOP tax priorities: acceleration of the individual income tax rate cuts of 2001, more-generous first-year write-offs for business investment and lower taxes on investment earnings. *(Investment breaks, p. 78; highlights, p. 80)*

"This is a Congress which is able to identify problems facing the American people," Bush said. "This bill I'm going to sign is good for American workers, it is good for American families, it is good for American investors, and it's good for American entrepreneurs and small-business owners."

House Republicans, who like Bush had insisted on tax cuts totaling at least $550 billion, embraced the smaller package as a healthy first step in a newly invigorated tax

Quick Contents

The tax cut debate became a struggle among Republicans. In the end, the White House largely determined the shape of a compromise that President Bush called a victory, and that was acceptable to both House conservatives and Senate moderates.

CQ PHOTO / SCOTT J. FERRELL

White House backing gave Thomas, right, the upper hand in his tax cut struggle with Grassley. Finance GOP aide Mark A. Prater looks on during the May 22 conference.

Who Benefits From New Rates For Dividends, Capital Gains

The centerpiece of the 2003 tax cut package is a six-year dividend and capital gains tax cut that would have a relatively small short-term impact on the economy, although it might encourage more companies to issue dividends.

At a cost of $148 billion, it would lower dividend taxes, currently taxed at individual income tax rates, to 15 percent. Capital gains, currently taxed at 20 percent for investments held longer than one year, also would be taxed at 15 percent.

The new rates apply to dividends received after Jan. 1, 2003, and capital gains realized after May 5, 2003. A shareholder would have to own a stock for 60 days before dividends were issued to take advantage of the new 15 percent rate.

For low-income taxpayers — those in the 10 percent and 15 percent tax brackets who make less than $28,400 in adjusted gross income a year ($47,450 for married couples) — the rate on dividends and capital gains is reduced to 5 percent in 2003 through 2007, and to zero in 2008.

As short-term stimulus measures to perk up the sluggish economy, the investor tax breaks are relatively small in a $10 trillion economy. In calendar year 2003, the provisions offer just $8 billion in tax relief, according the Treasury Department.

As long-term engines of growth, the prospects are unknown. To help reduce the cost of the tax package, dividend and capital gains taxes are scheduled to jump back up to their current rates in 2009. Future Congresses will decide whether the nation should extend them.

Double Taxation

Earlier this year, President Bush and his supporters on Capitol Hill spoke frequently of the need to end the "double taxation" of corporate profits. They argued that in addition to hurting economic growth, the current system is simply unfair.

The legislation, however, will do nothing to address that issue. Companies will continue to pay income taxes at the corporate level, and shareholders will continue to pay taxes — albeit at a lower rate — on those profits which are distributed to them as dividends.

Bush's original zero-dividend tax idea would have been a fundamental overhaul of the tax code. It not only would have ended double taxation, it also would have made sure companies paid corporate taxes on their income in the first place before distributing tax-free dividends.

Bush's plan was intended to crack down on the widespread use of tax shelters, and it would have reduced the attractiveness of many special credits used by corporations to reduce their tax bills.

In the bill (HR 2) cleared by Congress on May 23, there is no requirement for businesses to pay corporate taxes in order for shareholders to benefit from the new 15 percent rate. Theoretically, a company could pay no corporate taxes and still distribute dividends that would be taxed at 15 percent.

Corporations might be inclined to distribute more dividends now that dividend and capital gains rates are

---

cut drive that they promised would continue until Election Day 2004.

Only one House Republican, Jim Leach of Iowa, voted against the final deal, which seven House Democrats supported. Three Senate Republicans opposed it: Lincoln Chafee of Rhode Island, John McCain of Arizona and Olympia J. Snowe of Maine. Two Senate Democrats voted for it: Ben Nelson of Nebraska and Zell Miller of Georgia.

House Ways and Means Committee Chairman Bill Thomas, R-Calif., charmed no one during the final week of the tax negotiations, but he came away with a clear victory over his Senate counterpart, Finance Committee Chairman Charles E. Grassley, R-Iowa. The final bill included Thomas' alternative to Bush's dividend tax plan — a new 15 percent top rate on both dividends and capital gains that enjoyed the support of many business groups.

The final compromise also dropped Senate-passed revenue-raising offsets opposed by business lobbyists and House Republicans, substituting expiration dates as early as the end of 2004. Those will surely provide the starting point for an election-year tax bill that would extend expiring tax breaks.

Though three of them spurned the deal, Senate GOP moderates also had something to show for their efforts to limit the tax cut: They were successful in preventing the net cost of the package from exceeding $350 billion. The moderates' April 10 agreement with Grassley to limit the package stands as the turning point in this year's debate.

Divisive Conference Averted

After the Senate passed its version of the reconciliation package May 15, the White House stepped in to head off a lengthy and divisive conference with the House, which had passed a $550 billion measure. Bush met with Thomas, Grassley, and House and Senate GOP leaders at the White House on May 19.

But that presidential intervention could not prevent friction between the two chambers. Grassley came away convinced the final bill would feature a limited version of Bush's plan to make dividends tax-free. And he reacted angrily when Thomas and the White House agreed the following day to drop the dividend plan in favor of a variation on the House's approach.

With the tax-writing chairmen at odds, Cheney became the lead broker of the bill's final form.

The final hours in the talks were a bitter experience for Grassley, who had set aside his personal reservations to include a temporary dividend tax elimination in the Senate bill. "I know there's a great deal of resentment

the same.

Currently, tax experts say, there is a bias in the system toward retaining earnings and against distributing dividends to shareholders because dividend taxes are so much higher than capital gains.

Although there is no extra tax imposed on retained earnings, tax experts assume that retained earnings will be reflected in a company's stock price and eventually taxed as capital gains when investors sell their shares.

Some in Congress are concerned that companies might issue too many dividends if they fear the dividend tax cut will expire after 2008.

"If you're a closely held corporation," in which the company's executives own most of the shares, said one Senate aide, "why don't you just pay all your dividends out now?"

From a corporate governance perspective, it may not be wise for a company to drain all its cash. But it could stimulate the economy if shareholders go shopping with their dividend windfalls.

Mutual Funds

Not all income from mutual funds currently categorized broadly as dividend distributions will be entitled to the 15 percent rate. Only dividends from stocks held by the mutual fund can be passed on to mutual fund shareholders at the 15 percent rate.

A new "qualified dividend" box on the 1099-DIV form would show shareholders which dividend income was eligible for the new rate.

As before, mutual funds would break out capital gains distributions from underlying shares that were sold, and that income would be eligible for the new 15 percent capital gains rate. Also, when an investor sells his mutual fund shares, the new 15 percent capital gains rate would apply as it does for other investments, from financial instruments to real estate.

Nearly all foreign company dividends would be entitled to the 15 percent rate.

Earlier this month, as preliminary versions of the tax bills moved through Congress, foreign company dividends had been excluded from the tax break. But after a loud outcry from business lobbyists, including the U.S. Chamber of Commerce, legislators backed down.

However, to be eligible, a foreign company must be based in a country that has a tax treaty with the United States or have stock traded on a U.S. exchange.

Bermuda has no tax treaty with the United States, but many of the U.S. companies that have moved to the tax haven continue trading their shares in the United States. However, Barbados is specifically excluded.

Real Estate

Real estate investment trusts, or REITs, are real estate mutual funds that do not pay corporate income taxes and distribute nearly all their income to shareholders.

For the most part, REIT dividend income will not be eligible for the 15 percent rate and will still be taxed at individual income tax rates.

There are a few exceptions. REITs that invest in taxable subsidiaries and regular stocks can pass on dividends from those entities at the 15 percent rate. Also, in rare circumstances in which REITs do pay corporate taxes on income, dividend distributions on that income will be taxed at 15 percent.

REITs are expected to change the way they report income on 1099 tax forms to shareholders to distinguish dividend income which is and is not eligible for the 15 percent rate.

Investors will get to take advantage of the 15 percent rate on real estate gains and other capital gain distributions from REIT funds.

among Republicans that worked so hard," he told reporters May 21. "I presume that a lot of my colleagues feel somewhat undercut by the White House just for the sake of getting something done this week."

The fight pitting Grassley and the moderates against the House GOP hierarchy and the White House is probably a harbinger of more disputes between Republican moderates and conservatives this summer. But the final compromise also suggested that the administration and GOP leaders have sufficient leverage to persuade the party's factions to set aside their differences in order to address issues including a prescription drug benefit under Medicare and new tax incentives for retirement savings.

A strong push to build public support and increase pressure on moderate lawmakers in both parties helped the White House win enactment of the 2001 tax cut. But that victory came at the cost of alienating Senate GOP moderates, including James M. Jeffords of Vermont, who bolted the party to become an independent. *(2003 CQ Weekly, p. 1235)*

This time, Bush abandoned his uncompromising position on tax policy and allowed each side to see its own handiwork in the final product.

The key to the deal was language phasing in tax cuts and setting early expiration dates in order to reflect the cuts in the more expensive House package under the $350 billion ceiling set by the more closely divided Senate.

Few Republicans sounded completely satisfied. House lawmakers grumbled that the package was less than half what Bush proposed. Senators complained that they were whipsawed by the White House on the dividend plan they initially supported but that was eventually abandoned.

But in the end, most were happy to vote for a new round of tax cuts.

House Majority Leader Tom DeLay, R-Texas, called the bill a prelude to additional GOP tax cut efforts, including more generous tax incentives for retirement savings. "It was awesome," he said of the conference report. "And it's only the beginning."

But the House majority's drive for additional cuts will probably face strong resistance in the Senate, where Grassley cautioned that it will be difficult to obtain the 60 votes that would be needed to extend indefinitely the 2001 tax cuts without the filibuster protection provided by the budget reconciliation procedure.

Grassley said bills providing additional tax breaks for married couples, enhancing the child tax credit or eliminating the estate tax could probably move through the Senate later this year.

Majority Leader Bill Frist, R-Tenn., agreed with Grassley's assessment that weariness with the bitter tax cut debate — and a calendar filled with other priorities — will make it difficult to enact most of Bush's other proposed cuts. "But we're going to fight for as much as we can," he said.

Even staunch Senate tax cut advocates such as Trent Lott, R-Miss., said the deep divide between moderates and conservatives and a crowded calendar will block other major tax bills this year. "I think it's more likely we'll see these things done next year," he said.

Moderate senators who provided key votes for the reconciliation bill appear unlikely to sign on for other big tax cuts this year. "At some point, we are going to have to have offsets. The deficit is growing. The next tax bills are likely to be political gestures," Nelson said.

Or, as pivotal GOP Sen. George V. Voinovich of Ohio put it, "Any other consideration of tax cuts this year is foolhardy and a waste of time."

Bush's Intervention

Both representatives of rural constituents, Thomas and Grassley got to know each other as members of the House Agriculture Committee in the 1970s. But as chairmen of the House and Senate tax committees, they have pursued divergent agendas.

Thomas wanted a tax cut this year that would be deep enough to satisfy the GOP's conservative base, while Grassley envisioned a deal designed to win votes in the closely divided Senate by adding sweeteners such as aid to state and local governments. Those differing objectives seemed certain to produce arduous negotiation.

Bush moved to shortcut the process, telling lawmakers he wanted a conference agreement written and cleared within days, not weeks or months. To expedite the process, he agreed to live with the Senate's $350 billion ceiling on the bill's net cost and urged negotiators to work out their other differences.

That framework initially appeared to be a defeat for Thomas and the House, who had initially backed Bush's $726 billion proposal but had scaled it back to $550 billion to keep House GOP moderates from rebelling.

But by shifting his focus away from the content of the package to its timing, Bush provided an opening for Thomas. The House bill appeared a

Highlights of the Tax Bill

The reconciliation bill (HR 2) cleared May 23 would cut projected federal tax revenue by $320 billion and increase outlays by $30 billion by the conclusion of fiscal 2013. Some cuts would be retroactive to the start of 2003, but most would expire within five years. Below are the highlights of the measure, which President Bush has promised to sign, and who the principal beneficiaries would be.

INVESTORS	
Dividends	Currently taxed the same as other earned income — with a top rate of 38.6 percent — dividends would instead be taxed at 15 percent for most taxpayers through 2008. Lower-income investors would pay 5 percent through 2007 and nothing in 2008. Expires after 2008. *Cost: $126 billion*
Capital gains	The current 20 percent top rate on the profits from the sale of investments held at least a year would drop to 15 percent through 2008. Lower-income investors would pay 5 percent through 2007 and nothing in 2008. Expires after 2008. *Cost: $22 billion*
INDIVIDUALS	
Individual rates	The four top income tax brackets — 38.6 percent, 35 percent, 30 percent and 27 percent — would drop to 35 percent, 33 percent, 28 percent and 25 percent retroactively to Jan. 1. Under the 2001 tax cut (PL 107-16), the lower rates were set to take effect in 2006. Under the 2001 law, the rate cuts expire after 2010. *Cost: $74 billion*
Lowest bracket	The amount of income taxed at the 10 percent rate would increase to $7,000 in 2003 and 2004, after which it would revert to the current $6,000. *Cost: $12 billion*
Child tax credit and refund	The per-child credit would be $1,000 in 2003 and 2004, then would revert to $700 as provided by the 2001 tax law. Parents would receive refunds of up to $400 per child this summer. *Cost: $32 billion, including $9.5 billion in refund outlays*
'Marriage penalty'	For married couples filing jointly, the standard deduction and the amount of income taxed at the 15 percent rate would be twice that of a single person in 2003 and 2004, after which the gradual reductions of the "marriage penalty" set to begin in 2005 would start. *Cost: $35 billion*
Alternative minimum tax	Through 2004, married taxpayers filing jointly would be exempt from the AMT for their income up to $58,000, a $9,000 increase. Single taxpayers would be exempt for income up to $40,250, a $4,500 increase. *Cost: $18 billion*
BUSINESSES	
Depreciation	All businesses would be permitted to take a 50 percent depreciation deduction, up from 30 percent, for new equipment and other capital investments in 2003 and 2004. *Cost: $9 billion*
Expensing	Small businesses would be permitted to expense $100,000 worth of new equipment purchases annually, up from $25,000. Expires after 2005. *Cost: $952 million*
STATES	
General and Medicaid aid	The federal government would provide $10 billion for a general relief fund to be used by states for government services in 2003 and 2004. An additional $10 billion would be earmarked for state-run Medicaid programs. *Cost: $20 billion*

SOURCE: Joint Committee on Taxation

better bet for quick action because it enjoyed broad support both in Congress and among K Street's business lobbyists. The Senate bill, a product of Grassley's agreement with the moderates, had deeply divided the party and was opposed by business lobbyists because it included $101 billion in revenue-raising offsets.

Another factor was that House negotiators had more than a week to prepare for the talks, while senators were still coming to understand the details of their just-passed bill.

If the House accepted a smaller tax bill, Thomas argued, then the House deserved a dominant role in determining the bill's content.

In a surprising turnabout, Bush agreed, abandoning the dividend exclusion and embracing Thomas' proposal for a combined capital gains and dividend tax cut.

His proposal had emerged in March. Grover Norquist, president of Americans for Tax Reform, said Thomas had hoped to equalize tax rates for estates, capital gains and dividends. The estate tax cut was dropped when it appeared to conflict with the GOP's desire to end the tax altogether.

Thomas initially suggested setting the rate for capital gains and dividends at about 18 percent. But he found that the rate could be pushed even lower as part of a $550 billion tax plan. Word spread that the number Thomas ultimately selected happened to match the No. 15 jersey he wore as a high school football player.

That aside, the plan to cut both capital gains and dividend taxes quickly gained support in the House, where lawmakers concluded it would benefit investors in virtually all companies. Rural lawmakers liked the plan because it would save their constituents money on sales of livestock, timber, land and small businesses, including hair salons and restaurants.

After the Senate squeezed a scaled-back version of Bush's dividend plan into its bill, Thomas' plan appeared to be a long shot. But the Senate had actually undermined Bush's plan. An amendment by Budget Committee Chairman Don Nickles, R-Okla., dropped Bush's language limiting the exclusion to dividends paid from after-tax corporate income and offering a capital gains tax break to investors in companies that retain earnings instead of paying dividends.

The administration's proposal had focused on ending "double taxation" of corporate profits — first as corporate income and then as dividend income to individuals. Critics charged that the broader Senate proposal would encourage companies to shield profits from tax and make exorbitant tax-free dividend payments to executives and other investors.

The Senate plan took another blow when Grassley revealed that a drafting error in the Senate dividend exclusion had made it even broader than supporters had desired and had boosted its 11-year cost to $194 billion — or $70 billion more than expected.

Voinovich's Stand

The strategy for the 2003 tax debate endgame initially looked like the game plan for the 2001 tax law: A unified House majority backed by heavy White House lobbying was trying to force concessions by Republicans in the closely divided Senate.

Grassley had hoped for a far different outcome after the Senate adopted its version of the bill, 51-49, on May 15. The deal he cut with Voinovich and Snowe to limit the size of the package to $350 billion had enraged House conservatives. But Grassley said there was an obvious compromise: limiting tax cuts to $350 billion, while allowing some spending sought by senators who were potential swing votes.

Grassley also hoped that such a package would allow room for one of his own top priorities, more generous Medicare reimbursements for hospitals and doctors in rural areas.

But Grassley soon discovered that Snowe and Voinovich would not accept a $380 billion package of tax cuts and spending he had negotiated with Thomas on May 20. It included $20 billion in state aid and $9.5 billion in outlays to increase the refundability of the child tax credit for low-income parents.

Voinovich said flatly he would not support any package with a net cost of more than $350 billion.

In a rapid series of talks, the already tense relations between Thomas and Grassley grew more strained. Thomas refused to accept a $17.5 billion extension of customs fees, and he ended a meeting with Grassley by abruptly walking out of his own office.

After a meeting with Thomas, Cheney brokered a deal with Voinovich to fit both the tax cuts and additional spending under the $350 billion ceiling by moving up the expiration date of the capital gains and dividend tax cut proposal from 2009 to 2008, saving $29 billion.

Grassley attributed the rush to complete a bill to "anxiety about the economy." The senator, who is expected to seek a fifth term next year, said Republicans wanted to provide quick stimulus for growth that taxpayers could see this summer.

By the time the conference report was completed, Thomas and Grassley were acting as though their hard feelings will not be forgotten. On May 22, during the only meeting of the tax bill conferees, the chairmen had little to say to one another. But they may need to work together this summer, as their committees will be considering legislation focusing on a prescription drug benefit for seniors and legislation aimed at changing a tax break for U.S. exporters that the World Trade Organization has ruled amounts to an illegal trade subsidy.

Thomas took a philosophical view, attributing the tough bicameral negotiations to constitutional differences in the makeup of each chamber. That did little to mollify Grassley, who was still complaining publicly a day later. "I hope to educate Mr. Thomas in the next month that he ought to show a little more respect to a person of equal rank," he said. ◆

Supreme Court's Copyright Ruling Could Mean Broad Powers for Congress

Fair use doctrine trumps concerns about piracy, but future arguments could fail on First Amendment grounds

The Supreme Court affirmed Congress' power to legislate on intellectual property with its Jan. 15 ruling on copyright extensions, but the court also delivered a gentle reminder: Without a strong right to "fair use" of copyrighted material for individuals, future copyright regulations could fail on First Amendment grounds.

The decision highlighted the importance of the fair use doctrine, which permits limited access to and duplication of copyrighted material for noncommercial uses. And in doing so, the ruling could have significant implications for the 108th Congress, which once again is set to weigh the rights of creators to profit from their copyrighted works and the rights of the public to reasonably free access to the material.

In joining the fight over public access to copyright-protected works, the high court said Congress did not overstep its power under the Constitution when it passed legislation adding 20 years to the life of copyrights. The 7-2 ruling in *Eldred v. Ashcroft* marked a rare instance in which the court broadened the reach of Congress' legislative powers, and it created the potential, at least, for Congress to use copyright extensions to wall off original works from the public domain forever.

"If we thought it was important to look to . . . fair use before *Eldred*, it's even more important now," said Peter Jaszi, an American University law professor who specializes in intellectual property issues. "We are now going to live for our lifetimes under a reign of continuously extended copyrights, so we have to begin to look at where else or in what other ways the public interest in this copyright system can be realized. The stakes around the fair use doctrine are now higher than ever."

The ruling focused principally on Congress' power to legislate on copyright issues. But in the majority opinion, Justice Ruth Bader Ginsburg implied that the public's ability to access original works is necessary for copyright laws to withstand First Amendment challenges.

The question of what constitutes fair use of copyrighted material — as opposed to the pirating of proprietary work — is a critical one because of the capabilities of digital reproduction. Copyrighted works ranging from traditional media, such as printed books, to digital music and video files now can be swapped thousands of times every hour on the Internet.

The Supreme Court decision could embolden the 108th Congress to strengthen intellectual property protections over the objections of technology industries, whose stock in trade is hardware and software capable of flawless duplication and distribution. But sharp divisions exist on the Hill over such questions as how to regulate protected works in cyberspace. Although Congress debated the issue in the last session, no consensus was reached. (*Background, 2002 CQ Weekly, p. 894*)

The case took up the 1998 Copyright Term Extension Act (PL 105-298), which aligned U.S. copyrights with European standards, extending by 20 years the existing 75-year limit on copyrights held by companies. The law — passed partly to honor Sonny Bono, a songwriter who served in Congress from 1995 to 1998 — also boosted by 20 years the limit on copyrights originally held by individual writers of songs and books to 70 years after a creator's death.

Opponents of the law led by a New Hampshire online book publisher sued, arguing on two grounds that Congress had exceeded its power to legislate in this area. First, they said Congress erred in granting the extensions to both existing and future copyrights. They contended the law in force at the time a copyright was granted ought to set the time for the protection. They also claimed the law violated the First Amendment.

Congress draws its authority on copyright issues from Article I, Section 8, clause 8 of the Constitution, commonly known as the Copyright and Patent Clause. The clause says Congress may grant protections for "limited times." Until this case, there had been no serious challenges to the right of Congress to set standards for the granting of patents and copyrights, despite three previous major changes to the lengths of copyrights, in 1831, 1909 and 1976. (*1976 Almanac, p. 494*)

Big Win For Hollywood

The decision represented a major victory for the Walt Disney Co. and other large entertainment companies that sought the 1998 law and held copyrights that would have expired without it.

The entertainment industry lobbied hard for the law, fearing the copyrights that protected works such as "The Wizard of Oz" and the 1928 Mickey Mouse cartoon "Steamboat Willie" would expire, allowing the works to enter the public domain and limiting the industry's ability to make profits from the copyrighted material. AOL Time Warner holds the copyrights for "The Wizard of Oz" and Disney owns the copyright for "Steamboat Willie."

The high court not only upheld the 1998 copyright extension but left no doubt that, at least when it comes to copyright, Congress has wide power and discretion to make the laws: "Text, history and precedent . . . confirm that the Copyright Clause empowers Congress to prescribe 'limited times' for copyright protection and to secure the same level and duration of copyright protection for all copyright holders, present and future," Ginsburg wrote.

"We are not at liberty to second-guess congressional determinations and policy judgments of this order, however debatable or arguably unwise they may be," she noted.

Ginsburg also asserted that the law did not tread on individuals' First Amendment rights to access copyrighted information, largely because of the legal concept of fair use.

The principle of fair use was established by the Supreme Court in its 1984 decision in *Sony Corp. v. Universal City Studios*, the so-called Betamax case. In that ruling, the high court established consumers' rights to make copies of copyrighted material they legitimately and legally purchased as long as those copies are for personal and not commercial use.

Critics, including librarians and researchers, maintain the decision could lead to further incremental extensions. Even Justice Stephen G. Breyer, in his dissent, warned against the possibility, noting that the extension made copyrights last so long that it made them "virtually perpetual."

Ginsburg on *Eldred v. Ashcroft*

"Beneath the facade of their inventive constitutional interpretation, petitioners forcefully argue that Congress pursued very bad policy. . . . We are not at liberty to second-guess congressional determinations and policy judgments of this order, however debatable or arguably unwise they may be."

"The wisdom of Congress' action . . . is not within our province to second-guess."

"Text, history and precedent, we conclude, confirm that the Copyright Clause empowers Congress to prescribe 'limited times' for copyright protection and to secure the same level and duration of protection for all copyright holders, present and future."

"It is generally for Congress, not the courts, to decide how best to pursue the Copyright Clause's objectives."

"We defer substantially to Congress."

"The Copyright Clause and First Amendment were adopted close in time. This proximity indicates that, in the Framer's view, copyright's limited monopolies are compatible with free speech principles."

Two Sides in Congress

The debate over fair use was reignited when Congress passed the 1998 Digital Millennium Copyright Act (PL 105-304). The DMCA clarified rules for making copyrighted material available on the Internet and extended protection to software and compact discs. The issue has resonated further with the development of technology that allows works to be transferred into digital form and copied repeatedly without any degradation in quality. *(1998 Almanac, p. 22-3)*

Numerous bills that touch on this issue were introduced late last Congress; this year, debate on the legislation is sure to be fierce, in part because of the court's *Eldred* ruling. *(Background, 2002 Weekly, p. 894)*

The two bills most likely to attract comment deal with the DMCA. One bill (HR 107) would turn back some of the law's restrictions and aims to bolster the fair use rights of consumers who buy copyrighted material, such as musical compact discs.

The legislation, cosponsored by Reps. Rick Boucher, D-Va., and John T. Doolittle, R-Calif., would relax language in the DMCA that makes it a crime to circumvent — or make tools to circumvent — technological protections designed to bar access to copyrighted material. Boucher's and Doolittle's proposal would make it legal for individuals to bypass copyright protection technologies as long as they are doing so for personal use and not for widespread dissemination.

For example, under their bill, it would be legal for someone with a DVD player to duplicate a copyrighted DVD so it could be watched on another home device, even if that means skirting blocks on electronics equipment installed by manufacturers.

"We support vigorously enforcing laws against piracy," Boucher said. "But we don't want to extinguish fair use."

The Boucher-Doolittle legislation has the backing of consumer groups, such as the Consumers Union, as well as some library associations. But it faces fierce opposition from the Recording Industry Association of America (RIAA) and the Motion Picture Association of America, groups that lobbied heavily for the DMCA.

On the opposite side of the debate is a proposal from Rep. Howard L. Berman, D-Calif., that would build on existing intellectual property protections and address new technologies that have come into vogue since 1998.

Berman's bill, as introduced in the 107th Congress, would, among other things, allow copyright holders to engage in "self-help" measures to try to block illegal copying of protected material by, for example, searching data networks or planting false information, without liability.

The measure has strong support from Berman's constituents in Hollywood and from the recording industry, which argues that computer file-sharing programs such as Napster and Gnutella have allowed computer users to illegally trade copyrighted music.

"These uploaders supplying millions of files on a daily basis are having a negative impact on record sales and the livelihoods of hundreds of thousands of songwriters, musicians, artists and everyone who supports their work in the production, marketing, manufacturing, promotion, broadcast and distribution businesses," said Hilary Rosen, CEO of the RIAA, which has supported using technological locks to bar consumers from illegally copying and distributing digital music.

But such technological safeguards have many concerned, particularly in light of the Supreme Court's affirmation of Congress' authority to extend copyrights.

"We take it for granted . . . that you can go into your public library and your university library and fully use the items that have been purchased by your library to use," said Miriam Nisbet, legislative counsel for the American Library Association. "But as technology clamps down on the uses, if what we turn to is a pay-per-word, pay-per-byte society, we've really lost something as a society." ◆

A New Level of Acrimony In Parties' War of Procedure

Are filibusters of judicial nominations dangerous — or just democracy at work?

CQ PHOTOS / SCOTT J. FERRELL; KRT PHOTO / CHUCK KENNEDY

In the escalating Senate battle over judicial confirmations, Republican leaders such as Orrin G. Hatch of Utah, at microphones, upper left, say Democrats are misusing the filibuster to block two of President Bush's nominees. Democrats such as Charles E. Schumer of New York, upper right, and Patrick J. Leahy of Vermont, left, point to the fact that 123 of Bush's nominees have been confirmed, evidence that the system is not 'broken.'

The day Senate Democrats first decided to filibuster appeals court nominee Miguel A. Estrada early this year, they knew they were crossing a new threshold in the judicial nomination wars.

Some were even quite hesitant: Only once in history had a minority party in the Senate used the filibuster to block action on a judicial nomination, and that was 30 years ago, when an associate justice of the Supreme Court with a troubled financial background was nominated for promotion to chief justice. No minority party had ever kept a nominee approved by the Judiciary Committee from floor consideration. What would be the implications, some Democrats asked, of being first?

Now they know.

An escalating war of procedure is unfolding, and no one is sure where it will stop. The president has accused the Senate of an "abdication of constitutional responsibility." Senate Majority Leader Bill Frist, R-Tenn., has put on the table a plan that would ultimately forbid the use of a 60-vote Senate filibuster on executive branch nominees, essentially surrendering to the White House a traditional chamber prerogative that can be powerful even as a threat.

Some in the party are pushing for lawsuits or floor challenges. There is even talk of a "nuclear" option, so-called because, if employed, it would bring about mutually assured destruction of the legislative process and near-certain paralysis in the Senate.

"This is a prelude to potentially something much more momentous," said Norman Ornstein, a resident scholar at the American Enterprise Institute. He and other scholars are concerned about the level of acrimony in this fight, and the potential implications of any effort to "fix" the system. At stake is the balance of power between the Senate and the president on executive nominations, in addition to long-term relations between the parties.

Since January, Democrats have blocked a vote on Estrada six times, and have twice blocked appeals court nominee Priscilla Owen, as well. A third judge, Carolyn Kuhl, has been marked by some as a likely third target of Democrats who say their unprecedented use of the filibuster is in response to the White House's unprecedented effort to appoint

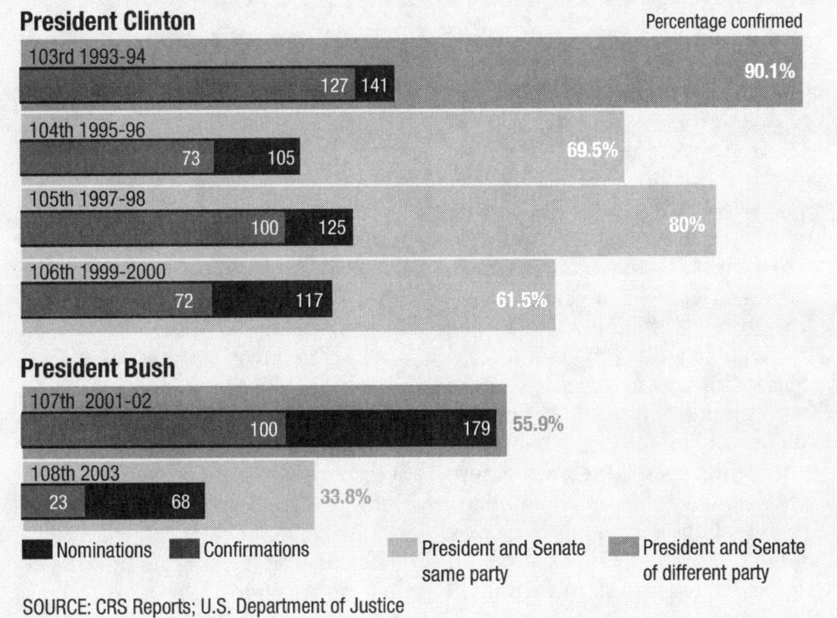

conservative ideologues to the federal bench.

While Democrats insist they are targeting only nominees they consider extreme, the string of blocked votes has begun to normalize the once-rare filibuster, increasing the chances — and, in fact, demonstrating the likelihood — that Democrats will employ the filibuster on a nominee to the Supreme Court.

"They're making it clear: They're playing hardball now," said Sheldon Goldman, a political science professor at the University of Massachusetts at Amherst and the author of a book on the judicial selection process.

At least one Supreme Court justice is expected to step down as early as June. If that happens, Democrats will demand that Bush send the Senate a nominee who can win the support of 60 members. If he does not — a distinct possibility — they will filibuster. And that could throw the nation's highest court into limbo.

"It would basically shut [the court] down," said Thomas E. Mann, a scholar at the Brookings Institution.

With a potential blowup over a Supreme Court nomination in mind, Republicans are looking for ways to loosen the Democrats' grip on the process. "If they can get away with these filibusters, they're going to make it very difficult to replace any Supreme Court justice that retires," said Judiciary Chairman Orrin G. Hatch, R-Utah.

War Escalates

The week of May 5 opened with a win for each side of this issue. The Senate voted 66-25 to confirm the nomination of Deborah L. Cook to the U.S. Court of Appeals for the 6th Circuit. *(2003 CQ Weekly, p. 1148)*

Then, Republicans sought, for the fifth time, cloture on the nomination of Estrada to the U.S. Court of Appeals for the D.C. Circuit. A cloture motion is a procedural move to end debate on an issue, thus clearing the way for a vote on the issue itself, but the motion must pass by 60 votes. The cloture motion on Estrada failed, 52-39. Later in the week, another motion to close debate on Estrada failed 54-43, and one to force a vote on the nomination of Owen to the 5th Circuit was rejected 52-45. *(2003 CQ Weekly, p. 1148; p. 1149)*

Cook's confirmation had been assured by a deal worked out the week of April 28, in which she and John G. Roberts Jr., nominated to the D.C. Circuit, would be approved on the floor despite some concerns among Democrats. Roberts was confirmed May 8 by voice vote. *(2003 CQ Weekly, p. 1034)*

Off the floor, the debate grew more bitter as Republicans tossed out proposals to change the system and end the stalemate. Those included rewriting Senate Rule XXII, which governs cloture votes, so that it no longer would apply to presidential nominations. At least one freshman senator said he might even file a lawsuit to stop the filibusters.

Another idea, termed "going nuclear" by a Senate aid, referred to a possible tactic in which Republicans would invoke the Constitution to circumvent a rule that makes it easy for the Democrats to block rule changes. Such a procedural move, which Ornstein said "would cause extraordinarily deep damage to the fabric of the United States Senate," was tried once before. *(2003 CQ Weekly, p. 1084)*

Bush ended the week with a Rose Garden speech, timed to mark the second anniversary of his first batch of nominations, in which he implored senators to solve the impasse.

"Today, we are facing a crisis in the Senate, and, therefore, a crisis in our judiciary," Bush said. "The obstructionist tactics of a small group of senators are setting a pattern that threatens judicial independence."

Earlier that day, Frist announced his move to change the rules governing cloture just in the cases of judicial nominations. Under his proposal, motions to invoke cloture on presidential nominations would be subject to declining majority votes. The first motion would, as under current rules, require 60 votes to prevail. A second motion would need 57 votes, and a third would require 54. The fourth cloture motion could be approved with 51.

Debate on motions to cut off debate would not begin until 12 hours after a nomination reached the Senate floor, and motions for each subsequent cloture vote could not be filed until after previous motions had been voted upon.

"We have entered upon a new era, damaging to the Senate as an institution, where a majority will be denied its right to consent to a nomination because a minority will filibuster to hold that nomination hostage," he said on the floor while introducing his proposal. "The need to reform the filibuster on nominations is obvious, and it is now urgent."

Democrats said such "reform" is not necessary. "It ain't broke," Minority Leader Tom Daschle of South Dakota said.

Democrats Take Careful Aim When Attacking Nominees

Both Priscilla Owen and Jeffrey S. Sutton, high-profile nominees to the U.S. Appeals Court, were opposed by a broad swath of liberal interest groups.

Owen, tapped for a seat on the 5th Circuit, caught flak for dissenting opinions she wrote as a justice on the Texas Supreme Court in cases involving a state law that required minors to get parental consent before they could obtain abortions.

Sutton, nominated to the 6th Circuit, drew fire for his arguments before the Supreme Court that it is unconstitutional to allow disabled state employees to sue their employers under the Americans with Disabilities Act (PL 101-336).

But the week of April 28, the Senate confirmed Sutton to a lifetime seat on the appeals court. Senate Democrats, meanwhile, launched a filibuster of Owen.

The choice of Owen over Sutton as a filibuster target by Democrats illustrates the minority party's strategy of being selective in picking their fights. In the end, Owen's parental choice decisions were deemed too offensive to one of the Democrats' major backers: the abortion rights lobby.

A main distinction between Owen and Sutton was the way they came out of the Senate Judiciary Committee. Every panel Democrat voted against Owen's nomination. In Sutton's case, Dianne Feinstein, D-Calif., broke party ranks and sided with Republicans for the nominee.

That alone was enough to ensure Democrats probably would not be able to mount a filibuster against Sutton.

As Democrats and interest groups survey the field of judicial nominees, it is clear that to successfully block a candidate for the federal courts, all Judiciary Democrats must be unified on the strategy.

But there are other factors that play a role in how Democrats choose which nominees will face the fiercest fights — and filibusters on the Senate floor.

To some extent, Democrats and the lobby groups who support them are only going after those nominees they believe they have a shot at defeating.

"You have to pick your battles very carefully, and you have to win those you pick — or you at least have to have a shot at winning them," said Kate Michelman, president of NARAL Pro-Choice America.

Generally, that means prime targets are those nominees who have extensive writings, arguments or opinions that help document a view most Democrats would find objectionable.

"For our own intense work, we have decided we're going to concentrate on those that are the most overtly threatening, or the most overtly threatening to reproductive rights through speeches and writings," Michelman said.

So far, the Democrats have won their fights against Owen, as well as against Miguel A. Estrada, nominated to the U.S. Court of Appeals for the D.C. Circuit. Two other nominees — Carolyn Kuhl, tapped for the 9th Circuit, and Charles W. Pickering Sr., nominated for a seat on the 5th Circuit — also are expected to be filibustered on the Senate floor.

Democrats object to the four nominees on ideological grounds. One rea-

"Any time you can confirm 124 judicial nominees in the course of 2fi years, I don't see much broken."

Since the administration of President Bill Clinton, both parties have employed procedural maneuvers with greater frequency to fight nominations. "With each change in power, we've seen an escalation of the tactics," said Nancy Scherer, a professor at the University of Miami who studies judicial confirmation. "They're treating lower court nominees like Supreme Court nominees."

The 1987 defeat of Supreme Court nominee Robert H. Bork — reported out of the Senate Judiciary Committee with a negative recommendation and rejected 42-58 by the full Senate — launched the current struggle over the shape of the federal judiciary. Supreme Court Justice Clarence Thomas' difficult confirmation battle in 1991 took the discord to a new level by showing that the opposition party — the party not in the White House — would demand a role in determining the direction of the federal courts.

Thomas made it through the Senate with just 52 votes; his nomination reached the Senate floor only after the Judiciary Committee reported it without a recommendation.

In the 12 years since Thomas, both parties have grown bolder in demanding a say over who gets lifetime appointments to the federal bench. Nominees for lower courts have been held up at the Judiciary Committee, stalled by anonymous holds on the floor and even rejected by the full Senate.

In the 107th Congress, when Democrats controlled the Senate for 18 months, Leahy, then chairman of the Judiciary Committee, moved a raft of Bush's least-controversial nominees. Ultimately, the Senate confirmed 100 judges to the U.S. Court of Appeals and federal district courts during the 107th.

At the same time, many of the highest-profile nominees — including six of Bush's first batch of 11 nominees announced two years ago, on May 9, 2001 — never received panel votes.

And then, in November 2002, Republicans regained control of the Senate, and, ostensibly, of the judicial confirmation process. Bush issued his first challenge to Democrats in January when he renominated Owen and Charles W. Pickering Sr. to seats on the U.S. Court of Appeals for the 5th Circuit. Both had been rejected by the Judiciary Committee when the Democrats ran it. It was the first time any president had renominated a rejected federal court candidate.

Because Democrats no longer had the ability to control nominations at the

son they have criticized Kuhl is her work against the landmark abortion ruling *Roe v. Wade* while she was in the Reagan administration.

But they are other issues at play, GOP senators suggest.

With the exception of Pickering, all three are potential contenders for any vacancy on the Supreme Court. If nominated for and confirmed to the high court, Estrada would be the first Hispanic justice.

"I don't think our colleagues on the other side are prejudiced against Hispanic nominees, but I think that they are prejudiced against a Republican, conservative they-think-pro-life Hispanic nominee, especially one who everyone has to know is on the fast track to the Supreme Court," said Senate Judiciary Chairman Orrin G. Hatch, R-Utah.

If potential Supreme Court nominees are blocked from getting lifetime seats on the appeals court, they might be viewed as too inexperienced for the high court.

And, Hatch said, the lower court confirmation battles can be so damaging that they erode a potential Supreme Court nominee's chances.

"They want to damage some of these people, so they can't go on to the Supreme Court," Hatch said. "That's what's really entering into this; I'm sure that that's part of what the game is here — to damage these people so they cannot be considered for the Supreme Court."

CQ PHOTO / SCOTT J. FERRELL

Senate Democrats chose to target Priscilla Owen, nominated for the U.S. Court of Appeals for the 5th Circuit, because of her rulings on a Texas abortion law.

Still, another theory is that there is a personal reason Democrats are passionately fighting some nominees, particularly Owen and Pickering.

Owen served on the Texas Supreme Court during President Bush's time as governor of the state. She is also a friend of Bush adviser Karl Rove.

With Owen, "Democrats could hit Bush where it counts," a Senate GOP aide said.

In the case of Pickering, the ties were not to the White House, but to former Senate Majority Leader Trent Lott, R-Miss., who recommended Pickering for the appellate judgeship.

Lott and Pickering are close friends; the nominee's son, Charles W. "Chip" Pickering Jr., R-Miss., a legislative aide in Lott's office.

When the then-Democratic-controlled Senate Judiciary Committee rejected Pickering on a party-line vote last year, Lott said he took the defeat as a personal insult.

committee level, the fight over Bush's judicial nominees moved to the floor.

They started with Estrada. Debate opened Feb. 5, but it was more than a month before Republicans filed a cloture motion. They fell five votes short, and in five subsequent attempts have not rounded up more than 55 votes.

Republicans held the first cloture attempt on Owen's nomination May 1, and that time only two Democrats voted with the GOP.

Democrats are expected to add to their filibuster scorecard the nominations of Kuhl for the 9th Circuit and of Pickering, if the Judiciary Committee sends his name to the floor. The panel voted May 8 along party lines to send Kuhl's nomination to the floor.

Until now, there has never been a successful filibuster against a nominee for a seat on the district or appeals courts. Senators have tried to filibuster such lower court candidates, but until this year, no lower court nominee has been shut out by an extended debate.

Some Republicans tried unsuccessfully in 2000 to mount a filibuster against two of Clinton's lower court nominees — Richard A. Paez and Marsha L. Berzon, whose nominations to the 9th Circuit were held up for years.

At the time, some in the Republican caucus, including Hatch and then-Majority Leader Trent Lott of Mississippi, warned that a filibuster would set a dangerous precedent. Ultimately, enough Republicans backed off from the strategy, and cloture votes on Paez and Berzon succeeded by lopsided margins. *(2000 Almanac, p. 15-41)*

Perhaps one reason Democrats are succeeding with this strategy now is that GOP leaders are allowing the Senate to handle other business at the same time, so little pressure is building to end the filibuster and move on to other issues.

These filibusters are not the traditional technique of a single senator holding the floor for days to force an issue. After an initial weeklong debate on Estrada, GOP leaders decided to essentially dual-track Senate business, putting Estrada's nomination and other executive calendar business on the floor only when legislative matters were not being considered.

The result is that the Senate's other business — and the GOP's legislative priorities — are not being pushed aside by the extended debate. Another, perhaps unintentional consequence is that the filibusters of Estrada and Owen are no longer drawing significant attention.

Zell Miller, D-Ga., who has voted in favor of ending debate on both the Estrada and the Owen nominations and who has a proposal to revamp the

Nomination Debates Through the Years

Judicial nominations were a source of controversy even before the Constitution was drafted, and have continued to be a source of friction between the executive branch and Congress.

George Washington addresses the Constitutional Convention

LIBRARY OF CONGRESS

1787
Delegates to the Constitutional Convention vote to give the Senate sole responsibility for the appointment of judges, but after considerable debate opt to turn in the direction of increased presidential power and assign the task of nominating to the president, with the advice and consent of the Senate.

1801
The Judiciary Act of 1801 increases the number of federal judgeships. President John Adams' administration hurriedly fills the positions through "midnight" appointments before leaving office.

1803
Democratic-Republican President Thomas Jefferson battles the Federalist-appointed judiciary. The dispute comes to a head in *Marbury v. Madison*, after Jefferson's secretary of State, James Madison, refuses to deliver appointed Justice of the Peace William Marbury's commission. In the ensuing legal case, the Supreme Court establishes the precedent of judicial review. Soon after, Jefferson tries unsuccessfully to remove Supreme Court Justice Samuel Chase by impeachment.

1869
Congress sets the number of Supreme Court justices at the current level of nine.

1916
Progressive Boston attorney Louis D. Brandeis is denounced by the American Bar Association and business interests after President Woodrow Wilson nominates him to the Supreme Court. Brandeis eventually wins confirmation, 47-22, and begins a 23-year career on the bench.

1937

Roosevelt

Stung by high court decisions that struck down pieces of the New Deal, President Franklin D. Roosevelt proposes that Congress reorganize the judiciary and add one Supreme Court justice (up to a total of 15) for every justice over the age of 70 who does not resign. Conservatives and many liberals view the proposal as a blatant attempt to exert political influence on the court and undermine judicial independence. The effort fails, but the high court soon appears more sympathetic to Roosevelt's legislative objectives.

1969
After Justice Abe Fortas resigns over financial improprieties, the Senate rejects two of President Richard M. Nixon's Supreme Court nominees. Supreme Court nominee Clement Haynsworth is rejected, 45-55, due to concerns over his civil rights and civil liberties record and the discovery of financial and other improprieties. Florida appellate court judge G. Harrold Carswell is nominated, but rejected, 45-51, after investigations show that at one time he firmly supported racial segregation.

1987
President Ronald Reagan nominates appeals court judge Robert H. Bork to the Supreme Court, triggering an unprecedented public debate, complete with direct-mail campaigns by liberal and conservative groups. Bork abandons the practice of allowing his record to speak for itself, instead defending his views during nearly 30 hours of testimony before the Senate Judiciary Committee. The Senate rejects Bork, 42-58 — the widest margin of disapproval in the history of Supreme Court nominations.

1991

Thomas

CQ FILE PHOTO

President George Bush nominates appellate judge Clarence Thomas to the Supreme Court, and his administration begins to steer the nomination through the Democratic-controlled Senate. A former employee, Anita Hill, charges Thomas with sexual harassment and airs allegations in a series of incendiary televised Judiciary Committee hearings. Thomas denies the allegations, leaving lawmakers unable to resolve the charges. The Senate eventually confirms Thomas, 52-48.

1995-2000
Senate Republicans periodically put holds on some of President Bill Clinton's judicial nominees, preventing them from advancing out of the Judiciary Committee.

2003
Senate Democrats for the first time successfully use the filibuster to stall appeals court nominees, holding up President Bush's nominations of Miguel A. Estrada and Priscilla Owen.

Robert H. Bork Nomination

AP PHOTO / CHARLES TASNADI

filibuster process, calls the dual-track strategy a "filibuster lite."

"With this devious device, you avoid the inconvenience and pain of a real filibuster, but it still can go on ad nauseam," Miller said. "It's just that the public doesn't notice it as much. And that's the point — public debate is turned down real low. I'd much rather have the old all-night filibuster — a bunch of them — than this charade."

Republicans now have labeled the current impasse over Estrada and Owen "a constitutional crisis."

The filibusters "demean the process," and "are a violation of the comity between the Senate and the president," said Judiciary Republican Jon Kyl of Arizona. And, Kyl said, "These are real people. These nominations have been pending now for two years. They've been hanging out there, they don't know what their future is, and real people's lives are being directly affected by this, and that's not fair to them."

But GOP senators say the biggest and most dangerous consequence of the Democrats' filibusters of some lower court candidates is that it rewrites the Senate's constitutional obligation to give "advice and consent" on judicial nominees.

"This is really a ratcheting up, a changing of the ground rules of huge proportions that's leading us into a serious crisis," said Jeff Sessions, R-Ala., whose own bid for the U.S. District Court was rejected by the Senate Judiciary Committee in 1986.

Although the Constitution specifically enumerates that a supermajority is needed in four separate instances, such as ratifying treaties, the document — in Article II, Section 2 — does not lay out a specific vote threshold for the confirmation of federal judges.

Senate Republicans say that means the framers intended for judges to be confirmed by a simple majority.

"Just two lines above the Advice and Consent Clause in Article II is a requisite two-thirds vote for the ratification of treaties," Hatch said. "So by implication, the Advice and Consent Clause in the Constitution means an up-or-down vote."

The Constitution does not discuss arcane Senate procedure, such as filibusters and cloture votes. And Republicans draw a distinction between filibustering legislation and filibustering nominees.

"A nomination comes from the president, and we have a constitutional obligation to act on it one way or another," Kyl said. "When we present a bill to our colleagues, the president isn't involved yet, and the judicial branch isn't involved yet. That's just our intramural fight, and the rules have always recognized that.

"We clearly have had a tradition of comity with the president, and frankly with the judicial branch, in acting on nominations to fill the courts that would be violated if this filibuster number gets fixed in stone," Kyl said.

The meaning of "advice and consent," is ambiguous, said Scherer, the University of Miami professor.

"Does the Senate have a co-equal role or are they a rubber stamp?" Scherer said. "Frankly, we don't know much about this from the constitutional debates and the Federalist Papers."

Notably, the constitutional language giving the Senate the right to give advice and consent on nominees was added during the closing days of the Constitutional Convention. Initially, the framers were leaning toward a proposal from James Madison that the Senate alone have the power to appoint judges. At one point, the Senate's power was to "reject and approve" judicial nominees. Ultimately, in the final days of the convention, the framers decided to give the president the power to nominate judges, and task the Senate with giving its "advice and consent."

"When you go back and read the debates of the Constitutional Convention, you see that the framers struggled to find the right balance of power when it came to selecting judges," said New York Sen. Charles E. Schumer, a member of the Judiciary Committee and one of the most visible Democrats on this issue. "History tells us that the framers did not reach this delicate balance easily."

Senate Democrats insist the framers intended for the Senate to have an equal role in selecting judges.

"The convention, having repeatedly rejected proposals that would lodge exclusive power to select judges with the executive branch, could not possibly have intended to reduce the Senate to a rubber-stamp role," said Edward M. Kennedy, D-Mass. "The debates make clear that while the president had the power to nominate judges, the Senate still had a central role."

The partisan fights over judicial nominees threaten the Senate's comity on other unrelated issues. During the 107th Congress, the sniping over the handling of Bush's judicial nominees translated to holds on legislation advanced by Judiciary Democrats. *(2002 CQ Weekly, p. 806)*

This year, the bickering has spilled over into the Judiciary Committee, heightening partisan tensions and breaking down communication among staff members. *(2003 CQ Weekly, p. 944)*

But experts say the current judicial confirmation battles, though rancorous, do not constitute a crisis.

"The crisis would be if no justices were being confirmed, if the filibuster is kind of a blanket thing that it's not," said Elliot Slotnick, an Ohio State University political science professor who studies the selection and confirmation of federal judges. He noted that the filibuster tool is being used sparingly. "These are not like Scud missiles; they're more like smart bombs. When that changes, you've got a problem."

The Stats Favor Bush

Democrats assert that they are picking their battles. Already this year, two appellate nominees — Timothy Tymkovich, nominated for the 10th Circuit, and Jeffrey S. Sutton, tapped for the 6th — have been confirmed, despite receiving 41 "no" votes. *(Choosing fights, p. 86)*

And Bush is winning confirmation of most of his judicial nominees. So far during the 107th and 108th Congresses, the Senate has confirmed 123 of Bush's 170 nominees. The rate of vacant federal judgeships, at 5.7 percent, is the lowest in 13 years.

When Democrats took over the Senate Judiciary Committee in the summer of 2001, they note, there were more than 100 vacancies. Now, there are 47 judgeships left unfilled.

"Right now in terms of advice and consent — and this is a very unorthodox thing to say now — it's a nice shining moment for democracy, to see it out in the open, to see it being discussed, to have the Democrats holding filibusters on nominees but not holding up the works entirely," said Goldman of the University of Massachusetts. "This is government at its best, where people see what's going on; where, if you're opposed to a nominee, you've got to justify it."

Democrats have complained bitterly

that Republicans bottled up many of Clinton's nominees in the Senate Judiciary Committee. Then, nominees opposed by Republicans were disposed of quietly, without contentious votes in the Judiciary Committee or on the Senate floor. *(2002 CQ Weekly, p. 2304)*

Holding up nominees in the Judiciary Committee might have been a less public, and to some a more civilized, way of blocking their confirmation, but Democrats say the end result is the same: With either strategy, the nominee does not make it to the bench.

"Is there any meaningful constitutional difference between a filibuster on the one hand and, on the other hand, a hold on the Senate floor, or a wink and a nod between a committee chairman and a member who just doesn't like a nominee?" asked Russell D. Feingold, D-Wis.

Neither side shows any sign of surrendering ground in this newly defined battle.

Republicans have scheduled cloture vote after cloture vote on Owen and Estrada. They vow to hold regular cloture votes — there have been eight so far — as long as it takes.

By their refusal to back down on specific nominees, the administration and Senate Republicans are challenging Democrats on the issue.

"Bush, whether he's doing it deliberately or not, is testing the Democrats: 'Do you have a backbone, or are you going to fold?' " Goldman said.

The administration also has not made major shifts in the way it picks nominees for federal judgeships.

"The president has thrown the gauntlet down, saying, 'I dare you to stop me,' because his nominees continue to be more and more far right, more and more ideological," said Kate Michelman, president of NARAL Pro-Choice America, which has opposed many of Bush's nominees.

Bush is distinguishing himself from Clinton, who appears not to have placed the same priority on judicial nominees, either as a way to reward party loyalists or to ensure that a legislative agenda remains intact after court challenges.

Many judicial-selection experts say Bush's nominees are further to the right than Clinton's were to the left. When Republicans took control of the Senate two years into Clinton's eight-year presidency, the administration started advancing nominees who were slightly more conservative than the picks chosen during the first two years of his first term in office.

Where Bush has demonstrated that he will not back down from messy judicial confirmation battles — and his belief that the president has an absolute prerogative to decide who belongs in federal judgeships — Clinton appeared to avoid conflict.

"If the Clinton administration ran into opposition, they tended to fold," said Slotnick of Ohio State University. "It wasn't worth pursuing one judge at the expense of other judges going forward. This administration has a greater commitment to who they decide to choose, and once they choose them, they're sticking to them."

Supreme Debate

Clinton is generally praised for sending two consensus nominees to the Supreme Court. While far from conservative, Slotnick said, neither Ruth Bader Ginsburg nor Stephen G. Breyer was extremely liberal. Republicans also are credited with widely supporting the candidates.

Ginsburg was approved unanimously by the Senate Judiciary Committee and ultimately confirmed by a vote of 96-3 in 1993. Breyer, who also won a unanimous recommendation by the Judiciary Committee, was confirmed 87-9 in 1994. *(Ginsburg, 1993 Almanac, p. 318; Breyer, 1994 Almanac, p. 303)*

The relatively easy confirmations were soothing for the Judiciary Committee, which had gone through two tough Supreme Court confirmation fights in the previous six years — the unsuccessful nomination of Bork and Thomas' narrow approval in the face of accusations of sexual harassment of a former employee. *(1991 Almanac, p. 274)*

But no one expects the attempt to fill expected Supreme Court vacancies to be as easy as it was in 1993 and 1994.

The highly anticipated high court vacancies would be the first in nine years — the longest stretch without an opening on the Supreme Court in nearly 200 years.

But a vacancy is by no means assured. Given the political war over judicial nominees, the justices believed to be weighing retirement — Chief Justice William H. Rehnquist and Associate Justices Sandra Day O'Connor and John Paul Stevens — might decide against leaving the court this year.

In making such a calculation, the justices would have to consider whether the current bitterness surrounding the judicial confirmation process would ease with time — and whether they are comfortable rolling the dice on the outcome of the 2004 elections. All three were appointed by Republican presidents, and they may have an interest in ensuring that their successors are as well.

"Everyone is expecting Rehnquist to step down at the end of June," Goldman said. "He might see what's happening now and come to the conclusion that 'I have to wait until after 2004.' Or he might say 'It's now or never; I'm going to try it now.' "

With neither Democrats nor Republicans likely to give any ground in the fight to fill a high court opening, a vacancy could be left pending for years. If an associate justice seat were left open, it wouldn't be the first time the Supreme Court was understaffed.

But the court has always operated with a chief justice. If Rehnquist steps down and is not replaced before the Supreme Court begins its 2003-04 term in October, the panel will be entering uncharted territory. ◆

Liberals, Conservatives Both Bracing For A Supreme Court Vacancy

Lawmakers and lobbyists are doing advance work to prepare campaigns for and against Bush's potential nominees in the event of a summer retirement

Speculation about the next Supreme Court vacancy is one of Washington's most enduring parlor games. But this year, the guesswork is taking on added urgency.

Lobbyists and Capitol Hill staff are furiously preparing for the possibility that at least one — and perhaps two — justices will retire when the current Supreme Court terms ends in June.

Such an announcement would mark the high court's first vacancy in nine years — the longest period of time the court's makeup has remained constant since 1823, when 12 years elapsed between vacancies.

It also would touch off a fierce fight over the ideological balance of the nation's most powerful court — particularly if either Sandra Day O'Connor or John Paul Stevens, frequent swing votes on issues such as abortion, steps down.

Though a vacancy is far from assured, conservative and liberal lawmakers and lobbyists are making battle plans. Preparations range from mundane scheduling decisions — some congressional staff have canceled August vacations — to hashing out political and procedural tactics.

Both sides are looking to the Democrats' recent successful filibusters against appeals court candidates Miguel A. Estrada and Priscilla Owen as a blueprint for any fight over a Supreme Court nominee. *(2003 CQ Weekly, p. 1034)*

The preparations for a Supreme Court vacancy — and the rumors spreading that there will be one soon — have been intensifying all year.

Chief Justice William H. Rehnquist, 78, and Associate Justices O'Connor, 73, and Stevens, 83, are viewed as the most likely to retire, in part because all three were Republican nominees and have a presumed interest in ensuring that their successor is selected by a Republican president. Rehnquist and O'Connor also have had health ailments.

This line of reasoning also holds that justices who do not step down after the term ends in June are effectively volunteering for another two years on the high court and gambling that President Bush will be re-elected. Because next year is an election year, when presidents have historically done poorly filling Supreme Court vacancies, politically astute justices presumably will not retire.

BLOOMBERG NEWS PHOTO/ DAVID SCULL

Rehnquist is one of three high court justices rumored to be pondering retirement.

The Rumors

Washington has buzzed with similar rumors before. "We went through this last year in May — everyone got agitated and in a lather, and then nothing happened," said Richard Lessner, executive director of American Renewal, the grass-roots lobbying arm of the conservative Family Research Council.

But the current speculation is more intense, whatever the cause: battles over Bush's judicial nominees, the age of the justices in question, the long interval since the last vacancy, or some combination of those factors.

"The stars seem to be aligned in a way that makes [a retirement] a lot more likely," said Louis Bograd, legal director of the Alliance for Justice, a coalition of liberal advocacy groups.

The rumor mill is particularly busy this year "partly because it has been so long. It's just a very long time for one group to be together on the Supreme Court, which makes it something that is a very significant possibility," said Elliot Mincberg, legal director for the liberal-leaning People For The American Way. "And the stakes are so incredibly high, because the Supreme Court is closely divided on so many issues that are so important to our future."

"No one knows what will happen, with the exception of nine people, for sure, and even some of those nine may not know," Mincberg said. "But I think in light of how long it has been since there was a Supreme Court vacancy, we do feel it's important to at least anticipate the possibility and to alert our members to that possibility — that it's something they need to be concerned about."

Groups that have opposed many of Bush's judicial nominees, such as the Alliance for Justice and People For The American Way, are researching the records of potential Supreme Court nominees and formulating campaigns against those they perceive as outside the mainstream. Some oft-mentioned potential nominees include J. Harvie Wilkinson III, chief justice of the 4th Circuit Court of Appeals in Richmond, Va.; J. Michael Luttig, a judge on the 4th Circuit; and White House counsel Alberto Gonzales.

"We have read the same articles everyone else has about who the likely nominees are, and we are doing as much research as we can on those nominees," Bograd said. "We want to know as much as we can about who they are."

Researchers are focusing on rulings issued by potential candidates who currently are judges, or cases argued by candidates who are practicing attorneys.

"The other thing we're trying to do is collect as much paper on those most likely nominees as possible, including any law review articles they've written, and if they've previously had a confirmation hearing, the old transcripts," Bograd said. "Even if we don't have

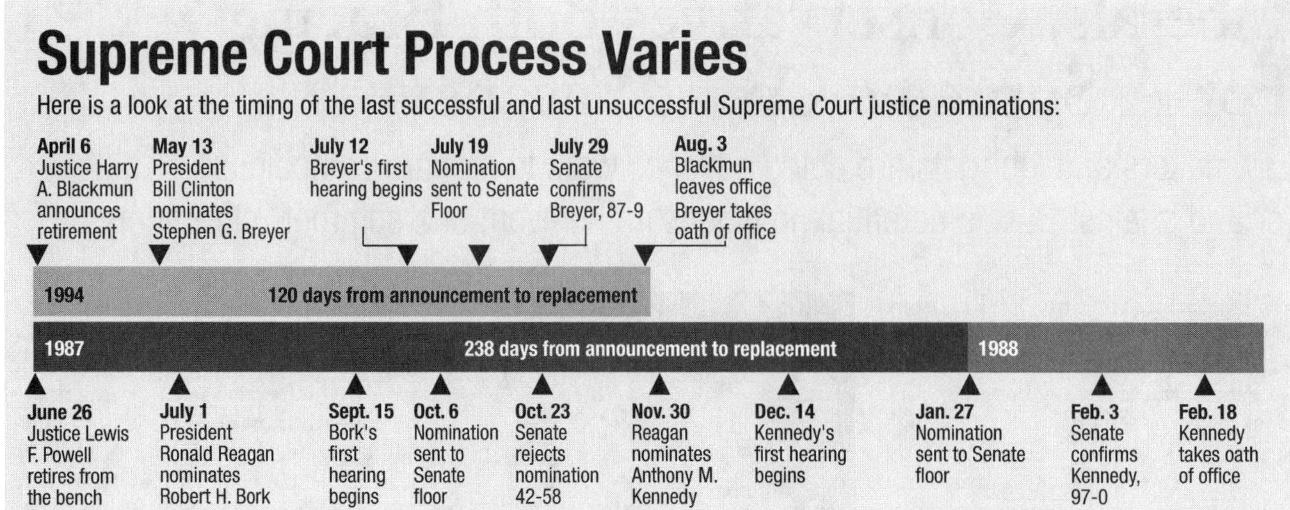

time to fully analyze and evaluate the less significant parts of the record, we want to have it so that if they should be nominated, we don't have to spend a lot of time tracking it down."

Liberal groups are mobilizing supporters in anticipation of a confirmation fight. The Democratic National Committee has undertaken one visible effort, aware that battles over judicial nominees are a potent way of mobilizing party bases. The DNC has launched a "Supreme Court Countdown" section on its Web site where supporters can donate money, sign a petition, and learn how to start their own "Supreme Court Action Team" to help "defeat President Bush's ultraconservative nominees."

Conservatives Mobilize

Conservatives also are expecting a vacancy and a confirmation battle. Some are motivated by a nagging sense that they have been outmaneuvered by media-savvy liberal groups in past battles over the judiciary.

"For folks on the right, there's a real inferiority complex on the issue. There's a sense that the folks on the left have mastered this and that those groups are really tough and well-funded," said a lobbyist with a conservative organization, who asked not to be identified.

Groups such as the Concerned Women for America say they are preparing to publicly refute anticipated Democratic criticisms of any Bush Supreme Court nominee. Democrats have charged that Estrada, Owen and some of Bush's other lower-court nominees are too conservative and represent views that are out of the mainstream.

Conservative activists will play the role of a "truth squad," said Mike Schwartz, a lobbyist with the Concerned Women for America.

"We'll be following Ralph Neas around with the rest of the story," Schwartz said, referring to the president of People For The American Way.

"Our big-picture goal . . . is saying the things that the White House and the Senate staff can't say," the conservative lobbyist said. "If the other side is flinging mud, the White House and the Senate staff can't do that. But we can."

Conservatives expect the White House to nominate reliably right-leaning jurists, who will not deviate on such bedrock issues as abortion and civil rights. They are mindful that Bush's father, President George Bush, nominated David H. Souter, an associate justice who has shown an independent streak that rankles many on the political right. Any such move would probably trigger fierce Democratic opposition.

Current Battles a Dry Run

Both sides in the debate over Bush's judicial nominees acknowledge that the current struggles to confirm nominees to the U.S. Court of Appeals — particularly the battle over appellate candidates Owen and Estrada — will serve as a guide for any fight over a Supreme Court vacancy.

With the successful filibusters of Owen and Estrada, Senate Democrats sent the White House a message about their ability to block judicial nominees they found particularly objectionable. *(2003 CQ Weekly, p. 556)*

"We've been laying the groundwork for the Supreme Court fight," said Nancy Zirkin, a lobbyist with the Leadership Conference on Civil Rights.

The filibusters have frustrated Republicans in the Senate, where Majority Leader Bill Frist, R-Tenn., has proposed changing chamber rules to minimize the ability of a minority party to filibuster executive branch nominations. The Senate Rules and Administration Committee will consider the proposal the week of June 2.

But the filibusters also have energized the GOP base — and helped motivate loyalists to fight for any conservative Supreme Court nominee, said Sean Rushton, executive director of the Committee for Justice, a group that lobbies for Bush's judicial nominees. "They won't need three months of getting up to speed time when we hit the big fight," Rushton said.

Even so, the process of filling a vacancy on the Supreme Court is certain to be lengthy. Senate Judiciary Committee Chairman Orrin G. Hatch, R-Utah, has said preparing for confirmation hearings could take two months.

Likewise, the hearings themselves are sure to be protracted, though five of the past six Supreme Court nominees spent less than a week being questioned by the Judiciary panel.

Liberal lobbyists are bracing for the possibility that Hatch will fast-track hearings by holding them during the August recess, which might undermine opposition efforts.

"I think there's a lot of concern that Republicans, led by Sen. Hatch, will push for hearings much more quickly than [usually is the case]," Mincberg said. "The tradition is to have the summer to prepare and have hearings in early September, and we think that is very important." ◆

Politics and Public Policy

The term *public policymaking* refers to action taken by the government to address issues on the public agenda; it also refers to the method by which a decision to act on policy is reached. The work of the president, Congress, the judiciary and the bureaucracy is to make, implement and rule on policy decisions. Articles in this section discuss major policy issues that came before the federal government in the first half of 2003.

The first article investigates what Congress is doing to combat spam, the flood of unsolicited bulk e-mail that clogs most Americans' electronic in-boxes. Internet service providers are pushing for legislation, saying one federal standard would be preferable to the 30 state anti-spam statutes that have been passed so far. But even companies that are urging Congress to act this year doubt that any law will have much effect. A federal anti-spam law might just drive spammers overseas and possibly make the problem worse. Legislative action is widely expected this year, but lawmakers are far from consensus.

Congress is readily aware that doctors are paying huge sums for malpractice insurance, but, as the second article in this section explains, legislators disagree whether a federal law is the solution. Republicans generally favor limiting legal liability for doctors by placing caps on jury awards, while Democrats fear that such legislative action could open the door to a larger debate over tort reform. Although Congress is unsure how or if a compromise can be forged, it agrees that confronting the medical malpractice issue is a priority.

The third article explores the multiple decisions that Congress faces in revamping Medicare. In March 2003, President Bush offered broad outlines for overhauling Medicare and asked Congress to handle the details. But Congress first must resolve a central question that Bush's outline raises: If seniors can choose between a government-run plan and a private insurance provider that is likely to offer better benefits, is that arrangement in keeping with the Medicare mission of equality for every senior?

The fourth article addresses Congress' recent debates over energy legislation. Bush's energy plan, first proposed in 2001, is focused primarily on raising domestic energy production, with oil exploration in Alaska's Arctic National Wildlife Refuge as the centerpiece of that strategy. However, the Senate voted by a narrow margin against allowing oil exploration in ANWR, thus making it unlikely that the proposal will be part of the broader energy debate in 2003.

As frequent fliers and champions of an industry that often employs significant portions of their constituencies, members of Congress want to help the airlines survive a recession. The final article in this section examines why that close relationship is becoming strained, now that the help means bailout money to protect the nation's largest airlines from financial ruin rather than airport expansion money to keep traffic moving.

Is 'There Oughta Be a Law' A Real Answer to 'Spam'?

Glut of unwanted e-mail has millions angry and Congress determined to step in

Burns, author of one of the anti-spam bills Congress will consider this year, figures he receives about 100 unsolicited e-mail pitches a day — everything from auto loans to mortgage advice and, of course, pornography. He calls the electronic onslaught a "toxic sea."

When Virginia Democratic Gov. Mark Warner signed his state's tough new law against "spam" at the end of April, he did so at the suburban headquarters of America Online Inc., which had lobbied for the statute, helped to draft it and planned to make the most of it.

"It's high noon for junk mailers," AOL Vice Chairman Ted Leonsis declared at the signing ceremony, "and it's time to let law enforcement take them from behind their computer screens and put them behind bars."

That's tough talk for an industry that for years has held government at arm's length and put its faith in technology to police the Internet and protect its commercial potential.

But the flood of unsolicited bulk e-mail — nearly half of all traffic by some estimates, and growing exponentially — has swept away that self-assurance.

Computer users are fed up with a seemingly endless inbox of ads such as: "Sleep away pounds for a healthier body," or "RE: I will cheat on my husband with you" — all part of what Sen. Conrad Burns, R-Mont., calls a "toxic sea of spam."

Some government agencies and members of Congress have even pulled the plug on their usual e-mail systems in favor of electronic form letters for constituents to fill out.

The cost of storing and processing spam on computer servers has driven Internet service providers such as AOL — which blocks up to 2.4 billion pieces of spam a day on its networks — and software giant Microsoft Corp. to cooperate in seeking state and congressional help. Some analysts worry that the Internet itself, though designed to withstand a nuclear attack because it is so decentralized, could succumb to a relative handful of artful spammers.

Federal Trade Commissioner Orson Swindle told the Senate Commerce, Science and Transportation Committee on May 21: "I am concerned that spam is about to kill the 'killer app' of the Internet, specifically, consumer use of e-mail. . . . I am not convinced industry has made the commitment" to stop it.

The anger and frustration of computer users and companies has built to a critical mass on Capitol Hill, where legislative action is widely expected this year.

"It's time to get going, folks," Oregon Democrat Ron Wyden told colleagues at the May 21 Senate hearing on spam. "We've always had a lot of arguments that now wasn't the time for congressional action. People said spam legislation would stunt the growth of e-commerce. . . . But we absolutely have to have a strong, enforceable national law."

Six bills are circulating, and more are expected, but lawmakers are far from consensus — an example of the difficulty Congress has in trying to regulate the Internet. Lawmakers have not reached agreement on taxing Internet commerce, for instance, or on regulating or banning Internet gambling. *(2003 CQ Weekly, p. 1267; p. 1266)*

To control or eradicate spam, Congress would first have to define it. What, for instance, is the difference between unsolicited e-mail sent by an established department store chain and those sent by a computer hacker in central Asia? Even in Congress, a constituent lobbying letter could be legitimate government business to one person but spam to another.

"I don't think there will ever be a 100 percent solution," said Rep. Zoe Lofgren, D-Calif., who represents Silicon Valley and has her own anti-spam bill (HR 1933).

If a federal law is enacted this year, it could supersede the 30 state anti-spam statutes passed so far, most of them to little effect. Delaware banned unsolicited bulk commercial e-mails to its residents nearly four years ago, for instance, but no one has yet been charged with a crime.

Internet service providers, forced to navigate this thicket of state civil and criminal laws, would prefer a federal statute.

"A big piece of what's driving this is the state laws," said Ari Schwartz, associate director of the Center for Democracy and Technology, a civil liberties group in Washington. "The individual states having different standards have driven companies to ask for a national standard."

Laws May Not Rein In Spammers

Several anti-spam bills have been introduced and most share a common goal of forcing bulk e-mailers to identify themselves. But experts in law and technology say each of the proposals carries a fundamental flaw that might hinder its effectiveness. House chairmen Billy Tauzin, R-La., of Energy and Commerce, and F. James Sensenbrenner Jr., R-Wis., of Judiciary, along with Richard M. Burr, R-N.C., have introduced the most recent measure.

BILL	WORKAROUNDS
S 877 Sponsored by Sens. Conrad Burns, R-Mont., and Ron Wyden, D-Ore. Would outlaw false and deceptive subject lines in unsolicited e-mails and require legitimate return addresses, as well as opt-out alternatives for future pitches. Would impose fines and up to one year in prison.	Enforcing a legitimate return address rule may be impossible as technology allows astute spammers to create mirage accounts with ease.
HR 1933 Sponsored by Rep. Zoe Lofgren, D-Calif. Would outlaw false and deceptive subject lines, require labeling e-mails for advertising and adult advertising, require legitimate return addresses and the opt-out alternative. Would impose fines and up to a year in prison on violators; the first to identify them could receive a bounty.	Like the return address requirement, enforcing a labeling law would be difficult and has not worked in California and other states. Also, managing a system that encourages e-mail users to report spam violators with the lure of a bounty would be an enormous, and likely expensive, task.
S 563 Sponsored by Sen. Mark Dayton, D-Minn. Would create a "Do Not Spam" database through the Federal Trade Commission where people could register their e-mail addresses. Would impose fines.	Legitimate marketers would honor the registry, but shadowy spammers might plunder the centralized list of e-mail addresses.
HR 122 Sponsored by Rep. Rush D. Holt, D-N.J. Would prohibit sending unsolicited e-mails to wireless phones.	The same legislative limitations apply to spam sent to any digital device.
HR2214 Sponsored by Reps. Richard M. Burr, R-N.C.; Billy Tauzin, R-La., and F. James Sensenbrenner Jr., R-Wis. Would prohibit false and deceptive subject headers and routing and would require spammers to have a valid return address. Contains opt-out provisions and would outlaw harvesting of e-mail addresses.	Each opt-out would be good for three years, after which a spammer could try the address again. Class action lawsuits against spammers would be prohibited.

Targeting the Bad Guys

The Virginia law has fines and prison terms of up to five years for bulk mailers who persist in concealing their identities or falsifying mail routing data, and AOL hopes to use it against spammers across the country who send mail through its computer servers in Northern Virginia.

What AOL and other major companies want from Congress more than anything else is tough sanctions against the most egregious bulk mailers. Many Internet analysts say that a relatively small number of people — 150 to 250 — are responsible for 90 percent of the world's spam. But the estimates are as elusive as the spam itself, and as difficult to trace. Some spam even appears as though it was sent by the person receiving it, or that of a co-worker.

The growth and persistence of spam has even led the Direct Marketing Association, which in the past has opposed legislation on Internet marketing, to get behind a bill to control spam. The group worries that all Internet solicita-

Capitol Takes Cautious Approach To Filtering Lawmakers' E-Mail

In the mid-1990s, Rep. Vernon J. Ehlers was recruited by Speaker Newt Gingrich, R-Ga. (1979-99) to help House members make better use of the Internet, which was just then coming into its own.

But this January, Michigan Republican Ehlers, a veteran research scientist and resident expert on e-mail, pulled the plug on his own electronic address, in a manner of speaking.

Anybody who wants to send an e-mail to Ehlers' office now must go through a centralized House system known as "Write Your Rep."

It requires a writer to fill in his name, address and ZIP code, then routes the message to a single member's office.

Some state and local officials have adopted similar systems.

The change has drastically curtailed the 150 unwanted e-mails a day that Ehlers' office had been receiving. But it is debatable whether the messages were "spam" in the first place.

Most were mass electronic mailings from interest groups, organized writing campaigns about such issues as the North American Free Trade Agreement, or letters from individuals who lived outside Ehlers' Michigan district.

Many senders "are actually writing their congressmen and sending copies to everyone else," he said. "That's not really spam so much as ignoring the fact that congressmen don't tend to respond to people who are outside their district."

As Congress considers legislation enacting laws to regulate unwanted e-mail, it will find that defining exactly what spam is can be a political minefield.

For instance, could a grass-roots organization be prohibited from sending out 20 million e-mails about a civil rights issue?

"There are some real questions of constitutionality — what limits you can put on people, particularly if they're not trying to sell products but are sending out information," Ehlers said.

Wait for Complaints

Administrators of the e-mail networks in the House and Senate — each has its own system — are grappling with that question as well. While they are aggressive about protecting the networks from computer viruses and hackers, technicians take a more light-handed approach when it comes to spam.

Senate technicians will try to block specific messages such as pornographic advertisements, but only after receiving a complaint from a senator's office.

"We're not in the habit of monitoring individual office e-mails," said a Senate aide. "One office will think one thing is spam, and another will say, 'No, that's not spam.' "

The Senate's network, which serves more than 7,000 e-mail addresses, does not use anti-spam software. If individual offices want a spam filter, they must install it on their own.

"There is software out there that can do a better job of filtering spam," the staffer said. "But it's not perfect either. A lot of those packages will actually filter out e-mail that is valid."

The House's e-mail network, which serves about 12,000 addresses, also does not use anti-spam software. The main objectives, a staff member said, are to provide constituents with simple e-mail access to lawmakers and protect network security.

Despite the limited protection, aides say lawmakers in both chambers have not been overwhelmed by the flood of commercial e-mail that has outraged many of their constituents.

"A lot [of spam] has to do with individual surfing habits and browser settings," said the House staffer.

Ehlers said that dedicated spammers will continue to find ways around electronic roadblocks.

"I think they're doing a great disservice to a very fine meat product by calling it spam," he quipped. "I don't know where that came from. When we first got it, it wasn't called spam. It was just a bother."

SPECIAL PHOTO / REP. VERNON J. EHLERS

Ehlers, who used a Powerpoint presentation during budget testimony in 2002, has switched his e-mail to a more restrictive system because of unsolicited messages.

tions are being condemned as spam, hurting legitimate marketers.

"We thought we could find some sort of silver bullet to kill spam, but over the years we have decided there is no silver bullet," said Louis Mastria, a spokesman for the direct marketers group. "Now we are pushing for federal legislation. We're working to see what we can do to offer up spammers on a silver platter."

Critics say the direct marketers group has had too much influence over anti-spam legislation (HR 2214) introduced by House Energy and Commerce Committee Chairman Billy Tauzin, R-La., Judiciary Committee Chairman F. James Sensenbrenner Jr., R-Wis., and Richard M. Burr, R-N.C.

The bill would outlaw false or misleading e-mail routing headers and give recipients the chance to opt out of future e-mails. But the consumer's opt-out request would expire after three years. The bill also would not allow individuals to file class-action lawsuits against spammers.

There is more progress in the Senate, where Wyden and Burns have sponsored a similar bill (S 877) that has broad support and is expected to reach the floor by summer. It would ban deceptive e-mail and require marketers to allow recipients to opt out of future mail.

But each of those is controversial, as are other proposed measures — particularly in how they define spam and how they would enforce sanctions.

Even some of those urging Congress to act this year doubt that any law will have much effect on spam. Its producers are too cagey, able to rapidly adjust their mail to avoid spam filters and legal restraints. Many already operate overseas, from the Caribbean to Kazakhstan, and have an uncanny ability to morph their identities and remain on the fringes of the Internet and out of reach of any U.S. law.

Ronald Scelson, a self-described spammer from Slidell, La., told the Senate Commerce Committee on May 21 that he prepares 120 million to 180 million e-mails a day for distribution and can easily crack sophisticated filtering software.

"If you pass these laws," he said, "we will go outside the U.S."

"It's time to let law enforcement take [spammers] from behind their computer screens and put them behind bars."

— Ted Leonsis, AOL vice chairman

"If you pass these laws we will go outside the U.S."

— Ronald Scelson, self-described spammer

The Wild Web

The Internet's attraction for users and spammers alike is that it is essentially limitless, unregulated and all but free. There are no stamps to buy, parcels to weigh or paper to print. Rent a connection to a computer network and send pretty much what you want, as often as you want and to as many people as you like, whether you know them or not.

It is this repetitiveness that earned spam its name, not any resemblance to the Hormel luncheon meat called SPAM. In a 1970 sketch by the British comedy group Monty Python, about a restaurant that serves SPAM with all its dishes, a background chorus of Vikings singing "SPAM SPAM SPAM SPAM. Lovely SPAM! Wonderful SPAM!" nearly drowns out conversation. Spam seeped into Internet culture as a catch phrase for oppressive, repetitive messages.

In its early days, spam was considered a quirk of the Internet's free-wheeling nature — ads for Russian brides or Nigerian money schemes. But like an ornamental vine that takes over the yard and then the house, spam has become a problem for nearly everyone, including members of Congress.

Burns, like many of his colleagues in the Senate and House, is tethered to his e-mail as a way to stay connected to his home state of Montana and keep track of staff memos and the concerns of constituents. *(Congress, p. 96)*

But judging from the senator's e-mail in-box, constituent letters are in danger of being swallowed up in a sea of spam. Burns estimates he gets about 100 unsolicited e-mail pitches a day, for everything from auto loans to mortgage advice, and of course pornography.

Anyone with a Yahoo! or Hotmail address is all too familiar with the problem. Some users find their accounts full of spam before they send their first message. Although some spammer programs collect addresses from Internet Web sites, others simply guess at possible combinations of log-on names and send mail blindly.

A survey by San Francisco-based Brightmail, which sells spam filtering software to businesses, recently showed that 22 billion of the 55 billion e-mails its software filtered were spam. Brightmail software now processes about 10 percent of the country's e-mail, according to the company. Just two years ago spam accounted for only 8 percent of all e-mail.

"By September it could be over 50 percent," Brightmail CEO Enrique Salem said. "We do need federal legislation. It may not stop spam, but it will reduce it."

At AOL, the world's largest Internet service provider, a team of specialists is engaged in a constant war with major spammers on the AOL network, trying to get a handle on between 1.2 billion and 2.4 billion spam messages a day that the company's system handles, said Joe Barrett, senior vice president of systems operations. The company receives 10 million complaints a day from its users about spam.

A Federal Trade Commission study of 1,000 spam emails found nearly 66 percent that "appeared to contain at least one form of deception."

This volume of junk mail creates expenses for all companies, even if it is the time employees spend hitting the delete key on their computers. For Internet companies, it is a major expense. Earthlink, which has had a 500 percent increase in spam in the past 18 months, spends between $10 million and $15 million a year in anti-spam efforts, including technology and personnel to track the problem, according to Dave Baker, vice president of law and public policy for the company.

Ferris Research Inc., a San Francisco-based market and technology research firm specializing in digital communications, estimates that spam will cost U.S. corporations $10 billion in 2003. Such statistics may prove to be a turning point in the debate over spam legislation before Congress.

Prohibitions on Mass Mailings

Mass mailings in any form are hard for governments to regulate, and digital duplication is proving particularly difficult because computers can reproduce and transmit hundreds of millions of identical copies at light speed. Here are the restrictions on e-mail spam and its predecessors.

JUNK MAIL

There is little regulation, but the volume is self-limited by postal rates. Fraudulent or obscene advertising is subject to Federal Trade Commission and U.S. Postal Service regulations.

JUNK FAX

The 1991 Telephone Consumer Protection Act (PL 102-243) prohibits the sending of unsolicited faxes. The law has survived multiple challenges in federal courts, most recently in March. More court challenges are expected.

TELEPHONE SOLICITATIONS

Starting July 1, anyone in the United States will be able to register over the Internet or by phone to be placed on a Federal Trade Commission "do not call" registry that telemarketers must honor. The commission plans to begin enforcing the rule in October. Violators will be subject to a fine of up to $11,000 per call. Political candidates and groups, polling firms, banks, long distance phone companies and airlines are exempted. The rule is under challenge by direct marketers and life insurance companies in federal courts in Colorado, Oklahoma and the District of Columbia.

E-MAIL SPAM

Since 1997, 31 states have enacted laws targeting fraudulent spam. Virginia has the toughest punishment, up to five years in prison for persistent offenders. Delaware's law is the most far-reaching, essentially prohibiting unsolicited commercial email.

SOURCES: The Media Institute, The First Amendment Center, Federal Trade Commission

Searching for Weapons

As the spam war escalates, an arms race of sorts has emerged, as Internet and e-mail providers constantly try to develop new filters and other technical solutions to outwit spammers. The bulk e-mailers, meanwhile, are known for constantly changing their identities, deceptively routing e-mails and co-opting overseas computer servers so messages cannot be traced to the sender. Some spammers have begun to omit sexual or sales-related terms from e-mails so they do not get flagged by corporate spam filters.

In the battle for technical solutions, Earthlink this month plans to release a program called "spamblocker," which automatically bounces the first e-mail to a recipient back to the sender, asking the sender to verify that he is a real person. This "challenge response" system then recognizes that the sender is a legitimate person from whom the recipient is willing to receive e-mails.

If the sender does not respond using certain visual cues indicated in the bounce-back e-mail, his address can be blocked.

"We have 12 full-time people devoted to this" spam problem, Baker said. "Spam is everywhere. It's not like if you leave Earthlink you'll get less spam elsewhere."

Lobbyists, lawmakers and technologists all say that such technical solutions are no longer enough, calling for legislation that gives the Federal Trade Commission, U.S. attorneys and Internet service providers the legal tools to punish and sue major spam producers.

"We are at a tipping point, where something has to be done about spam before the medium of e-mail as a communications and commerce tool is destroyed," said Brian Huseman, a staff attorney at the Federal Trade Commission who specializes in spam.

But there is a deepening divide over how far legislation should go, what techniques should be used to stop spam and how the laws would be enforced. Then there is the fundamental question of whether anti-spam measures will be anything more than feel-good legislation.

"There is no one bill that's going to cure the spam problem," said Earthlink's Baker. "We need to fight spam on several fronts. Legislation is just one front."

Mixed Success

In the short history of the Internet, Congress has had mixed success grappling with the societal and business problems that have emerged with the technology.

Previous laws, such as the copyright protections of the 1998 Digital Millennium Copyright Act (PL 105-304), have proved to be difficult to enforce over the years and have been challenged in courts. Spam laws may be even harder to enforce. *(1998 Almanac, p. 22-3)*

When Internet use first hit the mainstream in the mid-1990s, many in the tech industry and in Congress took a more libertarian approach, assiduously avoiding taxing or regulating anything that had to do with the new medium.

Since then, Congress has had limited experience in regulating aspects of the Internet. The copyright act was an attempt to protect copyright holders from having their works pirated and distributed electronically. That law was used as a vehicle to sue and eventually shut down the music-trad-

The Fight to Slam Spam

Spam is everywhere. And it could soon become the majority of Internet e-mail traffic. It is costly and hard to stop even with the best technology. Spammers have so far been able to skirt state laws and corporate spam filters, and now many in Congress believe a national law could help. Critics say otherwise.

Spam as a Percentage of all Internet E-mails

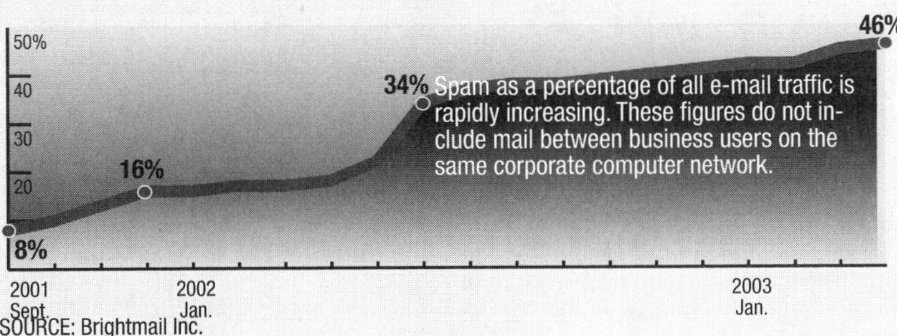

SOURCE: Brightmail Inc.

The Cost of Spam

Corporations and Internet service providers bear most of the cost created by spam. Where the costs are:

CORPORATE WORKERS (costs per month)	
Lost productivity	$4.51
IT resources	4.13
Help desk cost	1.25
TOTAL	**$9.89**

(NOTE: For a firm with 500 employees, the cost of dealing with spam would be nearer to $60,000 per year)

ISP (costs per subscriber per month)	
Lost revenue from subscriber defections	3 cents
Help desk costs	6 cents
IT resources	5 cents
TOTAL	**14 cents**

(NOTE: For an ISP with 1 million subscribers, costs of spam total nearly $1.7 million per year)

SOURCE: Ferris Analyzer Information Service

Types of Spam Sent

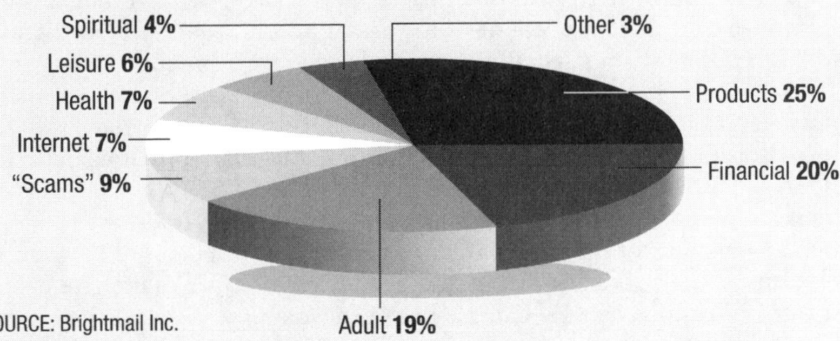

SOURCE: Brightmail Inc.

How Spammers Get Their Target E-mail Addresses

While there are many ways for companies or individuals to collect e-mail addresses, three are employed by large-scale spam operations:

DICTIONARY ATTACK: Program sends out millions of e-mails to every possible letter-number combination at large-scale servers. For instance: jdoe @ Yahoo.com; jdoe1 @ Yahoo.com; jdoe3 @ Yahoo.com; etc.

SCRAPING OR HARVESTING: Automated "robot" programs crawl the worldwide network picking up any and all e-mail addresses they find at Web sites or chat rooms.

PURCHASE: E-mail lists are readily available from companies and sites throughout the Internet world. And the addresses are cheap. According to one news account, 100 million addresses can be purchased for $100.

SOURCE: CQ research

ing service Napster, but it has not been able to stop the next generation of music-swapping services such as Morpheus and Kazaa, which are more decentralized.

Congress also tried unsuccessfully to regulate Internet pornography with the Communications Decency Act, part of the telecommunications overhaul of 1996 (PL 104-104). The decency act was overturned in 1997 by the Supreme Court, which said the law was too broad and covered too wide a range of adult content. *(Law, 1996 Almanac, p. 3-43; court decision, 1997 Almanac, p. 5-25)*

The Child Online Protection Act (PL 105-277), designed to protect children from adult content, was overturned earlier this year by the 3rd U.S. Circuit Court of Appeals in Philadelphia. *(2002 CQ Weekly, p. 3031)*

Congress has had more success in regulating other modern communications. The 1991 Telephone Consumer Protection Act (PL 102-243) banned telemarketing to cellular phones and all but stopped junk faxes. *(1991 Almanac, p. 163)*

None of the spam legislation being considered this year would be as restrictive as the junk fax and wireless phone rules, which outright prohibited solicitations rather than allowing consumers to opt out.

The bill sponsored by Burns and Wyden is meant to separate legitimate e-mail marketers from the pornographers and pharmaceutical peddlers.

"It's going to be hard to write a law that's one-size-fits-all," Burns said in an interview. "But if we don't do this, it's going to be harder to keep this as a free and open service."

Lofgren's bill would put a bounty on spammers and require bulk e-mailers to label their messages as advertisements or as "adult" content. Sen. Charles E. Schumer, D-N.Y., meanwhile, hopes to replicate the recently implemented no-call list for telemarketers with a national no-spam list. Members of the public who put their names on the list could not legally be solicited.

The House Republican bill introduced by Tauzin, Sensenbrenner and Burr would impose fines and prison terms on spammers who did not take people off lists when they requested to opt out of mass e-mailings.

The backing of two influential House chairmen almost guarantees that this bill will reach the floor.

The problems with passing such legislation lie in the technical details and the practicality of enforcement. As the states that have passed anti-spam laws have found out, they can be difficult or impossible to enforce.

Even if the 108th Congress is poised to pass the first-ever national anti-spam law, experts say any legislation needs to be accompanied by litigation, technical solutions, consumer education and funding for federal agencies to enforce the laws.

"They [Congress] are deluding their constituents if they're saying they can kick this," said the direct marketers' spokesman, Mastria. "This can't be legislated away. . . . This problem comes from all over the world."

Across Party Lines

Whether there should be some anti-spam legislation is not a partisan issue, and in the corporate world traditional foes such as the direct marketing group and Internet service providers have been working together to some extent.

However, the divisions emerge in the details. Nearly every legislative idea, critics say, has flaws that spammers would be able to exploit once it was enacted.

Tauzin's bill is similar to the one proposed by Burns and Wyden in the Senate in that it relies on an opt-out rule, meaning spammers must honor customer requests to be taken off the spam list.

However, opting out gives the entire universe of spammers one shot at virtually every e-mail user before they ask to be excluded from the list. And the list can keep changing.

The Tauzin-Sensenbrenner and Burns-Wyden proposals both call for prison terms and fines of $500,000 to $1.5 million for violators, and would require a valid return address for all e-mail solicitations, a move the lawmakers believe would separate legitimate marketers from the frauds.

Critics raise a red flag on the Tauzin legislation because it is supported by the Direct Marketing Association. In essence, Tauzin's legislation would allow spam if it came from legitimate businesses, critics say.

"The underlying problem here is marketers want to legitimize spam," said Chris Hoofnagle, an attorney with the Electronic Privacy Information Center, a public interest research center in Washington.

"To the recipient there is no difference between a legitimate and illegitimate sender," he said. "At the end of the day, consumers will have no protections."

Other legislative ideas pending in Congress also have potential weaknesses, critics say. Lofgren's idea of forcing spammers to carry an "ADV" label may work with reputable marketers, but spammers are not likely to follow such rules, said Jason Catlett, president of the anti-spam advocacy group Junkbusters.

"It would be better to do nothing than to pass a weak law," Catlett said.

Schumer's concept of a "no spam" list modeled after the anti-telemarketing "no call" lists is another potentially popular legislative concept. But technology experts say such a list would create a huge database with tens of million of e-mail addresses, which would have to be maintained, monitored and secured by the Federal Trade Commission.

The FTC is skeptical that such a no-spam list could work, given that one out of every three e-mail users changes his electronic address every year. There are also security concerns. "Would the list be a source of new-e-mail [addresses] for spammers?" the FTC's Huseman asked.

The other big question mark in writing spam legislation is dealing with foreign spammers.

Whether it is a pitch from an African benefactor with millions he needs to transfer to your account or a Caribbean online casino operator who wants you to play blackjack, such spam is difficult to trace and would be difficult to banish using any U.S. laws.

John R. Patrick, a former vice president of Internet technology at IBM and a founding member of the World Wide Web Consortium at the Massachusetts Institute of Technology, said Congress will not be able to write spam legislation that cuts across international borders.

"It's not that legislation is bad, it just won't work," said Patrick, author of "Net Attitude," a book of advice for tailoring companies to the Internet culture.

"We're dealing with a global issue, and a U.S. law isn't going to solve the problem," Patrick said. "The spammer in Tajikistan doesn't really care about the laws that you pass in America."

Tough to Pin Down

Even the entry-level question of what is and is not spam is sure to set off debate in Congress this year. While the definition may seem obvious in most cases — pornography and get-rich-quick offers are clearly spam to most people — there is a gray area for legitimate marketers and mass e-mailers.

For example, Lofgren says her neighborhood association newsletter goes to more than 500 people. Is that an unsolicited e-mail if a homeowner has not signed up for it? Are public advocacy groups who send mass e-mails to Congress supporting certain positions on bills considered spammers or legitimate lobbyists?

Tauzin is seeking to allow unsolicited e-mails from sources with which the user has a pre-existing relationship. If a person bought a book from Amazon.com, for example, that would serve as a basis for a business relationship, and Amazon would be allowed to send e-mail offers unless the buyer opted out at the beginning.

However, even defining what constitutes a pre-existing relationship could be difficult. Under Tauzin's bill, if a Web surfer requested information on a Web site but did not purchase anything, that could be considered a pre-existing relationship, opening the door to spam.

One expert said that allowing the marketing industry to have input on legislative language is a bad precedent.

"A lot of mainstream marketers would like to see spam go away, because they want to send their own spam," said David E. Sorkin, a law professor at John Marshall Law School in Chicago who specializes in Internet and privacy law. "Some of the bigger marketers are generally embracing forms of legislation that would only focus on fraud."

Sorkin warns that laws that essentially allow legitimate marketers to send spam could make the problem even worse.

Regardless of the criticisms of the anti-spam bills, Tauzin and Sensenbrenner, along with Burns and Wyden in the Senate, are likely to see their bills marked up and sent to the chambers' floors in some form.

"We believe this will be the strongest bill to date," said Ken Johnson, a spokesman for the Energy and Commerce Committee.

Lofgren, whose measure may be overshadowed by Tauzin's, is taking a more realistic approach.

"All of us are a little in the dark on this," she said. "We're just making our best guess." ◆

For First Time, Fighting Odds For Malpractice Awards Cap

Reform proponents buoyed by doctors' walkouts, GOP control of Congress

The image is compelling: doctors carrying picket signs instead of stethoscopes. In a handful of states recently, physicians staged walkouts to protest the latest rise in malpractice insurance premiums, which they say are driving them out of business and leaving vulnerable patients without health care.

For congressional Republicans, this picture is both dire and helpful. As longtime advocates of legislation that would cap jury awards of all kinds, they say the spectacle of physicians threatening to leave their profession over malpractice insurance costs graphically illustrates what is at stake for a society whose court system offers unlimited financial opportunities for even the most suspect arguments.

Democrats, though, see a different problem in a different picture. For them, what is at stake is crystallized in the image of 17-year-old Jesica Santillan, the organ transplant patient from Mexico who died Feb. 22 after doctors at Duke University Medical Center mistakenly gave her a heart and lung transplant of an incompatible blood type. Congressional Democrats see the courts, and their potential for hefty jury awards, as a necessary check on the power of wealth, a place for the weak to teach a lesson to the strong, and a way to maintain accountability from health care providers and insurance companies.

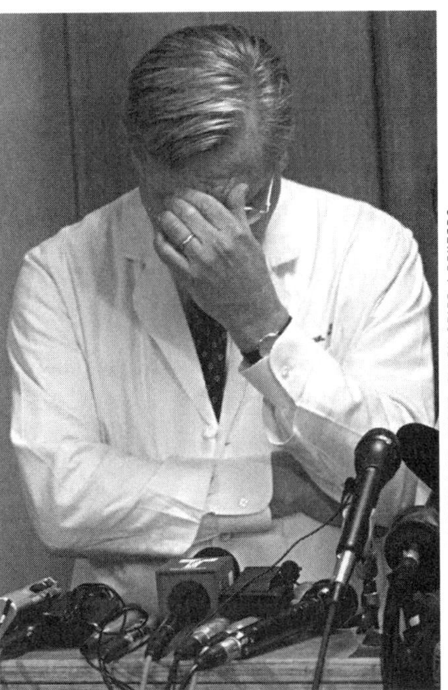

PHOTOS: LEFT, MIKE DERER / AP; RIGHT, ELLEN OZIER / REUTERS

Republicans say public protests by doctors such as Belleville, N.J., neurologist Steven Lomazow, left, make the case for caps on malpractice awards. But Democrats point to the death of 17-year-old Jesica Santillan at Duke University Hospital, whose chief executive, William Fulkerson, right, reacts at a recent news conference about her surgery.

The simplified version of the medical malpractice debate is embodied in this war of images. Republicans can add the potential for voter outrage over striking doctors to a confluence of other factors that have given legislation to limit medical malpractice its best chance of becoming law in nearly a decade. The GOP now controls both chambers of Congress, the president mentioned the urgency of the issue in his State of the Union address, and the majority leader in the Senate happens to be a physician himself.

But the true tale of the medical malpractice debate is more complex than that; the politics far less certain. To begin, the link between malpractice insurance premiums and big jury awards is uncertain at best. Second, efforts to rope this issue into the larger debate of rising health care costs — which does have the voters' attention — are undermined by studies showing that drug prices and increased consumer demand are probably the biggest reasons for the rise in health care spending.

And engaging in a real legislative debate on this issue is complicated because limiting legal liability for one industry or group cracks open the door for a broader consideration of caps, or limits, on jury awards — known as "tort reform" — a subject that always splits the parties and inflames the passions of special interests. Other tort reform initiatives, such as efforts to move more class action lawsuits from state to federal court or to establish a federal system to compensate asbestos victims, usually end in stalemate. *(History, p. 84)*

Any serious consideration of malpractice insurance legislation will quickly provoke a lobbying and advertising frenzy. The issue pits doctors and insurance companies — who had been on opposite sides of the issue during debate over a patients' bill of rights — against trial lawyers and patient advocacy groups.

As a practical matter, Democrats may be the minority party, but they have enough votes in the Senate to keep the GOP from doing much of anything without their consent. As long as Republicans insist on capping non-economic damages, such as those to cover pain and suffering, it will be difficult for them to win Democratic support.

Yet advocates of medical malpractice insist that it is the one area where GOP lawmakers could engage the opposition in a debate because it can be so easily brought home to voters.

"If you talk about asbestos tort reform, most people don't go through their daily lives encountering difficulties because of asbestos litigation," said James C. Greenwood, R-Pa., sponsor of the House medical liability bill (HR 5). "But when their obstetrician tells them he can't deliver their baby, when their trauma center closes, when their neurosurgeon can't fix their spinal injury, it becomes very real. They can get a very visceral grasp that this is a life and death issue."

Indeed, the group to watch on this issue may be the moderates, such as Democratic Sen. Dianne Feinstein, whose home state of California has a 28-year-old cap on the books that she would like to see become the model for federal legislation. On the Republican side, some members such as Gordon Smith of Oregon have signaled a willingness to compromise on the issue.

"The climate for civil justice reform is better now than it has been," said Victor Schwartz, general counsel to the American Tort Reform Association and an author of one of the nation's most popular tort law case books. "But that does not mean just anything . . . will pass."

Malpractice Awards Rise, Settlements Drop

Rising malpractice insurance premiums concern medical care providers to the point that some are walking off the job. The charts below show median jury awards and settlements in medical malpractice cases.

Jury awards*

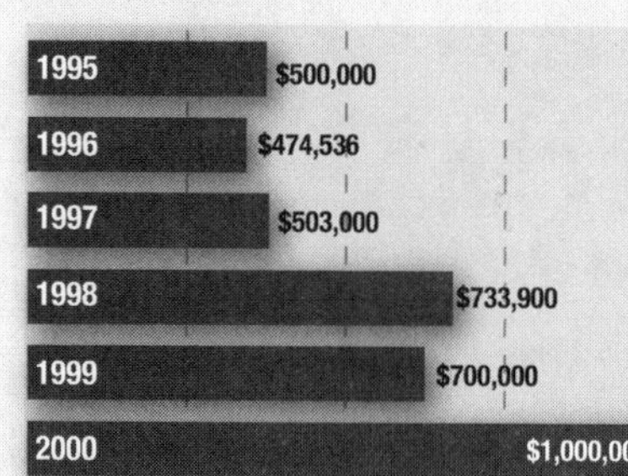

Settlements*

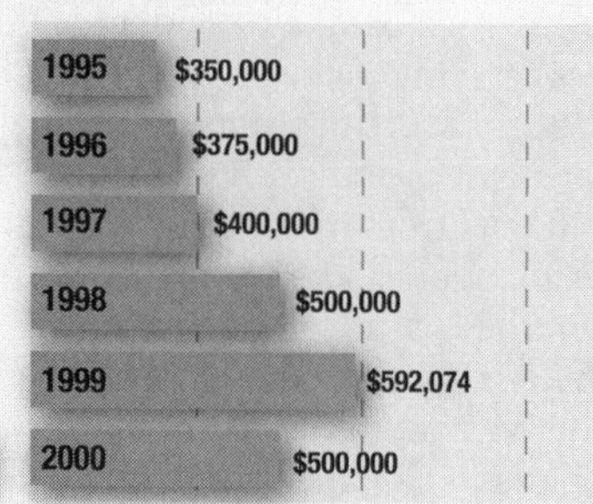

The three largest malpractice awards of 2002:

$94.8 million

Perez v. St. John's Episcopal Hospital – mother of premature baby born with cerebral palsy claimed doctors failed to administer corticosteroids to speed maturation of the baby's lungs. Post-trial motions are pending.

$91 million

Wise v. McCalla – Five-year-old girl born with cerebral palsy claimed hospital was negligent for failing to diagnose a rare condition in her mother. The girl contended she was delivered by Caesarean section though the mother may not have been in labor. Suit was settled for $6 million.

$80 million

Brenner v. Spector, et. al. – Defendants delivered a woman's twins 10 weeks prematurely and one of the babies had cerebral palsy. The suit claimed doctors arrived late and did not respond to complaints about uterine cramps. Suit later settled for an undisclosed amount.

*These numbers are based on incomplete data

SOURCE: Jury Verdict Research

Region by Region

Republicans and Democrats both use the term "crisis" in discussing the rise in medical malpractice insurance rates. But the extent of the "crisis" seems to vary from region to region and from specialty to specialty.

Malpractice premiums for obstetrician-gynecologists — considered a high-risk group because of the possibility of problem births — rose an average 19.6 percent last year, more than double the 9.2 percent rise of 2001, according to the Medical Liability Monitor, which tracks premiums for about 65 percent of the medical malpractice insurance market.

Rates rose an average 25 percent for surgeons last year and 24.7 percent for internists, both more than double the increases in 2001 for those specialties.

But because different states have different laws and market conditions, the premiums and salaries for doctors vary widely. Internists in South Dakota paid an annual rate of $2,906 last year, but Miami-Dade County, Fla., internists had to pay $56,153. The difference for surgeons was even larger, according to the Medical Liability Monitor. Minnesota surgeons could buy annual policies that cost $8,717, but in Miami, the most expensive policy was $174,268.

During the 1970s and 1980s, congressional Democrats deflected efforts to curb malpractice insurance lawsuits, and so states took action instead. More than three dozen states have passed damage caps, although some have been repealed or ruled as unconstitutional. All states have passed some sort of limits on tort litigation, such as a requirement that defendants must pay only the share of damages for which they are responsible; limits on attorneys' fees; provisions to allow periodic payments of awards; or caps on some awards, according to the National Council of State Legislatures.

Democrats, who generally agree there is a problem, question whether looking at jury awards is the right approach in addressing malpractice costs. Some, such as Sen. Edward M. Kennedy of Massachusetts, believe rate increases stem more from attempts by insurance companies to recover losses from stocks, bonds and other investments in recent years.

The problem of malpractice costs began to grow in the 1970s, when a number of private insurers stopped offering coverage, saying the costs were prohibitive. At that time, several states — led by California — passed legislation capping awards. And doctors who hoped to stave off rising rates in the future banded together to create physician-owned insurance companies.

A decade later, when premiums once again started to rise, state legislatures passed more laws. California addressed the issue again with comprehensive insurance regulations through an initiative known as

"Proposition 103," which affected a wide range of industries including health care. *(2003 CQ Weekly, p. 486)*

Rates remained steady throughout the 1990s, and insurers benefited from healthy investment returns.

Several reasons account for that. Insurers had expected to cover more significant losses, so they built up reserves during the 1990s, said James Hurley, the chairman of a medical malpractice subcommittee of the American Academy of Actuaries, the trade group for actuaries. The companies did not have to tap into their reserves much because claims were not as frequent and awards were not as high as they had expected. Profits rose for insurers, who then were able to invest the money, mostly in bond markets. Reinsurance companies, which insurers use to cover high awards, also were lowering their rates during this time — all of which drove down rates.

In the past two years, economic conditions changed and investment returns declined, awards grew and reinsurance costs increased. Some of the companies that had lowered rates found themselves in a precarious fiscal situation.

The median loss ratio for insurance companies — the direct losses that a company incurred divided by the premiums that it earned — was 54.2 in 1997, according to the National Association of Insurance Commissioners (NAIC). By 2001, the ratio had risen to 97.8, meaning losses were eating up most of the premiums that companies took in. The NAIC does not collect data from all insurers, but collects the data that companies must report to state insurance commissioners.

Physicians have staged at least five high-profile walkouts — in West Virginia, Nevada, New Jersey, Florida and Mississippi — since late 2002. A crisis was averted in Pennsylvania when Gov. Edward G. Rendell, a Democrat, reacted with a proposal to curb costs.

Republicans say the public nature of those protests gives Congress impetus to try to change medical liability law.

The concern over malpractice insurance rates "was a problem a couple of years ago. Today, it is a crisis," Senate Majority Leader Bill Frist, R-Tenn., the chamber's only doctor, said at a Feb. 11 hearing on the issue. "We need to recognize that we, at the federal level, absolutely must respond."

The atmosphere in Congress has changed in several potentially significant ways since last year, when an attempt to cap jury awards in malpractice cases died in the Democratic-led Senate. The House had passed a medical liability bill, 217-203, that mirrored a proposal by President Bush. That bill included caps on attorneys fees and a $250,000 cap on non-economic damages. It also would have limited punitive damages in certain circumstances. But the Senate tabled an amendment to an unrelated bill that would have capped punitive damages in malpractice cases at twice the compensatory damages and would have limited attorneys' fees. *(2002 CQ Weekly, p. 3197)*

Sharper GOP Focus

This year, Bush and congressional Republicans are elevating the issue as a priority in a much more focused way. At a party retreat in early February, Bush spoke at length about his interest in driving down medical malpractice premiums through caps on damages. His words echoed the tone he adopted during his Jan. 28 State of the Union speech, say Republicans.

"To improve our health care system we must address one of the prime causes of higher cost: the constant threat that physicians and hospitals will be unfairly sued," Bush said in the State of the Union address. "Because of excessive litigation, everybody pays more for health care, and many parts of America are losing fine doctors. No one has ever been healed by a frivolous lawsuit."

Additionally, advocacy groups are stoking public concern about access to health care. Physicians' organizations, health industry groups and business associations are devoting far more lobbying muscle to the issue this year as doctors become more frustrated over the rising cost of doing business.

The American Medical Association is substituting its interest in patients' rights legislation with a greater focus on medical malpractice legislation — which now ranks as the group's greatest priority in this session. The AMA can command attention: It contributed $2.7 million to congressional candidates last year, 60 percent of it to Republicans. This year, the AMA hopes to raise $15 million through its Fund for America's Liability Reform, which will finance a national media campaign to promote the issue.

Insurance organizations, which also support limits on jury awards, gave nearly $17 million in the 2002 election cycle to congressional candidates, about 65 percent to Republicans. For plaintiffs' attorneys, among the Democrats' closest political allies, blocking legislation that would cap awards is their most critical interest this year. The Association of Trial Lawyers of America gave $3.7 million in the last cycle, 89 percent of it to Democrats.

Republicans vow to move quickly on the issue. The House Energy and Commerce Committee has scheduled votes on the bill the week of March 3.

In addition to a $250,000 cap on non-economic damages, the measure also would cap punitive damages at twice the economic damages, or $250,000, whichever was greater. The jury would not be informed of this limit, and the defendant could pay the judgment in periodic increments. Punitive damages are intended to punish the defendant for a wrongdoing that caused an injury. They differ from other types of awards, which are intended to compensate victims for financial losses and suffering incurred because of the injury. The jury would not be informed of this limit and the defendant could pay damages awarded for future expenses in periodic payments.

In addition, no punitive damages would be allowed in cases in which no compensatory award was granted, and the bill would require courts to find "a substantial probability" that the plaintiff could win punitive damages before a request for such damages could be filed. To win punitive damages, plaintiffs would have to show "by clear and convincing evidence" that a health care professional "acted with malicious intent to injure" a patient, or that a doctor "deliberately failed to avoid unnecessary injury" to a patient. The punitive damages provisions were also in last year's bill and are tougher than those of many state laws, including California's.

The measure would affect only the dozen states that have no caps on damages already, sponsors said.

Congressional backers say they see no problem with a law that may impose federal regulations in an area that has been traditionally up to states to oversee. They cite the government's constitutional right to regulate interstate commerce, which they say could apply in malpractice cases.

Senate GOP leaders also hope to have legislation ready this spring, but they need to write a bill that can win support from Democrats. The biggest obstacle will still be deciding whether, and by how much, to cap jury awards — a concept most Democratic lawmakers, even many of those in states affected by physician walkouts — staunchly oppose.

"The idea of putting caps on what people can receive for their pain and suffering is just a non-starter," said Democrat Christopher J. Dodd, whose state of Connecticut is home to a number of major insurance companies. "I guarantee a lot of us will fight that tooth and nail."

Democrats, along with patient advocacy groups and trial lawyers, say that people who are harmed by medical negligence deserve compensation, even if they are not employed or if the injury does not affect their ability to work. And they say that capping punitive damages and pain-and-suffering awards would be unfair to children and women, who might not be able to recover as much in lost wages.

CQ PHOTO / SCOTT J. FERRELL

House Democrats Sheila Jackson-Lee of Texas, third from left, and Diana DeGette of Colorado, right, join Kurt Dixon, a lawyer for the Santillans, to oppose malpractice legislation.

A Front-Page Example

In the case of Jesica Santillan, opponents of awards caps say that under the House bill her family would have had little hope of recovering substantial damages from Duke. The 17-year-old would get far less than a wage-earning adult.

"Just as the tort reform advocates used the cup-of-McDonald's-coffee case to beat up on trial lawyers, sadly, the tragedy of the Santillan girl is going to be front and center evidence of why we have to be careful when we talk about changing medical malpractice laws," said Richard J. Durbin, D-Ill., a member of the Senate Judiciary Committee, which will take the lead on a Senate bill.

Even some moderate Republicans, such as Smith of Oregon, have said flat proposals of $250,000 are too restrictive. Smith, who voted against last year's Senate amendment to cap awards, now says he would consider some sort of limit — if a compromise can be reached.

And GOP leaders already are saying that legislation could include exclusions on caps for certain cases such as the Santillan family's.

Democrats point to insurers, not jury awards, as the culprit behind rising rates. They say insurance companies are using a handful of cases to justify their rate increases. Insurers, Democrats argue, drive up revenue from premiums to cushion against investment losses.

"Malpractice was a very lucrative line of insurance for the industry throughout the 1990s," said Kennedy, the top Democrat on the Senate Health, Education, Labor and Pensions Committee. "Doctors, especially those in high-risk specialties whose malpractice premiums have increased dramatically over the past year, do deserve premium relief. That relief will only come as a result of tougher regulation of the insurance industry."

As a result, Democrats are working on plans to toughen laws for insurers. One plan by Kennedy, Durbin and Patrick J. Leahy of Vermont — members of the Senate Judiciary Committee — would strip insurers of antitrust exemptions under the 1945 McCarran-Ferguson law. *(1945 Almanac, p. 105)*

The Democratic supporters of such a plan say they want "to ensure that medical malpractice insurers cannot drive up doctors' premiums by engaging in price fixing, bid rigging or market allocations." The insurance commissioners group counters that states already have adequate laws to regulate the industry and that a federal law would be redundant.

Some studies do show that the rates are not one of the main factors affecting the nation's overall increase in health insurance premiums. Litigation and extraneous medical measures that doctors may take to inoculate themselves from potential suits account for about 1 percent of the nation's medical costs, health care economists say.

An April 2002 study by PricewaterhouseCoopers for the American Association of Health Plans found that among the factors affecting health costs, medical malpractice litigation accounted for 7 percent of an increase. That was behind almost every other category, including drug costs, costs of providers, general inflation, government regulations and increased consumer demand.

House Republicans have indicated they would be willing to compromise on the amounts of limits as long as some sort of cap would be imposed.

"I've been a legislator for 22 years, so I understand the importance of compromise, but I have to have actuaries tell me at the end of this process that the bill will in fact have the desired effect on rates — that they will go down," said Greenwood.

The most likely area of consensus, given Republicans' insistence on some type of caps, might be a sliding scale that includes a set cap for most routine claims but the opportunity for higher awards in egregious cases of malpractice. Hatch, in particular, is sympathetic to concerns that malpractice victims who suffer from gross negligence should receive greater damages.

If a bill with some kind of caps survives the Senate, then Republicans say that the pressure from the public and the administration could force a bill through conference negotiations and onto the president's desk.

Although no one is clear how or if a compromise could be forged, there is still consensus on one issue: that there is some kind of crisis to be addressed.

"There's unanimity on this panel that we have a problem," Democratic Sen. Hillary Rodham Clinton of New York said at a joint hearing of the Senate HELP and Judiciary committees. "Even if it's a problem that ebbs and flows with the economic conditions and the marketplace, it still is a problem." ◆

Medicare Overhaul Proposals Put Difficult Trade-Offs on Table

Lawmakers try to avoid perception that 'some options are more equal than others'

Medicare was established under the premise of equality—the notion that all the nation's elderly and disabled should receive the same type of assistance to cover their health care needs and expenses. But President Bush's drive to overhaul the program and inject private competition into the system has raised important questions about whether such parity can continue to exist.

The administration and its mostly Republican congressional allies hope to lure more seniors to private insurance, including managed-care plans, by offering more-generous benefits — especially in the area of prescription drug coverage — than those offered by Medicare's traditional fee-for-service program. Nearly 90 percent of beneficiaries are enrolled in fee-for-service. *(Administration's plan, CQ Weekly, p. 255)*

To accomplish that goal, lawmakers first must get comfortable with a new definition of "equality" that accepts the likelihood that, while all beneficiaries may be guaranteed a specific set of benefits from private plans or the government, private insurers will probably offer additional benefits.

Beyond that conundrum, lawmakers also must decide how to apportion the $400 billion that the administration has allocated to create a Medicare drug benefit. The GOP is split between a majority that believes Medicare must deliver a benefit that would cover all seniors, and a faction including fiscal conservatives in the House and Senate that believes the vast majority of dollars should be spent on the neediest beneficiaries, who lack drug coverage through employer-related plans. About 24 percent of Medicare beneficiaries — about 10 million — have no drug coverage.

Making such pivotal decisions "involves trade-offs that are very difficult to make," said Robert D. Reischauer, president of the Urban Institute and former director of the Congressional Budget Office. "The consensus you might have had [to generally make changes to the system] starts to fall apart."

Bush put the difficult questions squarely in Congress' path on March 4, when he released a conceptual "framework" for overhauling the 37-year-old entitlement program. The president's plan calls for offering drug coverage in either the traditional fee-for-service program or through private plans participating in a program called "Enhanced Medicare." Bush also would rely on managed-care plans to offer coverage to beneficiaries in a third option called "Medicare Advantage."

Defining Parity

The proposal would give seniors in the traditional Medicare plan a drug discount card, an unspecified cap on out-of-pocket expenses and $600 to the poorest seniors to help them pay for their prescription drugs. Private insurers would offer more comprehensive benefits.

Democrats said the plan would force seniors to leave traditional Medicare in order to receive an acceptable level of drug coverage.

"The overwhelming majority of seniors chose traditional Medicare," said Sen. Debbie Stabenow, D-Mich. "Now, the White House is saying, 'Well, even though you had a choice, we don't like the choice you made.' That's not a choice. That's coercion."

Republicans, too, have misgivings about aspects of Bush's proposal that create the potential for their writing legislation that favors one class of beneficiaries over another.

The debate over how to provide parity in prescription drug coverage between fee-for-

Quick Contents

Now that President Bush has outlined his principles for overhauling Medicare, Congress must confront difficult questions about equal treatment for all beneficiaries and the scope of a prescription drug benefit.

BLOOMBERG NEWS / CHRIS KLEPONIS

Bush on March 4 outlined principles for overhauling Medicare that raise questions about whether the program will continue to offer equal benefits for all seniors.

service Medicare and the private sector will be "the No. 1 issue for Congress to deal with," said Sen. Susan Collins, R-Maine. "I think it's a major sticking point."

The soaring cost of administering the traditional Medicare program is driving Bush's call for an overhaul. The Office of Management and Budget estimates that Medicare spending will rise to $349.4 billion by fiscal 2008, a 51 percent increase from the $230.9 billion spent in fiscal 2002. That compares with a forecast of a 35 percent overall increase for total federal expenditures over that period.

Many Republicans believe having private insurers administer program benefits would dramatically reduce expenses. Such changes also would reduce political pressures on lawmakers, who now are subject to perennial lobbying from health care providers upset about what they characterize as excessively low government reimbursements.

But not all Republicans see managed care as a panacea. Collins and other lawmakers from rural states recall past efforts to steer Medicare beneficiaries into managed care that failed when many private insurers left the program, citing excessive costs and low government reimbursements. *(Medicare+Choice, 2002 CQ Weekly, p. 3070)*

Against this backdrop, lawmakers are only beginning to reconcile the push for privatization with the program's guarantee of equal benefits for all.

Senate Finance Committee Chairman Charles E. Grassley, R-Iowa, envisions a new criterion, one centered on "more parity, but I'm not saying absolute parity, between what's offered on old Medicare vs. new Medicare." As he and other lawmakers design a drug bill, Grassley said, they must ask a simple question: "Does this take care of the needs of enough people so there's not a club over their head to go into the new plan?"

Senate Majority Leader Bill Frist, R-Tenn., said Republicans must be able to convince seniors that they will have drug coverage no matter what Medicare plan they pick.

"If the perception is that in order to get substantial drug coverage you've got to go into an HMO, it's dead," said Frist, the Senate's only physician.

But even though lawmakers want to make all options equal, Frist acknowledged that parity will be in the eye of the beholder.

Bush Leaves It to Congress

President Bush offered a broad outline of an overhaul of Medicare that would include creating prescription drug coverage. But he left the details for Congress to work out.

WHAT THE PRESIDENT IS ASKING FOR:	WHAT CONGRESS HAS TO FIGURE OUT:
• All Medicare recipients should have help buying prescription drugs, with extra help for those who can least afford them.	• Congress will have to decide whether to target more assistance to the neediest, which may prevent certain others from obtaining coverage.
• All recipients should have access to full coverage of preventive benefits, and protection from high out-of-pocket costs.	• Congress has to define what preventive services Medicare should cover. Lawmakers also have to decide whether to cap out-of-pocket costs and when catastrophic coverage begins.
• Seniors should be able to stay in the current system and receive help with catastrophic prescription drug costs. There would be a drug discount card and annual limits on out-of-pocket costs for drugs plus a $600 annual subsidy for low-income seniors.	• Congress has to decide whether the traditional system should stop at this or be more generous.
• Seniors who want more coverage will be able to choose an enhanced form of fee-for-service Medicare similar to coverage enjoyed by members of Congress.	• Congress will have to guarantee that all seniors — particularly those in outlying areas — will always have a choice of at least two options.

For example, Bush envisions giving Medicare beneficiaries choices similar to those offered to members of Congress and federal workers through the Federal Employees Health Insurance Benefit Plan. But that program actually consists of many health insurance plans that each offer different levels of coverage. Some restrict beneficiaries' choices of health care providers.

"I don't know what the same coverage is," Frist said, because "each plan is a little bit different."

The same scenario is likely if Bush's overhaul brings more private insurers into the system. Some may focus more on preventive care, while others could cater to people with chronic medical conditions. Certain plans would have a more tightly controlled network of providers, which could provide services at less cost to beneficiaries and help shore up the program's financial condition. But it would be difficult to establish whether the plans were "equal" to each other and to the benefits offered in the fee-for-service program.

One legislative solution could involve Congress establishing a baseline of essential services that would be covered by both traditional Medicare and private plans.

But if Bush and his allies develop a framework that guarantees parity in drug coverage between the fee-for-service program and private insurers, it will be expensive and could actually undermine their efforts to steer beneficiaries away from traditional Medicare.

"The current Medicare system and a generous drug benefit will be unsustainable from a fiscal standpoint," said Rep. Jim McCrery, R-La., a House Ways and Means Committee member who has worked extensively on Medicare drug issues.

'A Schizophrenic Position'

McCrery and many other Republicans believe it is essential to offer beneficiaries in private plans more generous benefits, because having the government administer an equivalent drug benefit would be staggeringly expensive. Democratic plans to offer a government-administered benefit would cost as much as $900 billion over a decade.

Offering the same level of drug coverage also would reduce the incentive for beneficiaries to move out of traditional Medicare, Reischauer noted.

"Taking that step may make those [private] plans not viable," Reischauer said. "It really puts [Republicans] in a schizophrenic position."

Some Democrats believe that making private plans administer a drug benefit will wind up costing the government more. This line of thinking holds that the government will have to reimburse private plans more than what it would cost the government to provide drug coverage through traditional Medicare, or the private plans will withdraw, citing inadequate reimbursements.

"The argument has always been that private plans are more efficient; they're not," said Bruce Vladeck, director of the Institute for Medicare Practice at the Mt. Sinai School of Medicine in New York City, who ran the Health Care Financing Administration, now known as the Centers for Medicare and Medicaid Services, in the Clinton administration.

Vladeck and others argue that the administration should offer more generous drug coverage through traditional Medicare. Advocates of managed care, however, say those plans could provide drug coverage in a more cost-effective way.

The overwhelming popularity of the fee-for-service plan may nonetheless force Republicans to compromise and at least initially guarantee that the government program will provide coverage on par with private insurers.

The majority of fee-for-service enrollees spent most of their working lives with traditional insurance plans. They chose their doctors, and the insurance company paid for the visit. Many remain uncomfortable with the concept of managed care, and limited choices in providers.

Lawmakers may get an opportunity to scale back the traditional program as more Baby Boomers retire. Later generations will have spent decades in managed-care plans, which have grown in popularity with employers over the past decade.

Who Gets Covered

Beyond consideration of what is equal coverage, there is the difficult question of whether there is enough money to pay for everyone.

Some Republicans, including Sen. Trent Lott of Mississippi, believe the party should spend the majority of the $400 billion the Bush administration is proposing to set aside for a limited Medicare drug benefit for the low-income elderly.

Many fiscal conservatives like the idea of targeted relief. It would give the majority of help to those who need it most and would make it easier to tame future increases than if the benefit were given to all of the more than 40 million Medicare beneficiaries.

"To what extent is [Medicare drug legislation] helping the needs of [seniors] who don't have anything?" Grassley asked. Though the lawmaker supports a benefit for all Medicare beneficiaries, he said, "It seems to me to be very necessary to respond to those who do not have any drug coverage at all."

It still might be difficult for Republicans to produce anything but a universal benefit. Medicare drug coverage is a high-profile political issue for the GOP, which would love to pass legislation and take primacy on an issue long dominated by Democrats in time for the 2004 elections.

"I don't think [a limited bill] is where we'll come out," McCrery said.

But there are perils in that politically palatable approach.

As Republicans and Democrats both decide to cover more people, chances increase that some employers facing financial difficulties will decide to cut costs by abandoning drug coverage for their retirees — a phenomenon known as "employer crowd-out." That could make administering a drug benefit even more expensive for the federal government.

Policymakers could try to add incentives for employers to maintain coverage, perhaps by giving companies a subsidy to help them continue to provide the benefit. But the ongoing economic slump and lower corporate earnings could prompt companies to curtail or drop retiree health care coverage.

"I don't know how you discourage the displacement of private insurance," Vladeck said. "The former employers say, 'Why should we keep doing it?' "

Uwe Reinhardt, a Princeton University professor of political economy and an authority on the nation's health care system, agreed that a Medicare drug benefit may mean that "corporations will refuse to provide the elderly with the generous benefit they have so far."

Such fears are not likely to stop the momentum on Capitol Hill for Medicare drug coverage, though. The issue remains popular with both parties, which are sure to compete to take credit for any new benefit.

If lawmakers need another nudge, Frist said, they should think about the tidal wave of Baby Boomers who will begin to flood the program beginning in 2010. By 2031, Medicare enrollment is expected to reach 77 million.

"The thing that is going to drive this is the demographic shift," Frist said. "It's imminent, it's powerful, it's immutable, you can't change it." ◆

Medicare's Chances on the Hill

The Bush administration and its congressional allies are spending the early weeks of the 108th Congress pursuing two signature health care initiatives: overhauling Medicare and capping medical malpractice awards.

But if the administration has its way, it also will reshape the federal-state Medicaid program and enact tough bans on human cloning and on a procedure opponents call "partial birth abortion."

Of all the issues, medical malpractice may have the best chance of becoming law, although partisan differences still could derail the issue in the Senate. The issue goes to the floor of the House the week of March 10, where Republican legislation (HR 5) is expected to win passage. (Malpractice, p. 566)

Odds of overhauling Medicare are longer, though most Republicans and Democrats support the idea of creating a prescription drug benefit. With debate expected to take months, there may not be enough time to take up Medicaid.

The Senate takes up the abortion issue the week of March 10. The House passed a cloning ban Feb. 27.

Vote Against ANWR Drilling Hits Core of Bush Energy Plan

Democratic victory will invigorate debate over alternative fuels, electricity regulation

The Senate voted against allowing oil exploration in Alaska's Arctic National Wildlife Refuge, which probably takes the issue off the table for this year. Energy legislation still faces difficult debates over electricity and ethanol, however.

In the 107th Congress, the Bush administration found that it could not break a Democratic filibuster of its signature energy plan to allow oil drilling in a wilderness area of Alaska's Arctic coast. When the vote finally came, in fact, President Bush's allies could not even manage a simple majority in the Senate. Public opinion was clearly against the idea.

This year, with Republicans in control of both the House and Senate, the GOP strategy was to sidestep a Democratic filibuster and the 60 votes that cloture would require. Instead, Senate leaders included a provision in their budget resolution assuming future revenue from oil and gas leases in the Arctic National Wildlife Refuge (ANWR), which would be de facto authority for drilling.

But the Senate voted 52-48 on March 19 to remove the language, dealing a blow to Bush and to the prospects for any substantive energy legislation this year.

Bush's energy plan, first proposed in 2001 and largely embodied in Republican energy bills, is focused primarily on raised domestic energy production, including oil, gas and coal. Opening ANWR is the centerpiece of that strategy. Though supporters of drilling in the refuge, led by Alaska Republican Sen. Ted Stevens, say they will continue to pursue the issue — "It's never decided until we win," Stevens growled before the vote — others say the battle is over for now. *(2001 Almanac, p. 9-3)*

CQ Weekly March 22, 2003

CQ PHOTO / SCOTT J. FERRELL

Even before the Senate vote against drilling for oil in the Arctic National Wildlife Refuge, Debbie Stabenow of Michigan, center, and other Democrats claimed victory.

"They are going to have to come to a realization that one side has won this one," said Frank Maisano, an energy industry lobbyist, who said the fight was more "symbolic" than substantive.

Senate Energy and Natural Resources Committee Chairman Pete V. Domenici, R-N.M., appears ready to start assembling a new energy bill without an ANWR provision, rather than slogging through more debate on the refuge. The bill would incorporate a tax package (S 597) of $16 billion in incentives to encourage production of traditional and alternative supplies of energy and tax credits to spur conservation.

"If the commitment to filibuster is real, this is the best shot," Domenici said after the amendment vote. "We lost it — could easily have won it."

An omnibus energy bill in Bush's image has other problems. Environmental groups that have focused most of their lobbying and advertising on preserving ANWR now probably will shift their attention to the rest of the legislation, including provisions to open more federal lands up to energy production.

In addition, debate over electricity regulation and alternative fuels, such as ethanol, that complicated the energy bill conference in 2002 have again emerged as trouble spots.

The House Energy and Commerce Subcommittee on Energy and Air Quality, which approved a draft omnibus bill March 19, left out a section on fuels because of disagreement over ethanol subsidies and other issues. *(Provisions, p. 109)*

'Voting Against Me'

Republican leaders touted the ANWR budget provision as a matter of national security. They argued that at a time when the United States is sending troops into Iraq, Congress should act to expand domestic supplies of oil.

But Jeff Bingaman of New Mexico, ranking Democrat on the Energy and Natural Resources Committee, dismissed that reasoning and said Congress should not risk spoiling the refuge for its oil.

"The most compelling reason for not opening the refuge is that it will do very little, if anything, to further our national energy security," he said. "Not a single drop of oil would come from the Arctic Refuge for at least seven years and more likely 10 or 12 years."

A Bingaman spokesman said later that ANWR would be a "poison pill" for any energy bill.

Domenici said the ANWR drilling provision was defeated by senators who "don't understand the link between abundant, affordable energy and a vigorous economy."

But Stevens, in an angry, emotional floor speech before the vote, said his colleagues were not keeping a commitment made to him in 1980 by the late Sens. Henry M. Jackson, D-Wash. (1953-83), and Paul Tsongas, D-Mass. (1979-85), that the coastal plain of ANWR would eventually be opened to oil and gas development.

Referring to posters of Arctic caribou that opponents of drilling have used on the floor, Stevens said oil production in neighboring Prudhoe Bay did not bother the wildlife.

"We did not disturb the caribou," he said, pointing to his own photo of herds in the region. "There is the caribou right near Port McIntyre field. . . . I have been up there, and there are so many on the runway we had to wait until they decided to leave because they get first call on the runway."

Stevens, the chairman of the Appropriations Committee, then turned personal.

"My last comment is this," he said just before the vote. "In the time I have served here, many people have made commitments to me, and I have never broken a commitment in my life. I make this commitment: People who vote against this today are voting against me, and I will not forget it."

The anti-ANWR amendment's author, California Democrat Barbara Boxer, said the vote signaled that it was time to turn to the broader debate on energy and how to strike a balance between expanding production and creating new incentives to conserve oil.

"We have to make a choice," she said before the vote. "Do we want to change the policy and go into this beautiful refuge or do we want to look at other ways to get more energy?"

ANWR, How They Voted

The Senate again rejected a proposal that would have allowed oil drilling in the Arctic National Wildlife Refuge (ANWR) by agreeing 52-48 to strip the proposal from a budget resolution. Last spring, the Senate took a similar position, voting 46-54 to continue a filibuster on the idea. Below is a breakdown of advocates and foes for the last two Senate votes.

HOW NEW MEMBERS OF THE 108TH CONGRESS VOTED

Republicans voting for drilling: Alexander (Tenn.), Chambliss (Ga.), Cornyn (Texas), Dole (N.C.), Graham, L. (S.C.), Murkowski (Alaska), Sununu (N.H.), Talent, (Mo.)

Republican voting against drilling: Coleman (Minn.)

Democrats voting against drilling: Lautenberg (N.J.), Pryor (Ark.)

VOTING FOR ANWR DRILLING IN BOTH THE 107TH AND 108TH CONGRESS

REPUBLICANS

Allard (Colo.)
Allen (Va.)
Bennett (Utah)
Bond (Mo.)
Brownback (Kan.)
Bunning (Ky.)
Burns, C. (Mont.)
Campbell (Colo.)
Cochran (Miss.)
Craig (Idaho)
Crapo (Idaho)
Domenici (N.M.)
Ensign (Nev.)
Enzi (Wyo.)
Frist (Tenn.)
Grassley (Iowa)
Gregg (N.H.)
Hagel (Neb.)
Hatch (Utah)
Hutchison (Texas)
Inhofe (Okla.)
Kyl (Ariz.)
Lott (Miss.)
Lugar (Ind.)
McConnell (Ky.)
Nickles (Okla.)
Roberts (Kan.)
Santorum (Pa.)
Sessions, J. (Ala.)
Shelby (Ala.)
Specter (Pa.)
Stevens (Alaska)
Thomas (Wyo.)
Voinovich (Ohio)
Warner (Va.)

DEMOCRATS

Akaka (Hawaii)
Breaux (La.)
Inouye (Hawaii)
Landrieu (La.)
Miller (Ga.)

VOTING AGAINST ANWR DRILLING IN BOTH THE 107TH AND 108TH CONGRESS

REPUBLICANS

Chafee (R.I.)
Collins (Maine)
DeWine (Ohio)
Fitzgerald (Ill.)
McCain (Ariz.)
Smith (Ore.)
Snowe (Maine)

DEMOCRATS

Baucus, M. (Mont.)
Bayh (Ind.)
Biden (Del.)
Bingaman (N.M.)
Boxer (Calif.)
Byrd (W.V.)
Cantwell (Wash.)
Carper (Del.)
Clinton (N.Y.)
Conrad (N.D.)
Corzine (N.J.)
Daschle (S.D.)
Dayton (Minn.)
Dodd (Conn.)
Dorgan (N.D.)
Durbin (Ill.)
Edwards, J. (N.C.)
Feingold (Wis.)
Feinstein (Calif.)
Graham, B. (Fla.)
Harkin (Iowa)
Hollings (S.C.)
Johnson (S.D.)
Kennedy (Mass.)
Kerry (Mass.)
Kohl (Wis.)
Leahy (Vt.)
Levin (Mich.)
Lieberman (Ct.)
Lincoln (Ark.)
Mikulski (Md.)
Murray (Wash.)
Nelson, Ben (Neb.)
Nelson, Bill (Fla.)
Reed (R.I.)
Reid (Nev.)
Rockefeller (W.V.)
Sarbanes (Md.)
Schumer (N.Y.)
Stabenow (Mich.)
Wyden (Ore.)

INDEPENDENT

Jeffords (Vt.)

Source: CQ Floor Votes

House Energy Bill Reshapes Electricity Regulation

The first take on an energy bill for the 108th Congress, approved by a House subcommittee March 19, includes some of the most sweeping changes in electricity market regulation in decades, along with many provisions from earlier legislation that died in conference in 2002.

Under a 310-page draft approved by the Energy and Commerce Subcommittee on Energy and Air Quality, the Federal Energy Regulatory Commission (FERC) would gain broad authority over power transmission by some utilities it does not now regulate, while the industry would have more flexibility to expand and enter new areas of business with repeal of a Depression-era antitrust law.

Sponsor Joe L. Barton, R-Texas, the Energy and Air Quality Subcommittee's chairman, said it is crucial to pass an energy bill that includes language to create a "rational wholesale transmission system that has open access to all willing providers and consumers."

But ranking Democrat John D. Dingell of Michigan and other critics say the measure would deregulate too aggressively at a time when FERC is struggling to respond to cases of market manipulation by Enron Corp. and other energy traders that helped send prices soaring in California and elsewhere two years ago.

Following are some areas addressed in the draft bill:

PUHCA Repeal

The measure would repeal the Public Utility Holding Company Act (PUHCA) of 1935, which limits who can own electric and gas utilities and prevents utilities from subsidizing unregulated parts of their business with profits from regulated activities. The law was passed to break up huge utility holding companies that used complicated pyramid structures to dominate the industry and manipulate prices through self-trading.

Power companies say the law limits investment in utilities, crimping their ability to expand transmission capacity. Opponents of repeal say the law is needed more than ever in the wake of the Enron scandal.

FERC would retain power to review mergers of electric and gas utilities under the Federal Power Act.

Energy Trading

The draft bill includes language to crack down on energy market manipulation. It would prohibit "round-trip" trading practices that energy conglomerates use to drive up prices, and would increase criminal and civil penalties for violations of the Federal Power Act.

It would require FERC to establish rules improving transparency of the operations of wholesale electric power markets.

Power Transmission

The bill is aimed at accelerating construction of new transmission lines the Energy Department considers crucial. A power company could obtain a construction permit from FERC for "critical transmission lines" and exercise eminent domain if, after one year, a state was unable or refused to approve a site for the line. A state that had approved a transmission line would be able to exercise federal authority to grant right of way if a federal land management agency could not or refused to do so within one year.

The measure would unify FERC authority over interstate power transmission, including lines of utilities it does not now regulate, such as municipal utilities, rural electric cooperatives and federal utilities. Federal utilities, including the Tennessee Valley Authority and the Bonneville Power Administration, would have explicit authority to participate in regional transmission organizations, and the bill would encourage all utilities to join such arrangements.

Oil and Gas

The bill includes permanent authority for the Strategic Petroleum Reserve and Northeast Home Heating Oil Reserve. In addition it would authorize $1.5 billion to expand the petroleum reserve's capacity to 1 billion barrels.

The measure would enable the siting of a natural gas pipeline from Alaska's North Slope and would direct FERC to consider only applications that followed the southern route negotiated in 2002 by energy bill conferees.

The bill would direct the Environmental Protection Agency to complete its study on the regulation of hydraulic fracturing processes for recovering coal bed methane, and it expresses the sense of Congress that the federal government should not regulate hydraulic fracturing unless there is sufficient scientific evidence of the need to do so.

Price-Anderson

The bill includes a 15-year reauthorization of the Price-Anderson Act (PL 100-408), limiting the liability of nuclear power plants built in the future. Current plants are already protected.

Hydroelectric Relicensing

The bill would expedite the relicensing of hydroelectric facilities by requiring federal environmental agencies to consider alternatives proposed by a power company when imposing conditions or fish ways on a hydropower project. If the alternative met wildlife and water protection requirements, the lower-cost alternative would have to be approved. The section allows disputes to be referred to FERC's Dispute Resolution Service, which may issue a non-binding advisory opinion.

Knowing the vote would be close, Republican leaders had targeted four senators they thought might be wavering — Arkansas Democrats Mark Pryor and Blanche Lincoln, along with Republicans Gordon H. Smith of Oregon and Norm Coleman of Minnesota. But all four voted in favor of removing the ANWR provision.

Coleman — who said in his 2002 campaign that he was opposed to drilling in ANWR —waited until the end of the voting period to announce his decision. He said later that he voted "aye" with mixed emotions.

Republicans still could include an ANWR instruction to the House Resources Committee in reconciliation or simply pass it under broader energy legislation to be merged with the bill that Energy Committee Chairman Billy Tauzin, R-La., plans to mark up April 1.

The House budget resolution (H Con Res 95) does not mention ANWR, but it instructs the Resources Committee to save $1.1 billion over 10 years — funds that could come from ANWR royalties.

But such a provision could have a hard time making it through budget conference, where controversial elements that might delay the package are likely to be taken out.

House GOP Strategy

The same could be said of the energy bill. Though ANWR also will be in the portion of the House GOP energy bill marked up in the Resources Committee, Republicans might let it slide in conference in the interest of passing the rest of the omnibus legislation.

The House will probably pass a separate ANWR bill, if only to keep the issue alive for political purposes.

"We don't have to do it through the budget," a GOP energy aide said. "We can do this as regular legislation on the floor in front of the TV cameras."

Pragmatists on both sides say that electricity issues and other matters not settled in conference last year will probably be greater sticking points to passing an omnibus energy bill than ANWR.

A preview of the broader energy debate was provided when the House Energy and Commerce Subcommittee on Energy and Air Quality approved a sweeping bill that would shake up the electricity industry in a way that has not happened since the Depression.

But the subcommittee deferred until full committee markup any action on a proposal by the Federal Energy Regulatory Commission (FERC) to impose a "Standard Market Design" that would create a single energy trading market in place of a patchwork of state regulations. The bill is silent on the issue.

Domenici plans to include a provision on market design in his energy bill, but he intends to avoid the battle over FERC's jurisdiction by creating an alternative to federal regulation with regional electricity markets. A draft he is circulating would grant states the authority to create and coordinate their own transmission and market design by forming regional energy services commissions.

John D. Dingell of Michigan, ranking Democrat on the Energy and Commerce Committee, referred to the market plan as the "elephant in the room" that was the largest issue but one GOP leaders did not want to talk about. Dingell said failure to come to bipartisan terms with the electricity provision bodes ill for final passage of legislation.

But Republican Joe L. Barton of Texas, the subcommittee's chairman, and Tauzin maintained discipline among GOP ranks, and the bill passed with nine of 15 Democrats voting against it.

However, the measure was approved only after Barton dropped provisions of his bill that would have addressed renewable fuels, such as ethanol, which is derived from corn.

The hang-up was a debate in both chambers over a mandate to increase use of ethanol as an additive to gasoline to increase its oxygen content and thus reduce air pollution. The fight is over a parallel effort to phase out the additive methyl tertiary butyl ether (MTBE), which also cuts emissions but is blamed for polluting water.

One lobbyist described the issue as setting off a "battle royal," pitting corn growers against fuel refineries. The issue helped scuttle agreement on comprehensive energy legislation in 2002.

Midwestern lawmakers, including House Speaker J. Dennis Hastert, R-Ill., and Senate Minority Leader Tom Daschle, D-S.D., have been pushing for a tougher renewable-fuels standard that would assist the ethanol industry, which produces fuel from corn.

A Senate bill would require that production of renewable fuel additives, including ethanol, be tripled to 5 billion gallons by 2012 and that MTBE be phased out in four years.

Tauzin said the question will be taken up in full committee, but legislative aides and lobbyists suggested that no deal will be reached before the bill hits the House floor.

CAFE Standards

A similar fight is brewing once again over efforts by Democrats and some Republicans to increase the Corporate Average Fuel Economy (CAFE) standard for motor vehicles. The House and Senate included modest CAFE increases in their last energy bills. *(2002 CQ Weekly, p. 697)*

Rep. Edward J. Markey, D-Mass., sought to make an end-run around the CAFE debate with a subcommittee amendment that would have required new rules mandating a reduction of 5 percent in the total amount of petroleum demand for motor vehicles over the years 2010 through 2014. His amendment also would have required an additional annual 5 percent cut in oil consumption beginning in 2015.

The amendment was rejected on a 6-24 vote.

Dingell, an auto industry ally, said Markey's plan was not feasible and could be achieved only by the production of cars nobody would want to buy.

The amendment, Dingell said, would "condemn people to drive around in something that looks like a roller skate or perhaps a kiddie car or a motor scooter." ◆

Lawmakers Face Airline Dilemma: Bailout Now, Crowded Skies Later

Wild financial swings dog the industry

Before Sept. 11, 2001, Congress was trying to find ways to expand the nation's aviation system amid a crush of passengers. Now it is debating how much to help airlines survive a recession. Though many lawmakers are skeptical of airline demands for aid, they will not let the industry collapse.

Like most members of Congress, Harold Rogers of Kentucky sees the airline industry up close at least twice a week. Sometimes too close.

It takes Rogers about six hours to commute from his home in southeastern Kentucky to Washington, much of the time on airplanes — a turbo-prop flight from Lexington to either Pittsburgh or Cincinnati, then a jet to Reagan National Airport.

Before the Sept. 11 terrorist attacks, the planes were full and the skies were crowded, so crowded that Rogers was sometimes stranded waiting for a connecting flight. "The problem was too many planes carrying too many passengers," he said.

It used to be that the House Transportation Appropriations Subcommittee, which Rogers chaired for two years, worried about how to expand the air traffic system and improve air service.

Today, the issue is whether Congress should do more to protect the nation's largest airlines from financial ruin.

The major carriers faced tough times even before Sept. 11. Smaller upstart airlines had begun taking their market share, aided by lower labor costs and an ability to avoid serving less-profitable rural routes.

Now, on top of the competition, the majors are reeling from a one-two punch of higher security costs and fewer travelers during wartime. Most major carriers are now or on the brink of, if not in, bankruptcy.

The trouble feeds on itself: As fewer business travelers fly, services get cut, which dissuades high-margin passengers from flying. US Airways, which Rogers flies via Pittsburgh, and Delta, his connection in Cincinnati, have each cut costs on shorter runs by replacing larger jets with small propeller-driven planes. "There's been a fundamental change in the business travel community," he said. "Although planes are full, they're full of low-fare travelers. I don't know if that will ever turn around."

No other industry is as intertwined with the livelihood of lawmakers as the airlines, providing most with relatively quick and convenient transportation between Washington and their homes. For many, airlines and the airports they serve are vital local industries that members of Congress go out of their way to protect. *(Atlanta, p. 113)*

Immediately after Sept. 11, Congress enacted a $15 billion bailout package (PL 107-42) to help the airlines recover from the period when they were grounded, even though the White House considered the aid excessive. *(2001 Almanac, p. 20-3)*

Last fall, Congress granted carriers some temporary assistance with insurance coverage and security costs as part of a homeland security law (PL 107-296). *(2002 CQ Weekly, p. 3072)*

Now, conferees on a supplemental spending bill have agreed to a $3.5 billion package of airline aid, including relief from more security costs and an extension of war risk insurance. The conferees also included 26 weeks of additional unemployment insurance for laid-off aviation workers. *(2003 CQ Weekly, p. 862)*

Though Congress and the administration continue to debate the degree to which the government should help the industry, lawmakers have made clear they will step in to keep airlines flying. The oft-repeated phrase "too big to fail" summarizes the attitude of many lawmakers toward the airline industry

CQ PHOTO / SCOTT J. FERRELL

'Although planes are full, they're full of low-fare travelers,' said Rogers, shown at a March 20 hearing of his new Appropriations Subcommittee on Homeland Security.

Georgia Serves as Template for Airline Industry's Economic Problems

"When you die," according to an old Southern saying, "whether you go to heaven or hell, you have to change planes in Atlanta."

Few cities are as closely identified with air travel as Atlanta. The city's main airport, Hartsfield Atlanta International, is the second busiest in the world, sprawling over 3,750 acres of runways, concourses, hangars, roads, parking lots and grass 10 miles south of downtown.

And one air carrier in particular is identified with Atlanta and its airport — Delta Air Lines.

Delta and Hartsfield "are important for the national economy, not just the Southeastern region," said Rep. John Lewis, a Democrat whose otherwise urban district includes the airport. "There are hundreds of thousands of people traveling and moving around, a lot of business deals made by people going from one destination to another."

But Delta has recently come to symbolize another aspect of the airline business — expensive management. Delta's questionable compensation packages and other corporate decisions aren't helping any airlines as they seek relief on Capitol Hill from excise taxes and security fees.

The airlines contend that the Sept. 11 terrorist attacks — and now the war with Iraq and the health scare in the Far East — have so reduced their business that government help is essential.

Watching Over Constituents

Lewis and the other members of the Georgia congressional delegation, nearly all of them Republicans, are fiercely protective of the airport and Delta because they are the state's largest source of jobs and because they are so important for other industries.

Atlanta's airport is central to its role as a regional distribution center, with companies such as Coca-Cola Inc., United Parcel Service Inc., BellSouth Corp. and CNN, headquartered in the area.

Delta chairman and CEO Leo F. Mullin has been the chief spokesman for the airlines to lawmakers. But reports that Mullin was paid $2.2 million in salary and bonuses in 2002, on top of stock worth $5.5 million, have angered many in Congress — so much so that lawmakers included restrictions on executive compensation in the latest airline aid package that was being negotiated as part of a supplemental spending bill.

Micro-Managing?

Some opposed the restriction. "I don't think we should be trying to micro-manage businesses," said Rep. Mac Collins, a Republican whose Georgia district borders Hartsfield and is home to thousands of its workers.

But Collins added that he and other lawmakers he'd spoken with are "fed up with the boards, bonuses and pensions" of the major carriers, including Delta.

"That was poor judgement," he said of Mullin's pay package, noting that a number of former Delta board members had argued against it.

Mullin did give up the bonus, as Atlanta-area Republican Rep. Johnny Isakson pointed out to House colleagues who opposed supplemental airline aid because of the executive compensation issue.

The pay issue is not likely to affect the relationship between most members of Congress and their local airlines. Most of the Georgia delegation commutes weekly to Washington —

dating back to the growth of the network carrier and hub-and-spoke system after the 1978 industry deregulation.

The airlines are "like a national necessity," said Sen. John D. Rockefeller IV, D-W.Va., ranking Democrat on the Commerce, Science and Transportation Subcommittee on Aviation.

If the industry collapses, Rockefeller said, it would have the same effect on the economy as "if you take the interstates and roll them up like carpets."

But even as Congress considers how to help the airlines regain their health, some aviation experts warn that once the nation's economy recovers, lawmakers will face the same problem they had two years ago: gridlock in the air.

The Federal Aviation Administration's annual air travel forecast released March 18 predicts a return to pre-Sept. 11 levels by 2005-06 — later than the FAA predicted last year. But the agency expects steady growth in aviation demand.

The government should be planning for growth now, especially since red tape can stretch out regulatory approval for new runways for a decade, said Greg Principato, a Washington-based transportation specialist who served as executive director of a 1993 commission created by Congress to study the airline industry's woes after the last recession. "This would be a great time to do it," he said.

The immediate outlook, however, is bleak. Airlines will begin rolling out their first-quarter earnings results the week of April 14, and Wall Street is expecting grim news.

"It will be a disaster," said Ray Niedl, an analyst at Blaylock & Partners. "Everyone has been raising their loss estimates."

On April 10, JPMorgan Chase raised its estimate of the industry's quarterly operating loss by 45 percent to $3.5 billion — approaching the $3.8 billion U.S. airlines lost in the quarter that followed the Sept. 11 attacks.

"We thought that was as bad as it could possibly get for the airlines," said JPMorgan Chase analyst Jamie Baker.

There are four major network carriers — American, United, Delta and Northwest, in order of size — with na-

Delta has hourly flights between Hartsfield and Reagan National — and lawmakers develop a close relationship with carriers and even crews.

Members of the delegation often find themselves on the same Delta flight, sometimes with colleagues from neighboring states who connect at Hartsfield from smaller cities.

Isakson said he regularly flies with fellow Republicans Collins and Nathan Deal, although they refrain from talking politics. "I mostly sleep and catch up on mail," he said.

Atlanta used to have two big carriers, but Eastern Airlines went broke in 1991. Lewis recalls picketing the White House to try to persuade President George Bush to intervene and save Eastern Airlines, to no avail.

Now Lewis considers Delta's employees "like an extension of my family."

When Hartsfield was reopened to traffic after the Sept. 11 terrorist attacks, Lewis said "we all hugged and kissed a little bit."

Atlanta's Hartsfield International Airport is the nation's second busiest, with more than 36 million people boarding planes annually.

GRAPHIC / YOLIE DAWSON

Big Business

Isakson said the economic impact of Delta and Hartsfield on the state has been immeasurable.

"One of the unknown things is the value of the cargo they fly," he said, noting that Delta's shipping capacity had helped the area's recent high-tech boom.

The airport and its airlines are so important, in fact, that when the state legislature was drawing new congressional districts in 2001, there was a lively competition over who should represent Hartsfield.

Delta had a lobbyist at the state capitol to look after its interests. Lewis hung onto the airport, thanks mainly to the intervention of then-state House Speaker Tom Murphy, a Democrat who subsequently lost his own re-election race.

Collins, whose Middle Georgia district adjoins the airport and is home to thousands of its workers, has been one of the most stalwart supporters of the airport and Delta.

He has introduced a bill (HR 1467) that would reimburse airlines for all security costs as well as suspend security fees imposed by the post-Sept. 11 aviation security law (PL 107-71) for two years. And he is a cosponsor of legislation (HR 1380) that would give the airlines their fondest wish this year — a two-year moratorium on the excise tax on jet fuel. After labor, fuel is the industry's largest cost.

Collins also wrote President Bush urging support for airline aid.

"In order to support the stimulation of the economy, while we are undertaking military action in Iraq, I encourage you to request a moratorium on the passenger security tax and the air carrier security fee" imposed by the law, Collins wrote March 20.

The delegation's loyalty to Delta extends to the fierce competition among travel Web sites.

The carrier is a partner along with the other "Big Five" airlines in Orbitz, which competitors such as Travelocity.com have criticized for having an unfair advantage.

At a hearing last year before a House Energy and Commerce panel, Deal blasted executives from Orbitz's competitors for conducting a smear campaign and called the hearing "a public lynching."

tionwide service and international routes. Continental Airlines and US Airways, the fifth and sixth-largest, respectively, also have significant ridership and are economic engines in their hub areas.

It is those airlines that have faced the worst financial difficulties, with United operating under bankruptcy protection, US Airways having recently emerged from bankruptcy and American seeking labor concessions to stave off bankruptcy. But even that may not be enough, American's Chief Executive Officer Donald Carty warned employees on Feb. 10. "I must tell you honestly, that given the impact of the war in Iraq and a continued weak economy, the possibility of a bankruptcy filing remains," Carty said.

The Air Transport Association, the industry's main trade group, estimates that the war will add another $4 billion to the industry's losses for the year, which already could exceed $6 billion.

But most analysts say the congressional aid package is only a Band-Aid that will help the industry cope with lower traffic because of the Iraq conflict and the outbreak of the severe acute respiratory syndrome (SARS) virus in Asia. It would do little to solve the industry's structural problems, they say.

"We would not expect the government aid package as currently proposed to materially alter the earnings or bankruptcy outlook for most legacy carriers," said Baker.

Principato called the latest aid package "a Botox injection to smooth out the wrinkles for a little while."

The industry's recovery, analysts say, will hinge on the ability of older airlines to cut costs to better compete with low-cost carriers, such as Southwest Airlines and JetBlue Airways.

"The costs have gotten completely out of line, particularly in the labor area," said Niedl.

During the roaring economy of the late 1990s, airlines could sustain higher costs by charging sky-high prices to business travelers. But Baker said that lucrative market already was waning months before the Sept. 11 attacks knocked the industry flat.

"There was a discernable shift upon

Airlines' Financial Tumble and Its Causes

Terrorism and international tensions have caused millions of people to avoid flying and sent the nation's airlines into a financial tailspin. A look at recent airline losses and their causes:

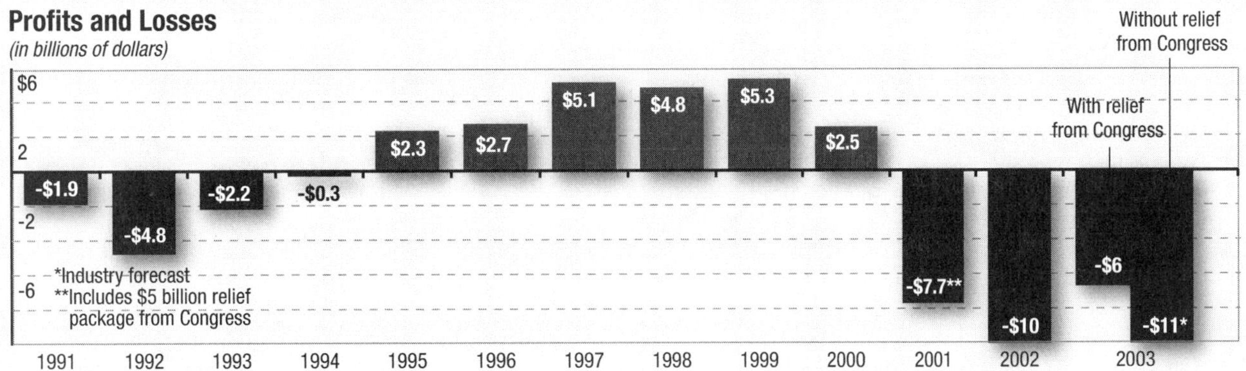

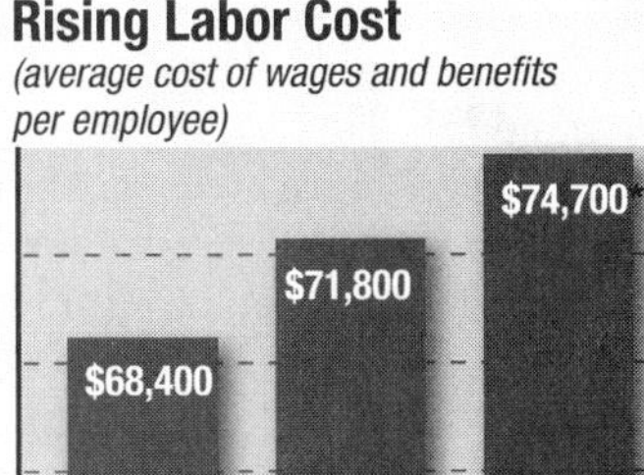

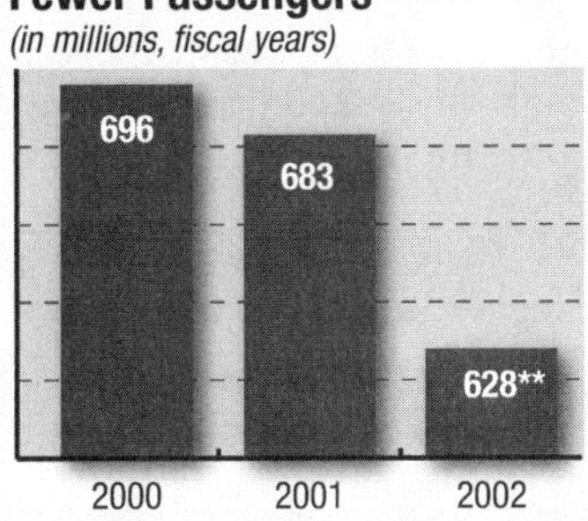

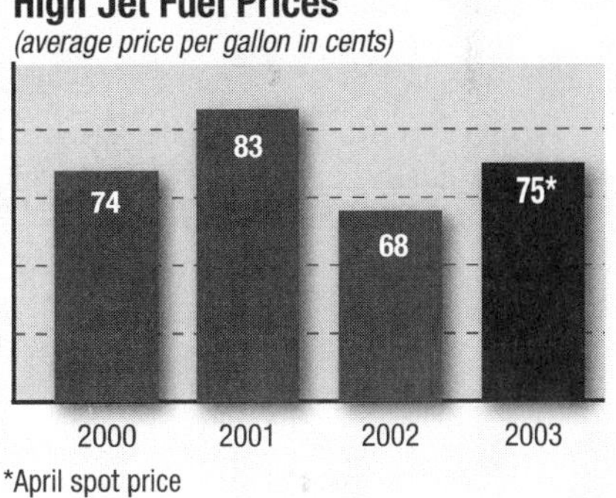

**Projections

SOURCES: U.S. Department of Transportation, Air Transport Association

CQ GRAPHIC / MARILYN GATES-DAVIS

the bursting of the tech bubble" in 2000, he said. A spike in jet-fuel prices did not help things, either.

Michael Roach, an airline consultant for Unisys R2A, said Congress' aid package is justified to help airlines cope with a decline in passengers because of the war, fears of terrorism and worries abut SARS. But Congress should not be in the business of bailing out the industry, he warned, when the big problem is the failure of legacy carriers to cut costs to compete with low-cost operators. A Unisys study Roach wrote last November found that United Airlines' per-hour pilot costs were double those of Southwest.

Niedl predicted the major carriers would survive the year, but said consolidation will occur in the long run.

"I bet in two to five years we have three less big carriers," he said. "I think we will be down to a system of three major network carriers and up to a half-dozen low-cost carriers."

The puzzle for Congress is how to deal with an industry that performs a vital public service but is still a business enterprise.

Short-Term or Long-Term?

The administration takes the view, articulated by Office and Management Budget Director Mitchell E. Daniels Jr. and backed by Treasury Secretary John W. Snow, that the airline industry's problems are deep-rooted and that any aid should be narrowly tailored to meet immediate security costs brought on by the war in Iraq.

The White House did not include assistance for the airline industry in its supplemental spending request.

But the president has not threatened to veto the $80 billion bill over airline aid, and a number of lawmakers and lobbyists have said it would be practically impossible for him to do so given the importance of the wartime bill.

In a statement of administration policy, Daniels wrote that "the industry is undergoing a period of fundamental restructuring to align costs and capacity to the demands of the marketplace, and excessive, generalized assistance would only delay and disrupt this important and inevitable process."

Sen. John McCain, R-Ariz., chairman of the Commerce, Science and Transportation Committee, has been critical of some airlines for letting costs get out of control, but he acknowledged that "this is an established service Americans have to use."

However, McCain sounded a note of caution about future bailouts. With the deficit increasing, McCain said, "There's just not enough money."

Administration officials have indicated that since some of the low-fare carriers, such as Southwest Airlines and JetBlue, have made money, failing carriers should not be propped up in their current incarnation.

The major network carriers are

built on a hub-and-spoke model developed after deregulation to make airlines more efficient. Airlines previously had operated point-to-point, whether or not there were enough passengers to fill the planes.

Routing flights through hubs allowed airlines to make the best use of their planes, thus saving money, while allowing passengers a wider range of choices. It also allowed carriers to better connect with overseas flights.

The result was the development of network carriers who served most of the nation. Though they had competition from point-to-point carriers that might pick selected routes, they remained the dominant force in aviation.

The system worked fairly well until the economic downturn of 1990-91 and the first Persian Gulf War, when three airlines ended up in liquidation.

R.W. Mann, a former airline executive turned industry analyst, said the administration was misguided in its sink-or-swim policies.

"Despite the draconian nature of these cuts it, doesn't get their costs anywhere close to Southwest or JetBlue" that do not serve small markets in the first place, he said. "If the country really wants a national transportation system which keeps the economy moving . . . you can't let [the majors] fail."

He added that Snow and Daniels "don't have to go home to see constituents. If those businesses lose service, there's going to be hell to pay."

Playing the Slots

Another limiting factor for all airlines has been the federally run air traffic control system. Just as highway traffic congestion can limit the expansion of trucking companies, crowded skies and airports make it difficult for airlines to operate when and how they like.

In particularly busy airports such as Reagan National in Washington or Chicago's O'Hare International, the number of takeoff and landing slots has been strictly controlled. That has made it difficult for startup carriers to break into some major metropolitan markets. And it has turned some lawmakers into advocates for carriers back home.

McCain, for instance, had for years sought to ease flight restrictions out of Reagan National, saying it would lead to lower airfares and more competition.

During negotiations over reauthorizing of the FAA in 2000, when air travel was at a peak, McCain brokered a deal which led to six daily flights out of the airport for airlines with hubs located beyond a 1,250-mile limit.

After the measure became the law commonly known as AIR-21 (PL 106-181), the Transportation Department awarded three of the slots to America West Holdings Inc., parent company of Tempe, Ariz.-based America West Airlines. One is a direct flight to Las Vegas, and two are to McCain's hometown of Phoenix.

The legislation was enacted in the thick of the Arizonan's failed presidential bid, and McCain was savaged in the media for what many saw as favoritism towards his hometown airline. Reports cited America West's campaign contributions to the senator, some $15,250, according to the Center for Responsive Politics.

McCain, however, vowed never to fly that America West route. "I swore I would never ride it, because everyone thought it looked bad," he said. To this day, he flies United Airlines out of Phoenix's Sky Harbor International Airport to the more inconveniently located Dulles International, and he often takes indirect flights home, including on American Airlines.

He has said repeatedly he did not have anything to do with the Transportation Department decision to award the slots, but the arrangement has come to symbolize some of the cozy relationships between members of Congress and the airline industry.

It is the major network carriers that have taken the lead in the lobbying campaign for both post-Sept. 11 federal aid, and the Iraq war supplemental as well, most observers agree, although low-fare carriers were invited to join the coalition to avoid the appearance of opportunism.

The all-hands-on-deck effort has paid off, although one needs look no further than the home bases of the major network carriers to understand the political clout they carry.

American Airlines is based in Dallas, where Dallas-Ft. Worth International Airport is a major domestic and international hub. The airline employs just under 24,000 people in the area, coupled with the workers, shops and concessionaires at the airport itself.

From 1985 to 2003, Republican Dick Armey, who was House majority leader before his retirement in January, represented the Dallas area.

Continental Airlines is based in Houston, backyard of current House Majority Leader Tom DeLay.

Airline Bailout

Both Texans were key factors in enacting what became known as the first airline "bailout" — although the carriers prefer the term "aid package." That law, passed 11 days after the terrorist attacks, is generally regarded as an unrivaled lobbying coup and a testament to the airlines' clout.

House Speaker J. Dennis Hastert, R-Ill., also was a major proponent of the original bailout. Chicago is home to O'Hare International Airport and United Airlines. O'Hare is the nation's only dual hub with a heavy American Airlines presence as well.

Hastert's presence has been a major boon to United and O'Hare even beyond the aid bill. He has fought for an expansion of O'Hare that has been sought by United and American, as well as a loan guarantee for troubled United. Both efforts have thus far been unsuccessful, the latter due to White House opposition.

But Hastert was the architect of the current airline assistance package, which would reimburse carriers for security costs dating back to Sept. 11, and he pushed it through over White House objections.

Not all lawmakers are happy with the airlines' lobbying efforts.

"I think more members are more dubious than we've been in a long time," said Sen. Ron Wyden, D-Ore., who for years fought a losing battle to enact a "passengers' bill of rights" to ensure certain standards of customer service and timely air travel.

"But it's always uphill when you're going up against such a powerful set of interests," Wyden said.

Even Republican Sen. Kay Bailey Hutchison of Texas has expressed some skepticism of the industry's efforts, even though her state has the nation's highest concentration of aviation interests — popular low-fare carrier Southwest Airlines is also headquartered there.

The major airlines, she said, "have to lower their cost-structures" before Congress considers any additional assistance after the supplemental.

"There will be nothing else for some time," she said. ◆

Appendix

The Legislative Process in Brief

Note: Parliamentary terms used below are defined in the glossary.

Introduction of Bills

A House member (including the resident commissioner of Puerto Rico and nonvoting delegates of the District of Columbia, Guam, the Virgin Islands and American Samoa) may introduce any one of several types of bills and resolutions by handing it to the clerk of the House or placing it in a box called the hopper. A senator first gains recognition of the presiding officer to announce the introduction of a bill.

As the usual next step in either the House or Senate, the bill is numbered, referred to the appropriate committee, labeled with the sponsor's name and sent to the Government Printing Office so that copies can be made for subsequent study and action. House and Senate bills may be jointly sponsored and carry several senators' names. A bill written in the executive branch and proposed as an administration measure usually is introduced by the chairman of the congressional committee that has jurisdiction, as a courtesy to the White House.

Bills—Prefixed with HR in the House, S in the Senate, followed by a number. Used as the form for most legislation, whether general or special, public or private.

Joint Resolutions—Designated H J Res or S J Res. Subject to the same procedure as bills, with the exception of a joint resolution proposing an amendment to the Constitution. The latter must be approved by two-thirds of both houses and is then sent directly to the administrator of general services for submission to the states for ratification instead of being presented to the president for his approval.

Concurrent Resolutions—Designated H Con Res or S Con Res. Used for matters affecting the operations of both houses. These resolutions do not become law.

Resolutions—Designated H Res or S Res. Used for a matter concerning the operation of either house alone and adopted only by the chamber in which it originates.

Committee Action

With few exceptions, bills are referred to the appropriate standing committees. The job of referral formally is the responsibility of the Speaker of the House and the presiding officer of the Senate, but this task usually is carried out on their behalf by the parliamentarians of the House and Senate. Precedent, statute and the jurisdictional mandates of the committees as set forth in the rules of the House and Senate determine which committees receive what kinds of bills. Bills are technically considered "read for the first time" when referred to House committees.

When a bill reaches a committee it is placed on the committee's calendar. Failure of a committee to act on a bill is equivalent to killing it and most fall by the legislative roadside. The measure can be withdrawn from the committee's purview only by a discharge petition signed by a majority of the House membership on House bills, or by adoption of a special resolution in the Senate. Discharge attempts rarely succeed and the Senate procedure has not been used for decades.

The first committee action taken on a bill usually is a request for comment on it by interested agencies of the government. The committee chairman may assign the bill to a subcommittee for study and hearings, or it may be considered by the full committee. Hearings may be public, closed (executive session) or both. A subcommittee, after considering a bill, reports to the full committee its recommendations for action and any proposed amendments.

The full committee then votes on its recommendation to the House or Senate. This procedure is called "ordering a bill reported." Occasionally a committee may order a bill reported unfavorably; most of the time a report, submitted by the chairman of the committee to the House or Senate, calls for favorable action on the measure since the committee can effectively "kill" a bill by simply failing to take any action.

After the bill is reported, the committee chairman instructs the staff to prepare a written report. The report describes the purposes and scope of the bill, explains the committee revisions, notes proposed changes in existing law and, usually, includes the views of the executive branch agencies consulted. Often committee members opposing a measure issue dissenting minority statements that are included in the report.

Usually, the committee "marks up" or proposes amendments to the bill. If the amendments are substantial and the measure is complicated, the committee may order a "clean bill" introduced, which will embody the proposed amendments. The original bill then is put aside and the clean bill, with a new number, is reported to the floor.

The chamber must approve, alter or reject the committee amendments before the bill itself can be put to a vote.

Floor Action

After a bill is reported back to the house where it originated, it is placed on the calendar.

There are five legislative calendars in the House, issued in one cumulative calendar titled *Calendars of the United States House of Representatives and History of Legislation*. The House calendars are:

The Union Calendar to which are referred bills raising revenues, general appropriations bills and any measures directly or indirectly appropriating money or property. It is the Calendar of the Committee of the Whole House on the State of the Union.

How a Bill Becomes a Law

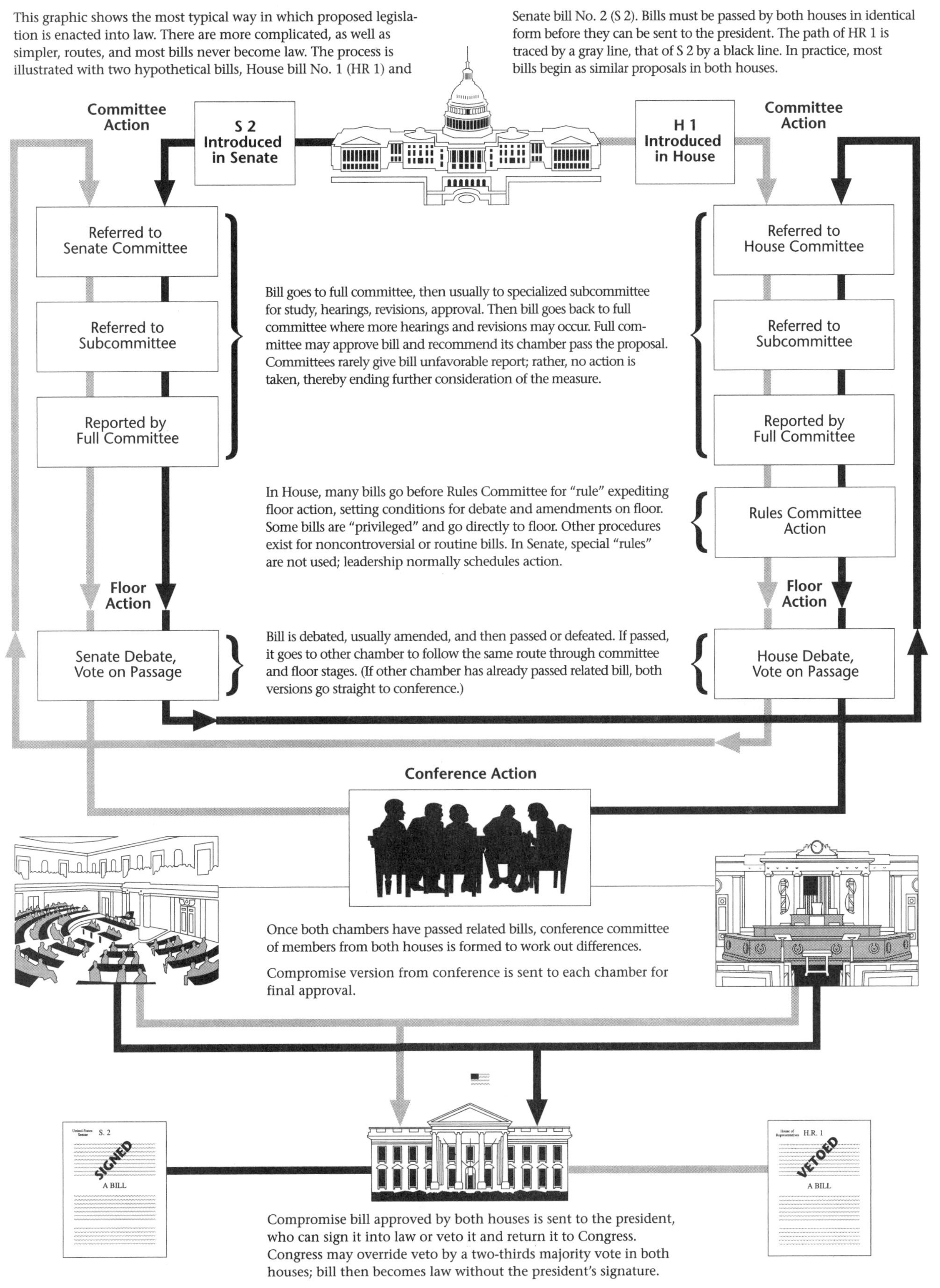

The House Calendar to which are referred bills of public character not raising revenue or appropriating money.

The Corrections Calendar to which are referred bills to repeal rules and regulations deemed excessive or unnecessary when the Corrections Calendar is called the second and fourth Tuesday of each month. (Instituted in the 104th Congress to replace the seldom-used Consent Calendar.) A three-fifths majority is required for passage.

The Private Calendar to which are referred bills for relief in the nature of claims against the United States or private immigration bills that are passed without debate when the Private Calendar is called the first and third Tuesdays of each month.

The Discharge Calendar to which are referred motions to discharge committees when the necessary signatures are signed to a discharge petition.

There is only one legislative calendar in the Senate and one "executive calendar" for treaties and nominations submitted to the Senate.

Debate. A bill is brought to debate by varying procedures. In the Senate the majority leader, in consultation with the minority leader and others, schedules the bills that will be taken up for debate. If it is urgent or important it can be taken up in the Senate either by unanimous consent or by a majority vote.

In the House, precedence is granted if a special rule is obtained from the Rules Committee. A request for a special rule usually is made by the chairman of the committee that favorably reported the bill. The request is considered by the Rules Committee in the same fashion that other committees consider legislative measures. The committee proposes a resolution providing for immediate consideration of the bill. The Rules Committee reports the resolution to the House where it is debated and voted on in the same fashion as regular bills.

The resolutions providing special rules are important because they specify how long the bill may be debated and whether it may be amended from the floor. If floor amendments are banned, the bill is considered under a "closed rule."

When a bill is debated under an "open rule," amendments may be offered from the floor. Committee amendments always are taken up first but may be changed, as may all amendments up to the second degree; that is, an amendment to an amendment to an amendment is not in order.

Duration of debate in the House depends on whether the bill is under discussion by the House proper or before the House when it is sitting as the Committee of the Whole House on the State of the Union. In the former, the amount of time for debate is allocated with an hour for each member if the measure is under consideration without a rule. In the Committee of the Whole the amount of time agreed on for general debate is equally divided between proponents and opponents. At the end of general discussion, the bill is often read section by section for amendment. Debate on an amendment is limited to five minutes for each side; this is called the "five-minute rule." In practice, amendments regularly are debated more than ten minutes, with members gaining the floor by offering pro forma amendments or obtaining unanimous consent to speak longer than five minutes.

Senate debate usually is unlimited. It can be halted only by unanimous consent or by "cloture," which requires a three-fifths majority of the entire Senate except for proposed changes in the Senate rules. The latter requires a two-thirds vote.

The House considers almost all important bills within a parliamentary framework known as the Committee of the Whole. It is not a committee as the word usually is understood; it is the full House meeting under another name for the purpose of speeding action on legislation. Technically, the House sits as the Committee of the Whole when it considers any tax measure or bill dealing with public appropriations. Upon adoption of a special rule, the Speaker declares the House resolved into the Committee of the Whole and appoints a member of the majority party to serve as the chairman. The rules of the House permit the Committee of the Whole to meet when a quorum of 100 members is present on the floor and to amend and act on bills. When the Committee of the Whole has acted, it "rises," the Speaker returns as the presiding officer of the House and the member appointed chairman of the Committee of the Whole reports the action of the committee and its recommendations. The Committee of the Whole cannot pass a bill; instead it reports the measure to the full House with whatever changes it has approved. The full House then may pass or reject the bill — or, on occasion, recommit the bill to committee. Amendments adopted in the Committee of the Whole may be put to a second vote in the full House.

Votes. Voting on bills may occur repeatedly before they are finally approved or rejected. The House votes on the rule for the bill and on various amendments to the bill. Voting on amendments often is a more illuminating test of a bill's support than is the final tally. Sometimes members approve final passage of bills after vigorously supporting amendments that, if adopted, would have scuttled the legislation.

The Senate has three different methods of voting: an untabulated voice vote, a standing vote (called a division) and a recorded roll call to which members answer "yea" or "nay" when their names are called. The House also employs voice and standing votes, but since January 1973 yeas and nays have been recorded by an electronic voting device, eliminating the need for time-consuming roll calls.

After amendments to a bill have been voted upon, a vote may be taken on a motion to recommit the bill to committee. If carried, this vote is usually a death blow to the bill. If the motion is unsuccessful, the bill then is "read for the third time." After the third reading a vote on passage is taken. The final vote may be followed by a motion to reconsider, and this motion may be followed by a move to lay the motion on the table. Usually, those voting for the bill's passage vote for the tabling motion, thus safeguarding the final passage action. With that, the bill has been formally passed by the chamber.

Action in Second Chamber

After a bill is passed it is sent to the other chamber. This body may then take one of several steps. It may pass the bill as is — accepting the other chamber's language. It may send the bill to committee for scrutiny or alteration, or reject the entire bill, advising the other chamber of its actions. Or it simply may ignore the bill submitted while it continues work on its own version of the proposed legislation. Frequently, one chamber may approve a version of a bill that is greatly at variance with the version already passed by the other chamber, and then substitute its contents for the language of the other, retaining only the latter's bill number.

Often the second chamber makes only minor changes. If these are readily agreed to by the other chamber, the bill then is routed to the president. However, if the opposite chamber significantly alters the bill submitted to it, the measure usually is "sent to conference." The chamber that has possession of the "papers" (engrossed bill, engrossed amendments, messages of transmittal) requests a conference and the other chamber may agree to it. If the second chamber does not agree, the bill dies.

Examples of Legislative Documents
H.R. 67
A BILL
H. CON. RES. 385
CONCURRENT RESOLUTION
S. J. RES. 14
JOINT RESOLUTION
H.R. 4660
A BILL
S. CON. RES. 11
CONCURRENT RESOLUTION
S. 2452
A BILL
S. RES. 187
RESOLUTION
H. J. RES. 29
JOINT RESOLUTION

Conference Action

A conference works out conflicting House and Senate versions of a legislative bill. The conferees usually are senior members from the committees that managed the legislation who are appointed by the presiding officers of the two houses. Under this arrangement the conferees of one house have the duty of trying to maintain their chamber's position in the face of amending actions by the conferees (also referred to as "managers") of the other house.

The number of conferees from each chamber may vary, the range usually being from seven to nine members in each group, depending on the length or complexity of the bill involved. But a majority vote controls the action of each group so that a large representation does not give one chamber a voting advantage over the other chamber's conferees.

Theoretically, conferees are not allowed to write new legislation in reconciling the two versions before them, but this curb sometimes is bypassed. Many bills have been put into acceptable compromise form only after new language was provided by the conferees. Frequently the ironing out of difficulties takes days or even weeks. Conferences on involved, complex and controversial bills sometimes are particularly drawn out.

As a conference proceeds, conferees reconcile differences between the versions, but generally they grant concessions only insofar as they remain sure that the chamber they represent will accept the compromises. Occasionally, uncertainty over how either house will react, or the positive refusal of a chamber to back down on a disputed amendment, results in an impasse, and the bills die in conference even though each was approved by its sponsoring chamber.

When the conferees have reached agreement, they prepare a conference report embodying their recommendations (compromises) and a joint explanatory statement. The report, in document form, must be submitted to each house. The conference report must be approved by each house. Consequently, approval of the report is approval of the compromise bill. In the order of voting on conference reports, the chamber that asked for a conference yields to the other chamber the opportunity to vote first.

Final Action

After a bill has been passed by both the House and Senate in identical form, all of the original papers are sent to the enrolling clerk of the chamber in which the bill originated. The clerk then prepares an enrolled bill, which is printed on parchment paper.

When this bill has been certified as correct by the secretary of the Senate or the clerk of the House, depending on which chamber originated the bill, it is signed first (no matter whether it originated in the Senate or House) by the Speaker of the House and then by the president of the Senate. It is next sent to the White House to await action.

If the president approves the bill, he signs it, dates it and usually writes the word "approved" on the document. If the president does not sign it within 10 days (Sundays excepted) and Congress is in session, the bill becomes law without his signature.

If Congress adjourns *sine die* at the end of the second session the president can pocket veto a bill and it dies without Congress having the opportunity to override.

A president vetoes a bill by refusing to sign it and, before the ten-day period expires, returning it to Congress with a message stating his reasons. The message is sent to the chamber that originated the bill. If no action is taken on the message, the bill dies. Congress, however, can attempt to override the president's veto and enact the bill, "the objections of the president to the contrary notwithstanding." Overriding a veto requires a two-thirds vote of those present in each chamber, who must number a quorum and vote by roll call.

If the president's veto is overridden by a two-thirds vote in both houses, the bill becomes law. Otherwise it is dead.

When bills are passed finally and signed, or passed over a veto, they are given law numbers in numerical order as they become law. There are two series of numbers, one for public and one for private laws, starting at the number "1" for each two-year term of Congress. They are then identified by law number and by Congress — for example, Private Law 10, 105th Congress; Public Law 33, 106th Congress (or PL 106-33).

The Budget Process in Brief

Through the budget process, the president and Congress decide how much to spend and tax during the upcoming fiscal year. More specifically, they decide how much to spend on each activity, ensure that the government spends no more than that and spends it only for that activity and report on that spending at the end of each budget cycle.

The President's Budget

The law requires that, by the first Monday in February, the president submit to Congress his proposed federal budget for the next fiscal year, which begins on October 1. To accomplish this the president establishes general budget and fiscal policy guidelines. Based on these guidelines, executive branch agencies make requests for funds and submit them to the White House's Office of Management and Budget (OMB) nearly a year before the start of a new fiscal year. The OMB, receiving direction from the president and administration officials, reviews the agencies' requests and develops a detailed budget by December. From December to January the OMB prepares the budget documents, so that the president can deliver it to Congress in February.

The president's budget is the executive branch's plan for the next year — but it is just a proposal. After receiving it, Congress has its own budget process to follow from February to October. Only after Congress passes the required spending bills — and the president signs them — has the government created its actual budget.

Action in Congress

Congress first must pass a "budget resolution" — a framework within which the members of Congress will make their decisions about spending and taxes. It includes targets for total spending, total revenues and the deficit, and allocations within the spending target for the two types of spending — discretionary and mandatory.

Discretionary spending, which currently accounts for about 33 percent of all federal spending, is what the president and Congress must decide to spend for the next year through the thirteen annual appropriations bills. It includes money for such activities as the FBI and the Coast Guard, for housing and education, for NASA and highway and bridge construction and for defense and foreign aid.

Mandatory spending, which currently accounts for 67 percent of all spending, is authorized by laws that have already been passed. It includes entitlement spending — such as for Social Security, Medicare, veterans' benefits and food stamps — through which individuals receive benefits because they are eligible based on their age, income or other criteria. It also includes interest on the national debt, which the government pays to individuals and institutions that hold Treasury bonds and other government securities. The only way the president and Congress can change the spending on entitlement and other mandatory programs is if they change the laws that authorized the programs.

Currently, the law requires that legislation that would raise mandatory spending or lower revenues — compared to existing law — be offset by spending cuts or revenue increases. This requirement, called "pay-as-you-go" is designed to prevent new legislation from increasing the deficit.

Once Congress passes the budget resolution, legislators turn their attention to passing the 13 annual appropriations bills and, if they choose, "authorizing" bills to change the laws governing mandatory spending and revenues.

Congress begins by examining the president's budget in detail. Scores of committees and subcommittees hold hearings on proposals under their jurisdiction. The House and Senate Armed Services Authorizing Committees, and the Defense and Military Construction Subcommittees of the Appropriations Committees, for instance, hold hearings on the president's defense budget. The White House budget director, cabinet officers and other administration officials work with Congress as it accepts some of the president's proposals, rejects others and changes still others. Congress can change funding levels, eliminate programs or add programs not requested by the president. It can add or eliminate taxes and other sources of revenue, or make other changes that affect the amount of revenue collected. Congressional rules require that these committees and subcommittees take actions that reflect the congressional budget resolution.

The president's budget, the budget resolution and the appropriations or authorizing bills measure spending in two ways — "budget authority" and "outlays." Budget authority is what the law authorizes the federal government to spend for certain programs, projects or activities. What the government actually spends in a particular year, however, is an outlay. For example, when the government decides to build a space exploration system, the president and Congress may agree to appropriate $1 billion in budget authority. But the space system may take ten years to build. Thus, the government may spend $100 million in outlays in the first year to begin construction and the remaining $900 million during the next nine years as the construction continues.

Congress must provide budget authority before the federal agencies can obligate the government to make outlays. When Congress fails to complete action on one or more of the regular annual appropriations bills before the fiscal year begins on October 1, budget authority may be made on a temporary basis through continuing resolutions. Continuing resolutions make budget authority available for limited periods of time, generally at rates related through some formula to the rate provided in the previous year's appropriation.

Monitoring the Budget

Once Congress passes and the president signs the federal appropriations bills or authorizing laws for the fiscal year, the government monitors the budget through (1) agency program managers and budget officials, including the Inspectors General, who report only to the agency head; (2) the Office of Management and Budget; (3) congressional committees; and (4) the General Accounting Office, an auditing arm of Congress.

This oversight is designed to (1) ensure that agencies comply with legal limits on spending and that agencies use budget authority only for the purposes intended; (2) see that programs are operating consistently with legal requirements and existing policy; and (3) ensure that programs are well managed and achieving the intended results.

The president may withhold appropriated amounts from obligation only under certain limited circumstances — to provide for contingencies, to achieve savings made possible through changes in requirements or greater efficiency of operations or as otherwise provided by law. The Impoundment Control Act of 1974 specifies the procedures that must be followed if funds are withheld. Congress can also cancel previous authorized budget authority by passing a rescissions bill — but it also must be signed by the president.

Glossary of Congressional Terms

AA—(See Administrative Assistant.)

Absence of a Quorum—Absence of the required number of members to conduct business in a house or a committee. When a quorum call or roll-call vote in a house establishes that a quorum is not present, no debate or other business is permitted except a motion to adjourn or motions to request or compel the attendance of absent members, if necessary by arresting them.

Absolute Majority—A vote requiring approval by a majority of all members of a house rather than a majority of members present and voting. Also referred to as constitutional majority.

Account—Organizational units used in the federal budget primarily for recording spending and revenue transactions.

Act—(1) A bill passed in identical form by both houses of Congress and signed into law by the president or enacted over the president's veto. A bill also becomes an act without the president's signature if he does not return it to Congress within ten days (Sundays excepted) and if Congress has not adjourned within that period. (2) Also, the technical term for a bill passed by at least one house and engrossed.

Ad Hoc Select Committee—A temporary committee formed for a special purpose or to deal with a specific subject. Conference committees are ad hoc joint committees. A House rule adopted in 1975 authorizes the Speaker to refer measures to special ad hoc committees, appointed by the Speaker with the approval of the House.

Adjourn—A motion to adjourn is a formal motion to end a day's session or meeting of a house or a committee. A motion to adjourn usually has no conditions attached to it, but it sometimes may specify the day or time for reconvening or make reconvening subject to the call of the chamber's presiding officer or the committee's chairman. In both houses, a motion to adjourn is of the highest privilege, takes precedence over all other motions, is not debatable and must be put to an immediate vote. Adjournment of a house ends its legislative day. For this reason, the House or Senate sometimes adjourns for only one minute, or some other very brief period of time, during the course of a day's session. The House does not permit a motion to adjourn after it has resolved into Committee of the Whole or when the previous question has been ordered on a measure to final passage without an intervening motion.

Adjourn for More Than Three Days—Under Article I, Section 5 of the Constitution, neither house may adjourn for more than three days without the approval of the other. The necessary approval is given in a concurrent resolution to which both houses have agreed.

Adjournment *Sine Die*—Final adjournment of an annual or two-year session of Congress; literally, adjournment without a day. The two houses must agree to a privileged concurrent resolution for such an adjournment. A sine die adjournment precludes Congress from meeting again until the next constitutionally fixed date of a session (Jan. 3 of the following year) unless Congress determines otherwise by law or the president calls it into special session. Article II, Section 3 of the Constitution authorizes the president to adjourn both houses until such time as the president thinks proper when the two houses cannot agree to a time of adjournment. No president, however, has ever exercised this authority.

Adjournment to a Day (and Time) Certain—An adjournment that fixes the next date and time of meeting for one or both houses. It does not end an annual session of Congress.

Administration Bill—A bill drafted in the executive office of the president or in an executive department or agency to implement part of the president's program. An administration bill is introduced in Congress by a member who supports it or as a courtesy to the administration.

Administrative Assistant (AA)—The title usually given to a member's chief aide, political advisor and head of office staff. The administrative assistant often represents the member at meetings with visitors or officials when the member is unable (or unwilling) to attend.

Adoption—The usual parliamentary term for approval of a conference report. It is also commonly applied to amendments.

Advance Appropriation—In an appropriation act for a particular fiscal year, an appropriation that does not become available for spending or obligation until a subsequent fiscal year. The amount of the advance appropriation is counted as part of the budget for the fiscal year in which it becomes available for obligation.

Advance Funding—A mechanism whereby statutory language may allow budget authority for a fiscal year to be increased, and obligations to be incurred, with an offsetting decrease in the budget authority available in the succeeding fiscal year. If not used, the budget authority remains available for obligation in the succeeding fiscal year. Advance funding is sometimes used to provide contingency funding of a few benefit programs.

Adverse Report—A committee report recommending against approval of a measure or some other matter. Committees usually pigeonhole measures they oppose instead of reporting them adversely, but they may be required to report them by a statutory rule or an instruction from their parent body.

Advice and Consent—The Senate's constitutional role in consenting to or rejecting the president's nominations to executive branch and judicial offices and treaties with other nations. Confirmation of nominees requires a simple majority vote of senators present and voting. Treaties must be approved by a two-thirds majority of those present and voting.

Aisle—The center aisle of each chamber. When facing the presiding officer, Republicans usually sit to the right of the aisle, Democrats to the left. When members speak of "my side of the aisle" or "this side," they are referring to their party.

Amendment—A formal proposal to alter the text of a bill, resolution, amendment, motion, treaty or some other text. Technically, it is a motion. An amendment may strike out (eliminate) part of a text, insert new text or strike out and insert — that is, replace all or part of the text with new text. The texts of amendments considered on the floor are printed in full in the Congressional Record.

Amendment in the Nature of a Substitute—Usually, an amendment to replace the entire text of a measure. It strikes out everything after the enacting clause and inserts a version that may be somewhat, substantially or entirely different. When a committee adopts extensive amendments to a measure, it often incorporates them into such an amendment. Occasionally, the term is applied to an amendment that replaces a major portion of a measure's text.

Amendment Tree—A diagram showing the number and types of amendments that the rules and practices of a house permit to be offered to a measure before any of the amendments is voted on. It shows the relationship of one amendment to the others, and it may also indicate the degree of each amendment, whether it is a perfecting or substitute amendment, the order in which amendments may be offered and the order in which they are put to a vote. The same type of diagram can be used to display an actual amendment situation.

Annual Authorization—Legislation that authorizes appropriations for a single fiscal year and usually for a specific amount. Under the rules of the authorization-appropriation process, an annually authorized agency or program must be reauthorized each year if it is to receive appropriations for that year. Sometimes Congress fails to enact the reauthorization but nevertheless provides appropriations to continue the program, circumventing the rules by one means or another.

Appeal—A member's formal challenge of a ruling or decision by the presiding officer. On appeal, a house or a committee may overturn the ruling by majority vote. The right of appeal ensures the body against arbitrary control by the chair. Appeals are rarely made in the House and are even more rarely successful. Rulings are more frequently appealed in the Senate and occasionally overturned, in part because its presiding officer is not the majority party's leader, as in the House.

Apportionment—The action, after each decennial census, of allocating the number of members in the House of Representatives to each state. By law, the total number of House members (not counting delegates and a resident commissioner) is fixed at 435. The number allotted to each state is based approximately on its proportion of the nation's total population. Because the Constitution guarantees each state one representative no matter how small its population, exact proportional distribution is virtually impossible. The mathematical formula currently used to determine the apportionment is called the Method of Equal Proportions. (See Method of Equal Proportions.)

Appropriated Entitlement—An entitlement program, such as veterans' pensions, that is funded through annual appropriations rather than by a permanent appropriation. Because such an entitlement law requires the government to provide eligible recipients the benefits to which they are entitled, whatever the cost, Congress must appropriate the necessary funds.

Appropriation—(1) Legislative language that permits a federal agency to incur obligations and make payments from the Treasury for specified purposes, usually during a specified period of time. (2) The specific amount of money made available by such language. The Constitution prohibits payments from the Treasury except "in Consequence of Appropriations made by Law." With some exceptions, the rules of both houses forbid consideration of appropriations for purposes that are unauthorized in law or of appropriation amounts larger than those authorized in law. The House of Representatives claims the exclusive right to originate appropriation bills — a claim the Senate denies in theory but accepts in practice.

At-Large—Elected by and representing an entire state instead of a district within a state. The term usually refers to a representative rather than to a senator. (See Apportionment; Congressional District; Redistricting.)

August Adjournment—A congressional adjournment during the month of August in odd-numbered years, required by the Legislative Reorganization Act of 1970. The law instructs the two houses to adjourn for a period of at least thirty days before the second day after Labor Day, unless Congress provides otherwise or if, on July 31, a state of war exists by congressional declaration.

Authorization—(1) A statutory provision that establishes or continues a federal agency, activity or program for a fixed or indefinite period of time. It may also establish policies and restrictions and deal with organizational and administrative matters. (2) A statutory provision, as described in (1), may also, explicitly or implicitly, authorize congressional action to provide appropriations for an agency, activity or program. The appropriations may be authorized for one year, several years or an indefinite period of time, and the authorization may be for a specific amount of money or an indefinite amount ("such sums as may be necessary"). Authorizations of specific amounts are construed as ceilings on the amounts that subsequently may be appropriated in an appropriation bill, but not as minimums; either house may appropriate lesser amounts or nothing at all.

Authorization-Appropriation Process—The two-stage procedural system that the rules of each house require for establishing and funding federal agencies and programs: first, enactment of authorizing legislation that creates or continues an agency or program; second, enactment of appropriations legislation that provides funds for the authorized agency or program.

Automatic Roll Call—Under a House rule, the automatic ordering of the yeas and nays when a quorum is not present on a voice or division vote and a member objects to the vote on that ground. It is not permitted in the Committee of the Whole.

Backdoor Spending Authority—Authority to incur obligations that evades the normal congressional appropriations process because it is provided in legislation other than appropriation acts. The most common forms are borrowing authority, contract authority and entitlement authority.

Baseline—A projection of the levels of federal spending, revenues and the resulting budgetary surpluses or deficits for the upcoming and subsequent fiscal years, taking into account laws enacted to date and assuming no new policy decisions. It provides a benchmark for measuring the budgetary effects of proposed changes in federal revenues or spending, assuming certain economic conditions.

Bells—A system of electric signals and lights that informs members of activities in each chamber. The type of activity taking place is indicated by the number of signals and the interval between them. When the signals are sounded, a corresponding number of lights are lit around the perimeter of many clocks in House or Senate offices.

Bicameral—Consisting of two houses or chambers. Congress is a bicameral legislature whose two houses have an equal role in enacting legislation. In most other national bicameral legislatures, one house is significantly more powerful than the other.

Bigger Bite Amendment—An amendment that substantively changes a portion of a text including language that had previously been amended. Normally, language that has been amended may not be amended again. However, a part of a sentence that has been changed by amendment, for example, may be changed again by an amendment that amends a "bigger bite" of the text — that is, by an amendment that also substantively changes the unamended parts of the sentence or the entire section or title in which the previously amended language appears. The biggest possible bite is an amendment in the nature of a substitute that amends the entire text of a measure. Once adopted, therefore, such an amendment ends the amending process.

Bill—The term for the chief vehicle Congress uses for enacting laws. Bills that originate in the House of Representatives are designated as HR, those in the Senate as S, followed by a number assigned in the order in which they are introduced during a two-year Congress. A bill becomes a law if passed in identical language by both houses and signed by the president, or passed over the president's veto, or if the president fails to sign it within ten days after receiving it while Congress is in session.

Bill of Attainder—An act of a legislature finding a person guilty of treason or a felony. The Constitution prohibits the passage of such a bill by the U.S. Congress or any state legislature.

Bills and Resolutions Introduced—Members formally present measures to their respective houses by delivering them to a clerk in the chamber when their house is in session. Both houses permit any number of members to join in introducing a bill or resolution. The first member listed on the measure is the sponsor; the other members listed are its cosponsors.

Bills and Resolutions Referred—After a bill or resolution is introduced, it is normally sent to one or more committees that have jurisdiction over its subject, as defined by House and Senate rules and precedents. A Senate measure is usually referred to the committee with jurisdiction over the predominant subject of its text, but it may be sent to two or more committees by unanimous consent or on a motion offered jointly by the majority and minority leaders. In the House, a rule requires the Speaker to refer a measure to the committee that has primary jurisdiction. The Speaker is also authorized to refer measures sequentially to additional committees and to impose time limits on such referrals.

Bipartisan Committee—A committee with an equal number of members from each political party. The House Committee on Standards of Official Conduct and the Senate Select Committee on Ethics are the only bipartisan, permanent full committees.

Borrowing Authority—Statutory authority permitting a federal agency, such as the Export-Import Bank, to borrow money from the public or the Treasury to finance its operations. It is a form of backdoor spending. To bring such spending under the control of the congressional appropriation process, the Congressional Budget Act requires that new borrowing authority shall be effective only to the extent and in such amounts as are provided in appropriations acts.

Budget—A detailed statement of actual or anticipated revenues and expenditures during an accounting period. For the national government, the period is the federal fiscal year (Oct. 1 to Sept. 30). The budget usually refers to the president's budget submission to Congress early each calendar year. The president's budget estimates federal government income and spending for the upcoming fiscal year and contains detailed recommendations for appropriation, revenue and other legislation. Congress is not required to accept or even vote directly on the president's proposals, and it often revises the president's budget extensively. (See Fiscal Year.)

Budget Act—Common name for the Congressional Budget and Impoundment Control Act of 1974, which established the basic procedures of the current congressional budget process; created the House and Senate Budget Committees; and enacted procedures for reconciliation, deferrals and rescissions. (See Budget Process; Deferral; Impoundment; Reconciliation; Rescission. See also Gramm-Rudman-Hollings Act of 1985.)

Budget and Accounting Act of 1921—The law that, for the first time, authorized the president to submit to Congress an annual budget for the entire federal government. Before passage of the act, most federal agencies sent their budget requests to the appropriate congressional committees without review by the president.

Budget Authority—Generally, the amount of money that may be spent or obligated by a government agency or for a government program or activity. Technically, it is statutory authority to enter into obligations that normally result in outlays. The main forms of budget authority are appropriations, borrowing authority and contract authority. It also includes authority to obligate and expend the proceeds of offsetting receipts and collections. Congress may make budget authority available for only one year, several years or an indefinite period, and it may specify definite or indefinite amounts.

Budget Enforcement Act of 1990—An act that revised the sequestration process established by the Gramm-Rudman-Hollings Act of 1985, replaced the earlier act's fixed deficit targets with adjustable ones, established discretionary spending limits for fiscal years 1991 through 1995, instituted pay-as-you-go rules to enforce deficit neutrality on revenue and mandatory spending legislation and reformed the budget and accounting rules for federal credit activities. Unlike the Gramm-Rudman-Hollings Act, the 1990 act emphasized restraints on legislated changes in taxes and spending instead of fixed deficit limits.

Budget Enforcement Act of 1997—An act that revised and updated the provisions of the Budget Enforcement Act of 1990, including by extending the discretionary spending caps and pay-as-you-go rules through 2002.

Budget Process—(1) In Congress, the procedural system it uses (a) to approve an annual concurrent resolution on the budget that sets goals for aggregate and functional categories of federal expenditures, revenues and the surplus or deficit for an upcoming fiscal year; and (b) to implement those goals in spending, revenue and, if necessary, reconciliation and debt-limit legislation. (2) In the executive branch, the process of formulating the president's annual budget, submitting it to Congress, defending it before congressional committees, implementing subsequent budget-related legislation, impounding or sequestering expenditures as permitted by law, auditing and evaluating programs and compiling final budget data. The Budget and Accounting Act of 1921 and the Congressional Budget and Impoundment Control Act of 1974 established the basic elements of the current budget process. Major revisions were enacted in the Gramm-Rudman-Hollings Act of 1985 and the Budget Enforcement Act of 1990.

Budget Resolution—A concurrent resolution in which Congress establishes or revises its version of the federal budget's broad financial features for the upcoming fiscal year and several additional fiscal years. Like other concurrent resolutions, it does not have the force of law, but it provides the framework within which Congress subsequently considers revenue, spending and other budget-implementing legislation. The framework consists of two basic elements: (1) aggregate budget amounts (total revenues, new budget authority, outlays, loan obligations and loan guarantee commitments, deficit or surplus and debt limit); and (2) subdivisions of the relevant aggregate amounts among the functional categories of the budget. Although it does not allocate funds to specific programs or accounts, the budget committees' reports accompanying the resolution often discuss the major program assumptions underlying its functional amounts. Unlike those amounts, however, the assumptions are not binding on Congress.

By Request—A designation indicating that a member has introduced a measure on behalf of the president, an executive agency or a private individual or organization. Members often introduce such measures as a courtesy because neither the president nor any person other than a member of Congress can do so. The term, which appears next to the sponsor's name, implies that the member who introduced the measure does not necessarily endorse it. A House rule dealing with by-request introductions dates from 1888, but the practice goes back to the earliest history of Congress.

Byrd Rule—The popular name of an amendment to the Congressional Budget Act that bars the inclusion of extraneous matter in any reconciliation legislation considered in the Senate. The ban is enforced by points of order that the presiding officer sustains. The provision defines different categories of extraneous matter, but it also permits certain exceptions. Its chief sponsor was Sen. Robert C. Byrd, D-W.Va.

Calendar—A list of measures or other matters (most of them favorably reported by committees) that are eligible for floor consideration. The House has five calendars; the Senate has two. A place on a calendar does not guarantee consideration. Each house decides which measures and matters it will take up, when and in what order, in accordance with its rules and practices.

Calendar Wednesday—A House procedure that on Wednesdays permits its committees to bring up for floor consideration nonprivileged measures they have reported. The procedure is so cumbersome and susceptible to dilatory tactics, however, that it is rarely used.

Call Up—To bring a measure or report to the floor for immediate consideration.

Casework—Assistance to constituents who seek assistance in dealing with federal and local government agencies. Constituent service is a high priority in most members' offices.

Caucus—(1) A common term for the official organization of each party in each house. (2) The official title of the organization of House Democrats. House and Senate Republicans and Senate Democrats call their organizations "conferences." (3) A term for an informal group of members who share legislative interests, such as the Black Caucus, Hispanic Caucus and Children's Caucus.

Censure—The strongest formal condemnation of a member for misconduct short of expulsion. A house usually adopts a resolution of censure to express its condemnation, after which the presiding officer reads its rebuke aloud to the member in the presence of his or her colleagues.

Chairman—The presiding officer of a committee, a subcommittee or a task force. At meetings, the chairman preserves order, enforces the rules, recognizes members to speak or offer motions and puts questions to a vote. The chairman of a committee or subcommittee usually appoints its staff and sets its agenda, subject to the panel's veto.

Chamber—The Capitol room in which a house of Congress normally holds its sessions. The chamber of the House of Representatives, officially called the Hall of the House, is considerably larger than that of the Senate because it must accommodate 435 representatives, four delegates and one resident commissioner. Unlike the Senate chamber, members have no desks or assigned seats. In both chambers, the floor slopes downward to the well in front of the presiding officer's raised desk. A chamber is often referred to as "the floor," as when members are said to be on or going to the floor. Those expressions usually imply that the member's house is in session.

Christmas Tree Bill—Jargon for a bill adorned with amendments, many of them unrelated to the bill's subject, that provide benefits for interest groups, specific states, congressional districts, companies and individuals.

Classes of Senators—A class consists of the thirty-three or thirty-four senators elected to a six-year term in the same general election. Because the terms of approximately one-third of the senators expire every two years, there are three classes.

Clean Bill—After a House committee extensively amends a bill, it often assembles its amendments and what is left of the bill into a new measure that one or more of its members introduces as a "clean bill." The revised measure is assigned a new number.

Clerk of the House—An officer of the House of Representatives responsible principally for administrative support of the legislative process in the House. The clerk is invariably the candidate of the majority party.

Cloakrooms—Two rooms with access to the rear of each chamber's floor, one for each party's members, where members may confer privately, sit quietly or have a snack. The presiding officer sometimes urges members who are conversing too loudly on the floor to retire to their cloakrooms.

Closed Hearing—A hearing closed to the public and the media. A House committee may close a hearing only if it determines that disclosure of the testimony to be taken would endanger national security, violate any law or tend to defame, degrade or incriminate any person. The Senate has a similar rule. Both houses require roll-call votes in open session to close a hearing.

Closed Rule—A special rule reported from the House Rules Committee that prohibits amendments to a measure or that only permits amendments offered by the reporting committee.

Cloture—A Senate procedure that limits further consideration of a pending proposal to thirty hours in order to end a filibuster. Sixteen senators must first sign and submit a cloture motion to the presiding officer. One hour after the Senate meets on the second calendar day thereafter, the chair puts the motion to a yea-and-nay vote following a live quorum call. If three-fifths of all senators (sixty if there are no vacancies) vote for the motion, the Senate must take final action on the cloture proposal by the end of the thirty hours of consideration and may consider no other business until it takes that action. Cloture on a proposal to amend the Senate's standing rules requires approval by two-thirds of the senators present and voting.

Code of Official Conduct—A House rule that bans certain actions by House members, officers and employees; requires them to conduct themselves in ways that "reflect creditably" on the House; and orders them to adhere to the spirit and the letter of House rules and those of its committees. The code's provisions govern the receipt of outside compensation, gifts and honoraria and the use of campaign funds; prohibit members from using their clerk-hire allowance to pay anyone who does not perform duties commensurate with that pay; forbids discrimination in members' hiring or treatment of employees on the grounds of race, color, religion, sex, handicap, age or national origin; orders members convicted of a crime who might be punished by imprisonment of two or more years not to participate in committee business or vote on the floor until exonerated or reelected; and restricts employees' contact with federal agencies on matters in which they have a significant financial interest. The Senate's rules contain some similar prohibitions.

College of Cardinals—A popular term for the subcommittee chairmen of the appropriations committees, reflecting their influence over appropriation measures. The chairmen of the full appropriations committees are sometimes referred to as popes.

Comity—The practice of maintaining mutual courtesy and civility between the two houses in their dealings with each other and in members' speeches on the floor. Although the practice is largely governed by long-established customs, a House rule explicitly cautions its members not to characterize any Senate action or inaction, refer to individual senators except under certain circumstances, or quote from Senate proceedings except to make legislative history on a measure. The Senate has no rule on the subject but references to the House have been held out of order on several occasions. Generally the houses do not interfere with each other's appropriations although minor conflicts sometimes occur. A refusal to receive a message from the other house has also been held to violate the practice of comity.

Committee—A panel of members elected or appointed to perform some service or function for its parent body. Congress has four types of committees: standing, special or select, joint, and, in the House, a Committee of the Whole. Committees conduct investigations, make studies, issue reports and recommendations and, in the case of standing committees, review and prepare measures on their assigned subjects for action by their respective houses. Most committees divide their work among several subcommittees. With rare exceptions, the majority party in a house holds a majority of the seats on its committees, and their chairmen are also from that party.

Committee Jurisdiction—The legislative subjects and other functions assigned to a committee by rule, precedent, resolution or statute. A committee's title usually indicates the general scope of its jurisdiction but often fails to mention other significant subjects assigned to it.

Committee of the Whole—Common name of the Committee of the Whole House on the State of the Union, a committee consisting of all members of the House of Representatives. Measures from the union calendar must be considered in the Committee of the Whole before the House officially completes action on them; the committee often considers other major bills as well. A quorum of the committee is 100, and it meets in the House chamber under a chairman appointed by the Speaker. Procedures in the Committee of the Whole expedite consideration of legislation because of its smaller quorum requirement, its ban on certain motions and its five-minute rule for debate on amendments. Those procedures usually permit more members to offer amendments and participate in the debate on a measure than is normally possible. The Senate no longer uses a Committee of the Whole.

Committee Ratios—The ratios of majority to minority party members on committees. By custom, the ratios of most committees reflect party strength in their respective houses as closely as possible.

Committee Report on a Measure—A document submitted by a committee to report a measure to its parent chamber. Customarily, the report explains the measure's purpose, describes provisions and any amendments recommended by the committee and presents arguments for its approval.

Committee Veto—A procedure that requires an executive department or agency to submit certain proposed policies, programs or action to designated committees for review before implementing them. Before 1983, when the Supreme Court declared that a legislative veto was unconstitutional, these provisions permitted committees to veto the proposals. Committees no longer conduct this type of policy review, and the term is now something of a misnomer. Nevertheless, agencies usually take the pragmatic approach of trying to reach a consensus with the committees before carrying out their proposals, especially when an appropriations committee is involved.

Concur—To agree to an amendment of the other house, either by adopting a motion to concur in that amendment or a motion to concur with an amendment to that amendment. After both houses have agreed to the same version of an amendment, neither house may amend it further, nor may any subsequent conference change it or delete it from the measure. Concurrence by one house in all amendments of the other house completes action on the measure; no vote is then necessary on the measure as a whole because both houses previously passed it.

Concurrent Resolution—A resolution that requires approval by both houses but does not need the president's signature and therefore cannot have the force of law. Concurrent resolutions deal with the prerogatives or internal affairs of Congress as a whole. Designated H. Con. Res. in the House and S. Con. Res. in the Senate, they are numbered consecutively in each house in their order of introduction during a two-year Congress.

Conferees—A common title for managers, the members from each house appointed to a conference committee. The Senate usually authorizes its presiding officer to appoint its conferees. The Speaker appoints House conferees, and under a rule adopted in 1993, can remove conferees "at any time after an original appointment" and also appoint additional conferees at any time. Conferees are expected to support the positions of their houses despite their personal views, but in practice this is not always the case. The party ratios of conferees generally reflect the ratios in their houses. Each house may appoint as many conferees as it pleases. House conferees often outnumber their Senate colleagues; however, each house has only one vote in a conference, so the size of its delegation is immaterial.

Conference—(1) A formal meeting or series of meetings between members representing each house to reconcile House and Senate differences on a measure (occasionally several measures). Because one house cannot require the other to agree to its proposals, the conference usually reaches agreement by compromise. When a conference completes action on a measure, or as much action as appears possible, it sends its recommendations to both houses in the form of a conference report, accompanied by an explanatory statement. (2) The official title of the organization of all Democrats or Republicans in the Senate and of all Republicans in the House of Representatives. (See Party Caucus.)

Conference Committee—A temporary joint committee formed for the purpose of resolving differences between the houses on a measure. Major and controversial legislation usually requires conference committee action. Voting in a conference committee is not by individuals but within the House and Senate delegations. Consequently, a conference committee report requires the support of a majority of the conferees from each house. Both houses require that conference committees open their meetings to the public. The Senate's rule permits the committee to close its meetings if a majority of conferees in each delegation agree by a roll-call vote. The House rule permits closed meetings only if the House authorizes them to do so on a roll-call vote. Otherwise, there are no congressional rules governing the organization of, or procedure in, a conference committee. The committee chooses its chairman, but on measures that go to conference annually, such as general appropriation bills, the chairmanship traditionally rotates between the houses.

Conference Report—A document submitted to both houses that contains a conference committee's agreements for resolving their differences on a measure. It must be signed by a majority of the conferees from each house separately and must be accompanied by an explanatory statement. Both houses prohibit amendments to a conference report and require it to be accepted or rejected in its entirety.

Congress—(1) The national legislature of the United States, consisting of the House of Representatives and the Senate. (2) The national legislature in office during a two-year period. Congresses are numbered sequentially; thus, the 1st Congress of 1789–1791 and the 106th Congress of 1999–2001. Before 1935, the two-year period began on the first Monday in December of odd-numbered years. Since then it has extended from January of an odd-numbered year through noon on Jan. 3 of the next odd-numbered year. A Congress usually holds two annual sessions, but some have had three sessions and the 67th Congress had four. When a Congress expires, measures die if they have not yet been enacted.

Congressional Accountability Act of 1995 (CAA)—An act applying eleven labor, workplace and civil rights laws to the legislative branch and establishing procedures and remedies for legislative branch employees with grievances in violation of these laws. The following laws are covered by the CAA: the Fair Labor

Standards Act of 1938; Title VII of the Civil Rights Act of 1964; Americans with Disabilities Act of 1990; Age Discrimination in Employment Act of 1967; Family and Medical Leave Act of 1993; Occupational Safety and Health Act of 1970; Chapter 71 of Title 5, U.S. Code (relating to federal service labor-management relations); Employee Polygraph Protection Act of 1988; Worker Adjustment and Retraining Notification Act; Rehabilitation Act of 1973; and Chapter 43 of Title 38, U.S. Code (relating to veterans' employment and reemployment).

Congressional Budget and Impoundment Control Act of 1974—The law that established the basic elements of the congressional budget process, the House and Senate Budget Committees, the Congressional Budget Office and the procedures for congressional review of impoundments in the form of rescissions and deferrals proposed by the president. The budget process consists of procedures for coordinating congressional revenue and spending decisions made in separate tax, appropriations and legislative measures. The impoundment provisions were intended to give Congress greater control over executive branch actions that delay or prevent the spending of funds provided by Congress.

Congressional Budget Office (CBO)—A congressional support agency created by the Congressional Budget and Impoundment Control Act of 1974 to provide nonpartisan budgetary information and analysis to Congress and its committees. CBO acts as a scorekeeper when Congress is voting on the federal budget, tracking bills to ensure they comply with overall budget goals. The agency also estimates what proposed legislation would cost over a five-year period. CBO works most closely with the House and Senate Budget Committees.

Congressional Directory—The official who's who of Congress, usually published during the first session of a two-year Congress.

Congressional District—The geographical area represented by a single member of the House of Representatives. For states with only one representative, the entire state is a congressional district. As of 2001 seven states had only one representative each: Alaska, Delaware, Montana, North Dakota, South Dakota, Vermont and Wyoming.

Congressional Record—The daily, printed and substantially verbatim account of proceedings in both the House and Senate chambers. Extraneous materials submitted by members appear in a section titled "Extensions of Remarks." A "Daily Digest" appendix contains highlights of the day's floor and committee action plus a list of committee meetings and floor agendas for the next day's session.

Although the official reporters of each house take down every word spoken during the proceedings, members are permitted to edit and "revise and extend" their remarks before they are printed. In the Senate section, all speeches, articles and other material submitted by senators but not actually spoken or read on the floor are set off by large black dots, called bullets. However, bullets do not appear when a senator reads part of a speech and inserts the rest. In the House section, undelivered speeches and materials are printed in a distinctive typeface. The term "permanent Record" refers to the bound volumes of the daily Records of an entire session of Congress.

Congressional Research Service (CRS)—Established in 1917, a department of the Library of Congress whose staff provide nonpartisan, objective analysis and information on virtually any subject to committees, members and staff of Congress. Originally the Legislative Reference Service, it is the oldest congressional support agency.

Congressional Support Agencies—A term often applied to three agencies in the legislative branch that provide nonpartisan information and analysis to committees and members of Congress: the Congressional Budget Office, the Congressional Research Service of the Library of Congress and the General Accounting Office. A fourth support agency, the Office of Technology Assessment, formerly provided such support but was abolished in the 104th Congress.

Congressional Terms of Office—A term normally begins on Jan. 3 of the year following a general election and runs two years for representatives and six years for senators. A representative chosen in a special election to fill a vacancy is sworn in for the remainder of the predecessor's term. An individual appointed to fill a Senate vacancy usually serves until the next general election or until the end of the predecessor's term, whichever comes first. Some states, however, require their governors to call a special election to fill a Senate vacancy shortly after an appointment has been made.

Constitutional Rules—Constitutional provisions that prescribe procedures for Congress. In addition to certain types of votes required in particular situations, these provisions include the following: (1) the House chooses its Speaker, the Senate its president pro tempore and both houses their officers; (2) each house requires a majority quorum to conduct business; (3) less than a majority may adjourn from day to day and compel the attendance of absent members; (4) neither house may adjourn for more than three days without the consent of the other; (5) each house must keep a journal; (6) the yeas and nays are ordered when supported by one-fifth of the members present; (7) all revenue-raising bills must originate in the House, but the Senate may propose amendments to them. The Constitution also sets out the procedure in the House for electing a president, the procedure in the Senate for electing a vice president, the procedure for filling a vacancy in the office of vice president and the procedure for overriding a presidential veto.

Constitutional Votes—Constitutional provisions that require certain votes or voting methods in specific situations. They include (1) the yeas and nays at the desire of one-fifth of the members present; (2) a two-thirds vote by the yeas and nays to override a veto; (3) a two-thirds vote by one house to expel one of its members and by both houses to propose a constitutional amendment; (4) a two-thirds vote of senators present to convict someone whom the House has impeached and to consent to ratification of treaties; (5) a two-thirds vote in each house to remove political disabilities from persons who have engaged in insurrection or rebellion or given aid or comfort to the enemies of the United States; (6) a majority vote in each house to fill a vacancy in the office of vice president; (7) a majority vote of all states to elect a president in the House of Representatives when no candidate receives a majority of the electoral votes; (8) a majority vote of all senators when the Senate elects a vice president under the same circumstances; and (9) the casting vote of the vice president in case of tie votes in the Senate.

Contempt of Congress—Willful obstruction of the proper functions of Congress. Most frequently, it is a refusal to obey a subpoena to appear and testify before a committee or to produce documents demanded by it. Such obstruction is a misdemeanor and persons cited for contempt are subject to prosecution in federal courts. A house cites an individual for contempt by agreeing to a privileged resolution to that effect reported by a committee. The presiding officer then refers the matter to a U.S. attorney for prosecution.

Continuing Body—A characterization of the Senate on the theory that it continues from Congress to Congress and has existed continuously since it first convened in 1789. The rationale for the theory is that under the system of staggered six-year terms for senators, the terms of only about one-third of them expire after each Congress and, therefore, a quorum of the Senate is always in office. Consequently, under this theory, the Senate, unlike the House, does not have to adopt its rules at the beginning of each Congress because those rules continue from one Congress to the next. This makes it extremely difficult for the Senate to change its rules against the opposition of a determined minority because those rules require a two-thirds vote of the senators present and voting to invoke cloture on a proposed rules change.

Continuing Resolution (CR)—A joint resolution that provides funds to continue the operation of federal agencies and programs at the beginning of a new fiscal year if their annual appropriation bills have not yet been enacted; also called continuing appropriations. Continuing resolutions are enacted shortly before or after the new fiscal year begins and usually make funds available for a specified period. Additional resolutions are often needed after the first expires. Some continuing resolutions have provided appropriations for an entire fiscal year. Continuing resolutions for specific periods customarily fix a rate at which agencies may incur obligations based either on the previous year's appropriations, the president's budget request, or the amount as specified in the agency's regular annual appropriation bill if that bill has already been passed by one or both houses. In the House, continuing resolutions are privileged after Sept. 15.

Contract Authority—Statutory authority permitting an agency to enter into contracts or incur other obligations even though it has not received an appropriation to pay for them. Congress must eventually fund them because the government is legally liable for such payments. The Congressional Budget Act of 1974 requires that new contract authority may not be used unless provided for in advance by an appropriation act, but it permits a few exceptions.

Correcting Recorded Votes—The rules of both houses prohibit members from changing their votes after a vote result has been announced. Nevertheless, the Senate permits its members to withdraw or change their votes, by unanimous consent, immediately after the announcement. In rare instances, senators have been granted unanimous consent to change their votes several days or weeks after the announcement. Votes tallied by the electronic voting system in the House may not be changed. But when a vote actually given is not recorded during an oral call of the roll, a member may demand a correction as a matter of right. On all other alleged errors in a recorded vote, the Speaker determines whether the circumstances justify a change. Occasionally, members merely announce that they were incorrectly recorded; announcements can occur hours, days or even months after the vote and appear in the Congressional Record.

Cosponsor—A member who has joined one or more other members to sponsor a measure.

Credit Authority—Authority granted to an agency to incur direct loan obligations or to make loan guarantee commitments. The Congressional Budget Act of 1974 bans congressional consideration of credit authority legislation unless the extent of that authority is made subject to provisions in appropriation acts.

C-SPAN—Cable-Satellite Public Affairs Network, which provides live, gavel-to-gavel coverage of Senate floor proceedings on one cable television channel and coverage of House floor proceedings on another channel. C-SPAN also televises important committee hearings in both houses. Each house also transmits its televised proceedings directly to congressional offices.

Current Services Estimates—Executive branch estimates of the anticipated costs of federal programs and operations for the next and future fiscal years at existing levels of service and assuming no new initiatives or changes in existing law. The president submits these estimates to Congress with the annual budget and includes an explanation of the underlying economic and policy assumptions on which they are based, such as anticipated rates of inflation, real economic growth and unemployment, plus program caseloads and pay increases.

Custody of the Papers—Possession of an engrossed measure and certain related basic documents that the two houses produce as they try to resolve their differences over the measure.

Dance of the Swans and the Ducks—A whimsical description of the gestures some members use in connection with a request for a recorded vote, especially in the House. When members want their colleagues to stand in support of the request, they move their hands and arms in a gentle upward motion resembling the beginning flight of a graceful swan. When they want their colleagues to remain seated to avoid such a vote, they move their hands and arms in a vigorous downward motion resembling a diving duck.

Dean—Within a state's delegation in the House of Representatives, the member with the longest continuous service.

Debate—In congressional parlance, speeches delivered during consideration of a measure, motion or other matter, as distinguished from speeches in other parliamentary situations, such as one-minute and special order speeches when no business is pending. Virtually all debate in the House of Representatives is under some kind of time limitation. Most debate in the Senate is unlimited; that is, a senator, once recognized, may speak for as long as he or she chooses, unless the Senate invokes cloture.

Debt Limit—The maximum amount of outstanding federal public debt permitted by law. The limit (or ceiling) covers virtually all debt incurred by the government except agency debt. Each congressional budget resolution sets forth the new debt limit that may be required under its provisions.

Deferral—An impoundment of funds for a specific period of time that may not extend beyond the fiscal year in which it is proposed. Under the Impoundment Control Act of 1974, the president must notify Congress that he is deferring the spending or obligation of funds provided by law for a project or activity. Congress can disapprove the deferral by legislation.

Deficit—The amount by which the government's outlays exceed its budget receipts for a given fiscal year. Both the president's budget and the annual congressional budget resolution provide estimates of the deficit or surplus for the upcoming and several future fiscal years.

Degrees of Amendment—Designations that indicate the relationships of amendments to the text of a measure and to each other. In general, an amendment offered directly to the text of a measure is an amendment in the first degree, and an amendment to that amendment is an amendment in the second degree. Both houses normally prohibit amendments in the third degree — that is, an amendment to an amendment to an amendment.

Delegate—A nonvoting member of the House of Representatives elected to a two-year term from the District of Columbia, the territory of Guam, the territory of the Virgin Islands or the territory of American Samoa. By law, delegates may not vote in the full House but they may participate in debate, offer motions (except to reconsider) and serve and vote on standing and select committees. On their committees, delegates possess the same powers and privileges as other members and the Speaker may appoint them to appropriate conference committees and select committees.

Denounce—A formal action that condemns a member for misbehavior; considered by some experts to be equivalent to censure. (See Censure.)

Dilatory Tactics—Procedural actions intended to delay or prevent action by a house or a committee. They include, among others, offering numerous motions, demanding quorum calls and recorded votes at every opportunity, making numerous points of order and parliamentary inquiries and speaking as long as the applicable rules permit. The Senate rules permit a battery of dilatory tactics, especially lengthy speeches, except under cloture. In the House, possible dilatory tactics are more limited. Speeches are always subject to time limits and debate-ending motions. Moreover, a House rule instructs the Speaker not to entertain dilatory motions and lets the Speaker decide whether a motion is dilatory. However, the Speaker may not override the constitutional right of a member to demand the yeas and nays, and in practice usually waits for a point of order before exercising that authority. (See Cloture.)

Discharge a Committee—Remove a measure from a committee to which it has been referred in order to make it available for floor consideration. Noncontroversial measures are often discharged by unanimous consent. However, because congressional committees have no obligation to report measures referred to them, each house has procedures to extract controversial measures from recalcitrant committees. Six discharge procedures are available in the House of Representatives. The Senate uses a motion to discharge, which is usually converted into a discharge resolution.

District Office—Representatives maintain one or more offices in their districts for the purpose of assisting and communicating with constituents. The costs of maintaining these offices are paid from members' official allowances. Senators can use the official expense allowance to rent offices in their home state, subject to a funding formula based on their state's population and other factors.

District Work Period—The House term for a scheduled congressional recess during which members may visit their districts and conduct constituency business.

Division Vote—A vote in which the chair first counts those in favor of a proposition and then those opposed to it, with no record made of how each member votes. In the Senate, the chair may count raised hands or ask senators to stand, whereas the House requires members to stand; hence, often called a standing vote. Committees in both houses ordinarily use a show of hands. A division usually occurs after a voice vote and may be demanded by any member or ordered by the chair if there is any doubt about the outcome of the voice vote. The demand for a division can also come before a voice vote. In the Senate, the demand must come before the result of a voice vote is announced. It may be made after a voice vote announcement in the House, but only if no intervening business has transpired and only if the member was standing and seeking recognition at the time of the announcement. A demand for the yeas and nays or, in the House, for a recorded vote, takes precedence over a division vote.

Doorkeeper of the House—A former officer of the House of Representatives who was responsible for enforcing the rules prohibiting unauthorized persons from entering the chamber when the House is in session. The doorkeeper was usually the candidate of the majority party. In 1995 the office was abolished and its functions transferred to the sergeant at arms.

Effective Dates—Provisions of an act that specify when the entire act or individual provisions in it become effective as law. Most acts become effective on the date of enactment, but it is sometimes necessary or prudent to delay the effective dates of some provisions.

Electronic Voting—Since 1973 the House has used an electronic voting system to record the yeas and nays and to conduct recorded votes. Members vote by inserting their voting cards in one of the boxes at several locations in the chamber. They are given at least fifteen minutes to vote. When several votes occur immediately after each other, the Speaker may reduce the voting time to five minutes on the second and subsequent votes. The Speaker may allow additional time on each vote but may also close a vote at any time after the minimum time has expired. Members can change their votes at any time before the Speaker announces the result. The House also uses the electronic system for quorum calls. While a vote is in progress, a large panel above the Speaker's desk displays how each member has voted. Smaller panels on either side of the chamber display running totals of the votes and the time remaining. The Senate does not have electronic voting.

Enacting Clause—The opening language of each bill, beginning "Be it enacted by the Senate and House of Representatives of the United States of America in Congress assembled..." This language gives legal force to measures approved by Congress and signed by the president or enacted over the president's veto. A successful motion to strike it from a bill kills the entire measure.

Engrossed Bill—The official copy of a bill or joint resolution as passed by one chamber, including the text as amended by floor action and certified by the clerk of the House or the secretary of the Senate (as appropriate). Amendments by one house to a measure or amendments of the other also are engrossed. House engrossed documents are printed on blue paper; the Senate's are printed on white paper.

Enrolled Bill—The final official copy of a bill or joint resolution passed in identical form by both houses. An enrolled bill is printed on parchment. After it is certified by the chief officer of the house in which it originated and signed by the House Speaker and the Senate president pro tempore, the measure is sent to the White House for the president's signature.

Entitlement Program—A federal program under which individuals, businesses or units of government that meet the requirements or qualifications established by law are entitled to receive certain payments if they seek such payments. Major examples include Social Security, Medicare, Medicaid, unemployment insurance and military and federal civilian pensions. Congress cannot control their expenditures by refusing to appropriate the sums necessary to fund them because the government is legally obligated to pay eligible recipients the amounts to which the law entitles them.

Equality of the Houses—A component of the Constitution's emphasis on checks and balances under which each house is given essentially equal status in the enactment of legislation and in the relations and negotiations between the two houses. Although the House of Representatives initiates revenue and appropriation measures, the Senate has the right to amend them. Either house may initiate any other type of legislation, and neither can force the other to agree to, or even act on, its measures. Moreover, each house has a potential veto over the other because legislation requires agreement by both. Similarly, in a conference to resolve their differences on a measure, each house casts one vote, as determined by a majority of its conferees. In most other national bicameral legislatures, the powers of one house are markedly greater than those of the other.

Ethics Rules—Several rules or standing orders in each house that mandate certain standards of conduct for members and congressional employees in finance, employment, franking and other areas. The Senate Permanent Select Committee on Ethics and the House Committee on Standards of Official Conduct investigate alleged violations of conduct and recommend appropriate actions to their respective houses.

Exclusive Committee—(1) Under the rules of the Republican

Conference and House Democratic Caucus, a standing committee whose members usually cannot serve on any other standing committee. As of 2000 the Appropriations, Energy and Commerce (beginning in the 105th Congress), Ways and Means and Rules Committees were designated as exclusive committees. (2) Under the rules of the two party conferences in the Senate, a standing committee whose members may not simultaneously serve on any other exclusive committee.

Executive Calendar—The Senate's calendar for committee reports on its executive business, namely treaties and nominations. The calendar numbers indicate the order in which items were referred to the calendar but have no bearing on when or if the Senate will consider them. The Senate, by motion or unanimous consent, resolves itself into executive session to consider them.

Executive Document—A document, usually a treaty, sent by the president to the Senate for approval. It is referred to a committee in the same manner as other measures. Resolutions to ratify treaties have their own "treaty document" numbers. For example, the first treaty submitted in the 106th Congress would be "Treaty Doc 106-1."

Executive Order—A unilateral proclamation by the president that has a policy-making or legislative impact. Members of Congress have challenged some executive orders on the grounds that they usurped the authority of the legislative branch. Although the Supreme Court has ruled that a particular order exceeded the president's authority, it has upheld others as falling within the president's general constitutional powers.

Executive Privilege—The assertion that presidents have the right to withhold certain information from Congress. Presidents have based their claim on (1) the constitutional separation of powers; (2) the need for secrecy in military and diplomatic affairs; (3) the need to protect individuals from unfavorable publicity; (4) the need to safeguard the confidential exchange of ideas in the executive branch; and (5) the need to protect individuals who provide confidential advice to the president.

Executive Session—(1) A Senate meeting devoted to the consideration of treaties or nominations. Normally, the Senate meets in legislative session; it resolves itself into executive session, by motion or by unanimous consent, to deal with its executive business. It also keeps a separate Journal for executive sessions. Executive sessions are usually open to the public, but the Senate may choose to close them.

Expulsion—A member's removal from office by a two-thirds vote of his or her house; the supermajority is required by the Constitution. It is the most severe and most rarely used sanction a house can invoke against a member. Although the Constitution provides no explicit grounds for expulsion, the courts have ruled that it may be applied only for misconduct during a member's term of office, not for conduct before the member's election. Generally, neither house will consider expulsion of a member convicted of a crime until the judicial processes have been exhausted. At that stage, members sometimes resign rather than face expulsion. In 1977 the House adopted a rule urging members convicted of certain crimes to voluntarily abstain from voting or participating in other legislative business.

Extensions of Remarks—An appendix to the daily Congressional Record that consists primarily of miscellaneous extraneous material submitted by members. It often includes members' statements not delivered on the floor, newspaper articles and editorials, praise for a member's constituents and noteworthy letters received by a member, among other material. Representatives supply the bulk of this material; senators submit very little. "Extensions of Remarks" pages are separately numbered, and each number is preceded by the letter "E." Materials may be placed in the Extensions of Remarks section only by unanimous consent. Usually, one member of each party makes the request each day on behalf of his or her party colleagues after the House has completed its legislative business of the day.

Federal Debt—The total amount of monies borrowed and not yet repaid by the federal government. Federal debt consists of public debt and agency debt. Public debt is the portion of the federal debt borrowed by the Treasury or the Federal Financing Bank directly from the public or from another federal fund or account. For example, the Treasury regularly borrows money from the Social Security trust fund. Public debt accounts for about 99 percent of the federal debt. Agency debt refers to the debt incurred by federal agencies such as the Export-Import Bank but excluding the Treasury and the Federal Financing Bank, which are authorized by law to borrow funds from the public or from another government fund or account.

Filibuster—The use of obstructive and time-consuming parliamentary tactics by one member or a minority of members to delay, modify or defeat proposed legislation or rules changes. Filibusters are also sometimes used to delay urgently needed measures to force the body to accept other legislation. The Senate's rules permitting unlimited debate and the extraordinary majority it requires to impose cloture make filibustering particularly effective in that chamber. Under the stricter rules of the House, filibusters in that body are short-lived and therefore ineffective and rarely attempted.

Fiscal Year—The federal government's annual accounting period. It begins Oct. 1 and ends on the following Sept. 30. A fiscal year is designated by the calendar year in which it ends and is often referred to as FY. Thus, fiscal year 1998 began Oct. 1, 1997, ended Sept. 30, 1998, and is called FY98. In theory, Congress is supposed to complete action on all budgetary measures applying to a fiscal year before that year begins. It rarely does so.

Five-Minute Rule—A House rule that limits debate on an amendment offered in Committee of the Whole to five minutes for its sponsor and five minutes for an opponent. In practice, the committee routinely permits longer debate by two devices: the offering of pro forma amendments, each debatable for five minutes, and unanimous consent for a member to speak longer than five minutes. Consequently, debate on an amendment sometimes continues for hours. At any time after the first ten minutes, however, the committee may shut off debate immediately or by a specified time, either by unanimous consent or by majority vote on a nondebatable motion. The motion, which dates from 1847, is also used in the House as in Committee of the Whole, where debate also may be shut off by a motion for the previous question.

Floor—The ground level of the House or Senate chamber where members sit and the houses conduct their business. When members are attending a meeting of their house they are said to be on the floor. Floor action refers to the procedural actions taken during floor consideration such as deciding on motions, taking up measures, amending them and voting.

Floor Manager—A majority party member responsible for guiding a measure through its floor consideration in a house and for devising the political and procedural strategies that might be required to get it passed. The presiding officer gives the floor manager priority recognition to debate, offer amendments, oppose amendments and make crucial procedural motions.

Frank—Informally, members' legal right to send official mail postage free under their signatures; often called the franking privilege. Technically, it is the autographic or facsimile signature used on envelopes instead of stamps that permits members and certain congressional officers to send their official mail free of charge. The franking privilege has been authorized by law since the first Congress, except for a few months in 1873. Congress reimburses the

U.S. Postal Service for the franked mail it handles.

Function or Functional Category—A broad category of national need and spending of budgetary significance. A category provides an accounting method for allocating and keeping track of budgetary resources and expenditures for that function because it includes all budget accounts related to the function's subject or purpose such as agriculture, administration of justice, commerce and housing and energy. Functions do not necessarily correspond with appropriations acts or with the budgets of individual agencies. As of 2000 there were twenty functional categories, each divided into a number of subfunctions.

Gag Rule—A pejorative term for any type of special rule reported by the House Rules Committee that proposes to prohibit amendments to a measure or only permits amendments offered by the reporting committee.

Galleries—The balconies overlooking each chamber from which the public, news media, staff and others may observe floor proceedings.

General Accounting Office (GAO)—A congressional support agency, often referred to as the investigative arm of Congress. It evaluates and audits federal agencies and programs in the United States and abroad on its initiative or at the request of congressional committees or members.

General Appropriation Bill—A term applied to each of the thirteen annual bills that provide funds for most federal agencies and programs and also to the supplemental appropriation bills that contain appropriations for more than one agency or program.

Germaneness—The requirement that an amendment be closely related — in terms of subject or purpose, for example — to the text it proposes to amend. A House rule requires that all amendments be germane. In the Senate, only amendments offered to general appropriation bills and budget measures or proposed under cloture must be germane. Germaneness rules can be waived by suspension of the rules in both houses, by unanimous consent agreements in the Senate and by special rules from the Rules Committee in the House. Moreover, presiding officers usually do not enforce germaneness rules on their own initiative; therefore, a nongermane amendment can be adopted if no member raises a point of order against it. Under cloture in the Senate, however, the chair may take the initiative to rule amendments out of order as not being germane, without a point of order being made. All House debate must be germane except during general debate in the Committee of the Whole, but special rules invariably require that such debate be "confined to the bill." The Senate requires germane debate only during the first three hours of each daily session. Under the precedents of both houses, an amendment can be relevant but not necessarily germane. A crucial factor in determining germaneness in the House is how the subject of a measure or matter is defined. For example, the subject of a measure authorizing construction of a naval vessel is defined as being the construction of a single vessel; therefore, an amendment to authorize an additional vessel is not germane.

Gerrymandering—The manipulation of legislative district boundaries to benefit a particular party, politician or minority group. The term originated in 1812 when the Massachusetts legislature redrew the lines of state legislative districts to favor the party of Gov. Elbridge Gerry, and some critics said one district looked like a salamander. (See also Congressional District; Redistricting.)

Gramm-Rudman-Hollings Act of 1985—Common name for the Balanced Budget and Emergency Deficit Control Act of 1985, which established new budget procedures intended to balance the federal budget by fiscal year 1991. (The timetable subsequently was extended and then deleted.) The act's chief sponsors were senators Phil Gramm (R-Texas), Warren Rudman (R-N.H.) Ernest Hollings (D-S.C.).

Grandfather Clause—A provision in a measure, law or rule that exempts an individual, entity or a defined category of individuals or entities from complying with a new policy or restriction. For example, a bill that would raise taxes on persons who reach the age of sixty-five after a certain date inherently grandfathers out those who are sixty-five before that date. Similarly, a Senate rule limiting senators to two major committee assignments also grandfathers some senators who were sitting on a third major committee before a specified date.

Grants-in-Aid—Payments by the federal government to state and local governments to help provide for assistance programs or public services.

Hearing—Committee or subcommittee meetings to receive testimony on proposed legislation during investigations or for oversight purposes. Relatively few bills are important enough to justify formal hearings. Witnesses often include experts, government officials, spokespersons for interested groups, officials of the General Accounting Office and members of Congress.

Hold—A senator's request that his or her party leaders delay floor consideration of certain legislation or presidential nominations. The majority leader usually honors a hold for a reasonable period of time, especially if its purpose is to assure the senator that the matter will not be called up during his or her absence or to give the senator time to gather necessary information.

Hold (or Have) the Floor—A member's right to speak without interruption, unless he or she violates a rule, after recognition by the presiding officer. At the member's discretion, he or she may yield to another member for a question in the Senate or for a question or statement in the House, but may reclaim the floor at any time.

Hold-Harmless Clause—In legislation providing a new formula for allocating federal funds, a clause to ensure that recipients of those funds do not receive less in a future year than they did in the current year if the new formula would result in a reduction for them. Similar to a grandfather clause, it has been used most frequently to soften the impact of sudden reductions in federal grants. (See Grandfather Clause.)

Hopper—A box on the clerk's desk in the House chamber into which members deposit bills and resolutions to introduce them. In House jargon, to drop a bill in the hopper is to introduce it.

Hour Rule—A House rule that permits members, when recognized, to hold the floor in debate for no more than one hour each. The majority party member customarily yields one-half the time to a minority member. Although the hour rule applies to general debate in Committee of the Whole as well as in the House, special rules routinely vary the length of time for such debate and its control to fit the circumstances of particular measures.

House As In Committee of the Whole—A hybrid combination of procedures from the general rules of the House and from the rules of the Committee of the Whole, sometimes used to expedite consideration of a measure on the floor.

House Calendar—The calendar reserved for all public bills and resolutions that do not raise revenue or directly or indirectly appropriate money or property when they are favorably reported by House committees.

House Manual—A commonly used title for the handbook of the rules of the House of Representatives, published in each Congress. Its official title is Constitution, Jefferson's Manual and Rules of the House of Representatives.

House of Representatives—The house of Congress in which states are represented roughly in proportion to their populations, but every state is guaranteed at least one representative. By law, the number of voting representatives is fixed at 435. Four delegates and one resident commissioner also serve in the House; they may vote in their committees but not on the House floor. Although the House and Senate have equal legislative power, the Constitution gives the House sole authority to originate revenue measures. The House also claims the right to originate appropriation measures, a claim the Senate disputes in theory but concedes in practice. The House has the sole power to impeach, and it elects the president when no candidate has received a majority of the electoral votes. It is sometimes referred to as the lower body.

Immunity—(1) Members' constitutional protection from lawsuits and arrest in connection with their legislative duties. They may not be tried for libel or slander for anything they say on the floor of a house or in committee. Nor may they be arrested while attending sessions of their houses or when traveling to or from sessions of Congress, except when charged with treason, a felony or a breach of the peace. (2) In the case of a witness before a committee, a grant of protection from prosecution based on that person's testimony to the committee. It is used to compel witnesses to testify who would otherwise refuse to do so on the constitutional ground of possible selfincrimination. Under such a grant, none of a witness's testimony may be used against him or her in a court proceeding except in a prosecution for perjury or for giving a false statement to Congress. (See also Contempt of Congress.)

Impeachment—The first step to remove the president, vice president or other federal civil officers from office and to disqualify them from any future federal office "of honor, Trust or Profit." An impeachment is a formal charge of treason, bribery or "other high Crimes and Misdemeanors." The House has the sole power of impeachment and the Senate the sole power of trying the charges and convicting. The House impeaches by a simple majority vote; conviction requires a two-thirds vote of all senators present.

Impeachment Trial, Removal and Disqualification—The Senate conducts an impeachment trial under a separate set of twenty-six rules that appears in the Senate Manual. Under the Constitution, the chief justice of the United States presides over trials of the president, but the vice president, the president pro tempore or any other senator may preside over the impeachment trial of another official.

The Constitution requires senators to take an oath for an impeachment trial. During the trial, senators may not engage in colloquies or participate in arguments, but they may submit questions in writing to House managers or defense counsel. After the trial concludes, the Senate votes separately on each article of impeachment without debate unless the Senate orders the doors closed for private discussions. During deliberations senators may speak no more than once on a question, not for more than ten minutes on an interlocutory question and not more than fifteen minutes on the final question. These rules may be set aside by unanimous consent or suspended on motion by a two-thirds vote.

The Senate's impeachment trial of President Clinton in 1999 was only the second such trial involving a president. It continued for five weeks, with the Senate voting not to convict on the two impeachment articles.

Senate impeachment rules allow the Senate, at its own discretion, to name a committee to hear evidence and conduct the trial, with all senators thereafter voting on the charges. The impeachment trials of three federal judges were conducted this way, and the Supreme Court upheld the validity of these rules in Nixon v. United States, 506 U.S. 224, 1993.

An official convicted on impeachment charges is removed from office immediately. However, the convicted official is not barred from holding a federal office in the future unless the Senate, after its conviction vote, also approves a resolution disqualifying the convicted official from future office. For example, federal judge Alcee L. Hastings was impeached and convicted in 1989, but the Senate did not vote to bar him from office in the future. In 1992 Hastings was elected to the House of Representatives, and no challenge was raised against seating him when he took the oath of office in 1993.

Impoundment—An executive branch action or inaction that delays or withholds the expenditure or obligation of budget authority provided by law. The Impoundment Control Act of 1974 classifies impoundments as either deferrals or rescissions, requires the president to notify Congress about all such actions and gives Congress authority to approve or reject them.

Inspector General (IG) In the House of Representatives—A position established with the passage of the House Administrative Reform Resolution of 1992. The duties of the office have been revised several times and are now contained in House Rule II. The inspector general (IG), who is subject to the policy direction and oversight of the Committee on House Administration, is appointed for a Congress jointly by the Speaker and the majority and minority leaders of the House. The IG communicates the results of audits to the House officers or officials who were the subjects of the audits and suggests appropriate corrective measures. The IG submits a report of each audit to the Speaker, the majority and minority leaders and the chairman and ranking minority member of the House Administration Committee; notifies these five members in the case of any financial irregularity discovered; and reports to the Committee on Standards of Official Conduct on possible violations of House rules or any applicable law by any House member, officer or employee. The IG's office also has certain duties to audit various financial operations of the House that had previously been performed by the General Accounting Office.

Instruct Conferees—A formal action by a house urging its conferees to uphold a particular position on a measure in conference. The instruction may be to insist on certain provisions in the measure as passed by that house or to accept a provision in the version passed by the other house. Instructions to conferees are not binding because the primary responsibility of conferees is to reach agreement on a measure and neither House can compel the other to accept particular provisions or positions.

Investigative Power—The authority of Congress and its committees to pursue investigations, upheld by the Supreme Court but limited to matters related to, and in furtherance of, a legitimate task of the Congress. Standing committees in both houses are permanently authorized to investigate matters within their jurisdictions. Major investigations are sometimes conducted by temporary select, special or joint committees established by resolutions for that purpose.

Some rules of the House provide certain safeguards for witnesses and others during investigative hearings. These permit counsel to accompany witnesses, require that each witness receive a copy of the committee's rules and order the committee to go into closed session if it believes the testimony to be heard might defame, degrade or incriminate any person. The committee may subsequently decide to hear such testimony in open session. The Senate has no rules of this kind.

Item Veto—Item veto authority, which is available to most state governors, allows governors to eliminate or reduce items in legislative measures presented for their signature without vetoing the entire measure and sign the rest into law. A similar authority was briefly granted to the U.S. president under the Line Item Veto Act of 1996. According to the majority opinion of the Supreme Court in its 1998 decision overturning that law, a constitutional amendment would be necessary to give the president such item veto authority.

Jefferson's Manual—Short title of Jefferson's Manual of Parliamentary Practice, prepared by Thomas Jefferson for his guidance when he was president of the Senate from 1797 to 1801. Although it reflects English parliamentary practice in his day, many procedures in both houses of Congress are still rooted in its basic precepts. Under a House rule adopted in 1837, the manual's provisions govern House procedures when applicable and when they are not inconsistent with its standing rules and orders. The Senate, however, has never officially acknowledged it as a direct authority for its legislative procedure.

Johnson Rule—A policy instituted in 1953 under which all Democratic senators are assigned to one major committee before any Democrat is assigned to two. The Johnson Rule is named after its author, Sen. Lyndon B. Johnson, D-Texas, then the Senate's Democratic leader. Senate Republicans adopted a similar policy soon thereafter.

Joint Committee—A committee composed of members selected from each house. The functions of most joint committees involve investigation, research or oversight of agencies closely related to Congress. Permanent joint committees, created by statute, are sometimes called standing joint committees. Once quite numerous, only four joint committees remained as of 2002: Joint Economic, Joint Taxation, Joint Library and Joint Printing. None has authority to report legislation.

Joint Resolution—A legislative measure that Congress uses for purposes other than general legislation. Similar to a bill, it has the force of law when passed by both houses and either approved by the president or passed over the president's veto. Unlike a bill, a joint resolution enacted into law is not called an act; it retains its original title. Most often, joint resolutions deal with such relatively limited matters as the correction of errors in existing law, continuing appropriations, a single appropriation or the establishment of permanent joint committees. Unlike bills, however, joint resolutions also are used to propose constitutional amendments; these do not require the president's signature and become effective only when ratified by three-fourths of the states. The House designates joint resolutions as H.J. Res., the Senate as S.J. Res. Each house numbers its joint resolutions consecutively in the order of introduction during a two-year Congress.

Joint Session—Informally, any combined meeting of the Senate and the House. Technically, a joint session is a combined meeting to count the electoral votes for president and vice president or to hear a presidential address, such as the State of the Union message; any other formal combined gathering of both houses is a joint meeting. Joint sessions are authorized by concurrent resolutions and are held in the House chamber, because of its larger seating capacity. Although the president of the Senate and the Speaker sit side by side at the Speaker's desk during combined meetings, the former presides over the electoral count and the latter presides on all other occasions and introduces the president or other guest speaker. The president and other guests may address a joint session or meeting only by invitation.

Joint Sponsorship—Two or more members sponsoring the same measure.

Journal—The official record of House or Senate actions, including every motion offered, every vote cast, amendments agreed to, quorum calls and so forth. Unlike the Congressional Record, it does not provide reports of speeches, debates, statements and the like. The Constitution requires each house to maintain a Journal and to publish it periodically.

Junket—A member's trip at government expense, especially abroad, ostensibly on official business but, it is often alleged, for pleasure.

Killer Amendment—An amendment that, if agreed to, might lead to the defeat of the measure it amends, either in the house in which the amendment is offered or at some later stage of the legislative process. Members sometimes deliberately offer or vote for such an amendment in the expectation that it will undermine support for the measure in Congress or increase the likelihood that the president will veto it.

King of the Mountain (or Hill) Rule—(See Queen of the Hill Rule.)

LA—(See Legislative Assistant.)

Lame Duck—Jargon for a member who has not been reelected, or did not seek reelection, and is serving the balance of his or her term.

Lame Duck Session—A session of a Congress held after the election for the succeeding Congress, so-called after the lame duck members still serving.

Last Train Out—Colloquial name for last must-pass bill of a session of Congress.

Law—An act of Congress that has been signed by the president, passed over the president's veto or allowed to become law without the president's signature.

Lay on the Table—A motion to dispose of a pending proposition immediately, finally and adversely; that is, to kill it without a direct vote on its substance. Often simply called a motion to table, it is not debatable and is adopted by majority vote or without objection. It is a highly privileged motion, taking precedence over all others except the motion to adjourn in the House and all but three additional motions in the Senate. It can kill a bill or resolution, an amendment, another motion, an appeal or virtually any other matter.

Tabling an amendment also tables the measure to which the amendment is pending in the House, but not in the Senate. The House does not allow the motion against the motion to recommit, in Committee of the Whole, and in some other situations. In the Senate it is the only permissible motion that immediately ends debate on a proposition, but only to kill it.

(The) Leadership—Usually, a reference to the majority and minority leaders of the Senate or to the Speaker and minority leader of the House. The term sometimes includes the majority leader in the House and the majority and minority whips in each house and, at other times, other party officials as well.

Legislation—(1) A synonym for legislative measures: bills and joint resolutions. (2) Provisions in such measures or in substantive amendments offered to them. (3) In some contexts, provisions that change existing substantive or authorizing law, rather than provisions that make appropriations.

Legislation on an Appropriation Bill—A common reference to provisions changing existing law that appear in, or are offered as amendments to, a general appropriation bill. A House rule prohibits the inclusion of such provisions in general appropriation bills unless they retrench expenditures. An analogous Senate rule permits points of order against amendments to a general appropriation bill that propose general legislation.

Legislative Assistant (LA)—A member's staff person responsible for monitoring and preparing legislation on particular subjects and for advising the member on them; commonly referred to as an LA.

Legislative Day—The day that begins when a house meets after an adjournment and ends when it next adjourns. Because the House of Representatives normally adjourns at the end of a daily session, its legislative and calendar days usually coincide. The Senate, however, frequently recesses at the end of a daily session, and its legislative day may extend over several calendar days, weeks or months. Among other uses, this technicality permits the Senate to save time by circumventing its morning hour, a procedure required at the beginning of every legislative day.

Legislative History—(1) A chronological list of actions taken on a measure during its progress through the legislative process. (2) The official documents relating to a measure, the entries in the Journals of the two houses on that measure and the Congressional Record text of its consideration in both houses. The documents include all committee reports and the conference report and joint explanatory statement, if any. Courts and affected federal agencies study a measure's legislative history for congressional intent about its purpose and interpretation.

Legislative Process—(1) Narrowly, the stages in the enactment of a law from introduction to final disposition. An introduced measure that becomes law typically travels through reference to committee; committee and subcommittee consideration; report to the chamber; floor consideration; amendment; passage; engrossment; messaging to the other house; similar steps in that house, including floor amendment of the measure; return of the measure to the first house; consideration of amendments between the houses or a conference to resolve their differences; approval of the conference report by both houses; enrollment; approval by the president or override of the president's veto; and deposit with the Archivist of the United States. (2) Broadly, the political, lobbying and other factors that affect or influence the process of enacting laws.

Legislative Veto—A procedure, declared unconstitutional in 1983, that allowed Congress or one of its houses to nullify certain actions of the president, executive branch agencies or independent agencies. Sometimes called congressional vetoes or congressional disapprovals. Following the Supreme Court's 1983 decision, Congress amended several legislative veto statutes to require enactment of joint resolutions, which are subject to presidential veto, for nullifying executive branch actions.

Limitation on a General Appropriation Bill—Language that prohibits expenditures for part of an authorized purpose from funds provided in a general appropriation bill. Precedents require that the language be phrased in the negative: that none of the funds provided in a pending appropriation bill shall be used for a specified authorized activity. Limitations in general appropriation bills are permitted on the grounds that Congress can refuse to fund authorized programs and, therefore, can refuse to fund any part of them as long as the prohibition does not change existing law. House precedents have established that a limitation does not change existing law if it does not impose additional duties or burdens on executive branch officials, interfere with their discretionary authority or require them to make judgments or determinations not required by existing law. The proliferation of limitation amendments in the 1970s and early 1980s prompted the House to adopt a rule in 1983 making it more difficult for members to offer them. The rule bans such amendments during the reading of an appropriation bill for amendments, unless they are specifically authorized in existing law. Other limitations may be offered after the reading, but the Committee of the Whole can foreclose them by adopting a motion to rise and report the bill back to the House. In 1995 the rule was amended to allow the motion to rise and report to be made only by the majority leader or his or her designee. The House Appropriations Committee, however, can include limitation provisions in the bills it reports.

Line Item—An amount in an appropriation measure. It can refer to a single appropriation account or to separate amounts within the account. In the congressional budget process, the term usually refers to assumptions about the funding of particular programs or accounts that underlie the broad functional amounts in a budget resolution. These assumptions are discussed in the reports accompanying each resolution and are not binding.

Line-Item Veto—(See Item Veto.)

Line Item Veto Act of 1996—A law, in effect only from January 1997 until June 1998, that granted the president authority intended to be functionally equivalent to an item veto, by amending the Impoundment Control Act of 1974 to incorporate an approach known as enhanced rescission. Key provisions established a new procedure that permitted the president to cancel amounts of new discretionary appropriations (budget authority), new items of direct spending (entitlements) or certain limited tax benefits. It also required the president to notify Congress of the cancellation in a special message within five calendar days after signing the measure. The cancellation would become permanent unless legislation disapproving it was enacted within thirty days. On June 25, 1998, in Clinton v. City of New York the Supreme Court held the Line Item Veto Act unconstitutional, on the grounds that its cancellation provisions violated the presentment clause in Article I, clause 7, of the Constitution.

Live Pair—A voluntary and informal agreement between two members on opposite sides of an issue, one of whom is absent for a recorded vote, under which the member who is present withholds or withdraws his or her vote to offset the failure to vote by the member who is absent. Usually the member in attendance announces that he or she has a live pair, states how each would have voted and votes "present." In the House, under a rules change enacted in the 106th Congress, a live pair is only permitted on the rare occasions when electronic voting is not used.

Live Quorum—In the Senate, a quorum call to which senators are expected to respond. Senators usually suggest the absence of a quorum, not to force a quorum to appear, but to provide a pause in the proceedings during which senators can engage in private discussions or wait for a senator to come to the floor. A senator desiring a live quorum usually announces his or her intention, giving fair warning that there will be an objection to any unanimous consent request that the quorum call be dispensed with before it is completed.

Loan Guarantee—A statutory commitment by the federal government to pay part or all of a loan's principal and interest to a lender or the holder of a security in case the borrower defaults.

Lobby—To try to persuade members of Congress to propose, pass, modify or defeat proposed legislation or to change or repeal existing laws. Lobbyists attempt to promote their preferences or those of a group, organization or industry. Originally the term referred to persons frequenting the lobbies or corridors of legislative chambers in order to speak to lawmakers. In a general sense, lobbying includes not only direct contact with members but also indirect attempts to influence them, such as writing to them or persuading others to write or visit them, attempting to mold public opinion toward a desired legislative goal by various means and contributing or arranging for contributions to members' election campaigns. The right to lobby stems from the First Amendment to the Constitution, which bans laws that abridge the right of the people to petition the government for a redress of grievances.

Lobbying Disclosure Act of 1995—The principal statute requiring disclosure of — and also, to a degree, circumscribing — the activities of lobbyists. In general, it requires lobbyists who spend more than 20 percent of their time on lobbying activities to register and make semiannual reports of their activities to the clerk of the House and the secretary of the Senate, although the law provides for a number of exemptions. Among the statute's prohibitions, lobbyists are not allowed to make contributions to the legal defense fund of a member or high government official or to reimburse for official travel. Civil penalties for failure to comply may include fines of up to $50,000. The act does not include grassroots lobbying in its definition of lobbying activities.

The act amends several other lobby laws, notably the Foreign Agents Registration Act (FARA), so that lobbyists can submit a single filing. Since the measure was enacted, the number of lobby registrations has risen from about 12,000 to more than 20,000. In 1998 expenditures on federal lobbying, as disclosed under the Lobbying Disclosure Act, totaled $1.42 billion. The 1995 act supersedes the 1946 Federal Regulation of Lobbying Act, which was repealed in Section 11 of the 1995 Act.

Logrolling—Jargon for a legislative tactic or bargaining strategy in which members try to build support for their legislation by promising to support legislation desired by other members or by accepting amendments they hope will induce their colleagues to vote for their bill.

Lower Body—A way to refer to the House of Representatives, which is considered pejorative by House members.

Mace—The symbol of the office of the House sergeant at arms. Under the direction of the Speaker, the sergeant at arms is responsible for preserving order on the House floor by holding up the mace in front of an unruly member, or by carrying the mace up and down the aisles to quell boisterous behavior. When the House is in session, the mace sits on a pedestal at the Speaker's right; when the House is in Committee of the Whole, it is moved to a lower pedestal. The mace is forty-six inches high and consists of thirteen ebony rods bound in silver and topped by a silver globe with a silver eagle, wings outstretched, perched on it.

Majority Leader—The majority party's chief floor spokesperson, elected by that party's caucus — sometimes called floor leader. In the Senate, the majority leader also develops the party's political and procedural strategy, usually in collaboration with other party officials and committee chairmen. The majority leader negotiates the Senate's agenda and committee ratios with the minority leader and usually calls up measures for floor action. The chamber traditionally concedes to the majority leader the right to determine the days on which it will meet and the hours at which it will convene and adjourn. In the House, the majority leader is the Speaker's deputy and heir apparent and helps plan the floor agenda and the party's legislative strategy and often speaks for the party leadership in debate.

Managers—(1) The official title of members appointed to a conference committee, commonly called conferees. The ranking majority and minority managers for each house also manage floor consideration of the committee's conference report. (2) The members who manage the initial floor consideration of a measure. (3) The official title of House members appointed to present impeachment articles to the Senate and to act as prosecutors on behalf of the House during the Senate trial of the impeached person.

Mandatory Appropriations—Amounts that Congress must appropriate annually because it has no discretion over them unless it first amends existing substantive law. Certain entitlement programs, for example, require annual appropriations.

Markup—A meeting or series of meetings by a committee or subcommittee during which members mark up a measure by offering, debating and voting on amendments to it.

Means-Tested Programs—Programs that provide benefits or services to low-income individuals who meet a test of need. Most are entitlement programs, such as Medicaid, food stamps and Supplementary Security Income. A few—for example, subsidized housing and various social services—are funded through discretionary appropriations.

Members' Allowances—Official expenses that are paid for or for which members are reimbursed by their houses. Among these are the costs of office space in congressional buildings and in their home states or districts; office equipment and supplies; postage-free mailings (the franking privilege); a set number of trips to and from home states or districts, as well as travel elsewhere on official business; telephone and other telecommunications services; and staff salaries.

Member's Staff—The personal staff to which a member is entitled. The House sets a maximum number of staff and a monetary allowance for each member. The Senate does not set a maximum staff level, but it does set a monetary allowance for each member. In each house, the staff allowance is included with office expenses allowances and official mail allowances in a consolidated allowance. Representatives and senators can spend as much money in their consolidated allowances for staff, office expenses or official mail, as long as they do not exceed the monetary value of the three allowances combined. This provides members with flexibility in operating their offices.

Method of Equal Proportions—The mathematical formula used since 1950 to determine how the 435 seats in the House of Representatives should be distributed among the fifty states in the apportionment following each decennial census. It minimizes as much as possible the proportional difference between the average district population in any two states. Because the Constitution guarantees each state at least one representative, fifty seats are automatically apportioned. The formula calculates priority numbers for each state, assigns the first of the 385 remaining seats to the state with the highest priority number, the second to the state with the next highest number and so on until all seats are distributed. (See Apportionment.)

Midterm Election—The general election for members of Congress that occurs in November of the second year in a presidential term.

Minority Leader—The minority party's leader and chief floor spokesman, elected by the party caucus; sometimes called minority floor leader. With the assistance of other party officials and the ranking minority members of committees, the minority leader devises the party's political and procedural strategy.

Minority Staff—Employees who assist the minority party members of a committee. Most committees hire separate majority and minority party staffs but they also may hire nonpartisan staff. Senate rules state that a committee's staff must reflect the relative number of its majority and minority party committee members, and the rules guarantee the minority at least one-third of the funds available for hiring partisan staff. In the House, each committee is authorized thirty professional staff, and the minority members of most committees may select up to ten of these staff (subject to full committee approval). Under House rules, the minority party is to be "treated fairly" in the apportionment of additional staff resources. Each House committee determines the portion of its additional staff it allocates to the minority; some committees allocate one-third; and others allot less.

Modified Rule—A special rule from the House Rules Committee that permits only certain amendments to be offered to a measure during its floor consideration or that bans certain specified amendments or amendments on certain subjects.

Morning Business—In the Senate, routine business that is to be transacted at the beginning of the morning hour. The business consists, first, of laying before the Senate, and referring to committees, matters such as messages from the president and the House, federal agency reports and unreferred petitions, memorials, bills and joint resolutions. Next, senators may present additional petitions and memorials. Then committees may present their reports, after which senators may introduce bills and resolutions. Finally, resolutions coming over from a previous day are taken up for consideration. In practice, the Senate adopts standing orders that permit senators to introduce measures and file reports at any time, but only if there has been a morning business period on that day. Because the Senate often remains in the same legislative day for several days, weeks or months at a time, it orders a morning business period almost every calendar day for the convenience of senators who wish to introduce measures or make reports.

Morning Hour—A two-hour period at the beginning of a new legislative day during which the Senate is supposed to conduct routine business, call the calendar on Mondays and deal with other matters described in a Senate rule. In practice, the morning hour very rarely, if ever, occurs, in part because the Senate frequently recesses, rather than adjourns, at the end of a daily session. Therefore the rule does not apply when the senate next meets. The Senate's rules reserve the first hour of the morning for morning business. After the completion of morning business, or at the end of the first hour, the rules permit a motion to proceed to the consideration of a measure on the calendar out of its regular order (except on Mondays). Because that normally debatable motion is not debatable if offered during the morning hour, the majority leader may, but rarely does, use this procedure in anticipating a filibuster on the motion to proceed. If the Senate agrees to the motion, it can consider the measure until the end of the morning hour, and if there is no unfinished business from the previous day it can continue considering it after the morning hour. But if there is unfinished business, a motion to continue consideration is necessary, and that motion is debatable.

Motion—A formal proposal for a procedural action, such as to consider, to amend, to lay on the table, to reconsider, to recess or to adjourn. It has been estimated that at least eighty-five motions are possible under various circumstances in the House of Representatives, somewhat fewer in the Senate. Not all motions are created equal; some are privileged or preferential and enjoy priority over others. Some motions are debatable, amendable or divisible, while others are not.

Multiple and Sequential Referrals—The practice of referring a measure to two or more committees for concurrent consideration (multiple referral) or successively to several committees in sequence (sequential referral). A measure may also be divided into several parts, with each referred to a different committee or to several committees sequentially (split referral). In theory this gives all committees that have jurisdiction over parts of a measure the opportunity to consider and report on them.

Before 1975, House precedents banned such referrals. A 1975 rule required the Speaker to make concurrent and sequential referrals "to the maximum extent feasible." On sequential referrals, the Speaker could set deadlines for reporting the measure. The Speaker ruled that this provision authorized him to discharge a committee from further consideration of a measure and place it on the appropriate calendar of the House if the committee fails to meet the Speaker's deadline. The Speaker also used combinations of concurrent and sequential referrals. In 1995 joint referrals were prohibited. Now each measure is referred to a primary committee and also may be referred, either concurrently or sequentially, to one or more other committees, but usually only for consideration of portions of the measure that fall within the jurisdiction of each of those other committees.

In the Senate, before 1977 concurrent and sequential referrals were permitted only by unanimous consent. In that year, a rule authorized a privileged motion for such a referral if offered jointly by the majority and minority leaders. Debate on the motion and all amendments to it is limited to two hours. The motion may set deadlines for reporting and provide for discharging the committees involved if they fail to meet the deadlines. To date, this procedure has never been invoked; multiple referrals in the Senate continue to be made by unanimous consent.

Multiyear Appropriation—An appropriation that remains available for spending or obligation for more than one fiscal year; the exact period of time is specified in the act making the appropriation.

Multiyear Authorization—(1) Legislation that authorizes the existence or continuation of an agency, program or activity for more than one fiscal year. (2) Legislation that authorizes appropriations for an agency, program or activity for more than one fiscal year.

Nomination—A proposed presidential appointment to a federal office submitted to the Senate for confirmation. Approval is by majority vote. The Constitution explicitly requires confirmation for ambassadors, consuls, "public Ministers" (department heads) and Supreme Court justices. By law, other federal judges, all military promotions of officers and many high-level civilian officials must be confirmed.

Oath of Office—Upon taking office, members of Congress must swear or affirm that they will "support and defend the Constitution...against all enemies, foreign and domestic," that they will "bear true faith and allegiance" to the Constitution, that they take the obligation "freely, without any mental reservation or purpose of evasion," and that they will "well and faithfully discharge the duties" of their office. The oath is required by the Constitution, and the wording is prescribed by a statute. All House members must take the oath at the beginning of each new Congress. Usually, the member with the longest continuous service in the House swears in the Speaker, who then swears in the other members. The president of the Senate or a surrogate administers the oath to newly elected or reelected senators.

Obligation—A binding agreement by a government agency to pay for goods, products, services, studies and the like, either immediately or in the future. When an agency enters into such an agreement, it incurs an obligation. As the agency makes the required payments, it liquidates the obligation. Appropriation laws usually make funds available for obligation for one or more fiscal years but do not require agencies to spend their funds during those specific years. The actual outlays can occur years after the appropriation is obligated, as with a contract for construction of a submarine that may provide for payment to be made when it is delivered in the future. Such obligated funds are often said to be "in the pipeline." Under these circumstances, an agency's outlays in a particular year can come from appropriations obligated in previous years as well as from its current-year appropriation. Consequently, the money Congress appropriates for a fiscal year does not equal the total amount of appropriated money the government will actually spend in that year.

Off-Budget Entities—Specific federal entities whose budget authority, outlays and receipts are excluded by law from the calculation of budget totals, although they are part of government spending and income. As of early 2001, these included the Social Security trust funds (Federal Old-Age and Survivors Insurance Fund and the Federal Disability Insurance Trust Fund) and the Postal Service. Government-sponsored enterprises are also excluded from the budget because they are considered private rather than public organizations.

Office of Management and Budget (OMB)—A unit in the Executive Office of the President, reconstituted in 1970 from the former Bureau of the Budget. The Office of Management and Budget (OMB) assists the president in preparing the budget and in formulating the government's fiscal program. The OMB also plays a central role in supervising and controlling implementation of the budget, pursuant to provisions in appropriations laws, the Budget Enforcement Act and other statutes. In addition to these budgetary functions, the OMB has various management duties, including those performed through its three statutory offices: Federal Financial Management, Federal Procurement Policy and Information and Regulatory Affairs.

Officers of Congress—The Constitution refers to the Speaker of the House and the president of the Senate as officers and declares that each house "shall chuse" its "other Officers," but it does not name them or indicate how they should be selected. A House rule refers to its clerk, sergeant at arms and chaplain as officers. Officers are not named in the Senate's rules, but Riddick's Senate Procedure lists the president pro tempore, secretary of the Senate, sergeant at arms, chaplain and the secretaries for the majority and minority parties as officers. A few appointed officials are sometimes referred to as officers, including the parliamentarians and the legislative counsels. The House elects its officers by resolution at the beginning of each Congress. The Senate also elects its officers, but once elected Senate officers serve from Congress to Congress until their successors are chosen.

Omnibus Bill—A measure that combines the provisions of several disparate subjects into a single and often lengthy bill.

One-Minute Speeches—Addresses by House members that can be on any subject but are limited to one minute. They are usually permitted at the beginning of a daily session after the chaplain's prayer, the pledge of allegiance and approval of the Journal. They are a customary practice, not a right granted by rule. Consequently, recognition for one-minute speeches requires unanimous consent and is entirely within the Speaker's discretion. The Speaker sometimes refuses to permit them when the House has a heavy legislative schedule or limits or postpones them until a later time of the day.

Open Rule—A special rule from the House Rules Committee that permits members to offer as many floor amendments as they wish as long as the amendments are germane and do not violate other House rules.

Order of Business (House)—The sequence of events prescribed by a House rule during the meeting of the House on a new legislative day that is supposed to take place, also called the general order of business. The sequence consists of (1) the chaplain's prayer; (2) reading and approval of the Journal; (3) the pledge of allegiance; (4) correction of the reference of public bills to committee; (5) disposal of business on the Speaker's table; (6) unfinished business; (7) the morning hour call of committees and consideration of their bills; (8) motions to go into Committee of the Whole; and (9) orders of the day. In practice, the House never fully complies with this rule. Instead, the items of business that follow the pledge of allegiance are supplanted by any special orders of business that are in order on that day (for example, conference reports; the corrections, discharge or private calendars; or motions to suspend the rules) and by other privileged business (for example, general appropriation bills and special rules) or measures made in order by special rules or unanimous consent. The regular order of business is also modified by unanimous consent practices and orders that govern recognition for one-minute speeches (which date from 1937) and for morning-hour debates, begun in 1994. By this combination of an order of business with privileged interruptions, the House gives precedence to certain categories of important legislation, brings to the floor other major legislation from its calendars in any order it chooses and provides expeditious processing for minor and noncontroversial measures.

Order of Business (Senate)—The sequence of events at the beginning of a new legislative day, as prescribed by Senate rules and standing orders. The sequence consists of (1) the chaplain's prayer; (2) the pledge of allegiance; (3) the designation of a temporary presiding officer if any; (4) Journal reading and approval; (5) recognition of the majority and minority leaders or their designees under the standing order; (6) morning business in the morning hour; (7) call of the calendar during the morning hour (largely obsolete); and (8) unfinished business from the previous session day.

Organization of Congress—The actions each house takes at the beginning of a Congress that are necessary to its operations. These include swearing in newly elected members, notifying the president that a quorum of each house is present, making committee assignments and fixing the hour for daily meetings. Because the House of Representatives is not a continuing body, it must also elect its Speaker and other officers and adopt its rules.

Original Bill—(1) A measure drafted by a committee and introduced by its chairman or another designated member when the committee reports the measure to its house. Unlike a clean bill, it is not referred back to the committee after introduction. The Senate permits all its legislative committees to report original bills. In the House, this authority is referred to in the rules as the "right to report at any time," and five committees (Appropriations, Budget, House Administration, Rules and Standards of Official Conduct) have such authority under circumstances specified in House Rule XIII, clause 5.

(2) In the House, special rules reported by the Rules Committee often propose that an amendment in the nature of a substitute be considered as an original bill for purposes of amendment, meaning that the substitute, as with a bill, may be amended in two degrees. Without that requirement, the substitute may only be amended in one further degree. In the Senate, an amendment in the nature of a substitute automatically is open to two degrees of amendment, as is the original text of the bill, if the substitute is offered when no other amendment is pending.

Original Jurisdiction—The authority of certain committees to originate a measure and report it to the chamber. For example, general appropriation bills reported by the House Appropriations Committee are original bills, and special rules reported by the House Rules Committee are original resolutions.

Other Body—A commonly used reference to a house by a member of the other house. Congressional comity discourages members from directly naming the other house during debate.

Outlays—Amounts of government spending. They consist of payments, usually by check or in cash, to liquidate obligations incurred in prior fiscal years as well as in the current year, including the net lending of funds under budget authority. In federal budget accounting, net outlays are calculated by subtracting the amounts of refunds and various kinds of reimbursements to the government from actual spending.

Override a Veto—Congressional enactment of a measure over the president's veto. A veto override requires a recorded two-thirds vote of those voting in each house, a quorum being present. Because the president must return the vetoed measure to its house of origin, that house votes first, but neither house is required to attempt an override, whether immediately or at all. If an override attempt fails in the house of origin, the veto stands and the measure dies.

Oversight—Congressional review of the way in which federal agencies implement laws to ensure that they are carrying out the intent of Congress and to inquire into the efficiency of the implementation and the effectiveness of the law. The Legislative Reorganization Act of 1946 defined oversight as the function of exercising continuous watchfulness over the execution of the laws by the executive branch.

Oxford-Style Debate—The House held three Oxford-style debates in 1994, modeled after the famous debating format favored by the Oxford Union in Great Britain. Neither chamber has held Oxford-style debates since then. The Oxford-style debates aired nationally over C-SPAN television and National Public Radio. The organized event featured eight participants divided evenly into two teams, one team representing the Democrats (then holding the majority in the chamber) and the other the Republicans. Both teams argued a single question chosen well ahead of the event. A moderator regulated the debate, and began it by stating the resolution at issue. The order of the speakers alternated by team, with a debater for the affirmative speaking first and a debater for the opposing team offering a rebuttal. The rest of the speakers alternated in kind until all gained the chance to speak.

Parliamentarian—The official advisor to the presiding officer in each house on questions of procedure. The parliamentarian and his or her assistants also answer procedural questions from members and congressional staff, refer measures to committees on behalf of the presiding officer and maintain compilations of the precedents. The House parliamentarian revises the House Manual at the beginning of every Congress and usually reviews special rules before the Rules Committee reports them to the House. Either a parliamentarian or an assistant is always present and near the podium during sessions of each house.

Party Caucus—Generic term for each party's official organization in each house. Only House Democrats officially call their organization a caucus. House and Senate Republicans and Senate Democrats call their organizations conferences. The party caucuses elect their leaders, approve committee assignments and chairmanships (or ranking minority members, if the party is in the minority), establish party committees and study groups and discuss party and legislative policies. On rare occasions, they have stripped members of committee seniority or expelled them from the caucus for party disloyalty.

Pay-as-You-Go (PAYGO)—A provision first instituted under the Budget Enforcement Act of 1990 that applies to legislation enacted before Oct. 1, 2002. It requires that the cumulative effect of legislation concerning either revenues or direct spending should not result in a net negative impact on the budget. If legislation does provide for an increase in spending or decrease in revenues, that effect is supposed to be offset by legislated spending reductions or revenue increases. If Congress fails to enact the appropriate offsets, the act requires presidential sequestration of sufficient offsetting amounts in specific direct spending accounts. Congress and the president can circumvent this requirement if both agree that an emergency requires a particular action or if a law is enacted declaring that deteriorated economic circumstances make it necessary to suspend the requirement.

Permanent Appropriation—An appropriation that remains continuously available, without current action or renewal by Congress, under the terms of a previously enacted authorization or appropriation law. One such appropriation provides for payment of interest on the public debt and another the salaries of members of Congress.

Permanent Authorization—An authorization without a time limit. It usually does not specify any limit on the funds that may be appropriated for the agency, program or activity that it authorizes, leaving such amounts to the discretion of the appropriations committees and the two houses.

Permanent Staff—Term used formerly for committee staff authorized by law, who were funded through a permanent authorization and also called statutory staff. Most committees were authorized thirty permanent staff members. Most committees also were permitted additional staff, often called investigative staff, who were authorized by annual or biennial funding resolutions. The Senate eliminated the primary distinction between statutory and investigative staff in 1981. The House eliminated the distinction in 1995 by requiring that funding resolutions authorize money to hire both types of staff.

Personally Obnoxious (or Objectionable)—A characterization a senator sometimes applies to a president's nominee for a federal office in that senator's state to justify his or her opposition to the nomination.

Pocket Veto—The indirect veto of a bill as a result of the president withholding approval of it until after Congress has adjourned sine die. A bill the president does not sign but does not formally veto while Congress is in session automatically becomes a law ten days (excluding Sundays) after it is received. But if Congress adjourns its annual session during that ten-day period the measure dies even if the president does not formally veto it.

Point of Order—A parliamentary term used in committee and on the floor to object to an alleged violation of a rule and to demand that the chair enforce the rule. The point of order immediately halts the proceedings until the chair decides whether the contention is valid.

Pork or Pork Barrel Legislation—Pejorative terms for federal appropriations, bills or policies that provide funds to benefit a legislator's district or state, with the implication that the legislator presses for enactment of such benefits to ingratiate himself or herself with constituents rather than on the basis of an impartial, objective assessment of need or merit. The terms are often applied to such benefits as new parks, post offices, dams, canals, bridges, roads, water projects, sewage treatment plants and public works of any kind, as well as demonstration projects, research grants and relocation of government facilities. Funds released by the president for various kinds of benefits or government contracts approved by him allegedly for political purposes are also sometimes referred to as pork.

Postcloture Filibuster—A filibuster conducted after the Senate invokes cloture. It employs an array of procedural tactics rather than lengthy speeches to delay final action. The Senate curtailed the postcloture filibuster's effectiveness by closing a variety of loopholes in the cloture rule in 1979 and 1986.

Power of the Purse—A reference to the constitutional power Congress has over legislation to raise revenue and appropriate monies from the Treasury. Article I, Section 8 states that Congress "shall have Power To lay and collect Taxes, Duties, Imposts and Excises, [and] to pay the Debts." Section 9 declares: "No Money shall be drawn from the Treasury, but in Consequence of Appropriations made by Law."

Preamble—Introductory language describing the reasons for and intent of a measure, sometimes called a whereas clause. It occasionally appears in joint, concurrent and simple resolutions but rarely in bills.

Precedent—A previous ruling on a parliamentary matter or a long-standing practice or custom of a house. Precedents serve to control arbitrary rulings and serve as the common law of a house.

President of the Senate—One constitutional role of the vice president is serving as the presiding officer of the Senate, or president of the Senate. The Constitution permits the vice president to cast a vote in the Senate only to break a tie, but the vice president is not required to do so.

President Pro Tempore—Under the Constitution, an officer elected by the Senate to preside over it during the absence of the vice president of the United States. Often referred to as the "pro tem," this senator is usually a member of the majority party with the longest continuous service in the chamber and also, by virtue of seniority, a committee chairman. When attending to committee and other duties the president pro tempore appoints other senators to preside.

Presiding Officer—In a formal meeting, the individual authorized to maintain order and decorum, recognize members to speak or offer motions and apply and interpret the chamber's rules, precedents and practices. The Speaker of the House and the president of the Senate are the chief presiding officers in their respective houses.

Previous Question—A nondebatable motion which, when agreed to by majority vote, usually cuts off further debate, prevents the offering of additional amendments and brings the pending matter to an immediate vote. It is a major debate-limiting device in the House; it is not permitted in Committee of the Whole in the House or in the Senate.

Private Bill—A bill that applies to one or more specified persons, corporations, institutions or other entities, usually to grant relief when no other legal remedy is available to them. Many private bills deal with claims against the federal government, immigration and naturalization cases and land titles.

Private Calendar—Commonly used title for a calendar in the House reserved for private bills and resolutions favorably reported by committees. The private calendar is officially called the Calendar of the Committee of the Whole House.

Private Law—A private bill enacted into law. Private laws are numbered in the same fashion as public laws.

Privilege—An attribute of a motion, measure, report, question or proposition that gives it priority status for consideration. Privileged motions and motions to bring up privileged questions are not debatable.

Privilege of the Floor—In addition to the members of a house, certain individuals are admitted to its floor while it is in session. The rules of the two houses differ somewhat but both extend the privilege to the president and vice president, Supreme Court justices, cabinet members, state governors, former members of that house, members of the other house, certain officers and officials of Congress, certain staff of that house in the discharge of official duties and the chamber's former parliamentarians. They also allow access to a limited number of committee and members' staff when their presence is necessary.

Pro Forma Amendment—In the House, an amendment that ostensibly proposes to change a measure or another amendment by moving "to strike the last word" or "to strike the requisite number of words." A member offers it not to make any actual change in the measure or amendment but only to obtain time for debate.

Pro Tem—A common reference to the president pro tempore of the Senate or, occasionally, to a Speaker pro tempore. (See President Pro Tempore; Speaker Pro Tempore.)

Procedures—The methods of conducting business in a deliberative body. The procedures of each house are governed first by applicable provisions of the Constitution, and then by its standing rules and orders, precedents, traditional practices and any statutory rules that apply to it. The authority of the houses to adopt rules in addition to those specified in the Constitution is derived from Article I, Section 5, clause 2, of the Constitution, which states: "Each House may determine the Rules of its Proceedings...." By rule, the House of Representatives also follows the procedures in Jefferson's Manual that are not inconsistent with its standing rules and orders. Many Senate procedures also conform with Jefferson's provisions, but by practice rather than by rule. At the beginning of each Congress, the House uses procedures in general parliamentary law until it adopts its standing rules.

Proxy Voting—The practice of permitting a member to cast the vote of an absent colleague in addition to his or her own vote. Proxy voting is prohibited on the floors of the House and Senate, but the Senate permits its committees to authorize proxy voting, and most do. In 1995, House rules were changed to prohibit proxy voting in committee.

Public Bill—A bill dealing with general legislative matters having national applicability or applying to the federal government or to a class of persons, groups or organizations.

Public Debt—Federal government debt incurred by the Treasury or the Federal Financing Bank by the sale of securities to the public or borrowings from a federal fund or account.

Public Law—A public bill or joint resolution enacted into law. It is cited by the letters "PL" followed by a hyphenated number. The digits before the hyphen indicate the number of the Congress in which it was enacted; the digits after the hyphen indicate its position in the numerical sequence of public measures that became law during that Congress. For example, the Budget Enforcement Act of 1990 became PL 101-508 because it was the 508th measure in that sequence for the 101st Congress. (See also Private Law.)

Qualification (of Members)—The Constitution requires members of the House of Representatives to be twenty-five years of age at the time their terms begin. They must have been citizens of the United States for seven years before that date and, when elected, must be "Inhabitant[s]" of the state from which they were elected. There is no constitutional requirement that they reside in the districts they represent. Senators are required to be thirty years of age at the time their terms begin. They must have been citizens of the United States for nine years before that date and, when elected, must be "Inhabitant[s]" of the states in which they were elected. The "Inhabitant" qualification is broadly interpreted, and in modern times a candidate's declaration of state residence has generally been accepted as meeting the constitutional requirement.

Queen of the Hill Rule—A special rule from the House Rules Committee that permits votes on a series of amendments, especially complete substitutes for a measure, in a specified order, but directs that the amendment receiving the greatest number of votes shall be the winning one. This kind of rule permits the House to vote directly on a variety of alternatives to a measure. In doing so, it sets aside the precedent that once an amendment has been adopted, no further amendments may be offered to the text it has amended. Under an earlier practice, the Rules Committee reported "king of the hill" rules under which there also could be votes on a series of amendments, again in a specified order. If more than one of the amendments was adopted under this kind of rule, it was the last amendment to receive a majority vote that was considered as having been finally adopted, whether or not it had received the greatest number of votes.

Quorum—The minimum number of members required to be present for the transaction of business. Under the Constitution, a quorum in each house is a majority of its members: 218 in the House and 51 in the Senate when there are no vacancies. By House rule, a quorum in Committee of the Whole is 100. In practice, both houses usually assume a quorum is present even if it is not, unless a member makes a point of no quorum in the House or suggests the absence of a quorum in the Senate. Consequently, each house transacts much of its business, and even passes bills, when only a few members are present. For House and Senate committees, chamber rules allow a minimum quorum of one-third of a committee's members to conduct most types of business.

Quorum Call—A procedure for determining whether a quorum is present in a chamber. In the Senate, a clerk calls the roll (roster) of senators. The House usually employs its electronic voting system.

Ramseyer Rule—A House rule that requires a committee's report on a bill or joint resolution to show the changes the measure, and any committee amendments to it, would make in existing law. The rule requires the report to present the text of any statutory provision that would be repealed and a comparative print showing, through typographical devices such as stricken-through type or italics, other changes that would be made in existing law. The rule, adopted in 1929, is named after its sponsor, Rep. Christian W. Ramseyer, R-Iowa. The Senate's analogous rule is called the Cordon Rule.

Rank or Ranking—A member's position on the list of his or her party's members on a committee or subcommittee. When first assigned to a committee, a member is usually placed at the bottom of the list, then moves up as those above leave the committee. On subcommittees, however, a member's rank may not have anything to do with the length of his or her service on it.

Ranking Member—(1) Most often a reference to the minority member with the highest ranking on a committee or subcommittee. (2) A reference to the majority member next in rank to the chairman or to the highest ranking majority member present at a committee or subcommittee meeting.

Ratification—(1) The president's formal act of promulgating a treaty after the Senate has approved it. The resolution of ratification agreed to by the Senate is the procedural vehicle by which the Senate gives its consent to ratification. (2) A state legislature's act in approving a proposed constitutional amendment. Such an amendment becomes effective when ratified by three-fourths of the states.

Reapportionment—(See Apportionment.)

Recess—(1) A temporary interruption or suspension of a meeting of a chamber or committee. Unlike an adjournment, a recess does not end a legislative day. Because the Senate often recesses from one calendar day to another, its legislative day may extend over several calendar days, weeks or even months. (2) A period of adjournment for more than three days to a day certain, especially over a holiday or in August during odd-numbered years.

Recess Appointment—A presidential appointment to a vacant federal position made after the Senate has adjourned sine die or has adjourned or recessed for more than thirty days. If the president submits the recess appointee's nomination during the next session of the Senate, that individual can continue to serve until the end of the session even though the Senate might have rejected the nomination. When appointed to a vacancy that existed thirty days before the end of the last Senate session, a recess appointee is not paid until confirmed.

Recommit—To send a measure back to the committee that reported it; sometimes called a straight motion to recommit to distinguish it from a motion to recommit with instructions. A successful motion to recommit kills the measure unless it is accompanied by instructions.

Recommit a Conference Report—To return a conference report to the conference committee for renegotiation of some or all of its agreements. A motion to recommit may be offered with or without instructions.

Recommit with Instructions—To send a measure back to a committee with instructions to take some action on it. Invariably in the House and often in the Senate, when the motion recommits to a standing committee, the instructions require the committee to report the measure "forthwith" with specified amendments.

Reconciliation—A procedure for changing existing revenue and spending laws to bring total federal revenues and spending within the limits established in a budget resolution. Congress has applied reconciliation chiefly to revenues and mandatory spending programs, especially entitlements. Discretionary spending is controlled through annual appropriation bills.

Recorded Vote—(1) Generally, any vote in which members are recorded by name for or against a measure; also called a record vote or roll-call vote. The only recorded vote in the Senate is a vote by the yeas and nays and is commonly called a roll-call vote. (2) Technically, a recorded vote is one demanded in the House of Representatives and supported by at least one-fifth of a quorum (forty-four members) in the House sitting as the House or at least twenty-five members in Committee of the Whole.

Recorded Vote by Clerks—A voting procedure in the House where members pass through the appropriate "aye" or "no" aisle in the chamber and cast their votes by depositing a signed green (yea) or red (no) card in a ballot box. These votes are tabulated by clerks and reported to the chair. The electronic voting system is much more convenient and has largely supplanted this procedure. (See Committee of the Whole; Recorded Vote; Teller Vote.)

Redistricting—The redrawing of congressional district boundaries within a state after a decennial census. Redistricting may be required to equalize district populations or to accommodate an increase or decrease in the number of a state's House seats that might have resulted from the decennial apportionment. The state governments determine the district lines. (See Apportionment; Congressional District; Gerrymandering.)

Referral—The assignment of a measure to committee for consideration. Under a House rule, the Speaker can refuse to refer a measure if the Speaker believes it is "of an obscene or insulting character."

Report—(1) As a verb, a committee is said to report when it submits a measure or other document to its parent chamber. (2) A clerk is said to report when he or she reads a measure's title, text or the text of an amendment to the body at the direction of the chair. (3) As a noun, a committee document that accompanies a reported measure. It describes the measure, the committee's views on it, its costs and the changes it proposes to make in existing law; it also includes certain impact statements. (4) A committee document submitted to its parent chamber that describes the results of an investigation or other study or provides information it is required to provide by rule or law.

Representative—An elected and duly sworn member of the House of Representatives who is entitled to vote in the chamber. The Constitution requires that a representative be at least twenty-five years old, a citizen of the United States for at least seven years and an inhabitant of the state from which he or she is elected. Customarily, the member resides in the district he or she represents. Representatives are elected in even-numbered years to two-year terms that begin the following January.

Reprimand—A formal condemnation of a member for misbehavior, considered a milder reproof than censure. The House of Representatives first used it in 1976. The Senate first used it in 1991. (See also Censure; Code of Official Conduct; Denounce; Ethics Rules; Expulsion; Seniority Loss.)

Rescission—A provision of law that repeals previously enacted budget authority in whole or in part. Under the Impoundment Control Act of 1974, the president can impound such funds by sending a message to Congress requesting one or more rescissions and the reasons for doing so. If Congress does not pass a rescission bill for the programs requested by the president within forty-five days of continuous session after receiving the message, the president must make the funds available for obligation and expenditure. If the president does not, the comptroller general of the United States is authorized to bring suit to compel the release of those funds. A rescission bill may rescind all, part or none of an amount proposed by the president, and may rescind funds the president has not impounded.

Reserving the Right To Object—Members' declaration that at some indefinite future time they may object to a unanimous consent request. It is an attempt to circumvent the requirement that members may prevent such an action only by objecting immediately after it is proposed.

Resident Commissioner from Puerto Rico—A nonvoting member of the House of Representatives, elected to a four-year term. The resident commissioner has the same status and privileges as delegates. Like the delegates, the resident commissioner may not vote in the House or Committee of the Whole.

Resolution—(1) A simple resolution; that is, a nonlegislative measure effective only in the house in which it is proposed and not requiring concurrence by the other chamber or approval by the president. Simple resolutions are designated H. Res. in the House and S. Res. in the Senate. Simple resolutions express nonbinding opinions on policies or issues or deal with the internal affairs or prerogatives of a house. (2) Any type of resolution: simple, concurrent or joint. (See Concurrent Resolution; Joint Resolution.)

Resolution of Inquiry—A resolution usually simple rather than concurrent calling on the president or the head of an executive agency to provide specific information or papers to one or both houses.

Resolution of Ratification—The Senate vehicle for agreeing to a treaty. The constitutionally mandated vote of two-thirds of the senators present and voting applies to the adoption of this resolution. However, it may also contain amendments, reservations, declarations or understandings that the Senate had previously added to it by majority vote.

Revenue Legislation—Measures that levy new taxes or tariffs or change existing ones. Under Article I, Section 7, clause 1 of the Constitution, the House of Representatives originates federal revenue measures, but the Senate can propose amendments to them. The House Ways and Means Committee and the Senate Finance Committee have jurisdiction over such measures, with a few minor exceptions.

Revise and Extend One's Remarks—A unanimous consent request to publish in the Congressional Record a statement a member did not deliver on the floor, a longer statement than the one made on the floor or miscellaneous extraneous material.

Revolving Fund—A trust fund or account whose income remains available to finance its continuing operations without any fiscal year limitation.

Rider—Congressional slang for an amendment unrelated or extraneous to the subject matter of the measure to which it is attached. Riders often contain proposals that are less likely to become law on their own merits as separate bills, either because of opposition in the committee of jurisdiction, resistance in the other house or the probability of a presidential veto. Riders are more common in the Senate.

Roll Call—A call of the roll to determine whether a quorum is present, to establish a quorum or to vote on a question. Usually, the House uses its electronic voting system for a roll call. The Senate does not have an electronic voting system; its roll is always called by a clerk.

Rule—(1) A permanent regulation that a house adopts to govern its conduct of business, its procedures, its internal organization, behavior of its members, regulation of its facilities, duties of an officer or some other subject it chooses to govern in that form. (2) In the House, a privileged simple resolution reported by the Rules Committee that provides methods and conditions for floor consideration of a measure or, rarely, several measures.

Rule Twenty-Two—A common reference to the Senate's cloture rule. (See Cloture)

Second-Degree Amendment—An amendment to an amendment in the first degree. It is usually a perfecting amendment.

Secretary of the Senate—The chief financial, administrative and legislative officer of the Senate. Elected by resolution or order of the Senate, the secretary is invariably the candidate of the majority party and usually chosen by the majority leader. In the absence of the vice president and pending the election of a president pro tempore, the secretary presides over the Senate. The secretary is subject to policy direction and oversight by the Senate Committee on Rules and Administration. The secretary manages a wide range of functions that support the administrative operations of the Senate as an organization as well as those functions necessary to its legislative process, including record keeping, document management, certifications, housekeeping services, administration of oaths and lobbyist registrations. The secretary is responsible for accounting for all funds appropriated to the Senate and conducts audits of Senate financial activities. On a semiannual basis the secretary issues the Report of the Secretary of the Senate, a compilation of Senate expenditures.

Section—A subdivision of a bill or statute. By law, a section must be numbered and, as nearly as possible, contain "a single proposition of enactment."

Select or Special Committee—A committee established by a resolution in either house for a special purpose and, usually, for a limited time. Most select and special committees are assigned specific investigations or studies but are not authorized to report measures to their chambers. However, both houses have created several permanent select and special committees and have given legislative reporting authority to a few of them: the Ethics Committee in the Senate and the Intelligence Committees in both houses. There is no substantive difference between a select and a special committee; they are so called depending simply on whether the resolution creating the committee calls it one or the other.

Senate—The house of Congress in which each state is represented by two senators; each senator has one vote. Article V of the Constitution declares that "No State, without its Consent, shall be deprived of its equal Suffrage in the Senate." The Constitution also gives the Senate equal legislative power with the House of Representatives. Although the Senate is prohibited from originating revenue measures, and as a matter of practice it does not originate appropriation measures, it can amend both. Only the Senate can give or withhold consent to treaties and nominations from the president. It also acts as a court to try impeachments by the House and elects the vice president when no candidate receives a majority of the electoral votes. It is often referred to as "the upper body," but not by members of the House.

Senate Manual—The handbook of the Senate's standing rules and orders and the laws and other regulations that apply to the Senate, usually published once each Congress.

Senator—A duly sworn elected or appointed member of the Senate. The Constitution requires that a senator be at least thirty years old, a citizen of the United States for at least nine years and an inhabitant of the state from which he or she is elected. Senators are usually elected in even-numbered years to six-year terms that begin the following January. When a vacancy occurs before the end of a term, the state governor can appoint a replacement to fill the position until a successor is chosen at the state's next general election or, if specified under state law, the next feasible date for such an election, to serve the remainder of the term. Until the Seventeenth Amendment was ratified in 1913, senators were chosen by their state legislatures.

Senatorial Courtesy—The Senate's practice of declining to confirm a presidential nominee for an office in the state of a senator of the president's party unless that senator approves.

Seniority—The priority, precedence or status accorded members according to the length of their continuous service in a house or on a committee.

Seniority Loss—A type of punishment that reduces a member's seniority on his or her committees, including the loss of chairmanships. Party caucuses in both houses have occasionally imposed such punishment on their members, for example, for publicly supporting candidates of the other party.

Seniority Rule—The customary practice, rather than a rule, of assigning the chairmanship of a committee to the majority party member who has served on the committee for the longest continuous period of time.

Seniority System—A collection of long-standing customary practices under which members with longer continuous service than their colleagues in their house or on their committees receive various kinds of preferential treatment. Although some of the practices are no longer as rigidly observed as in the past, they still pervade the organization and procedures of Congress.

Sequestration—A procedure for canceling budgetary resources — that is, money available for obligation or spending — to enforce budget limitations established in law. Sequestered funds are no longer available for obligation or expenditure.

Sergeant at Arms—The officer in each house responsible for maintaining order, security and decorum in its wing of the Capitol, including the chamber and its galleries. Although elected by their respective houses, both sergeants at arms are invariably the candidates of the majority party.

Session—(1) The annual series of meetings of a Congress. Under the Constitution, Congress must assemble at least once a year at noon on Jan. 3 unless it appoints a different day by law. (2) The special meetings of Congress or of one house convened by the president, called a special session. (3) A house is said to be in session during the period of a day when it is meeting.

Severability (or Separability) Clause—Language stating that if any particular provisions of a measure are declared invalid by the courts the remaining provisions shall remain in effect.

Sine Die—Without fixing a day for a future meeting. An adjournment sine die signifies the end of an annual or special session of Congress.

Slip Law—The first official publication of a measure that has become law. It is published separately in unbound, single-sheet form or pamphlet form. A slip law usually is available two or three days after the date of the law's enactment.

Speaker—The presiding officer of the House of Representatives and the leader of its majority party. The Speaker is selected by the majority party and formally elected by the House at the beginning of each Congress. Although the Constitution does not require the Speaker to be a member of the House, in fact, all Speakers have been members.

Speaker Pro Tempore—A member of the House who is designated as the temporary presiding officer by the Speaker or elected by the House to that position during the Speaker's absence.

Speaker's Vote—The Speaker is not required to vote, and the Speaker's name is not called on a roll-call vote unless so requested. Usually, the Speaker votes either to create a tie vote, and thereby defeat a proposal or to break a tie in favor of a proposal. Occasionally, the Speaker also votes to emphasize the importance of a matter.

Special Session—A session of Congress convened by the president, under his constitutional authority, after Congress has adjourned sine die at the end of a regular session. (See Adjournment Sine Die; Session.)

Spending Authority—The technical term for backdoor spending. The Congressional Budget Act of 1974 defines it as borrowing authority, contract authority and entitlement authority for which appropriation acts do not provide budget authority in advance. Under the Budget Act, legislation that provides new spending authority may not be considered unless it provides that the authority shall be effective only to the extent or in such amounts as provided in an appropriation act.

Spending Cap—The statutory limit for a fiscal year on the amount of new budget authority and outlays allowed for discretionary spending. The Budget Enforcement Act of 1997 requires a sequester if the cap is exceeded.

Split Referral—A measure divided into two or more parts, with each part referred to a different committee.

Sponsor—The principal proponent and introducer of a measure or an amendment.

Staff Director—The most frequently used title for the head of staff of a committee or subcommittee. On some committees, that person is called chief of staff, clerk, chief clerk, chief counsel, general counsel or executive director. The head of a committee's minority staff is usually called minority staff director.

Standing Committee—A permanent committee established by a House or Senate standing rule or standing order. The rule also describes the subject areas on which the committee may report bills and resolutions and conduct oversight. Most introduced measures must be referred to one or more standing committees according to their jurisdictions.

Standing Order—A continuing regulation or directive that has the force and effect of a rule, but is not incorporated into the standing rules. The Senate's numerous standing orders, like its standing rules, continue from Congress to Congress unless changed or the order states otherwise. The House uses relatively few standing orders, and those it adopts expire at the end of a session of Congress.

Standing Rules—The rules of the Senate that continue from one Congress to the next and the rules of the House of Representatives that it adopts at the beginning of each new Congress.

Standing Vote—An alternative and informal term for a division vote, during which members in favor of a proposal and then members opposed stand and are counted by the chair.

Star Print—A reprint of a bill, resolution, amendment or committee report correcting technical or substantive errors in a previous printing; so called because of the small black star that appears on the front page or cover.

State of the Union Message—A presidential message to Congress under the constitutional directive that the president shall "from time to time give to the Congress Information of the State of the Union, and recommend to their Consideration such Measures as he shall judge necessary and expedient." Customarily, the president sends an annual State of the Union message to Congress, usually late in January.

Statutes at Large—A chronological arrangement of the laws enacted in each session of Congress. Though indexed, the laws are not arranged by subject matter nor is there an indication of how they affect or change previously enacted laws. The volumes are numbered by Congress, and the laws are cited by their volume and page number. The Gramm-Rudman-Hollings Act, for example, appears as 99 Stat. 1037.

Straw Vote Prohibition—Under a House precedent, a member who has the floor during debate may not conduct a straw vote or otherwise ask for a show of support for a proposition. Only the chair may put a question to a vote.

Strike From the *Record*—Expunge objectionable remarks from the Congressional Record, after a member's words have been taken down on a point of order.

Subcommittee—A panel of committee members assigned a portion of the committee's jurisdiction or other functions. On legislative committees, subcommittees hold hearings, mark up legislation and report measures to their full committee for further action; they cannot report directly to the chamber. A subcommittee's party composition usually reflects the ratio on its parent committee.

Subpoena Power—The authority granted to committees by the rules of their respective houses to issue legal orders requiring individuals to appear and testify, or to produce documents pertinent to the committee's functions, or both. Persons who do not comply with subpoenas can be cited for contempt of Congress and prosecuted.

Subsidy—Generally, a payment or benefit made by the federal government for which no current repayment is required. Subsidy payments may be designed to support the conduct of an economic enterprise or activity, such as ship operations, or to support certain market prices, as in the case of farm subsidies.

Sunset Legislation—A term sometimes applied to laws authorizing the existence of agencies or programs that expire annually or at the end of some other specified period of time. One of the purposes of setting specific expiration dates for agencies and programs is to encourage the committees with jurisdiction over them to determine whether they should be continued or terminated.

Sunshine Rules—Rules requiring open committee hearings and business meetings, including markup sessions, in both houses, and also open conference committee meetings. However, all may be closed under certain circumstances and using certain procedures required by the rules.

Supermajority—A term sometimes used for a vote on a matter that requires approval by more than a simple majority of those members present and voting; also referred to as extraordinary majority.

Supplemental Appropriation Bill—A measure providing appropriations for use in the current fiscal year, in addition to those already provided in annual general appropriation bills. Supplemental appropriations are often for unforeseen emergencies.

Suspension of the Rules (House)—An expeditious procedure for passing relatively noncontroversial or emergency measures by a two-thirds vote of those members voting, a quorum being present.

Suspension of the Rules (Senate)—A procedure to set aside one or more of the Senate's rules; it is used infrequently, and then most often to suspend the rule banning legislative amendments to appropriation bills.

Task Force—A title sometimes given to a panel of members assigned to a special project, study or investigation. Ordinarily, these groups do not have authority to report measures to their respective houses.

Tax Expenditure—Loosely, a tax exemption or advantage, sometimes called an incentive or loophole; technically, a loss of governmental tax revenue attributable to some provision of federal tax laws that allows a special exclusion, exemption or deduction from gross income or that provides a special credit, preferential tax rate or deferral of tax liability.

Televised Proceedings—Television and radio coverage of the floor proceedings of the House of Representatives has been available since 1979 and of the Senate since 1986. They are broadcast over a coaxial cable system to all congressional offices and to some congressional agencies on channels reserved for that purpose. Coverage is also available free of charge to commercial and public television and radio broadcasters. The Cable-Satellite Public Affairs Network (C-SPAN) carries gavel-to-gavel coverage of both houses.

Teller Vote—A voting procedure, formerly used in the House, in which members cast their votes by passing through the center aisle to be counted, but not recorded by name, by a member from each party appointed by the chair. The House deleted the procedure from its rules in 1993, but during floor discussion of the deletion a leading member stated that a teller vote would still be available in the event of a breakdown of the electronic voting system.

Third-Degree Amendment—An amendment to a second-degree amendment. Both houses prohibit such amendments.

Third Reading—A required reading to a chamber of a bill or joint resolution by title only before the vote on passage. In modern practice, it has merely become a pro forma step.

Three-Day Rule—(1) In the House, a measure cannot be considered until the third calendar day on which the committee report has been available. (2) In the House, a conference report cannot be considered until the third calendar day on which its text has been available in the Congressional Record. (3) In the House, a general appropriation bill cannot be considered until the third calendar day on which printed hearings on the bill have been available. (4) In the Senate, when a committee votes to report a measure, a committee member is entitled to three calendar days within which to submit separate views for inclusion in the committee report. (In House committees, a member is entitled to two calendar days for this purpose, after the day on which the committee votes to report.) (5) In both houses, a majority of a committee's members may call a special meeting of the committee if its chairman fails to do so within three calendar days after three or more of the members, acting jointly, formally request such a meeting.

In calculating such periods, the House omits holiday and weekend days on which it does not meet. The Senate makes no such exclusion.

Tie Vote—When the votes for and against a proposition are equal, it loses. The president of the Senate may cast a vote only to break a tie. Because the Speaker is invariably a member of the House, the Speaker is entitled to vote but usually does not. The Speaker may choose to do so to break, or create, a tie vote.

Title—(1) A major subdivision of a bill or act, designated by a roman numeral and usually containing legislative provisions on the same general subject. Titles are sometimes divided into subtitles as well as sections. (2) The official name of a bill or act, also called a caption or long title. (3) Some bills also have short titles that appear in the sentence immediately following the enacting clause. (4) Popular titles are the unofficial names given to some bills or acts by common usage. For example, the Balanced Budget and Emergency Deficit Control Act of 1985 (short title) is almost invariably referred to as Gramm-Rudman (popular title). In other cases, significant legislation is popularly referred to by its title number (see definition (1) above). For example, the federal legislation that requires equality of funding for women's and men's sports in educational institutions that receive federal funds is popularly called Title IX.

Track System—An occasional Senate practice that expedites legislation by dividing a day's session into two or more specific time periods, commonly called tracks, each reserved for consideration of a different measure.

Transfer Payment—A federal government payment to which individuals or organizations are entitled under law and for which no goods or services are required in return. Payments include welfare and Social Security benefits, unemployment insurance, government pensions and veterans benefits.

Treaty—A formal document containing an agreement between two or more sovereign nations. The Constitution authorizes the president to make treaties, but the president must submit them to the Senate for its approval by a two-thirds vote of the senators present. Under the Senate's rules, that vote actually occurs on a resolution of ratification. Although the Constitution does not give the House a direct role in approving treaties, that body has sometimes insisted that a revenue treaty is an invasion of its prerogatives. In any case, the House may significantly affect the application of a treaty by its equal role in enacting legislation to implement the treaty.

Trust Funds—Special accounts in the Treasury that receive earmarked taxes or other kinds of revenue collections, such as user fees, and from which payments are made for special purposes or to recipients who meet the requirements of the trust funds as established by law. Of the more than 150 federal government trust funds, several finance major entitlement programs, such as Social Security, Medicare and retired federal employees' pensions. Others fund infrastructure construction and improvements, such as highways and airports.

Unanimous Consent—Without an objection by any member. A unanimous consent request asks permission, explicitly or implicitly, to set aside one or more rules. Both houses and their committees frequently use such requests to expedite their proceedings.

Uncontrollable Expenditures—A frequently used term for federal expenditures that are mandatory under existing law and therefore cannot be controlled by the president or Congress without a change in the existing law. Uncontrollable expenditures include spending required under entitlement programs and also fixed costs, such as interest on the public debt and outlays to pay for prior-year obligations. In recent years, uncontrollables have accounted for approximately three-quarters of federal spending in each fiscal year.

Unfunded Mandate—Generally, any provision in federal law or regulation that imposes a duty or obligation on a state or local government or private sector entity without providing the necessary funds to comply. The Unfunded Mandates Reform Act of 1995 amended the Congressional Budget Act of 1974 to provide a mechanism for the control of new unfunded mandates.

Union Calendar—A calendar of the House of Representatives for bills and resolutions favorably reported by committees that raise revenue or directly or indirectly appropriate money or property. In addition to appropriation bills, measures that authorize expenditures are also placed on this calendar. The calendar's full title is the Calendar of the Committee of the Whole House on the State of the Union.

Upper Body—A common reference to the Senate, but not used by members of the House.

U.S. Code—Popular title for the United States Code: Containing the General and Permanent Laws of the United States in Force on.... It is a consolidation and partial codification of the general and permanent laws of the United States arranged by subject under 50 titles. The first six titles deal with general or political subjects, the other forty-four with subjects ranging from agriculture to war, alphabetically arranged. A supplement is published after each session of Congress, and the entire Code is revised every six years.

User Fee—A fee charged to users of goods or services provided by the federal government. When Congress levies or authorizes such fees, it determines whether the revenues should go into the general collections of the Treasury or be available for expenditure by the agency that provides the goods or services.

Veto—The president's disapproval of a legislative measure passed by Congress. The president returns the measure to the house in which it originated without his signature but with a veto message stating his objections to it. When Congress is in session, the president must veto a bill within ten days, excluding Sundays, after the president has received it; otherwise it becomes law without his signature. The ten-day clock begins to run at midnight following his receipt of the bill. (See also Committee Veto; Item Veto; Line Item Veto Act of 1996; Override a Veto; Pocket Veto.)

favor a question answer aye in chorus, after which those opposed answer no in chorus, and the chair decides which position prevails.

Voting—Members vote in three ways on the floor: (1) by shouting "aye" or "no" on voice votes; (2) by standing for or against on division votes; and (3) on recorded votes (including the yeas and nays), by answering "aye" or "no" when their names are called or, in the House, by recording their votes through the electronic voting system.

War Powers Resolution of 1973—An act that requires the president "in every possible instance" to consult Congress before committing U.S. forces to ongoing or imminent hostilities. If the president commits them to a combat situation without congressional consultation, the president must notify Congress within forty-eight hours. Unless Congress declares war or otherwise authorizes the operation to continue, the forces must be withdrawn within sixty or ninety days, depending on certain conditions. No president has ever acknowledged the constitutionality of the resolution.

Well—The sunken, level, open space between members' seats and the podium at the front of each chamber. House members usually address their chamber from their party's lectern in the well on its side of the aisle. Senators usually speak at their assigned desks.

Whip—The majority or minority party member in each house who acts as assistant leader, helps plan and marshal support for party strategies, encourages party discipline and advises his or her leader on how colleagues intend to vote on the floor. In the Senate, the Republican whip's official title is assistant leader.

Yeas and Nays—A vote in which members usually respond "aye" or "no" (despite the official title of the vote) on a question when their names are called in alphabetical order. The Constitution requires the yeas and nays when a demand for it is supported by one-fifth of the members present, and it also requires an automatic yea-and-nay vote on overriding a veto. Senate precedents require the support of at least one-fifth of a quorum, a minimum of eleven members with the present membership of 100.

Congressional Information on the Internet

A huge array of congressional information is available for free at Internet sites operated by the federal government, colleges and universities and commercial firms. The sites offer the full text of bills introduced in the House and Senate, voting records, campaign finance information, transcripts of selected congressional hearings, investigative reports and much more.

THOMAS

The most important site for congressional information is THOMAS (*http://thomas.loc.gov*), which is named for Thomas Jefferson and operated by the Library of Congress. THOMAS' highlight is its databases containing the full text of all bills introduced in Congress since 1989, the full text of the *Congressional Record* since 1989 and the status and summary information for all bills introduced since 1973.

THOMAS also offers special links to bills that have received or are expected to receive floor action during the current week and newsworthy bills that are pending or that have recently been approved. Finally, THOMAS has selected committee reports, answers to frequently asked questions about accessing congressional information, publications titled *How Our Laws Are Made* and *Enactment of a Law* and links to lots of other congressional Web sites.

House of Representatives

The U.S. House of Representatives site (*http://www.house.gov*) offers the schedule of bills, resolutions and other legislative issues the House will consider in the current week. It also has updates about current proceedings on the House floor and a list of the next day's meeting of House committees. Other highlights include a database that helps users identify their representative, a directory of House members and committees, the House ethics manual, links to Web pages maintained by House members and committees, a calendar of congressional primary dates and candidate-filing deadlines for ballot access, the full text of all amendments to the Constitution that have been ratified and those that have been proposed but not ratified and lots of information about Washington, D.C., for visitors.

Another key House site is The Office of the Clerk On-line Information Center (*http://clerkweb.house.gov*), which has records of all roll-call votes taken since 1990. The votes are recorded by bill, so it is a lengthy process to compile a particular representative's voting record. The site also has lists of committee assignments, a telephone directory for members and committees, mailing label templates for members and committees, rules of the current Congress, election statistics from 1920 to the present, biographies of Speakers of the House, biographies of women who have served since 1917 and a virtual tour of the House Chamber.

One of the more interesting House sites is operated by the Subcommittee on Rules and Organization of the House Committee on Rules (*http://www.house.gov/rules/crs_reports. htm*). Its highlight is dozens of Congressional Research Service reports about the legislative process. Some of the available titles include *Legislative Research in Congressional Offices: A Primer, How to Follow Current Federal Legislation and Regulations; Investigative Oversight: An Introduction to the Law, Practice and Procedure of Congressional Inquiry*; and *Presidential Vetoes 1789 – Present: A Summary Overview.*

Senate

At least in the Internet world, the Senate is not as active as the House. Its main Web site (*http://www.senate.gov*) has records of all roll-call votes taken since 1989 (arranged by bill), brief descriptions of all bills and joint resolutions introduced in the Senate during the past week and a calendar of upcoming committee hearings. The site also provides the standing rules of the Senate, a directory of senators and their committee assignments, lists of nominations that the president has submitted to the Senate for approval, links to Web pages operated by senators and committees and a virtual tour of the Senate.

Information about the membership, jurisdiction and rules of each congressional committee is available at the U.S. Government Printing Office site (*http://www.access.gpo.gov/congress/index.html*). It also has transcripts of selected congressional hearings, the full text of selected House and Senate reports and the House and Senate rules manuals.

General Reference

The U.S. General Accounting Office, the investigative arm of Congress, operates a site (*http://www.gao.gov*) that provides the full text of its reports from 1975 to the present. The reports cover a wide range of topics: aviation safety, combating terrorism, counternarcotics efforts in Mexico, defense contracting, electronic warfare, food assistance programs, Gulf War illness, health insurance, illegal aliens, information technology, long-term care, mass transit, Medicare, military readiness, money laundering, national parks, nuclear waste, organ donation and student loan defaults, among others.

The GAO Daybook is an excellent current awareness tool. This electronic mailing list distributes a daily list of reports and testimony released by the GAO. Subscriptions are available by sending an e-mail message to *majordomo@www.gao.gov*, and in the message area typing "subscribe daybook" (without the quotation marks).

Current budget and economic projections are provided at the Congressional Budget Office Web site (*http://www.cbo.gov*). The site also has reports about the economic and budget outlook for the next decade, the president's budget proposals, federal civilian employment, Social Security privatization, tax reform, water use conflicts in the West, marriage and the federal income tax and the role of foreign aid in development, among other topics. Other highlights include monthly budget updates, historical budget data, cost estimates for bills reported by congressional committees and transcripts of congressional testimony by CBO officials.

Campaign Finance

Several Internet sites provide detailed campaign finance data for congressional elections. The official site is operated by the Federal Election Commission (*http://www.fec.gov*), which regulates political spending. The site's highlight is its database of campaign reports filed from May 1996 to the present by House and presidential candidates, political action committees and political party committees. Senate reports are not included because they are filed with the Secretary of the Senate. The reports in the FEC's database are scanned images of paper reports filed with the commission.

The FEC site also has summary financial data for House and Senate candidates in the current election cycle, abstracts of court decisions pertaining to federal election law from 1976 to 1997, a graph showing the number of political action committees in existence each year from 1974 to the present and a directory of national and state agencies that are responsible for releasing information about campaign financing, candidates on the ballot, election results, lobbying and other issues. Another useful feature is a collection of brochures about federal election law, public funding of presidential elections, the ban on contributions by foreign nationals, independent expenditures supporting or opposing a candidate for federal office, contribution limits, filing a complaint, researching public records at the FEC and other topics. Finally, the site provides the FEC's legislative recommendations, its annual report, a report about its first twenty years in existence, the FEC's monthly newsletter, several reports about voter registration, election results for the most recent presidential and congressional elections and campaign guides for corporations and labor organizations, congressional candidates and committees, political party committees and nonconnected committees.

The best online source for campaign finance data is Political Money Line (*http://www.tray.com*). The site's searchable databases provide extensive itemized information about receipts and expenditures by federal candidates and political action committees from 1980 to the present. The data, which are obtained from the FEC, are quite detailed. For example, for candidates contributions can be searched by Zip Code. The site also has lists of the top political action committees in various categories, lists of the top contributors from each state and much more.

Another interesting site is the American University Campaign Finance Website (*http://www1.soc.american.edu/campfin*), which is operated by the American University School of Communication. It provides electronic files from the FEC that have been reformatted in .dbf format so they can be used in database programs such as Paradox, Access and FoxPro. The files contain data on PAC, committee and individual contributions to individual congressional candidates.

More campaign finance data is available from the Center for Responsive Politics (*http://www.opensecrets.org*), a public interest organization. The center provides a list of all "soft money" donations to political parties of $100,000 or more in the current election cycle and data about "leadership" political action committees associated with individual politicians. Other databases at the site provide information about travel expenses that House members received from private sources for attending meetings and other events, activities of registered federal lobbyists and activities of foreign agents who are registered in the United States.

Index